Timber Connections

Timber Connections

THE JOYCE LUMBER STORY

SUSAN HAWKINSON

WARREN JEWETT

BLUEWATERS PRESS

Library of Congress Control Number: 2003094409
ISBN 0-9740971-0-1 (Hardcover)
ISBN 0-9740971-1-X (Softcover)

Printed in Canada

Bluewaters Press
Box 246
Grand Rapids, MN 55744
email: inquiries@bluewaterspress.com

Contents

The Joyce Estate Lodge on Trout Lake as it appeared in 1918. JOE WALESKI PRIVATE COLLECTION

Preface

WARREN AND I DID NOT INITIALLY plan to write *Timber Connections.* We had instead envisioned a much narrower focus—recording the history of the Joyce Estate, a 4,500-acre retreat built by David Gage Joyce on Trout Lake, north of Grand Rapids, Minnesota, in 1915. The impetus for the book was a conversation that took place ten years ago between Warren and Howard Zeman, who was a district ranger for the Chippewa National Forest at that time. These two felt that documenting the past events at the Joyce Estate would contribute to the public understanding of the historic site. We were all well aware that the estate and events marking its history had generated a considerable local folklore containing a confusing mix of fact and fiction.

I first saw the Joyce Estate in 1963, when I was sixteen years old. A high school classmate, Ellen Kean, drove me out to see the grounds and lodge and to meet her former sister-in-law, Beatrice Joyce Kean, who was the last living Joyce. I had heard that Beatrice Joyce Kean was fabulously rich, rumored at one time to be the third wealthiest woman in the world, and I anticipated arriving at a mansion as Ellen and I traveled a narrow dirt road through the pine and hardwood forest to the lodge. Walking up the stairs and across the screen porch, we entered a surprisingly rustic living area, where Beatrice and, I believe, her former husband, Dudley Kean, were seated, facing a fireplace, visiting. Ellen introduced me, but we did not join the conversation. Rather, we wandered through the grounds. While I pretended to admire the equally rustic cabins and other structures, I wondered why such a wealthy woman lived so simply and so isolated. It wasn't until decades later—as Warren and I unraveled the Joyce story—that I understood the seeming simplicity of the Joyce Estate.

Researching life at the Joyce Estate evolved into more general research about the Joyce family. We soon learned that the family not only had an intriguing personal history but an intriguing business history too. That discovery changed our focus. At that point, we knew we had taken on a book-length project.

Joyce lumbering in Itasca County, Minnesota—particularly in the Bigfork Valley— is the centerpiece of *Timber Connections.* This is the region where three generations of Joyces built and operated a mill and a railroad and afterwards sold their cutover lands.

The story of the Joyce family and their business enterprises is significantly intertwined with the early history of the county. Many small communities, some still in existence today, developed along the railroad tracks and adjacent to the mill in the late 1800s and early 1900s. Homesteaders arrived to cultivate the cutover lands and to work in the mill or on the railroad while lumberjacks came to cut timber for the Joyces. We also tell their stories.

Minnesota is not the only state in which the Joyces operated sawmills. They had significant business holdings in Iowa, Wisconsin, Mississippi, Louisiana, and Texas. What emerged for us was the realization that the communities in which the Joyces owned mills as well as the mills themselves shared connections in history that have not been generally known. The title of our book reflects the commonalities Warren and I discovered as we researched and wrote. The fact that the Joyces operated businesses for a century and a half, often in several states simultaneously, made it difficult to organize our book in a strict chronological order. We have, therefore, organized the chapters by geographic region.

It is important to note that the Joyce business history is even bigger than what is told in *Timber Connections.* The Joyces had holdings in Michigan and in British Columbia and in other locations. They also diversified by owning stock in Iowa and Louisiana banks, the Benjamin Manufacturing Company—a manufacturer of heavy sawmill equipment, a motorcycle company, a hotel in Hot Springs, Arkansas, and many other enterprises. Warren and I limited the content of the book to the major lumbering sites and history relevant to Minnesota for practical reasons.

Whenever possible, we have given glimpses of the Joyce family members' personalities and social lives along with their business roles. John Joyce (1799–1881), his son, David Joyce (1825–1894), and his grandson, William Joyce (1860–1909), were the family visionaries and entrepreneurs who worked hard, expanding their holdings and insuring the success of their various businesses. In the following generations, David Gage Joyce (1885–1937), his brother, Stanley Joyce (1886–1944), and his daughter, Beatrice Joyce Kean (1923–1972), loosened their hold on the managerial reins of their empire and enjoyed themselves, delegating more of the workload to the executives of the various companies. The five generations of Joyces sustained an important place in the lumber industry for approximately 150 years.

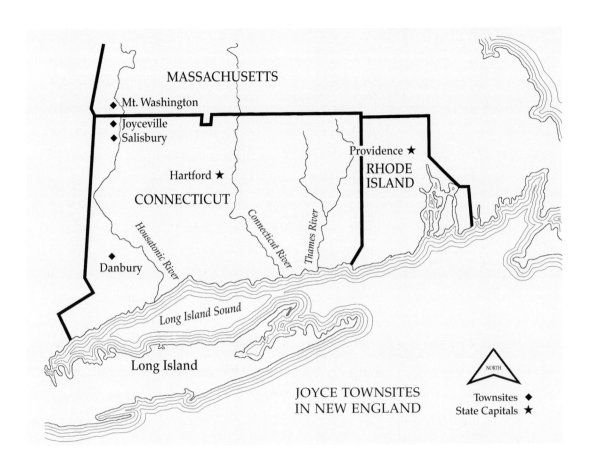

MASSACHUSETTS

◆ Mt. Washington
◆ Joyceville
◆ Salisbury

Providence ★

RHODE ISLAND

Hartford ★

CONNECTICUT

Housatonic River

Connecticut River

Thames River

◆ Danbury

Long Island Sound

Long Island

JOYCE TOWNSITES
IN NEW ENGLAND

NORTH

Townsites ◆
State Capitals ★

An Entrepreneurial Tradition

THE FIRST CLEAR FACTS ABOUT THE JOYCE FAMILY history begin with John Dibble Joyce, born in Danbury, southwestern Connecticut, in 1799, to David Joyce and Olive Dibble Joyce. Both the Joyces and the Dibbles had traveled to America sometime before the American Revolution. The families had been neighbors in Connecticut until the close of the war.

The ambitious John Dibble Joyce, who left home at fifteen, changed the occupational course of his family. While his ancestors had farmed in New England during the early part of the eighteenth century, young Joyce learned blacksmithing, apprenticing in the northwestern Connecticut village of Hammertown. He set up his first blacksmith shop in Mount Washington Township, in extreme southwestern Massachusetts, around the time he married Jerusha Jones, an event that occurred on April 1, 1819. His move to Mount Washington was a logical step, for both his grandparents and his wife's family called the area home. In 1821 Joyce purchased another piece of property in Mount Washington Township. On it, he built a larger shop, adding a forge and triphammer. He then developed a water supply by damming a brook on the property. On the large pond behind the dam he constructed a waterwheel-powered sawmill. The mill's vertical jig-rig saw processed hemlock, pine, chestnut, and oak into lumber. Such were the modest beginnings of the Joyce lumbering empire.

Lumbering secured the family fortune for future generations of Joyces, yet John Dibble Joyce's most profitable ventures were his foundry and machine shop. As a young businessman he made and repaired implements used by local farmers and forged harpoons for Hudson whalers. He produced iron chains in great quantity and manufactured equipment for raising and hauling immense blocks of marble from the Goodale Quarry in Egremont in southwestern Massachusetts. The marble blocks went to the famous Giraud College, located at Hudson in eastern Massachusetts.[1] This work was successful enough for Joyce to employ twenty laborers, including, at least for a time, his brothers, William and Ezra. The hired men farmed their own small acreages during the spring and the fall and worked in the mill or foundry the rest of the year.

Financially astute, the New Englander diversified his business dealings. He loaned money on mortgages and bought and sold farm, timber, and mineral land in Mount Washington and Sheffield, Massachusetts, as well as in Salisbury Township in Connecticut.[2] Later he opened a mercantile store. In time, he expanded his businesses until they became the industrial center of his township.

Portrayed as "stern, frugal, and a strong minded man of beliefs and practices" by Joyce business historian, Herbert O. Brayer, John Joyce was the most recognized name in Mount Washington with the exception of his grandfather, revolutionary war veteran Lt. John Dibble. Joyce not only acted as town moderator for four years, he also was elected five times as selectman, spent several years on the school committee, served a term as constable, collected taxes, and worked for two years as town treasurer.* In fact, his fellow citizens elected him to every unappointed office in his community. Finally, in 1844, he captured a unanimous vote for state representative from Mount Washington.[3]

During the 1840s, while the railroads were pushing west and the iron and steel industry of New England was booming, Joyce looked south for more investment opportunities in Salisbury, Connecticut, a few miles across the state boundary from Mount Washington. He was already sending much of what he manufactured to this community and planned to relocate his business there as soon as the Housatonic Railroad was completed. Salisbury—where the cannons were cast for General Washington's army—was a natural choice because it abounded in the natural resources needed for his foundry.[4]

John Joyce achieved his goal of settling near Salisbury on October 20, 1845, when he paid $3,300 to Ira and Simeon Sage for farming land, buildings, dams, water rights, and equipment. The property stretched across the borders of Massachusetts and Connecticut, a few miles north of Salisbury.[5] Joyce happily moved into his new home on Sage's Ravine, planting his farmland and buying cattle. Then he built a furnace for his foundry, a coalhouse, and a machine shop, for although he had divested himself of his Massachusetts property, he had taken the forge, sawmill, machinery, and tools with him. Out of necessity he put up his own mercantile store since he could no longer rely on Cyrus Lamson's General Store in Mount Washington Township, a long day's travel from Sage's Ravine.

In 1848 Joyce put his twenty-three year old son David in charge of the flourishing mercantile stores. This allowed the older Joyce to attend to his Connecticut lumbering and foundry operations as well as to his other business. By updating the sawmill with a reconstructed waterwheel powering his new circular saw, John Joyce produced lumber for the region's barns, bridges, and industrial businesses, while his foundry fashioned the requisite iron implements.[6] He also continued to profitably speculate in property throughout the

---

* Joyce's elected role as selectman is equivalent to a councilman. Town moderator is equivalent to the chairman of a governing body.

township. These diverse enterprises swelled the family fortune and would soon provide the springboard for David Joyce's lumbering adventures in the young state of Iowa.

In 1857, fifty-eight-year-old John Dibble Joyce also left his manufacturing businesses under the direction of his only son in order to devote himself solely to his large farm in what was now called Joyceville. John Joyce remained on his farm until July 19, 1881, when he succumbed to a heart attack at age eighty-two.

David Joyce

David Joyce, the family visionary who founded the Joyce lumber fortune, was born to John and Jerusha Joyce in their two-story slab house near Mount Washington on February 26, 1825. He was educated at the one-room school near town, where lessons were taught just five months a year. In 1837, at age twelve, he finished his formal instruction and was initiated into the family businesses. "John Joyce," wrote Herbert O. Brayer, "saw that the youngster learned every facet of the business from the sawmill and charcoal roasters to the foundry and machine shop. He cut hemlock logs in the hills and helped skid them to the millpond." He worked at the charcoal pits and as a wagon driver for the mill. "By the time he was fifteen Dave knew enough about the operations to be put in charge of the firm's books."[7]

Ambitious like his father, David Joyce supplemented the practical education that he had received in sawmilling and foundry work. On his own, as George Hotchkiss explained in his *History of the Lumber and Forest Industry of the Northwest*, Joyce "developed a taste for mathematics" and the mechanic arts, becoming a "practical civil engineer and surveyor" and forming the "instruments of this profession with his own hands." In 1848, however, under his father's directive, the twenty-three year old switched his professional interests to mercantiling, "assuming full control of [his father's] two general stores."[8]

David Joyce expanded his control in the family businesses, maintaining the working relationships begun by his father. In particular, two of Joyce's sisters, Hannah and Permelia, were married to men who assisted in Joyce enterprises. Hannah's husband, Jeremiah Dibble, and Permelia's husband, Sylvester Sardam, served as foremen under Joyce.

Just before the start of the Civil War, David Joyce uprooted his family from the security of the Connecticut businesses to attend to new investments in distant Iowa. His nephew, George Sardam, followed him to the Mississippi River town of Lyons, where the two men worked closely throughout David Joyce's life.

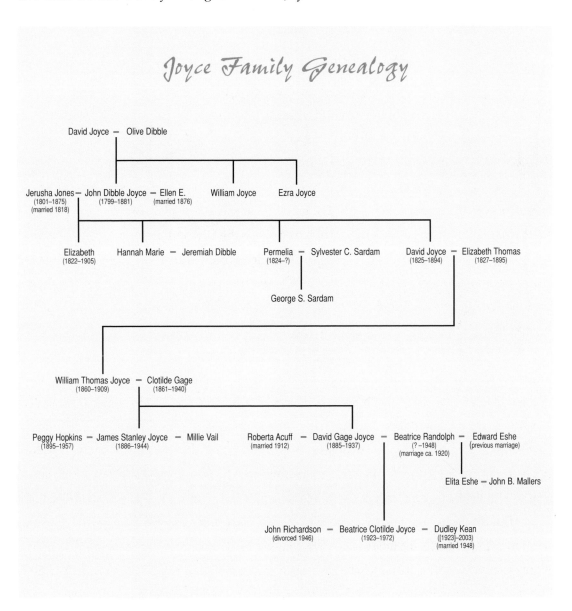

ITASCA
COUNTY

Deer River

Prairie River

Swan River

Mississippi River

LAKE SUPERIOR

MICHIGAN

Duluth

Mason

Shell Lake

Barronett

St. Croix River

Chippewa River

Minneapolis
St. Paul

Chippewa
Falls

Eau Claire

← BEEF SLOUGH

MINNESOTA

Madison

IOWA

WISCONSIN

Mississippi River

ILLINOIS

Carroll

Lyons

Fulton

Des Moines

Clinton

Omaha

Council
Bluffs

Rock Island

NORTH

Joyce Mill Town ◆
State Capitals ★
Other Cities ●

JOYCE LUMBERING SITES IN THE MIDWEST

Sawmill on the Mississippi

DAVID JOYCE FIRST BOARDED A WESTBOUND TRAIN in Connecticut in 1855 to search for land investments on the Iowa frontier. When he arrived at the Mississippi River, he ferried from Fulton, Illinois, to a well-situated river town on the Iowa bank called Lyons. A major stop for steamboats plying the Mississippi, Lyons boomed during the 1850s. Its population grew from 200 in 1852 to 5,000 in 1858. Lyons' location, just 130 miles due west of Chicago, encouraged its rapid growth. According to *History of Clinton County, Iowa*, by the mid-1850s "there were two banks, 53 stores and groceries, two sawmills, a planing and lath mill, a sash, door and blind factory, a marble works, an iron foundry and machine shop, a saddle and harness factory and a broom factory"[1] in the river town.

The fact that the Mississippi narrowed at Lyons, creating an ideal spot for a bridge, had caught the eyes of railroad men, subsequently boosting land sales and development. Unfortunately for Joyce, other entrepreneurs hungry for property had already recognized Lyons' favorable positioning and had acquired the best parcels. Little was left. Even as Joyce scouted for property, he must have heard news about competition developing for the river crossing. The Iowa Land Company had snapped up 500 acres just a few miles downstream and was promoting the spot known as Clinton for the bridge. Joyce decided to concentrate his search in Lyons, believing that the established community would have a better chance of attracting the crossing. (Joyce was wrong. The first rail bridge spanned the Mississippi at Clinton in 1865.[2] In 1895 Clinton annexed Lyons.)

David Joyce spent many months analyzing potential opportunities before he chose two safe investments for his $6,000, a sum he had accumulated managing his father's businesses. Orrin Sage and William Gibbs sold him a small tract of land in Lyons, but

Joyce also deviated from his plan to buy property by lending mill owner George Stambaugh most of the $6,000 to operate his business. The loan was not an unusual arrangement. Many mill owners faced a perennial problem of acquiring sufficient cash to purchase the flood of logs arriving during the spring drives and were always on the lookout for capital. Stambaugh was especially needy, for he had expended all of his reserves on the construction of a new mill following a fire and as collateral pledged his steam-driven sawmill in Lyons to guarantee the four-year loan.[3]

The soundness of the Stambaugh investment seemed evident to Joyce. Since Lyons was located on the Mississippi River, mill owners were assured of a constant log supply from the Wisconsin forests that lined the tributaries of the Mississippi. They could then sell their lumber to homesteaders in and around Lyons who needed material to build homes, barns, sheds, and fences. A second wave of settlers was expected to arrive as soon as railroads bridged the Mississippi River at Lyons or its vicinity. The rail lines would connect rural Iowa with the commercial center of the Midwest—Chicago. In addition to the needs of the new settlers, the railroads would demand ties for their tracks advancing westward. Equally as important as location and market was the fact that David Joyce knew the business of sawmilling firsthand. Confident of his investments, Joyce ferried back across the Mississippi River to Fulton, Illinois, and caught the train to Connecticut.

Business boomed in Iowa during 1856 while David Joyce guided his father's Connecticut enterprises. The following year, however, the country experienced the Panic of 1857 that depressed the economy, including the lumber market. Joyce was forced to extend his loan to Stambaugh for another twelve months, since Stambaugh had defaulted on the interest. Like other mill owners, Stambaugh had tied up his capital in a down payment on logs from the Wisconsin forests early in the year, expecting to recover and increase his investment after sawing the logs into lumber and selling them during the summer and fall. Because of the panic, his primary customers, the local farmers, could not dispose of their cattle and grain and, therefore, could not buy lumber. Whether Stambaugh even accepted his allotment of logs is uncertain. He might have chosen to lose his down payment rather than bankrupt himself buying logs that he knew he could not sell.

The situation with Stambaugh had still not improved in 1859, which forced Joyce to act. In 1860 he traveled to Lyons intending to divest himself of his holdings but found he could not do so without losing money. Furthermore, his Iowa friends were so optimistic about the future that their enthusiasm infected the Easterner. Joyce resolved at that moment to return to Connecticut and sell his father's businesses so that he could fully commit to the Iowa adventure.

The David Joyce home in Lyons (Clinton), Iowa. WARREN JEWETT PHOTO

Just before the outbreak of the Civil War, David Joyce brought his bride of two years, Elizabeth Thomas Joyce, and their one-year-old son William to Lyons. He built a two-story brick house on the bluffs of the Mississippi River with the busy frontier town stirring below. The location gave the home a splendid vista from which to view the river traffic. On a typical summer day, the family could watch forty to fifty steamboats traveling north and south as well as the log rafts floating downriver from Wisconsin or Minnesota.[4]

Sawmilling

A prairie state like Iowa seemed an unlikely place for the lumber production capital of the world, a distinction it would attain by 1877. But with the great river to link it to the unmatched white pine forests to the north and with rail transportation to nearby Chicago, the lumber trading capital of the world, the river towns of Lyons and Clinton bloomed. The sawmill industry, which spread out for five miles along the Mississippi from north of Lyons to south of Clinton, brought great wealth to these communities. In fact, the Lyons-Clinton area became home to thirteen millionaires, including David Joyce, Chancy Lamb, and William Young, who cooperated to promote the lumber industry in Iowa and later in

Wisconsin.[5] When Joyce arrived with his family in Iowa, the mills of Lamb and Young were already sawing lumber. Young's mill was once touted as the "largest saw mill in operation on the American continent," according to lumber industry historian George Hotchkiss.[6] Together, these two men manufactured as much as sixty-seven percent of the locally produced lumber.

Like Joyce, Chancy Lamb and William Young were men with a vision. Lamb increased productivity within the mill. In 1884 he operated the first band saw in the white pine industry in one of his Clinton mills, demonstrating to his doubting peers the superiority of the newly developed saw. The band saw could produce more board feet per log and less waste than the traditional circular saw. Lamb's innovation quickly became a standard in the industry. Young developed new log-driving techniques. He used steamboats to push and guide log rafts downstream to the mills. This saved weeks of travel time on the Mississippi, and that, in turn, saved money. Young also reduced the cost of transporting log rafts by developing the brailed raft system. An individual brail was formed by grouping logs with the same identifying marks—log stamps and bark marks that indicated ownership—together when they reached a sorting works on a river. Around each brail a brailing crew fitted overlapping logs, called boom sticks, held together by a peg and chain system. Every fifty feet along the length of the raft, quarter-inch diameter wire was stretched from side to side to hold logs tightly in place. A single brail was 45 feet wide by 600 feet long. Generally, six brails were linked

A typical brailed raft is guided downriver through St. Paul.
MINNESOTA HISTORICAL SOCIETY

together to form a larger raft—270 feet wide by 600 feet long.[7] Prior to the brailed system, the river men drove many more pins into the logs to create rafts. The older process devalued substantially more logs. With their bore marks, they were fit only for "coarser uses, such as sidewalk plank."[8]

As David Joyce settled his family in Lyons, he set his sights on improving the profitability of the Stambaugh lumber venture. The two men entered into a partnership. Stambaugh retained control of the sawmill, and Joyce concentrated on managing the retail side of the business. To promote trade in the midst of a national cash shortage, Joyce set up a lumberyard in Lyons and encouraged farmers to barter their grain and cattle for lumber until his customers could again pay in cash. Joyce astutely financed a distillery that would use the bartered grain to produce whiskey. He then fed the mash, a byproduct of whiskey production, to his growing herd of cattle. Joyce's innovations were successful. Whiskey was popular in Wisconsin where Stambaugh bought logs, and the fattened cattle went to market.[9]

Although the yard and cattle businesses were secure investments, the mill hobbled along. Joyce foreclosed on Stambaugh and assumed control of the mill during the spring of 1865. Soon after, he discovered that to make the mill monetarily sound would cost more than it was worth, but he kept it running two more years before selling it. Joyce relied on Wisconsin-sawed lumber to outfit his retail yard in Lyons until he built a new mill.[10]

David Joyce substantially increased his wealth during the boom years following the Civil War. European immigrants and war veterans were buying homesteads and demanding lumber products, spurring development in the Midwest. Lumber prices surpassed even the lucrative war years. Relying on this growing economy, Joyce collaborated with S. I. Smith, a New York lumber dealer, to build a $48,000 sawmill in 1869. The partners procured the highest ground along the Mississippi River in the Clinton-Lyons area for construction of this mill. It was the only sawmill to be built above the high water line, insurance against flood damage. Described in the July 21, 1869 issue of the *Lyons City Advocate*, the property perched on "a shallow and sluggish arm of the Mississippi River that swung around a low, mile-long island." Beyond the reaches of river current, the slough offered a convenient holding area for logs. (Joyce left his mark on the area, for even today these features are called Joyce's Slough and Joyce's Island.) Mill construction started early in the spring of 1869, and workers finished their task by August of that same year.[11]

When Joyce inspected the completed mill, he saw an imposing complex of buildings and machinery. On the south side of the mill stood the smokestack, boiler house, and engine house. The substantial smokestack was eighty-five feet tall, twelve feet square at the base, and about five feet square at the top. Constructed of brick and covered with iron, the seventeen-foot-by-forty-six-foot fireproof boiler room contained three horizontal boilers. The coal-fired boilers produced the steam piped to the 240 horsepower engine, which sported a flywheel weighing 5,000 pounds. The engine rotated the pulleys and belts on the lower floor of the mill to power mill machinery on the second floor. Belts transferred power to all the saw blades and conveyors. Steam-powered cylinders also manipulated logs in the initial sawing process.

As the numerous belts, pulleys, and shafts were set in motion by the steam coursing through the veins of the mill, skilled workers reduced mighty logs to lumber and sawdust. Mill men guided the logs out of the slough onto the endless chain conveyor at the east end of the mill. Once the logs reached the cutting deck on the upper floor, a double rotary saw squared the logs in preparation for running them through the gang of thirty-six saws that cut them into lumber. Edgers and other specialty equipment sized the lumber that was then moved out of the mill to be piled in the yard for the drying process. A year later the seasoned lumber was planed and re-stacked. Daily mill output tallied 40,000 board feet of lumber, 20,000 board feet of shingles, and 15,000 board feet of lath, the work of sixty men and several teams of horses.* Annual production over the years ranged from 8 to 18 million board feet of lumber, lath, and shingles. Whistling by the front door of the mill, a local railroad picked up the finished lumber on an adjoining sidetrack.

The completed mill allowed the partners to concentrate on their individual areas

---

* In this book, a board foot is defined as a quantity of lumber equal to 12 inches by 12 inches by 1 inch. This unit is used for finished lumber as well as for timber in the woods. In some cases, the word "board" is dropped, but the inference is always that of board feet.

of expertise. Smith supervised mill operation while Joyce focused on marketing. A store-room was added as an extension of the mill to sell lumber, shingles, and lath to local citizens. Buyers also found specialty items such as sash, doors, blinds, and other house construction materials produced onsite.* Joyce set up a new lumberyard in Clinton to augment the Lyons yard.[12]

The Joyce-Smith partnership only lasted a few years. Smith soon became interested in investing in a new paper mill in Lyons and requested that Joyce purchase his half of the sawmill. This proposition delighted the forty-eight-year-old David Joyce. For the first time he was the sole owner of a substantial sawmilling business. Joyce's contribution to the total annual cut produced by the many Lyons-Clinton mills ranged from 5 to 8 percent.[13]

Log Driving

Shortly after the Joyce-Smith mill was completed in 1869, the two men joined with other mill men to discuss the formation of a log-driving company to reduce the complexity and expense of their spring log drives. Every spring millions of logs, each with ownership marks, had to be guided downriver from the distant Wisconsin forests to the correct mills in Iowa and Illinois. As a result of the deliberations, David Joyce, S. I. Smith, Chancy Lamb, William Young, and lumber giant Frederick Weyerhaeuser (who created a lumber dynasty still in operation today) incorporated the Mississippi River Logging Company. The formation of this company promoted a steady stream of Wisconsin logs for the Iowa and Illinois mills. Two additional companies in which Joyce, Lamb, Young, and Weyerhaeuser all had membership, the Chippewa Logging Company (which later assumed some of the functions of the Mississippi River Logging Company) and the Beef Slough Manufacturing, Booming, Log Driving and Transportation Company, distributed the logs and drove them downriver. The history of these companies is embedded in a long-standing conflict on the Chippewa River in Wisconsin.

Prior to the Middle Mississippi lumbermen actually purchasing stumpage in Wisconsin, they relied on logs bought from Wisconsin timber owners. These logs were

* Sash is the lumber used for window and door frames. A blind refers to a window treatment, such as a Venetian blind.

floated down the Mississippi in rafts and dropped off at various Iowa and Illinois mills. This caused a stir among Wisconsin mill owners, who bickered with local timber owners and loggers over the distribution of the state's logs. The mill owners wanted to secure the stumpage exclusively for their own mills, while the timber owners and loggers wanted to sell their stumpage to both in-state and out-of-state lumbermen. The in-state mill owners feared that stumpage sales to out-of-state mills would dramatically increase the amount of manufactured lumber on the market, lowering the price of the finished product and diminishing profits. On the other hand, the timber owners and loggers wanted to increase their customer base by sending more logs to mill owners south of Wisconsin. This would generate more competition among buyers, driving up the price of timber. To further their goal, the timber owners purchased a tract on the Chippewa River, called Beef Slough, a natural spot for collecting, sorting and assembling log rafts before they were sent downstream to Iowa and Illinois.

Beef Slough was located at the mouth of the Chippewa and served as a second outlet for the river as it flowed into the Mississippi. Logs were channeled into the sluggish waters of the slough by placing a boom across the Chippewa. Once in the slough, logs were sorted and then organized into rafts by the unique log marks cut into each log to identify the purchase company. The rafts were then discharged into the Mississippi, where steamboats pushed the rafts to the appropriate downstream mills, such as the Joyce mill in Lyons, Iowa, or the Weyerhaeuser mill in Rock Island, Illinois. The acquisition of Beef Slough by the Wisconsin timber owners resulted in the formation of the Beef Slough Manufacturing, Booming, Log Driving and Transportation Company in 1867.

In 1868 Frederick Weyerhaeuser visited Wisconsin's Chippewa River Valley. He quickly discerned that this countryside, on which he already relied for white pine for his Illinois mill, was a "'loggers' paradise.'"[14] Thick stands of the finest quality pine grew adjacent to a multitude of lakes, tied together by navigable streams and rivers that fed into the Chippewa River, foremost among the pine-bearing tributaries of the Mississippi. Most of the land in the Chippewa River basin was still for sale, Weyerhaeuser discovered, and, if purchased, would offer the Middle Mississippi mill men like himself the assurance of continuous log supplies. Led by Frederick Weyerhaeuser, Iowa and Illinois mill owners started collectively buying large tracts of stumpage in the following decade.[15]

In 1870 Weyerhaeuser and his peers first leased and later acquired the Beef Slough Manufacturing, Booming, Log Driving and Transportation Company after it lost its financial solvency in the hands of the Wisconsin timber owners. With control of the sorting works at Beef Slough in the hands of the Middle Mississippi lumbermen, the way was clear in 1871 for the formation of the Mississippi River Logging Company. Each mill owner bought shares in the new company in accordance with the quantity of logs he expected to send through the slough. Joyce bought five percent of the company stock. Immediately the Mississippi River Logging Company invited the Wisconsin mill owners to join them in a cooperative sorting and driving effort on the Chippewa, but the Wisconsin men refused the opportunity.

As tensions grew between the two competitive groups throughout the 1870s, the Wisconsin men lobbied their legislature to halt the volume of logs traveling downstream to the Iowa and Illinois mills. They said that these logs obstructed river transportation. The legislature, however, did not support their state lumbermen, and the Iowa and Illinois mill owners were free to float their logs on the rivers as they had always done. According to the authors of *Timber and Men*, the Weyerhaeuser lumbering story, the legislative battle cost both groups considerable money and created "a feud so bitter that the entire history of lumbering could hardly show its like."[16] The conflict came to blows as log drivers and mill men intent on protecting their log investments faced off, armed with "axes, pike poles, peavies, and cant hooks" wrote Agnes Larson in her history of the white pine industry.[17]

Finally the terrible June rains of 1880 and the subsequent flooding that destroyed booms, sorting works, bridges, and other buildings in its path ended the conflict. During the rains, 180 million board feet of logs roared down the Chippewa for 125 miles, coming to rest sometimes from one to three miles off the banks of the river. For the Wisconsin lumbermen to recover these logs and haul them upstream to their mills at Chippewa Falls and Eau Claire was impossible. Instead, they needed to negotiate a log exchange with the Middle Mississippi lumbermen. The Wisconsin lumbermen fully expected their competitors to take advantage of the disaster, but the Middle Mississippi lumbermen surprised the Wisconsinites by using the situation to strengthen the relationship between the two groups. They enacted a plan to round up the logs stranded on the Chippewa and send them on down to their mills in Iowa and Illinois. In exchange, the Middle Mississippi men gave a like number of logs that they held on the upper Chippewa to the Chippewa Falls and Eau Claire mill owners.

This was the beginning of cooperation on the Chippewa. In November 1880 the two rival groups signed a provisional agreement. Gathering at the Grand Hotel in Chicago, they passed a resolution to form a new company "'for the purpose of uniting in one interest the purchasing, owning, driving, scaling, grading and distributing the several amounts of logs to each of the parties who shall subscribe and pay for them, in the best and cheapest manner.'"[18] The outcome of this new cooperative effort was the Chippewa Logging Company.

Joyce Contributions to Industry and Community

About the same time that David Joyce was constructing his mill with S. I. Smith in 1869 and also struggling with log-supply issues, Clinton and Lyons lumbermen addressed the difficulty of transporting their 2,000 mill laborers to work. To solve this problem, the Clinton and Lyons Horse Railway Company was incorporated by a number of men, including David Joyce, and shares in the horse railway uniting the two towns were offered. All $50 shares in the newly formed company quickly sold, raising the necessary $25,000 to begin the project. David Joyce served as president of the company with fellow lumbermen taking seats as other officers.

Upset by the high bids coming in for the railway construction, the financially prudent David Joyce proposed to lay the track himself for $28,000, undercutting the lowest bid by twenty percent. In less than three months, on December 6, 1869, the first narrow-gauge mule-drawn car conducted passengers the nearly five miles between Main Street in Lyons and the Clinton depot. The Clinton and Lyons Horse Railway made twelve trips per day. Regardless of how far passengers rode the railway, they paid five cents, and they could buy ten tickets in advance to save fifty percent or more on their fares. David Joyce later purchased controlling interest in the line.[19] The railway remained under his ownership for several years until the advent of electric streetcars.

Lyons citizens were impressed with how rapidly and efficiently David Joyce expedited the horse railway project and asked him to serve his community in the same tireless manner that he served the lumber industry. Joyce agreed to solicit funding for both the Lyons Female College and for a growing public-school system. In 1872 his fellow citizens drafted him as mayor of Lyons. Apparently he managed the city in an exemplary fashion. At the beginning of his four-year tenure, city bonds were worth just forty-five cents on the dollar. Following his years of service, city bonds were valued at one hundred cents per dollar. There were also sufficient funds in the treasury for the town of Lyons to pay all its debts. David Joyce returned to private life after serving as mayor. Lumber industry historian George Hotchkiss penned, however, "As a public-spirited man he was ever on the alert to add to the growth and prestige of the city of his adoption."[20]

In the 1880s Joyce bought nearly one hundred acres of land north of Lyons on the bluffs of the Mississippi from Elijah Buell. The high-perched land offered unparalleled vistas of the river hundreds of feet below. After extending his railway to this property, Joyce designated it as a public park. Admission was free. On Sunday afternoons park goers hopped on the railcars to attend parties, dances, and picnics at a large pavilion in the park and to enjoy the cultivated and natural beauty of the park setting, where, noted the *Clinton Herald,* the "flower gardens were so carefully tended that a spot of red never mixed with a sea of blue or white." The Joyce family maintained control of the park until 1925, when they offered it to the city for $20,000. (The park is still a popular destination today.)[21]

Not only were the citizens of Lyons and Clinton grateful for David Joyce's public benevolence, the men who worked for him appreciated the reliable employment and fair wages. By the 1880s he offered the highest mill wages in the area, a practice he probably started much earlier.[22] His mill employees worked the industry standard of eleven hours a day, six days a week, during the five-to-seven-month sawing season. Foremen earned $100 per month when the mill was in operation from May through October. Once the mill shut down, they repaired the machinery for $2.50 per day. Another skilled position was the sawyers who were paid an hourly rate of $.30 during mill operation and received a bonus if the year had been profitable. Experienced filers commanded as much as $.70 per hour to keep the mill sawing equipment honed to a razor-sharp edge. The apprentice filers' salaries came out of the pocket of the filers. These wages adequately covered the cost of living during the 1880s. A worker could rent a comfortable home for a monthly rate of between $5.00 and $8.00, and room and board for an unmarried employee cost $3.00 to $3.50 per week.[23]

The Burning and Rebuilding of the Mill

With so much sawdust and shavings flying in the midst of hot equipment, sawmill fires were common. David Joyce's mill burned in July 1888. The *Mississippi Valley Lumberman* trade journal described the fire in detail: "On Friday night at 9:30 o'clock fire broke out in the saw mill of David Joyce, located in the south part of the city. The mill was completely destroyed. It is presumed that a hot box was the cause of the fire, though there seems to be no definite knowledge on this point. A number of men were engaged in repairing the gang saws at the time, but before they could use the water the flames had gone beyond control. The lumberyard north of the mill was saved only by the most strenuous efforts. The yards of the Langford & Hall Lumber company of Fulton, a mile distant on the other side of the [Mississippi] River, caught [fire] from flying embers, but no serious damage was done. Mr. Joyce's loss will be $75,000." At the time of the conflagration, Joyce was in Minneapolis.[24]

David Joyce

The same issue of the *Mississippi Valley Lumberman* voiced the sympathy of Joyce's business peers: "There is probably none of the Middle Mississippi manufacturers who is so well known throughout all of the lumber region of Wisconsin and Minnesota as is D. Joyce, of Lyons, Ia. Mr. Joyce is interested in

William Joyce

the Barronett and Shell Lake Lumber companies [in Wisconsin]; is a frequent visitor, therefore, to St. Paul and at points along the North Wisconsin [railroad], and is always on hand when there is a gathering of lumbermen. He is as popular as he is well known, and there is, therefore, more than the usual number of men in the trade who will regret to learn of the destruction of his mill."[25]

Fire threatened lumbermen continuously. Sometimes it ended careers. David Joyce had to dig deeply into his own pockets to cover the expenses of a new mill, since insurance only paid for $15,000 of the fire's damage. Still, construction commenced quickly. David Joyce's twenty-eight-year-old son William supervised the erection of the new mill, with groundbreaking on September 1, 1888, less than two months after the fire. The larger and more modern mill was ready the following spring. A year later, the July 19, 1889 issue of the *Mississippi Valley Lumberman* reported, "David Joyce's new band[saw] mills are running nicely."[26]

The fire of 1888 showed the wisdom of lumbermen like Joyce who understood that survival demanded diversification. Joyce had continually invested in other companies to carry him through disasters like the mill fire. One of these was Langford & Hall, the prosperous lumber firm located across the river in Fulton, Illinois. In 1878 he had used his financial influence to install his nephew, George S. Sardam, as the firm's manager. Sardam, who had followed his uncle from New England to Iowa, joined Joyce as an investor in the Fulton mill. By the time that the Lyons mill burned, Joyce owned three quarters of Langford & Hall's stock. Even though his mill in Lyons lay in ashes, he was assured of a source of lumber for his retail lumberyards from the Fulton mill. Thus, the company across the river, which caught some flying embers from the Lyons mill fire, proved invaluable to the Joyce organization.[27]

In 1892 and 1893 local lumbermen faced another threat from nature—fluctuating water levels. The flooding Mississippi closed all mills during the summer of 1892 except for the Joyce mill, which had been built on the highest ground on the river. In spite of high water,

The *Gardie Eastman* paddlewheel steamer drove brailed rafts to the Joyce mill in Iowa.
MINNESOTA HISTORICAL SOCIETY

Joyce surpassed his previous year's cut by operating into late November 1892. The next year though he was forced to close for a couple of days in September because the water in the slough next to the mill was too low to float logs.[28]

By the 1890s there was a much more serious concern than either fire or fluctuating water. The Wisconsin log supply had diminished, crippling many of the Clinton-Lyons mills. Fortunately Joyce had envisioned the exhaustion of Wisconsin white pine and had bought stumpage in northern Minnesota during the 1880s. This foresight kept his Lyons and Fulton mills running throughout the 1894 season, when all other area mills shut down early. Part of that sawing season no logs were floated down the Mississippi on the open market. Only Joyce's private cuts fed his two mills.[29]

That same year, sixty-nine year old David Joyce died unexpectedly of a stroke with his only son William at his side. William had worked closely with his father for nearly two decades. During this time David had made all of the major decisions. However, William's training had been thorough, and he was more than capable of assuming leadership of his father's far-reaching endeavors.

William Joyce immediately set to work. In 1895 he overhauled the Lyons mill machinery, significantly boosting its production. The renovated mill, equipped with electric lighting, ran two shifts, employing 220 men. In spite of his new equipment, two problems challenged Joyce. The accumulation of twenty-five years of sawdust washing down the Mississippi from hundreds of mills operating north of Lyons silted up the slough. Workers struggled continuously to dredge this channel so they could float the logs to the mill. Then, just before the close of the season, a steamer called the *Gardie Eastman* approached the Lyons mill on the Mississippi River with the last one-half raft of logs and was stranded a half mile up river. There above the mill the steamer had to abandon the logs, which Joyce's employees unloaded and guided downstream. Nevertheless, Joyce reported a good year. The Fulton mill in Illinois performed well too. Commented the *Mississippi Valley Lumberman* in the March 8, 1895 issue, "Mr. Will Joyce seems to be imbued with the same spirit which made his father such a giant in the lumber business."[30] The mills in Clinton, Lyons, and Fulton closed one by one, as the timber supply ran out. W. J. Young shut down his mill in 1897 in the company of many other dying mills. The Lambs lasted through part of the 1904 cutting season. William Joyce's Fulton mill discontinued in 1904, but his Lyons mill did not quit operating until 1907 and was dismantled in 1909.[31]

Retail and Wholesale Yards: Marketing the Lumber

David Joyce had originally established a lumberyard in 1860 as a retail outlet for the Stambaugh mill in Lyons. Thereafter, his lumberyards continued as a growing adjunct to his sawmills. In 1877 David Joyce situated his first line yard—a retail yard built next to a railroad line—in Carroll in western Iowa. By 1897, fifteen Joyce yards dotted the lines of the Illinois Central and Chicago and Northwestern Railroads. Before the days of automobiles and trucks, when the slow pace of horse-drawn wagons limited the distance farmers could travel to purchase lumber, these farmers were a captive market for the closest retail yard.

The line yard, which evolved in the Midwest, developed because of two factors. New settlers needed lumber, and the lumber industry needed markets. The Joyces, as well as many other lumbermen, had devoted their fortunes to stumpage and mills. They established their line yards as markets for their investments. In 1899, the same year William Joyce moved his business headquarters and family to Chicago, he incorporated the W. T. Joyce Company in Illinois, which served as an umbrella for all eighteen

Joyce-owned retail yards. Generally these yards profited from centralized management because their capital could be pooled and more credit offered to farmers.[32]

That did not assure sales, however. If drought or floods damaged or destroyed crops, farmers avoided new building projects and missed payments for the lumber they had purchased earlier on credit. Thus, the weather conditions from the numerous retail yards dominated the managers' reports sent to the head office in Chicago.[33]

Line yards also signaled an increasing competition among lumbermen. An example of the spirited but straightforward manner with which William Joyce handled his

John W. Berger, manager of the Joyce Lumber Company retail store and lumberyard in Templeton, Iowa, circa 1938. Four generations of Bergers worked nearly a century for four generations of Joyces. In 1880 David Joyce purchased two-thirds share of a retail yard in Arcadia, Iowa, owned by G. L. S. Berger. Berger worked only briefly for the Joyces. His son John W. Berger began his nearly fifty-year career in 1910 in the same community. The Joyces eventually promoted him to manager of a retail yard at Templeton, Iowa. Grandson Orval spent twenty years with the Joyces. He started as a laborer in one of the yards at $15 per month. Disgusted with the pay, Orval Berger complained to Tom Fortune, manager of the Joyce retail and wholesale lumber businesses. Fortune then hired Berger as bookkeeper for the Carroll yard at $75 per month. (Berger paid one dollar a day or 40 percent of net salary for room and board.) Berger eventually became superintendent of the retail lumber business, known as the Joyce Lumber Company, in Clinton in 1960. In 1973 Orval Berger's son helped his father clean out the yards in preparation for the sale of Joyce Lumber to Fullerton Lumber. Orval Berger said that typically many people worked all their lives for the Joyce family. The pay was not great, but the work was steady. ORVAL BERGER PRIVATE COLLECTION

rivals is documented in a letter he wrote to a competitor. The W. T. Joyce Company had frequently butted heads with one particular lumber operation, Schull and Company, as both expanded their retail yards across western Iowa. After a few fractious encounters, Joyce sent the following message to Schull on December 18, 1899:

"We desire to grow and expand with the country, and in looking about with this idea in view, have found every new or proposed townsite had upon it the stake and notice that you intended to open a lumber yard there, and as we could not find any which you had not preempted in this way decided that we would have to go in with you and await future developments and 'survival of the fittest!'

"Now regarding [the small Iowa town of] Moseley [I] would say, I am not particularly anxious to open a yard there, but will not abandon the point just because you ask me to do so. There are a number of places in which I had as soon locate, but these you have also preempted with your sign. There are three points on the St. Paul road in which I would like to open a yard, but find you have the same intention. They are Lytton, Lavinia, and Verina. I'm willing to do so, and have been willing at any and all times to consider and agree upon a division of territory."[34]

Joyce's communication succeeded in its mission. The territory was divided between the two men.

Joyce was keen on vying for line yard locations, but he refused to enter into the lumber price-cutting fray. When Chicagoans and Minneapolitans shipped their finished lumber into western Iowa on the railroads, clamoring for their share of the Iowa lumber market, William Joyce's yard managers pointed out that Joyce lumber was priced higher. This news did not sway William Joyce. As he wrote to yard manager G. M. Stanton on October 22, 1899, "We do not base our prices on what we hear about what Minneapolis is doing or information as to the actions of the dealers in any other market. We base our prices on the condition of our own trade and stock."[35]

The letter to the yard manager reflected the Joyces' autonomous business practices. In 1891, when David Joyce was still alive, the Mississippi Valley Lumbermen's Association met to discuss establishing a uniformity of grades and prices. Neither David nor William Joyce attended this gathering. They continued to ignore any attempts on the part of the Middle Mississippi lumbermen to establish price lists and, for that matter, to regulate lumber grades for the Midwest industry in general.[36] David was well known for his cooperative style of lumbering; however, when it came to pricing the final product, he was inflexible. William followed that theme and only softened his hard line as the maturing lumber industry forced compliance.

The Joyce lumber pricing policy was successful until automobiles and trucks replaced horse-drawn wagons as the major mode of transportation. The advent of the automobile and better roads allowed farmers to shop further from home. Policy changed at this point. The Joyces competitively priced lumber in order to keep customers and stocked the yards with products requested by their clientele. While lumber had represented between 90 and 100 percent of the sales in Joyce yards before 1910, by 1940 lumber sales dropped below 30 percent of the total goods sold. Other merchandise, such as "paint, hardware, tools and lumber substitutes," replaced a large portion of previous lumber sales.[37]

The growth in the number of Joyce yards over the years encouraged William Joyce's two sons, David and Stanley, to develop a wholesale distributing center. Located in Council Bluffs, Iowa, directly across the Missouri River from Omaha, Nebraska, this new, centrally situated site offered lumber products at better prices to Joyce retail yards, which had spread across western Iowa into eastern Nebraska. Mr. Thielen, general manager of the retail yard business in 1921, noted that customers could now save money on building materials, "making it possible for anyone desiring to own a home to do so."[38] The general retail yard headquarters moved to Omaha, Nebraska, from Clinton, Iowa, to better accommodate the wholesale distributing center.

David and Elizabeth Joyce's son William married Clotilde Gage in 1884. Gage was the daughter of an affluent third-generation banking family. The couple might have met through their parents, since David Joyce had been involved in various local banks from the time he arrived in Lyons. The William Joyces had two children. David Gage was born in 1885, and James Stanley, in 1886.

Around 1887, during the peak of the lumber industry in Iowa, William Joyce built, what one observer called, "the last of the magnificent houses" next door to his father's brick home on the bluff. Just under 7,000 square feet, the three-story home had nineteen rooms and exterior decorative features, such as the curved plate glass windows and rounded turrets that dazzled onlookers. In 1899, when William Joyce moved his family to Chicago, he did not sell his Lyons mansion because he still had a mill and line yards in Iowa.

Leaving behind his hometown of Lyons, William Joyce looked forward to mingling more regularly with the numerous lumbermen making Chicago their home. At the time of Joyce's move, Chicago was the center of the lumber trade. Understandably then, Joyce set his sights on the city from which he could better direct his business. He soon joined the Chicago Athletic Club, the Chicago Yacht Club, and the Midlothian Country Club, probably for professional as well as social encounters. Joyce was also a Mason and an Elk.

The William Joyce home in Lyons (Clinton), Iowa.
ANN TUBBS PRIVATE COLLECTION

The retail branch of the Joyce lumber business operated for nearly one hundred years. This ancillary business proved successful for two reasons. It motivated the Joyces to seek another lumber source in the South for their Midwest line yards when they exhausted the white pine of Wisconsin and Minnesota. Moreover, yards often paid handsome dividends during their prosperous years, particularly those before the Great Depression.[39] It was not until the late 1960s or early 1970s that the last outlets were sold to Fullerton Lumber Company of Minneapolis.

Iowa had served David Joyce well. It was in Lyons that he bought his first sawmill and simultaneously developed markets for his milled lumber. In Iowa he formed lasting partnerships with other influential lumbermen and cooperatively incorporated log-sorting and driving companies. He also established his reputation as an astute and well-respected lumberman while his personal fortune mushroomed from $6,000 to more than $2 million. But Iowa alone was not enough for the ambitious David Joyce. From Lyons, he extended his reach northward to forests and mills in Wisconsin and Minnesota.

Pioneering a Logging Railroad

DAVID JOYCE HAD BEEN RELYING on logs floated down the Mississippi River from Wisconsin tributaries ever since he purchased an interest in the Stambaugh mill in Lyons in the mid-1850s. As he and other Iowa and Illinois lumbermen continually pushed further north to feed their ravenous mills in the late 1870s, they encountered promising new pine stocks situated midway between the watersheds of Wisconsin's St. Croix and Chippewa Rivers. While rich in white pine, this area lacked suitable driving streams to float the logs to the Mississippi and on to their existing mills, a fact that forced some lumbermen to consider a partnership to manufacture lumber at the timber source rather than at their mills downriver. Shell Lake, Wisconsin, located eighty miles northeast of Minneapolis and seventy miles south of Duluth, Minnesota, thus became the site of a bold venture to process timber at the stump.[1]

The lumbermen now had to find a way to deliver the logs from the woods to the future Shell Lake mill. The men knew that a great deal of timber could be hauled by sled to Shell Lake, floated across the water to a mill to be manufactured into lumber, and shipped out by rail. But they had their eyes on a region with valuable white pine lands that lay beyond practical sledding distances from the lake. In 1880 the lumbermen hatched a plan to build Wisconsin's first dedicated logging railroad as a feeder for a large mill on the shores of Shell Lake.[2]

The use of logging railroads in general quickened the pace of removing timber from the forests. They not only made remote pine stands more accessible they also avoided the difficulties accompanying the occasional mild winter. Traditional logging sleds were only

Left: The Shell Lake Lumber Company mill during the winter of 1897.

usable with ample snow and cold weather. Unseasonably warm winters left logs lying in the woods, sometimes until the following winter season. Many logs were lost forever or were damaged by insects and rot because of the delay. A logging railroad could extract logs year-round, regardless of weather conditions.

Joyce and his fellow lumbermen could also rely on rail transportation for shipping their finished lumber to Midwest markets since a major north-south railroad, commonly referred to as the Omaha Railway or Omaha Lumber Line, had just crossed the Shell Lake area. Prior to the arrival of the Omaha Lumber Line, lumbermen had suffered from the perpetual uncertainties accompanying log driving on the rivers, namely, low water, high water, log theft, sunken logs, and log jams. The loss of logs on a river drive in a good year averaged 10 to 15 percent; in a bad year, higher losses crippled some mills. In 1876—a good year—150 million board feet of sawlogs came down the Chippewa River into the Beef Slough sorting works. Low water in the following two years hampered the log drives and slashed the Beef Slough figures nearly in half, devastating the downriver mills. Floods visited the waterways of the Chippewa in subsequent years, stranding many sawlogs far from the riverbanks, where they could not be recovered.[3]

The Shell Lake Lumber Company

As soon as the problems of transporting timber from forest to mill and finished lumber from mill to market were solved, the men drew up the plans for the Shell Lake sawmill that would, of necessity, be colossal in size and capacity. Competition demanded that a successful mill convert the raw material into lumber as quickly and efficiently as possible. Southern, western, and Canadian mills were beginning to ship lumber into the Midwest, magnifying the competitive atmosphere for men like Joyce who marketed white pine lumber in the same area. The rising value of stumpage, government-taxing policies on timberland, and increasing losses of standing timber to wildfire also supported the need for a large mill. Lumbering of white pine had become a fevered race that the proposed Shell Lake sawmill was about to enter.

The newly formed Shell Lake Lumber Company became one of three affiliated companies located along the Omaha Railway in northern Wisconsin. Joyce's partners in these companies had their own large-scale milling operations and had joined forces before with Joyce in log driving and booming companies like the Mississippi River Logging Company. The lumbermen were Frederick Weyerhaeuser of Rock Island, Illinois; F. C. A. Denkmann, a son-in-law of Frederick Weyerhaeuser, also from Rock Island; Chancy Lamb of Clinton, Iowa; and Delos Moon of Eau Claire, Wisconsin. (Weyerhaeuser was the best known of the lumbermen, and members of logging companies with his name among the investors were often simply referred to as belonging to the Weyerhaeuser Syndicate.) These lumber giants were happy to pool resources. They knew that owning shares in many lumber operations reduced the financial risks associated with owning a single mill.[4]

The three Wisconsin companies shared the Joyces, the Lambs, and the Weyerhaeusers as major investors and members of the boards of directors. Each individual company also had a minor investor who managed the concern. John A. Humbird, a son-in-law of Weyerhaeuser, managed White River Lumber Company in Mason; Captain William R. Bourne, Barronett Lumber Company in Barronett; and A. H. Earle, Shell Lake Lumber Company in Shell Lake. Although David Joyce acted as secretary-treasurer of all three organizations, he concentrated his energy on the Barronett and Shell Lake Companies, while Frederick Weyerhaeuser focused on the White River Lumber Company in Mason. Joyce assigned his son William to manage a headquarters in Minneapolis. This office existed solely for advertising and marketing the products being manufactured in Wisconsin.

The incorporators convened at Shell Lake to develop plans for constructing a mill. They selected a level sixty acres on the northwest shore of the lake between the lake and the Omaha Railway tracks. A tremendous job lay ahead. These men needed not only an extensive mill works to process lumber and a narrow-gauge railroad to transport sawlogs but they also had to build an entire town to house the future workforce.

Joyce went beyond his role as a major investor and his official duties as secretary-treasurer, taking a special interest in the construction and operation of the Shell Lake

Lumber Company. In fact, he spent most of his time in Shell Lake during the construction process and served as the general manager of the mill during its first year of operation. His interests even extended to the systematic development of the burgeoning community.[5]

The first point of business at Shell Lake was to secure an enormous amount of lumber, timber, and piling in order to construct the huge sawmill, ancillary buildings, and housing. The question facing the investors was where the supply of materials would come from. A nearby source would be the most cost effective, and such an opportunity presented itself. N. C. Foster and Captain William R. Bourne, a Civil War veteran, had formed a lumber company known as Foster and Bourne at Barronett, Wisconsin. It appears that the two had a modest sawmill up and running when they learned of the plans for the large milling operation at Shell Lake, only nine miles to the north.[6] The Foster and Bourne sawmill was conveniently located but lacked the capacity and funding to supply the large quantity of lumber needed at Shell Lake. After entering into negotiations with the Joyce contingent, Bourne and Foster accepted an offer to buy them out. The quickly renamed and enlarged Barronett Lumber Company was manufacturing lumber for construction of the mill, shops, and housing at Shell Lake by late 1880.

The Barronett mill was only a bootstrap for the main mill at Shell Lake, yet it was a large mill in its own right once Joyce and his partners pumped in $125,000 to expand the original Bourne-Foster operation. With dimensions of 176 feet by 80 feet, Barronett became one of the more prominent mills of Wisconsin. After its initial job of producing material for Shell Lake, it went on to generate a significant amount of lumber for its owners, operating as an adjunct to the Shell Lake mill. Its output was approximately half of the sawing capacity of Shell Lake.[7]

Walter Hoar's *History Is Our Heritage,* the story of the Shell Lake area, describes the Barronett mill. It consisted "of a saw mill, planing mill, shingle and lath mill, dry shed for finished lumber, lath and shingles, a boarding house [for the workmen], blacksmith and carpenter shops." Three large barns sheltered the horses that were responsible for moving the logs. Water was pumped from a newly drilled well by steam power and "a large windmill was erected as an auxiliary power unit for water pumping purposes."[8] In order to accommodate its workforce, Barronett Lumber Company not only erected homes for its workers but also built and stocked a large company store that permitted employees to buy on credit. The town of Barronett swelled to nearly 500 individuals after the mill had operated for three years. At this time lumber production at Barronett averaged 13 million board feet of lumber annually.

While the Barronett mill churned out lumber in late 1880, the Omaha Railway shipped the material the short distance to Shell Lake for construction of that area's mill. The *Mississippi Valley Lumberman* trade journal documented the new mill's progress by reporting on May 13, 1881, "Shell Lake Lumber Company is pushing work with great activity. The boom is all in and piling for the mill is about driven. A large force of mechanics are erecting tenements, boarding houses and other buildings. They are laying side tracks, fitting machinery and doing everything necessary to get the mammoth establishment under way."[9]

Construction proceeded at a brisk rate to accommodate the owners who wished to activate the saws at the earliest possible date. The power plant and sawmill were the first mill components completed and were operational within a year's time. The power plant contained a brick-lined double boiler, enclosed in a one-story brick building. Motive power came from a 300 horsepower steam engine, fitted with a flywheel twelve feet in diameter. A dynamo supplied the power for electric lighting.* In addition, the power plant provided steam heat for most of the buildings on the site.

The mill was immediately fitted with a circular head saw, the norm for sawmills in 1881. Any large mill bristled with specialty machines using small circular saws. However, it was the head saw that wielded the size and power to make the first cuts in the raw logs as these reached the cutting deck from the holding pond. Only one head saw was installed in 1881, so the mill did not reach its full capacity during its first year of operation. The second head saw, installed in 1882, brought the mill output to its normal operating potential of 200,000 board feet per day, not including the output of shingles and lath.[10]

---

* According to Walter Hoar, electric lighting was in place at the mill. Other sources indicate that this was possible, although it certainly would not have been in common use. Incandescent lights were not available in 1881, but arc lights and dynamos were.

As the mill laborers cut the lumber, shingles, and lath, support buildings for planing and storage were started. The planing mill operated for the first time in 1882, processing the rough-cut lumber from the previous season. After planing, the finished lumber was stored in a 24-foot-by-214-foot weatherproof shed until it was loaded onto rail cars. Construction on the mill site concluded with the completion of another large shed for finished lath and shingles, machine shop, blacksmith shop, locomotive house, car house, turntable, and assorted smaller buildings. Rising above all of these other structures, a twenty-foot wide refuse burner stood 105 feet high. The burner was made of brick and was topped with a carefully maintained spark suppression screen. The prodigious output of waste bark, sawdust, and edgings were conveyed to this burner. Adjacent to the mill, a hot pond, heated by steam pipes, kept the mill operating early and late in the season when ice would have otherwise forced it to shut down.[11] Logs were always floated in the mill hot pond to clean them of dirt and rocks before they were sent on a conveyor chain up an incline to the head saws on the cutting deck.

Even as construction on the mill began, some workers were diverted to another important task—fire control. Their first priority was to clear a substantial firebreak between the surrounding forests and the mill site. The Shell Lake firebreak was probably similar to the one at the Barronett mill, a clearing three-quarters of a mile wide encompassing the mill site and town. The next action was to link all areas of the mill site to a system of piping and hoses. An eight-inch water main with strategically placed fire hydrants ran the length of the mill site. Four hose carts were kept at the ready, each with 500 feet of one-and-one-half-inch hose. These could be supplemented by an additional 3,000 feet of two-and-one-half-inch hose. Water pressure generated by the mill pumping plant could deliver 1,000 gallons per minute. Rounding out the company's fire-fighting arsenal were a number of water wagons, a larger tank wagon, and the company steamboat, which was equipped with a pump and 300 feet of hose. After a major fire swept through the Shell Lake business district in 1889, destroying more than twenty buildings, workers expanded the water system and extended it into town. Again, when the threat of major forest fires mounted in the 1890s, the company enhanced its fire-fighting arsenal by fitting wooden water tanks onto logging railway flat cars.

David Joyce and his partners constantly upgraded the mill and replaced sawing and processing equipment as sawing technology quickly improved throughout the late 1800s. By 1887 the band saw, one of the most important technical advancements, challenged the popularity of circular saws. David Joyce's praise for the band saws, installed in his Lyons, Iowa mill in 1888, promoted the purchase of the same for Shell Lake during 1889 and 1890. Although the band saw could not produce lumber any faster than a circular saw, the advantage came from the narrower kerf, which resulted in less sawdust and more lumber per sawlog. A band saw wasted only one board out of every eight, while a circular saw consumed about one board for every four that were cut. Stated differently, the band saw produced half as much sawdust as a circular saw. The replacement of circular saws by band saws probably happened more as a result of escalating timber prices than as a genuine desire to save the resource.[12]

Shell Lake enthusiastically milled its superior white pine that produced lumber of length and quality unavailable from competing mills. Some of the logs arriving at the mill measured more than four feet at the small end. Breaking its previous records on July 18, 1889, Shell Lake turned out 326,000 board feet of lumber from these magnificent trees, no doubt running two shifts. Normally, during an eleven-hour workday in 1891, the mill processed 100,000 to 175,000 board feet of lumber. An additional 28,000 to 30,000 board feet of lath and 70,000 to 75,000 board feet of shingles were processed from defective logs, lumber, and slabs. Lumber then was sent to the yard for the drying process. The huge stacks of neatly piled lumber were monitored for their moisture level. After drying sufficiently, the lumber received its final processing at the planing mill. Finished lumber, along with shingles and lath, were loaded onto railcars and sent to market on the Omaha Railroad.[13]

The lumber produced at Shell Lake was shipped chiefly to Nebraska, where it was sold through the numerous line yards, many of which were owned by Joyce. In 1887 the Shell Lake Lumber Company was dispatching, on average, 100 carloads of lumber per week to these line yards. Occasionally, Shell Lake shipped to a more distant

The Shell Lake Lumber Company lumberyard workmen. Note the tram tracks used for carting freshly cut lumber from the mill to the lumberyard to be stacked for drying. WASHBURN COUNTY HISTORICAL SOCIETY

destination. It sent one carload of lath to Los Angeles, California, on December 23, 1887. Advertisements run in the *Mississippi Valley Lumberman* trade journal by the sales office in the Twin Cities solicited orders nationwide.[14]

The Crescent Springs Railroad

It was at Shell Lake that David Joyce first explored methods of logging using a dedicated railroad, a strategy later copied and refined in his northern Minnesota operations. Joyce did have some previous experience with a horse railway that he had laid between his hometown of Lyons and the neighboring community of Clinton to transport employees to his mill and serve the public. Although horses provided the motive power, the other details of developing a railroad were similar.

Joyce's narrow-gauge logging railroad in Wisconsin became known as the Crescent Springs Railroad. Narrow-gauge railroads, defined as any railway whose gauge measures less than the standard forty-eight and one-half inches, offered significant advantages when compared to standard-gauge railroads. The thirty-six-inch gauge Crescent Springs operated for about 50 percent of the cost of a standard-gauge railway.[15] Another advantage of the narrow gauge was its lighter rails, ties, and equipment, which made tearing up and laying down track a relatively easy task. In a sense, the rails were brought to the trees instead of the trees to the rails, as was the case with standard-gauge rail lines. The disadvantage of narrow-gauge tracks was that engines and cars from the Crescent Springs Railroad could not transfer to the standard-gauge tracks of the Omaha Railway. A map produced by Walter G. Hoar in his book *History Is Our Heritage* shows a spider-web network of rail lines spreading out from the Shell Lake hub, covering an area of 120 square miles. In total, 84 miles of track were laid down, although at any one time the trackage was only a fraction of this amount.

The train equipment began arriving in 1881 during mill construction. Engine No. 1 was a Schenectady and No. 2, the larger engine, was a Baldwin Mogul. Both were purchased secondhand. The Schenectady hailed from the yellow pine regions of the southern states. The Baldwin had been refurbished in Philadelphia before being shipped to Shell Lake. Both engines were initially fired with waste or defective wood blocks from the shingle mill operation. Later, in 1887, the engines were fueled with coal. The Schenectady engine was apparently replaced at some point because other accounts describe two Baldwin engines and photos support this claim. Rolling stock was comprised of seventy Russell (or Russel) logging cars and a number of boxcars for shipping supplies to the logging camps. Several boxcars were also outfitted as mobile logging-camp housing.[16]

The Crescent Springs Railroad played only a minor part in the transport of logs as

The Crescent Springs Railroad traverses a burned section of forest. WASHBURN COUNTY HISTORICAL SOCIETY

long as ample pine remained in the vicinity of Shell Lake's sparkling waters. The first lumber produced by the Shell Lake Lumber Company was cut from logs harvested on and around the mill site. Logging then proceeded outward from the shores of Shell Lake and into the interior using conventional oxen and horse power to skid logs to the lake. A steamboat, the *Crescent*, was employed to raft logs to the mill booms.[17]

While the areas around Shell Lake were being logged, the first steel for the narrow-gauge railroad was laid in a westward direction from the mill and lake during 1881. The logging supervisor and chief accountant of the mill James Devereux acted as superintendent of the railway construction crew. Initially a compass and axe man blazed the right-of-way. Next the saw crews felled timber and fashioned railway ties. The stump blowers then dynamited the stumps from the narrow-gauge right-of-way in preparation for the grading crews, who employed oxen to power the primitive earth-moving tool called the hand-dump scoop. The process of grading and earth moving later accelerated as horses and wheeled scoops replaced the hand-dump scoop and oxen.

In 1885, when the lumberjacks had harvested nearly all of the timber around and west of Shell Lake, the narrow-gauge railroad tracks were expanded east of the lake and mill. Part of the expansion called for a remarkable trestle to cross Shell Lake's Corbits Bay.[18] The trestle works alone spanned 2,200 feet of water with additional earth-filled approaches at both ends. Pilings for the trestle were red pine, harvested along the western branch lines of the Crescent Springs Railway. As the trestle advanced into the lake, the pilings were quickly topped with rails, allowing the locomotive to continually creep along the leading edge of construction and supply steam power for operating the pile driver. The finished structure carried log-laden trains eight feet above the surface of the water.

After the completion of the trestle in 1886, rails were rapidly pushed on through hilly terrain toward an initial destination of Bear Lake. The building crew cut deeply through these hills in order to keep the grade inclines within the capabilities of the locomotives. In places the cuts reached a depth of 14 feet and stretched distances up to 300 feet. The supply of rails came, in part, by cannibalizing the company's older system of rails west of Shell Lake.

This photo of Shell Lake logging appeared in the February 2, 1894 issue of the *Mississippi Valley Lumberman*.

Woods Operation

The Shell Lake Lumber Company was the first Joyce enterprise that managed its own camps and woods operations. One of these camps was situated near the shores of Mud Lake, which was encircled by a majestic stand of white pine rivaling the finest in northern Wisconsin. After felling the stand, lumberjacks bucked the huge logs to length and then sledded them onto the lake ice, where they accumulated over the winter. Following spring breakup, a loading works hoisted logs out of the water and positioned them on rail cars.

An article in the *Shell Lake Watchman* chronicled logging statistics at the loading works: "A *Watchman* representative took a trip out to Mud Lake on the narrow gauge railroad last Monday and found the loading docks doing a rushing business under Mr. O. E. Stone's excellent management. A few figures obtained while at the works from Mr. Stone and others will be interesting to many of our readers. Imagine, if you can, 13,000,000 feet of logs piled three and four deep in and on the banks of this lake. During the spring and summer this amount has been reduced to such an extent as to leave only 5,000,000 feet now in the lake. One hundred and ten cars are loaded here daily, amounting to about 1100 logs or thereabout, which would scale in the neighborhood of 175,000 feet. All the logs are hauled in on the narrow gauge to the mill in this village by two trains which make four trips each, daily. So perfect is the system of machinery in use that only 18 men are employed in handling the logs. . . . The company has about 175 men working in the woods cutting from 30 to 35 million feet of logs per annum."[19]

More statistics of cuts on Mud Lake and Shell Lake appeared in a March 1889 article in the *Mississippi Valley Lumberman* trade journal: "Bergin's camp has 3,350,000 [board feet of lumber banked on the ice] on Shell Lake and is banking daily 55,000; the steam skidder lands in the neighborhood of 50,000, and Stone's camp 60,000, on the narrow gauge daily; Walsh's camp has over 1,600,000 feet on Mud Lake, and is hauling at the rate of 65,000 a day; and Ripley's camp is landing 100,000 a day on Mud Lake where he has 3,000,000 banked."[20] These logs eventually left the woods bound for the Shell Lake mill on the Crescent Springs Railway.

The use of a steam skidder, basically a steam engine geared to a large reel of cable, facilitated the movement of felled logs to rail side and could "skid all of the logs on a forty acre tract" at one setting, according to a July 1887 *Mississippi Valley Lumberman*.[21] Sometimes the logs were dragged across the ground. Sometimes a "dry flume" or skidway was constructed of logs for a greater degree of efficiency. In its most sophisticated configuration, the skidder was rigged for "high-lead" operation during which logs were actually hoisted into the air while being delivered to rail side. When rigged for high-lead logging, the skidder used a complicated system of cables, pulleys, and spar trees. This technique was frequently applied on a larger scale for logging operations among the mammoth trees of the Pacific coast.[22]

A description of the Shell Lake Lumber Company skidder engaged in high-lead operation was published in an 1891 issue of the Shell Lake newspaper, giving us a picture of the process. "We soon came to where the veteran logger, Mike Welch, was operating the steam skidder. This skidder consists of a steam engine of twenty-four horsepower, sitting side tracked on wheels. Near the skidder is a large pine tree, and attached to this at a distance above the ground of about forty feet, is a heavy wire cable. 600 feet off in the woods is a large oak tree and the end of the cable is attached to it, at a height of about twenty feet above the ground. Both trees are supported by heavy guy-ropes. Over the main wire extending from the pine to the oak is a hanging block working on pulleys and running down from this by means of ropes are grab hooks [which are similar to ice tongs]. The incline from the two [spar] trees to which the cable is attached is sufficient to carry the hanging block or velocipede to the oak tree where men fasten the grab hooks to the logs. The signal is then given to the engineer, and the rope which is attached to the logs is rapidly wound around a huge pulley, and the logs are raised from the ground. Three or four logs go rapidly through the air while the lower ends strike on stumps, logs and other obstructions. . . . We must not cease to look at wonders in mechanical science, and the steam skidder is surely one."[23]

Operation of the Shell Lake Lumber Company skidder required a crew of about twelve men under the direction of foreman Mike Welch. A mobile camp, composed of a dining car and a sleeping car, accompanied the crew to the skidding site. After work

Early logging operations at Shell Lake depended on oxen.
MISSISSIPPI VALLEY LUMBERMAN

was completed at one locale, the entire outfit swiftly relocated by rail to a new one. The steam skidder performed year round but proved particularly useful in the summer months when sledding logs was impossible. In 1891 the experienced crews at the loading works in the forest could fill a railroad car with 1,500 to 2,000 board feet of sawlogs in just four minutes.[24]

Sometimes logs needed to be retrieved beyond the reach of the steam skidder's cable. In those instances, a high wheel skidder assisted. Composed of two giant wagon-style wheels about twelve feet in diameter and connected by an axle, the high wheel skidder could skim the tops of stumps and underbrush. After the lumberjacks chained one end of a group of logs to the high axle, the high wheel skidder, pulled by oxen, could drag the logs across the ground to the steam skidder's cable. Its use was limited to the summer months.[25]

Company Town

When David Joyce invested in the Stambaugh mill in Lyons, Iowa, he did not have to provide housing to attract workers. Lyons was already a flourishing river town with a grain depot and a sawmill industry. This was not the case at the site of the Shell Lake mill. To attract workers, single-family homes were erected rather than barracks because Joyce and his partners sought married men to provide a stable workforce. Out of virtual wilderness, sixty company houses and a large company store appeared during the spring of 1881.[26]

Joyce himself developed the original plat for the village of Shell Lake, specifying the block, lot, and street dimensions and orientation for his surveyor. In the plat he reserved a site for a courthouse since he anticipated the formation of a new county for the area. The plat was approved and signed by company officers Chancy Lamb and David Joyce, and the plan was filed on June 23, 1881.

Even before the mill was up and running, workmen and their families occupied company houses and shopped at the company store, charging their purchases against future earnings. In Shell Lake's early days, not only company workers but also the entire community traded there. Eventually, five or six clerks worked in the 26-foot-by-80-foot building that had steam heat and electric lights powered by the company power plant. The clerks sold flour, feed, hay, crockery, tinware, lamps, and lanterns as part of the store inventory.

Many company towns offered amenities beyond the necessities of room and board. At Phelps, Wisconsin, there was an opera house; at Winegar, a pool hall and movie house; at Wichester, a bandstand and community hall. The Shell Lake Lumber Company provided a billiard hall and art gallery. Mill owners were keenly aware of the importance of a good community environment to attract and retain the skilled men needed to run a sawmill.[27]

Like other mill owners, Joyce and his partners strove unsuccessfully to deter the

The Shell Lake Lumber Company was one of the few logging companies in the Midwest to experiment with high-lead logging, shown here. A spar tree behind the locomotive supports an elaborate system of cables used to hoist logs to rail side. Also illustrated in this photo is one of the Crescent Springs Railway water tank cars used for fire suppression. WASHBURN COUNTY HISTORICAL SOCIETY

disruptive influence of saloons and liquor. Deeds for lots marketed by Shell Lake Lumber Company carried the stipulation that no liquor could be sold on the property. When the election for town officers took place in 1882, 153 out of 186 voters turned down the issue of allowing liquor licenses in Shell Lake. The majority of voters were company men and more than likely followed the suggestions of their superiors. Nevertheless, the saloons "came just the same."[28]

Situated on the Omaha Railroad and now boasting a large lumber mill and a picturesque lake, Shell Lake naturally drew more settlement and business development. In 1882 the community counted 500 inhabitants, and the company continued to build homes for employees. Merchants thrived, and the two hotels bustled with boarders, most commonly mill laborers.[29] Through its enthusiastic growth, the town of Shell Lake eventually shed its status as a company town and gained the stature of a self-sustaining community.

Joyce's belief that a new county would form proved to be correct. Two years later Washburn County separated from what had originally been Burnett County territory. In 1885 the newly organized government purchased the site that Joyce had reserved for a courthouse. Shell Lake Lumber Company received $1500 payment for the lot.

A Sea of Flames

The sandy pinelands of northern Wisconsin were prone to wild fire. A major conflagration, called the Peshtigo fire, had ripped through the area in 1871.[30] With this knowledge, David Joyce and his Shell Lake and Barronett business partners had taken elaborate measures to protect their company towns, mills, and lumber yards. Their lines of defense were put to the test during the summer of 1894 as a staggering number of fire storms tracked across the Minnesota and Wisconsin border area, the famous Hinckley (Minnesota) fire of 1894 being just a single incident during that fire season. All three of the Wisconsin lumbering operations in which Joyce had an interest suffered. But the biggest loss would be David Joyce's life, arguably an indirect result of the fires.

The year 1894 was unique for the extreme intensity of fires, but fire was always a threat during dry periods. A prelude to the conflagrations of 1894 took place in 1891. In September of that year a spark landed on the large building that stored Shell Lake Lumber Company's finished lumber prior to shipment. The fire quickly consumed the building and stored lumber and spread to several piles of drying lumber. Flames jumped the adjoining street and claimed one of the company housing units. The company's fire fighting equipment and water system certainly stalled the fire, but the southeast direction of the wind was more significant in preventing the fire from spreading into the mill and yard areas. Had the wind been blowing from any other direction the damage could have been much more serious. The total loss, estimated at $10,000, was covered by insurance.[31] Little did anyone suspect that the fires of 1891 would pale in comparison to what was coming in three years' time.

The magnitude of the firestorms was generally due to logging activity, which left large areas dry, covered with slash, and open to the wind. Sparse rainfall compounded the situation when accompanied by howling winds and high temperatures. In August 1894 these hazardous conditions led to widespread fires across the Midwest. Fires plagued not only forested regions but also places like Chicago. One of the most serious lumberyard fires in the country swept through forty acres of the Chicago lumber district, reducing the expansive lumber piles to "nothing but smoking embers." The resulting losses equaled $1.6 million. Fires also swept through several Minneapolis lumberyards a few days before the Chicago fire.[32] Fear was evident everywhere as fire after fire demolished forests, towns, and mills. The extent of damage was beyond belief.

The Shell Lake Lumber Company's sister mill, the White River Lumber Company in Mason, Wisconsin, was reduced to ashes by a fire in early August 1894, one of many mill towns to succumb during that month. Mill manager John Humbird had positioned his men around the perimeter of the mill site. They effectively fought off advancing flames until the gale of wind, blowing from the southwest, threw flaming brands high into the air. When these landed in the middle of the lumberyard, the area practically exploded in flames. Humbird lamented, "From that minute we were helpless."[33] Lost at

Mason were the sawmill, planing mill, 33 million feet of lumber, and employee housing. The loss was estimated at $700,000. The fire had so thoroughly scoured the site, noted Humbird, that "hardly a bushel of ashes was left."[34]

Flames advanced upon Barronett and Shell Lake on September 1, 1894, while Captain Bourne, who managed the Barronett Lumber Company, attended a meeting in Minneapolis with David Joyce and other lumbermen. Bourne was assuring them that "his mill was in no danger because all the timber within three-quarters of a mile of it had been cleared" when "word came that Barronett was on fire. Flames driven by a violent southwest wind had whipped across the protective area and were destroying the town and mill."[35]

The September 6, 1894 issue of the *Watchman* headlined the story: "BARRONETT. The Once Prosperous Village Wiped Entirely Out of Existence. The Loss About $350,000, and 500 People Driven from their Homes." The newspaper continued with the details: "Barronett was the worst sufferer in this section from the fire. A sea of flames swept over the place at 2:00 Saturday afternoon, and in 30 minutes the Company Store, the Mill, Depot, Lumberyards and in fact every place in the village was entirely wiped out. Nothing but burned poles and ashes now mark the site of this once thriving village." Strangely, a pile of ice remained where the icehouse had been. Protected by wet sawdust, the stacked ice survived the flames and remained for several days the only source of drinking water available after the fire.

Everyone in Barronett experienced unparalleled losses. Barronett Lumber Company lost everything:

13,500,000 feet of lumber . . . . $	130,000
13,000,000 shingles . . . . $	19,000
4,000,000 lath . . . . $	5,000
sawmill . . . . $	40,000
planing mill. . . . . $	10,000
boarding house. . . . . $	3,000

three barns.	$	2,000
dry shed.	$	1,000
company store, office and stock.	$	13,000
windmill.	$	2,000
blacksmith and carpenter shop with tools. . . .	$	10,000
logging sheds.	$	7,000
25 dwelling houses.	$	20,000
200 tons of hay and shed.	$	3,000
10,000 cords of slab.	$	10,000
Total Loss.	$	275,000[36]

The company as well as private individuals also lost livestock. Nevertheless, chickens survived the ordeal, apparently healthy but minus their feathers, which were burned off.[37]

The people of Barronett sacrificed all of their earthly possessions but escaped with their lives, primarily because of the evacuation route made possible by the Omaha Railroad. The railroad's passenger trains pulled into the town just as the fire blasted the edges of the community. Years later, Mrs. Frank (Marsh) Brookshaw remembered the fire that occurred when she was twelve years old: "When the trains finally arrived we [citizens of Barronett] boarded the southbound which went back through the fire. . . . Burning trees were falling in every direction. Paint on the coaches was blistering and the wooden trestles and bridges we crossed were beginning to burn."[38] The mill employees who had stayed behind to protect the mill avoided death by burying themselves in pits dug along the railroad tracks and remaining there until the following morning.[39] A large rutabaga field shielded some as they lay face down in the dirt, the rutabagas later sustaining the survivors.

Even as Barronett refugees poured into Shell Lake ahead of the inferno, Shell Lake braced for the onslaught of flames flying on the gale force winds. All of the company's superior fire fighting equipment and men readied for the fire still could not spare the town from tragedy. The fire approached from the southwest, breaking through one fire line after another, eventually entering the housing district of the village. According to Walter Hoar in *History Is Our Heritage*, "The fire fighters were forced to retreat, there being no further means of holding a line. The high wind now swept the fire with a great roar over 'Bible Hill', forcing the residents of this section to flee, leaving most of their household articles to burn. Seven blocks of buildings now lie in ashes . . . ."[40] The heroic efforts of the fire fighters and, probably to a greater extent, a shift in the wind direction safeguarded the mill area and most of Shell Lake from destruction. Only one person died as a direct result of the fire, which was amazing compared to the lives lost elsewhere.

The events of that day remained as vivid memories long after the fire. Emma Nell Stevenson, who lived in the company housing at Shell Lake, gave the following eyewitness account:

"That spring, Dunk, my husband, got a job in town at the mill. The summer was unusually dry; there were forest fires all around us. It was quite common for us to be awakened in the night with a call for Dunk to go out and fight fires. Then came the first of September. The sky was so thick with smoke, we could hardly breathe. We had not seen the sun for several days. On Saturday, the same day as the Hinckley fire, we heard that Barronett had burned to the ground. That was only nine miles away.

"They shut down the mill and all the men were out fighting fire. . . . When the orders came to rush to the depot to board a train, I stuck Angus [her infant son] into the old dilapidated baby buggy, also five loaves of bread, a pound of butter, two pies and a ring of bologna, as I figured that no matter what happened, we had to eat. I'll never forget the commotion at the depot. The train was made up of boxcars, cabooses, passenger cars and flat cars. There was everything loaded on, from dogs to family pictures. . . . I was the only one who had brought any food, so about midnight I brought out my 'loaves and fishes' and they went like hot cakes. Next morning we had orders to return to Shell Lake. We found the town the most dilapidated place I ever saw. We did not know what to expect but made a bargain between us that anyone who was not burned out, should befriend those that were. Sixty-five houses were burned, but the wind had changed in time to save most of the town. Our house was still there. Almost everyone who was not burned out had a family with them until they could put up some kind of a shelter. . . . The wells all dried up so we had to use lake water and consequently, a regular epidemic of typhoid fever broke out. In less than three weeks, there were forty cases of it and some people died."[41]

The Shell Lake Lumber Company, which escaped with only $2,200 in damages, did what it could to aid the families made homeless by the fire. The mill closed for seven days, allowing the men to help with relief efforts. Lumber was provided at less than cost for the rebuilding of homes while the company stock of mattresses for the lumber camps was offered to the victims seeking shelter at the Methodist church.[42]

The village of Shell Lake recovered rapidly from its damages totaling $63,470. Within a month of the fire, half of the burned section of town had been reconstructed, and most of the remaining construction was completed in the following month. Many of the new buildings were better than those they replaced. The people of Shell Lake were justly proud of their indomitable drive to repair the fire damage in such a short period. Praising their efforts, the Shell Lake newspaper crowed, "We question if there is a town in Northern Wisconsin, where more pluck has been displayed than we can proudly boast of in Shell Lake."[43]

David Joyce Meets His End

After the fire had swept across northern Wisconsin, David Joyce immediately set out for Shell Lake to assess the extent of damage to his mills and pinelands. He arrived directly from his business meetings in Minneapolis along with other owners of the Shell Lake Lumber Company, including the Lambs and Captain Bourne. Joyce would have been in Shell Lake anyway. He had previously scheduled an inspection trip to Shell Lake and Barronett following his business meetings and convention in Minneapolis. Frederick Weyerhaeuser, another owner, was vacationing in Europe at the time of the fires. Even though he cut his trip short, a month would elapse before his return to Wisconsin.[44]

Upon his arrival in northern Wisconsin, Joyce tramped through the countryside, looking over the still smoldering pinelands and the ashen remains of the Barronett mill with his thirty-four year old son William. William returned to Lyons to supervise the mill operations in Iowa and Illinois while his father stayed at Shell Lake for the next two months to deal with the aftermath of the fire. During this time Joyce determined which lands needed to be salvaged immediately. Fire-damaged trees are quickly attacked by insects, and the valuable stumpage could be lost if not harvested within the year. He then redirected tracks for the logging railroad into the salvage areas and decided where haul roads would have to be built. One new three-mile track was extended into a heavy stand of burned timber near the southwest end of Bear Lake. In addition to the frenzied workload at Shell Lake, David Joyce regularly commuted to St. Paul and Minneapolis, where he conducted business for his many other enterprises, even setting up a temporary office at the West Hotel.[45]

David Joyce and the other Barronett Lumber Company mill owners decided to forego rebuilding the Barronett mill. The 40 million board feet of standing timber left in the vicinity did not warrant such an expense, so the scorched timber that had been scheduled for sawing at the Barronett mill would be milled at Shell Lake instead.

The Omaha Railroad would ship the sawlogs from Barronett the nine miles to Shell Lake.[46]

By early November, after two months of non-stop activity, Joyce felt the operation of the Shell Lake Lumber Company was in order. The mill was about to shut down for the season, allowing him to return to his home in Lyons, Iowa. En route he stopped in Minneapolis at the West Hotel to rest. He suffered a stroke, and there, three weeks later, with his son and wife at his side, died on December 4, 1894. In a sense, David Joyce was one more victim of the 1894 fires.[47]

In retrospect, Joyce, then sixty-nine years old, was not physically strong enough for the demanding schedule following the fire at Shell Lake. His normal activities in the preceding years had been drastically limited by accident and illness. In August 1889, five years before the fire, "Mr. Joyce was seated in a buggy in front of his office in Lyons, Iowa," reported the *Mississippi Valley Lumberman*, "when a passing train frightened his horse, and Mr. Joyce was thrown out suffering a fracture of his right leg about an inch above the ankle."[48] Within a year he suffered another accident when he fell down a flight of stairs. Compounding his health problems were ongoing bouts of rheumatism that were at times severe enough to confine him to his home in Lyons.[49]

The *Mississippi Valley Lumberman* trade journal and the *Shell Lake Watchman* carried an unprecedented number of articles praising David Joyce for his business practices. The journal spoke of a man "respected and honored everywhere" whose name "will ever be a synonym for all that is the strongest and best in the world of the lumber trade."[50] The newspaper reported that the citizens of Shell Lake, Wisconsin, remembered David Joyce as "a man of esteemed worth and character, wise in counsel, discreet in judgment and kind and obliging to all, respected as a citizen and loved by his associates and employees." They grieved "the loss of a public spirited counselor" as well as a "faithful, kind and conscientious friend, one who has ever aided in building our houses and providing the sustenance of life."[51] As far as the Shell Lake Company employees were concerned, Joyce had been "looked upon more as a father than an employer."[52]

The Final Years at Shell Lake

William Joyce was eminently capable of managing the far-flung business empire left to him. But his new style of corporate management would not endear him to the employees and citizens of Shell Lake. While David Joyce had taken personal interest in the day-to-day activities of the Shell Lake Lumber Company, his son chose to let mill managers and other partners assume a higher level of control. Frederick Weyerhaeuser, a partner in the company, replaced David Joyce as secretary-treasurer.[53] William's detachment from Shell Lake was pragmatic. He would put his energies into his father's larger lumbering operations elsewhere that had a more promising future. The future of Shell Lake was clear. A simple calculation, based on the amount of unharvested timber and the production capacity of the mill, showed that the mill would only operate until 1900.

William Joyce was not the only new voice of authority at Shell Lake. The loss of the Barronett Lumber Company mill in the fire left Captain Bourne without a mill to manage. In 1895 he was transferred to Shell Lake to assume responsibility for the surviving mill, replacing Mr. Earle, who had been in charge of Shell Lake since David Joyce turned the position over to him in 1882. The Shell Lake employees resented this move. They liked the capable Mr. Earle. They credited him with saving the mill. And they suspected the overconfident Bourne was responsible for the town of Barronett as well as its mill going up in flames.

Bourne's life as a military man was apparent as he quite literally took command of Shell Lake. He instituted strict rules. Supplies and foodstuffs were tightly controlled. No longer would visitors to the logging camps be able to enjoy the tasty camp meals. An interview with logging camp cook William (Billie) Coleman in 1954 verifies this side of Bourne: "When I first went to work for Capt. Bourne, he said: 'Don't feed any women!' However, I used to set up food at one end of a table, and by a nod of my head or a flip of my hand (but without a murmur), indicate that they should help themselves."[54] Whatever his failings, a stern and autocratic Bourne successfully supervised the Shell Lake Lumber Company. Improvements to the mill and Crescent Springs Railroad were ongoing until the company exhausted the white pine.

After twenty years of logging, the last load on the Crescent Springs rolled into the mill on September 17, 1901. Slightly more than five weeks later, on October 24, 1901, the Shell Lake Lumber Company completed the dismantling of the narrow-gauge track. All that survived was the roadbed, which the company gave to the town of Shell Lake after reconditioning the surface for wagon travel. Captain Bourne negotiated this gift. Everything that could be sold was: the rolling stock, the buildings at the various camps, and all the timber and piling of the trestle works, with the exception of the piling across Corbits Bay.

Even before the mill had been built, the timber resources of the Shell Lake area had been carefully calculated, forecasting a twenty-year cutting cycle before depletion. In spite of ongoing fires that whittled away at the timber base, the twenty-year prediction held true, since additional purchases of pinelands and the harvesting of hardwoods offset the trees taken by fire. During its two decades of operation, the Shell Lake Lumber Company cut approximately 584 million board feet of lumber, 224 million board feet of shingles, and 113 million board feet of lath. The sawmill shut down in 1901, but the planing mill ran until October 1, 1902.

The company still held 20,000 acres of cutover land when the planing mill closed. This was after an aggressive sales campaign during which local settlers purchased only 200 parcels. Tired of these fruitless marketing attempts, Joyce allowed Captain Bourne to hastily sell the 20,000 acres to a land speculator "at a price between $2.50 and $3.00 an acre." Historian Joseph Ernst observed that Bourne's sale "proved to be a rash mistake."[55] Within a few years of the mill closing, the land around Shell Lake significantly grew in value in response to a growing resort industry. Regardless of this disappointment, David and William Joyce realized profits and garnered the necessary logging railroad expertise that allowed them to expand their lumbering operations into Minnesota, Texas, and Louisiana.

The Itasca Lumber Company on Swan River

IN ITS UPPERMOST REACHES, the Mississippi River begins a great arc to the west, bending under the influence of the continental divide in northern Minnesota. Here, men intent on harvesting the last vestiges of the Mississippi River white pine cast a calculating eye on the numerous tributaries leading northward, including the Swan River. The lumbermen's interest was warranted. In 1877 the nationally known *Mississippi Valley Lumberman* journal printed a lengthy description of the timber reserves of tributaries found along the upper reaches of the Mississippi River. This report estimated that the pine timber within the Swan River watershed amounted to 560 million board feet, enough timber to build a boardwalk four and one-half feet wide all around the earth at the equator.[1]

The headwaters of the Swan River are near the city of Hibbing. From there, several meager streams, called O'Brien, Hay, and Hart Creeks, trace a southerly course, eventually emptying into the large expanse of Swan Lake. Exiting Swan Lake, the Swan River proper begins, joining with the Mississippi River in the southeast quadrant of Itasca County. Unique for its location, the Swan watershed is perched squarely in the middle of the three great continental river systems of Minnesota. While the waters of the Swan flow to the Gulf of Mexico, its neighboring watersheds to the north and east flow to Hudson Bay or the Atlantic. Today's visitor to the area may miss the unremarkable Swan River as it ripples beneath the busy highways, but for a brief time it carried hundreds of millions of board feet of saw logs toward the Mississippi.

In 1882 the federal government, the largest landowner in the state of Minnesota at that time, sold a significant swath of land in the Duluth district that contained much of Itasca County. Minnesota's preeminent land speculators, John S. Pillsbury and T. B.

Walker, both of Minneapolis, added to their growing land holdings during this sale. In just five days, Pillsbury secured 8,385 acres while Walker, the third largest landowner in the state, gained 10,089 acres. Typical of T. B. Walker's property acquisitions was the purchase of eleven sections or eleven square miles in Lone Pine Township near Swan Lake on December 13, 1882.[2] The total land area involved in the timber deals with Walker and Pillsbury was truly enormous. These land sales precipitated the advent of large-scale logging in the region.

On February 16, 1886, Robert W. Turnbull of Wisconsin, Samuel B. Barker of Illinois, and Healy C. Akeley of Minnesota purchased the pine timber on the coveted Pillsbury property located in the Upper Mississippi region.[3] This purchase featured large holdings in the Swan River district. Supplementing the purchase were timber rights bought from T. B. Walker. Turnbull, Barker, and Akeley planned to log the timber and then drive it on the Mississippi to Minneapolis sawmills. They were not alone in the rush for timber. Many other individuals and companies competed for stumpage.

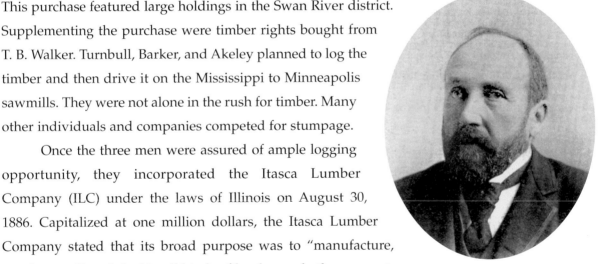

H. C. Akeley
MISSISSIPPI VALLEY LUMBERMAN

Once the three men were assured of ample logging opportunity, they incorporated the Itasca Lumber Company (ILC) under the laws of Illinois on August 30, 1886. Capitalized at one million dollars, the Itasca Lumber Company stated that its broad purpose was to "manufacture, purchase, sell, and deal in all kinds of lumber and other property, products and merchandise."[4] During its first years of existence, the ILC occupied itself with company organization and continued timber appropriation. In 1889 the *Mississippi Valley Lumberman* trade journal reported that the company controlled "a larger amount of stumpage on the Upper Mississippi waters than any single firm or individual."[5]

The partners had taken another measure to ensure their success. The narrow and shallow Swan River was not ideal for driving the masses of logs to be cut by the Itasca

Lumber Company as well as several other companies. To get all of the logs out required a torrent of water to swell the river. As early as 1877, the first loggers in the area built a dam at the outlet of Swan Lake for this purpose. Their crude dam created the artificially high head of water in Swan Lake necessary for the log drives. This dam needed rebuilding by the time the Itasca Lumber Company entered the scene ten years later. Recognizing the benefits that control of the dam would bring, the ILC took ownership of the site. Akeley and his partners then sought official government license to secure their investment. In 1887 the Itasca County government, based at that time in the town of Aitkin, granted the ILC an official charter for the construction of a logging dam at the outlet of Swan Lake. This charter was granted for a period of six years. Other logging companies, which had no recourse but to send their logs through the ILC dam, paid five cents per thousand-foot measure. More than a century later, this dam, even in its contemporary form, continues to be referred to as the "charter dam" by residents of the nearby town of Pengilly.[6]

David Joyce saw great potential for the company that now controlled in excess of 750 million board feet of pine on the northern Mississippi tributaries. On April 2, 1889, he bought out Robert Turnbull's third of the company stock.[7] Joyce took over the position of vice-president, Akeley retained his role as president, and Barker served as the secretary-treasurer. Joyce's affiliations with the Middle Mississippi lumbermen in Iowa and Illinois guaranteed markets for Itasca Lumber Company logs.

At about the same time, Healy C. Akeley, with funding from David Joyce and others—most notably, Charles Hackley and Thomas Hume of Muskegon, Michigan—incorporated the H. C. Akeley Lumber Company for the purpose of milling lumber at Minneapolis from the timber being cut by the Itasca Lumber Company on the Swan River.[8] The Akeley mill would soon gain the distinction of being the largest mill in the Midwest, consistently out producing all other competitors.

David Joyce's ability to provide operating capital was essential for the success of both the ILC and the H. C. Akeley Lumber Company. In fact, Joyce's partners remarked on his "rather deep pockets." Akeley, taking note of world affairs, quipped to Joyce, "If

Baring Brothers or any similar institution gets into financial trouble again, I shall refer them to you for help."*[9]

Having secured the necessary operating capital from Joyce, the lumbermen now had to figure out how to get the logs out of the Swan, which was problematic in spite of the dam and other improvements to the waterway. The company banked logs along the frozen Swan River and Swan Lake in preparation for the spring breakup when the high water would start the logs on their long journey to Minneapolis or beyond. In the spring of 1890, three hundred men toiled to keep the logs moving, more men than were working on any other tributary above Aitkin on the Upper Mississippi. The low volume of water that year tested the stamina of every man as 40 million board feet of logs dragged the river bottom the length of the Swan. Ten million board feet of logs were stranded high and dry in Swan Lake's western bay and never made it through the sluicing dam at the outlet. These would have to wait until the log drive the following season. Even though the large quantity of logs that were sluiced through the dam profited the company, it was discouraging to realize the impossibility of increasing the annual cut of timber because of the river's limited carrying capacity.[10]

This was just the kind of problem that David Joyce knew how to address. Since he had previous experience with logging railroads in Wisconsin and Texas, his entry into the Itasca Lumber Company immediately precipitated talk of the company building a railroad to access the timber in the Swan River country.[11] The construction of a logging railroad could potentially allow the lumbermen to eliminate river transportation on the Swan entirely. Logs could be dumped directly on the frozen Mississippi River from rail cars. From there they could be floated to the mills in Minneapolis during the traditional spring log drive. At a meeting in Minneapolis on July 26, 1889, ILC stockholders Joyce, Akeley, and Barker announced their decision to construct such a railroad. As reported in the *Mississippi Valley Lumberman* trade journal, the railroad would run from the Mississippi River near the current town of Jacobson, approximately twenty-five miles

*Baring Brothers refers to an English family of financiers and bankers who overextended themselves in loans made to the Argentine Republic and were bailed out by the British government.

into the standing timber at the headwaters of the Swan River. The trade journal claimed their proposal was probably the most significant one that "has yet been made on the upper waters of the Mississippi. Heretofore the mills have been dependent upon the spring freshets for their supply of logs. But the Itasca company doesn't propose to be wholly dependent upon the fickle waters hereafter." As put forth, this railroad would not only be the longest but one of the only lines in Minnesota built for the sole purpose of log transport. The journal speculated that such a venture would permit year-round logging.[12] The company would also benefit in another way. It could realize a profit from hauling the logs of its many competitors in the area.

Building the railroad was feasible, but the men struggled with the logistics of delivering machinery and equipment to the remote site. Overland roads and railroads did not exist in Itasca County at the time. The Duluth and Winnipeg Railroad was in the process of building its line from Duluth and would eventually reach Swan River, but the arrival date was uncertain. Joyce and his partners had posted an optimistic start date of spring 1890 for the construction of their railroad and wanted to be hauling logs by the middle of that same year, so they decided not to wait for the Duluth and Winnipeg. Rather, they planned to ship all of the rails, cars, locomotives, and other equipment by steamboat from the Mississippi River town of Aitkin, fifty miles by water downstream. The plan proved to be impractical. Possibly they miscalculated the viability of shipping standard-gauge railroad equipment on the meager fleet of boats plying the Upper Mississippi and were forced to wait for the advancing rails of the Duluth and Winnipeg Railroad, owned by Ami W. Wright and Charles H. Davis. These two men from Michigan also owned extensive timberlands in the Swan River area.

The Itasca Lumber Company never built the proposed logging railroad at Swan River. Instead, Wright and Davis did. Wright and Davis were negotiating a sale of their 45,000 acres of Swan River timber to Frederick Weyerhaeuser and his associates for $1.2 million. With this sale pending, Wright and Davis could see that they were in a good position to build their own logging railroad to carry the timber of the Weyerhaeuser group along with that of the ILC and other logging companies. They already owned the larger Duluth and Winnipeg Railroad, which would facilitate the construction of a secondary logging railroad. Furthermore, surveyors had been reporting dramatic compass deviations on land in this district for years. These deviations were a strong indication of iron deposits. Wright and Davis may have suspected that a logging railroad into the area might eventually profit by mining activity, yet another incentive for them to build the railroad.

Certainly Wright and Davis and the Itasca Lumber Company would have had to work out some mutually beneficial agreement. The result was that the Itasca Lumber Company agreed to abandon its planned railroad and relied upon the rail services of the Wright and Davis logging railroad once it was built. As Wright and Davis were beginning to survey a route for their logging railroad in 1891, they also extended the Duluth and Winnipeg Railroad tracks to the Swan River crossing and then continued to lay track to Bass Brook, another tributary of the Mississippi located approximately twenty-one miles northwest of Swan River. The extension allowed the Itasca Lumber Company to fulfill its desire to forge its own logging railroad northward in 1891 to company timber holdings in the Bass Brook area. The ILC's Bass Brook logging railroad was actually completed a year ahead of the Wright and Davis logging railroad.[13]*†

In 1892 Wright and Davis's logging railroad, incorporated as the Duluth, Mississippi River, and Northern Railroad, hauled its first logs for the Swan River Logging Company, the Itasca Lumber Company, and others. The railroad fueled an explosion in the quantity of timber coming out of the Swan River district. By 1894 the standard-gauge railroad used six locomotives and two hundred logging cars on some twenty-five miles

---

*According to Frank King, author of *Minnesota Logging Railroads*, the honor of the first logging railroad in Minnesota goes to J. M. Paine & Company, who built a short logging railroad near Duluth in 1886. Three other short logging railroads were built in 1890 elsewhere in the state. The Itasca Lumber Company Railroad at Bass Brook came next in 1891, followed by the Wright and Davis railroad in 1892.

†The Itasca Lumber Company did not confine its logging to the Swan River but also logged on many other tributaries of the Mississippi in northern Minnesota. According to a report in the 1892 *Mississippi Valley Lumberman*, the joint efforts of the H. C. Akeley Lumber Company and the Itasca Lumber Company "put 16 million feet into the Crow Wing, 20 million feet on the Pine, 15 million feet on Bass Brook, 5 million feet on Bear River, 20 million feet on Prairie River, 28 million feet on the Swan, 2 million feet in the Mississippi below Pokegama falls and 3 million feet on the river above." The two closely allied firms, essentially one-in-the-same, planned on sending 100 million board feet of logs downriver. Although these firms relied on their own crews to get the logs out, they also hired independent contractors such as Price Brothers, Powers and Dwyer, and John Frazier to assist in the mammoth cut ("Around The Twin Cities," *MVL*, 1 July 1892).

of track that extended to Swan Lake and surrounding lakes. The total haul on the logging railroad for 1894 hit the 145 million board feet mark, an amazing figure that prompted the *Mississippi Valley Lumberman* to exclaim, "The operations . . . have surpassed anything heretofore done on the [tributaries of the] Mississippi River."[14] The journal attributed 31.5 million board feet of this stupendous cut to the Itasca Lumber Company. A listing of Itasca Lumber Company camps, identified by the name of the camp foreman, detailed the harvest. On Beauty Lake, four miles southeast of Swan Lake, John Craig's camp was cutting 12 million board feet; J. Toppin's camp, 3.5 million board feet; William McDermott's camp, 3 million. John Chisholm's camp was cutting on Hart Lake, one mile south of Swan Lake, but the cut figure was not given.[15] There was additional output by Itasca Lumber Company camps banking logs along the Swan River.

In 1895 a reporter for the *Mississippi Valley Lumberman* stood at the log landing at the mouth of the Swan River on the Mississippi where the Itasca Lumber Company and other firms banked their

As enormous as the quantity of logs spewing out of the Swan River district was, the lumbermen focused solely on timber missed the bigger bonanza of wealth that lay beneath their feet. This would be a lesson that David Joyce and his descendants would never forget. Wright and Davis had originally offered mineral rights on their 45,000 acres to the Weyerhaeuser group for a mere $100,000, a tiny fraction of its true value. Weyerhaeuser wanted to buy the mineral rights along with the timber, but his associates outvoted him.

Business tycoon James J. Hill was willing to gamble on the mineral rights rejected by Weyerhaeuser and his associates and developed the properties for mining. He purchased the Duluth, Mississippi River and Northern Railroad in 1897, along with the Duluth and Winnipeg, absorbing them into his Great Northern railway system. Hill made millions in the process. Weyerhaeuser, upon seeing what had slipped through his hands, commented, "And to think we could have had all that land for $100,000!"[16] To insure that such a mistake would not befall Joyce, the Itasca Lumber Company, as well as his other lumbering companies around the country, religiously surveyed their lands for possible mineral value.

The Duluth, Mississippi River and Northern Railroad, which was hauling logs for the ILC and other companies in 1895, started hauling iron ore—250,000 tons of the ore—that year.[17] Ore cars were switched onto the tracks of the Great Northern for transport to Duluth and beyond. Eventually, the Duluth, Mississippi River and Northern Railroad, begun as a logging railroad, would carry iron ore almost exclusively.

logs for the spring log drives. Early in the spring he observed "more logs assembled than have ever been collected in any railway up to that time. There were over 45 million feet on the rollway, and the logs extended in a magnificent stretch for a mile down the stream, until lost to view by a bend in the Mississippi. They were piled nearly the full width of the stream, and were 25 to 30 tiers deep, reaching from the bottom of the river to the level of the tracks. The site was an impressive one and long to be remembered."[18]

This report was understated, for the logs continued to be banked at the rate of 400,000 board feet per day by the railway. The estimate for the total cut for the ten logging companies in the Swan River district in 1895 was 171 million board feet, surpassing the previous year's cut by 26 million board feet. The ILC's cut was estimated at 30 million board feet. Of the ten companies, the ILC had the second largest cut.[19] That year the quantity of logs pouring out of the Swan River district on the Wright and Davis railroad reached its zenith.

The innovations of the Itasca Lumber Company and Wright and Davis signaled a shift in the way logging was done. In six short years from the time the Itasca Lumber Company first proposed the construction of a railroad, logging methods statewide had shifted to the use of logging railroads with an astounding two-thirds of the entire cut in the Upper Mississippi region hauled by rail, either to landings on the Mississippi River or directly to sawmills.[20]

As the turn of the century approached, pine harvests on the Swan River ebbed rapidly. By 1908 the big loggers were all but gone, leaving only small, scattered lots of logs, cut by local farmers. Joyce's Itasca Lumber Company had long since moved further up the Mississippi to pursue the receding white pine frontier. *The Itasca County Independent* printed a brief epitaph in 1908, marking the end of an era. "Swan River, down which the finest kind of white pine floated by the millions of feet but a few years ago is done."[21]

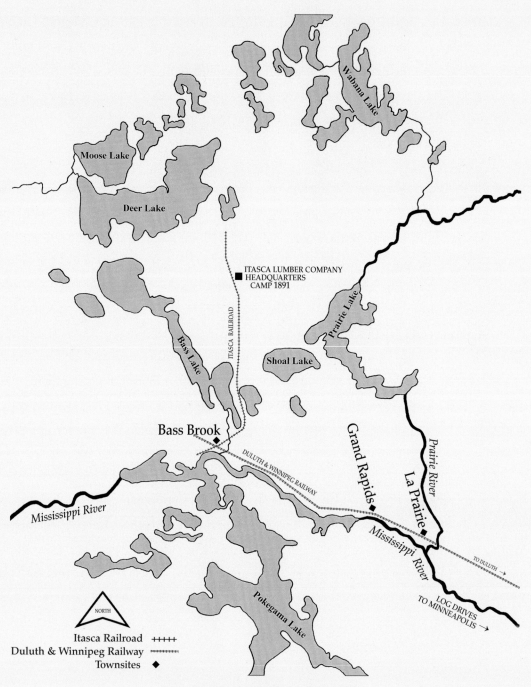

Moose Lake

Deer Lake

Wabana Lake

ITASCA LUMBER COMPANY
HEADQUARTERS
CAMP 1891

Prairie Lake

Bass Lake

ITASCA RAILROAD

Shoal Lake

Bass Brook

DULUTH & WINNIPEG RAILWAY

Grand Rapids

Prairie River

La Prairie

Mississippi River

Mississippi River

TO DULUTH →

LOG DRIVES
TO MINNEAPOLIS →

Pokegama Lake

NORTH

Itasca Railroad +++++
Duluth & Winnipeg Railway ┼┼┼┼┼
Townsites ◆

ITASCA RAILROAD 1891–1893

The Itasca Railroad

BASS BROOK FLOWS INTO THE MISSISSIPPI RIVER at the present town of Cohasset and is only about a mile in length. As early as the 1870s lumbermen working in northern Minnesota had begun logging the shorelines of seven-mile-long Bass Lake that formed the stream's headwaters. An estimated 50 million board feet of white and Norway pine, plus cedar stands, covered Bass Lake's immediate periphery.[1] In these early years the lumbermen first cut the pine within sight of the water's edge. After harvesting the shoreline, they reached surrounding pine stands by building ice roads that radiated outward from the lake. They sledded the logs to the shore on these temporary roadways. When the Itasca Lumber Company (ILC) arrived at Bass Lake in the late 1880s, the distance to the white pine had significantly increased with the largest remaining stands concentrated several miles to the east. The ILC owners knew that a logging railroad, built through the heart of the best stands, would greatly speed up logging by avoiding long sled hauls to the lake and drives down the small brook. A logging railroad would also make possible year-round logging. Logs loaded onto cars near the stump could be dumped directly into the Mississippi River near the mouth of Bass Brook. The railroad would again provide the solution to the perennial problem of extracting timber from an area without adequate log-driving streams.

Once a decision had been made to build the railroad, the most pressing obstacle was how to transport the heavy equipment needed to build and operate it. The area was not only a wilderness without roads, but falls and rapids blocked Mississippi River travel below Bass Brook. Fortunately for the ILC, the Duluth and Winnipeg Railroad continued to expand westward after it completed its line to Swan River on December 10, 1889. It reached Grand Rapids in July 1890. By the end of 1890, tracks had been laid to Bass Brook, the new end of the line. Now the Itasca Lumber Company could construct its railroad.[2]

Some indications suggest that Wright and Davis, builders of the Duluth and Winnipeg, extended the line to Bass Brook in the waning months of 1890 in order to help the establishment of the Itasca Lumber Company's logging railroad. As mentioned in the previous chapter, Wright and Davis and the Itasca Lumber Company seem to have cooperated with each other in their railroad and logging operations. Their adjacent tracts of timber in northern Minnesota encouraged a joint effort.

Itasca Lumber Company owners H. C. Akeley and Samuel Barker relied on David Joyce's railroad experience as the three men formulated their plans for a railroad at Bass Brook. Joyce's Shell Lake Lumber Company logging railroad at Shell Lake, Wisconsin— the Crescent Springs—and his Trinity County Lumber Company logging railroad at Groveton, Texas—the Groveton, Lufkin and Northern—gave him firsthand working knowledge that the other owners appreciated. Based on the information supplied by Joyce, the company chose lightweight (35 pounds per foot) rails that sped the rate at which the track could be laid or removed.[3] More importantly, the railroad crew laid a standard-gauge track and thereby eliminated the interchange problems experienced by the Crescent Springs narrow-gauge track. When plans for the Bass Brook logging operation were firm, owner Samuel Barker realized that he could not meet the necessary financial obligations to the ILC and subsequently sold his shares to the large Michigan lumber firm of Hackley and Hume, captained by Thomas Hume. Joyce, Akeley, and Hume would continue their association for many years.

Joyce was conspicuously absent from local news reports about the Itasca Lumber Company during the years that the Itasca Railroad was headquartered at Bass Brook (1891–1893). He was consulted for major decisions and provided capital as needed, but his energy was primarily directed toward his sawmills at Shell Lake, Wisconsin, and Lyons, Iowa. It was also during these years that David Joyce was afflicted with a serious health problem, described as inflammatory rheumatism, which very likely prevented him from visiting all of his widely spread ventures. Seeking a cure, he spent several months at Hot Springs, Arkansas, a well-known destination for those with health problems. There, Joyce took treatments at the hot baths, unable to attend to his business matters. At times his illness was so severe that he was bedridden.[4] As a result, Joyce's partner H. C. Akeley toured the Itasca County area on inspection trips with local manager J. P. Sims, and the two kept Joyce posted on current company progress.

J. P. Sims
MISSISSIPPI VALLEY LUMBERMAN

Organized as a separate company, the logging railroad functioned within the fold of the ILC, its owners holding executive positions in both companies. The reason for the separation of the railroad and lumber company is not documented. We can speculate, however, that separating the entities was expedient because of bookkeeping requirements, tax laws, and government regulation. This was also the era of rail transportation. Buyouts, consolidation, and expansion were commonplace among railroads. The owners would have considered the possibility that their railroad would one day be sold or become part of a larger system.

After christening the new line the Itasca Railroad, the Itasca Lumber Company hired a staff to build and run the railroad. Informally known by several other names, including the "Itasca Road" and the "Bass Brook Railroad," the Itasca Railroad operated with H. C. Akeley at the helm. J. P. Sims was the local manager. Superintendent R. T. Stett assisted Sims with its construction. A valuable asset to the ILC, Stett, trained in Michigan, had worked with a number of logging railroads and was also a lumberman. A. G. Bernard acted as passenger agent, W. Blaker as freight agent, and Oscar Mather as auditor. Arriving from Pittsburgh, William Byers joined the company as the locomotive mechanic. Head cook John Oslie and the cooks in his charge turned out hearty meals for the railroad crews from the base camp located near the outlet of Bass Brook on the Mississippi.[5]

The Itasca Lumber Company prepared for its railroad by surveying the right-of-way and establishing camps for the workmen. J. P. Sims coordinated the endeavor. By June 1891 the new rail was well under way and was expected to reach fifteen to thirty miles north of the fork of the Mississippi River and Bass Brook. Several camps had been set up for the men working on the grades and tracks, and additional camps had been created for the logging crews. Upon entering the future town site, commonly referred to as Bass Brook but eventually named Cohasset,* the tracks crossed the brook and then struck the Mississippi.† A spur track paralleled the riverfront so that logs could be rolled directly from the rail cars into the river.

By August 1891 the Itasca Railroad's engine and logging cars, known as Russell cars,‡ had arrived. During its operation at Bass Brook, the Itasca Railroad owned only one engine, No. 1, named the Itasca, which was built on order for the ILC by Porter the same year. It was a diamond-stacked Mogul that continued in service until it was retired in 1898. Small as locomotives go, No. 1 was, nonetheless, an attractive machine. The LaPrairie newspaper called it "a pretty plaything" when it was spotted steaming through LaPrairie on the Duluth and Winnipeg tracks. The Itasca Railroad engine frequently switched onto the Duluth and Winnipeg and made runs into Grand Rapids, LaPrairie, and beyond for supplies and men.[6]

---

* In 1891, this emerging community was not named Cohasset, as it is today. Instead the site went by various names, including Sims, Compton, Itasca and Bass Brook. Sims, of course, was the head man for the Itasca Lumber Company. Compton was the name of an original plat at the townsite, established in July 1891 by George Canfield and J. M. Markham. Compton was immediately misspelled, and reports sometimes referred to Compston, Crompton and Campton. For a brief time a post office operated under the name of Compton. Rufus Gale, also a bookkeeper for the Itasca Lumber Company, was employed as the first postmaster. The name Itasca seems to have been quite popular, for several other lumbering camps along the Mississippi River were called Itasca—a confusing situation. Bass Brook, however, was the name that defined the location and was most commonly used until the name Cohasset was applied to a plat on the riverfront several years later (Plat Map A23, Recorder Office, Itasca County Courthouse; "Local," *GRM*, 9 July 1891; "Local," *GRM*, 8 October 1891; "Local," *GRM*, 25 June 1891; Jessie M. Lawrence vs. Itasca Lumber Company, District Court transcript #236 [1893], MHS).

† The length of the main line north of Bass Brook probably never exceeded 8 miles. The predicted 15 to 30 miles of track was reached by including the length of the branching spur tracks ("Local," *GRM*, 18 June 1891).

‡ Russell cars used for hauling at that time consisted of two separate trucks or wheel sets. Imagine the flat car of today. Now disconnect the two ends by cutting out the central portion of the bed. The result would approximate the appearance of the Russell car. Logs were positioned so that both ends rested on the car's independent trucks and were then secured with chains. The independent trucks permitted this car to carry any length of log. Dangerous to use, the Russell cars were responsible for untold injury and death among log handlers and trainmen. Later the Russell cars were replaced with flat cars, which were more stable and thus much safer.

A special excursion for the local populace placed the participants aboard open logging cars at great risk.
GENE MADSEN PRIVATE COLLECTION

The Itasca Lumber Company delivered the first loads of logs to the Mississippi River at the rate of up to 1 million board feet per week shortly after receiving the engine. Some of the timber was harvested during the summer months—a practice unusual for that era of Minnesota logging—and hauled to rail side using a high-wheel skidder similar to those employed by the Shell Lake Lumber Company.[7] Horses or oxen supplied the motive power for the skidder.

Logging at Bass Brook Fosters a Community

After the Itasca Lumber Company established itself at Bass Brook, adventurous businessmen like Robert McCabe, who built a saloon to quench the thirsts of lumberjacks and railroad men, came to settle.[8] McCabe and others may have realized that Bass Brook showed promise as more than just another river logging town. Rumors of gold in the Rainy Lake region, just 100 miles to the north, and the potential extension of the Itasca Railroad toward that hard-to-reach area expanded the possibilities for the infant burg. Investors knew that if the rumors panned out, Bass Brook, at the junction of two railroads, could become a major transportation hub.

No roads yet connected Bass Brook with surrounding communities; the rail lines, therefore, assumed tremendous importance for the local population. The presence of a single railroad was sufficient to drive settlement, and Bass Brook now had two—the Duluth and Winnipeg and the Itasca Railroad. According to the *Grand Rapids Magnet*, "The effect [of the Itasca Railroad] has been magical with reference to settlement and the country [to the north] has taken a big boom with swarms of settlers and land lookers. The Grand Rapids Land and Improvement Company has located twenty-five settlers in that direction during the past month."[9] It is unclear how the Itasca Railroad carried settlers or their supplies north from Bass Brook during these first years. The railroad owned no passenger cars, so how were passengers carried? One early photo shows passengers precariously perched upon the Russell logging cars.

Even with the influx of newcomers, the growing population remained secondary in size to the large company camps that contained the primary population in the area. Two Itasca Lumber Company camps were, in fact, designated as the only local polling places for the November election of 1892: the camp at Bass Brook and what was then the Headquarters camp, six miles north of Bass Brook on the Itasca Railroad.[10]

A Public Excursion on the Itasca Railroad

The railroad occasionally scheduled public tours to commemorate the progress of both the railmen and the lumbermen. A lengthy news item in the *Grand Rapids Magnet* on June 7, 1892, detailed an excursion on the Itasca Railroad "to visit the native wilds brought under the conquering hand of man." J. P. Sims and his crew, consisting of conductor A. F. Bailey, engineer O. W. Merwin, and fireman C. H. Sweet, arranged to pick up the tourists who had arrived at LaPrairie from Duluth early Tuesday morning. These passengers were conveyed on a coach car supplied by the Duluth and Winnipeg Railroad. After the passengers in LaPrairie boarded, the Itasca steamed into Grand Rapids, where local citizens were invited to join the party, bringing the total number of travelers to approximately forty men, women, and children.

The Itasca Railroad engine #1, nicknamed the Itasca.
PETE BONESTEEL PRIVATE COLLECTION

The *Mississippi Valley Lumberman* also printed a feature about the trip.

At 11 o'clock Conductor Bailey shouted, 'all aboard'. A quick run to Pokegama dam was made, where the passengers were given an opportunity to view the picturesque scenery in that vicinity. The train then started for Bass Brook, where it was switched on to the Itasca Lumber Company tracks. The run to Headquarters camp was made in slow time in order to allow the passengers to obtain a full view of the country through which they were passing. At 12:50 the excursionists alighted at the camp [six miles north of Bass Brook]. The interval until dinner was announced, [and] was spent in looking over the Company's improvements. It is quite a village unto itself: a store, several dwelling houses, the eating house and sleeping rooms were all objects of interest. The farm was next visited, where several acres are under cultivation. [The company not only raised crops to feed the crews but also cultivated an abundant hay crop to feed the many horses used for logging operations.[11]]

When dinner was called, there was an orderly rush for the tables. The ride and the odor from the pine trees had evidently sharpened the appetites of the entire party. Had Mr. Sims been a less liberal provider, some would have gone hungry. How ham and eggs, beans, potatoes, fried pork and other camp food disappeared! The cooks must have thought they were trying to satisfy appetites of a very hungry logging crew.

At 3 o'clock the excursionists started homewards. At the head of Bass Brook a halt was made for the purpose of allowing the party to see the fish that inhabit this stream by the thousands. The run to Cohasset was made without further stop or incident and then on to Pokegama dam on the Duluth and Winnipeg tracks. At the dam the party alighted and was allowed a half-hour for the purpose of thoroughly inspecting the government works and enjoying a little fishing. At 5 o'clock the train stopped at Grand Rapids and its citizens reluctantly left the party after enjoying a very pleasant day.[12]

The Logging Railroad Steams Westward

The entertainment of the local populace was only a slight diversion for the Itasca Railroad as it labored under the weight of a seemingly endless stream of logs. On the first day of 1892 the *Mississippi Valley Lumberman* reported that the two Bass Brook lumber camps, each employing fifty lumberjacks, had been cutting logs for the past two and one half months. A crew of seventeen men worked at the river landing, where 1.5 million board feet of logs were tumbled weekly onto the frozen riverfront, adding to the mass of 10 million board feet of timber poised for the spring drive. By April 1892 the Itasca Lumber Company had successfully brought out its anticipated cut of 60 million board feet of logs and was gearing up for summer logging. At this time the railroad's mainline reached eight miles into the woods. The tracks extended northward from the river siding to the northeast corner of Deer Lake. By September 1892 Sims declared that the railroad had been extended five miles further with more track being laid daily.[13] These additions to the system were most probably temporary spurs.

As the following winter season of 1892–1893 began, the accumulation of logs banked along the railroad's river landing, waiting to be driven downstream, must have been an impressive site. The January 1893 *Grand Rapids Magnet* announced, "It will repay anyone to travel to Bass Brook and see the 7 million feet of logs belonging to the Itasca Lumber Company banked along the Mississippi River."[14] Logs accumulated at the Mississippi landing throughout the remainder of January, but the flurried activity of trains and work crews ceased as a new month dawned.

February of 1893 did not start with good news for the people of Bass Brook. Startling the public, the Itasca Lumber Company leased the locomotive and all thirty cars of the Itasca Railroad to the Northern Mill Company of Brainerd. The Itasca Railroad was not destined for another logging season at Bass Brook. By the end of 1893, after only two years of operation, the rails had vanished.[15]

The company had a number of reasons for pulling up stakes. On the south end of the railroad, legal action pended concerning the tract of land fronting the Mississippi River where the Itasca Lumber Company dumped and banked logs. This property was owned by Jessie Lawrence, who had allowed the ILC to use the land through an oral agreement. But her relationship with the logging company had become strained.

Lawrence, who lived in Minneapolis, sought damages to her property from the activities on the Itasca Lumber Company spur track and rollway at the river. She took legal action in May 1893 that continued until the end of the year.* According to affidavits filed in the district court for Itasca County, Lawrence wanted reimbursement for damages caused by the construction of the rail, removal of standing timber, storage of logs, and the obstruction of her river landing. She also requested an injunction to prevent the ILC from removing its rails, which she claimed she now owned because they had been put on her property without permission.[16] J. P. Sims, speaking for the ILC, claimed that all actions of the company on Lawrence's property had been undertaken with the full knowledge of Lawrence, after numerous consultations with Lawrence's father. Furthermore, he emphasized that the ILC was fully prepared to negotiate with her for compensation. The Court appointed a commission to determine the amount that would be awarded. Lawrence had originally demanded $4,400 in damages, but the final decision of the commission stipulated that the ILC owed her just $294. The Itasca Lumber Company was denied further use of Lawrence's property.

Another issue struck down Bass Brook as the center of the Itasca Lumber Company's logging effort. Rugged terrain and the many small lakes north of Deer Lake, an area now known as Suomi Hills, blocked the advance of the rails to company timberlands farther north, stifling the ILC, which had already harvested the best timber available to current rail penetration. The Itasca Lumber Company had to find another route to access the northern frontier of the county.

It could be argued that the Itasca Lumber Company had never considered

---

* On October 5, 1893, her large tract of property was platted as "Cohasset," thus permanently changing the name of the community of Bass Brook.

Cohasset as a permanent site for its logging railroad but had just been waiting for access to Deer River. Ten miles northwest of Cohasset, the town of Deer River afforded an excellent site for the railroad. The terrain north of the town was fairly level, and a rail could be constructed arrow straight to the ILC's untapped timber holdings that lay north of the Suomi Hills area. Deer River was on the edge of White Oak Lake, which would make an excellent holding pond with direct access to the Mississippi River. The lake had ample frontage available for the logging operation. No less important, the Duluth and Winnipeg Railroad had extended its tracks to Deer River, possibly with the intent of helping the Itasca Lumber Company relocate. The move seemed to have been in the ILC's long-range plan. In fact, J. P. Sims, ILC manager, platted the townsite of Deer River as a future logging town even as the Itasca Railroad was just up and running in Cohasset.

Jessie Lawrence and the other people of fledgling Cohasset were left in the dust as the last carload of rails headed up the Duluth and Winnipeg Railroad for Deer River. In the end it was just a matter of economics to the Itasca Lumber Company, whose business was to get the logs out. Construction on the new railhead at Deer River began immediately in 1893. Meanwhile, the Itasca Lumber Company was not quite done with the logging north of Cohasset. J. P. Sims saw to it that the sluicing dam on Bass Brook was rebuilt so that the timber remaining in the vicinity could be floated out the old fashioned way.[17]

Today, the only remnant of the Itasca Railroad when it was based in Cohasset is County Road 62, which follows much of the original railroad grade north.

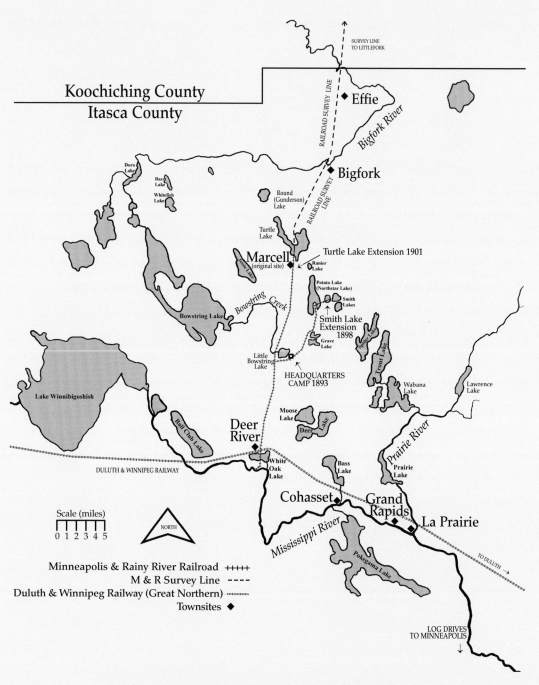

Koochiching County
Itasca County

SURVEY LINE
TO LITTLEFORK

◆ Effie

Bigfork River

RAILROAD SURVEY LINE

◆ Bigfork

Dora
Lake

Bass
Lake

Whitefish
Lake

Round
(Gunderson)
Lake

RAILROAD SURVEY LINE

Turtle
Lake

Marcell
(original site) ◆

Turtle Lake Extension 1901

○ Ranier
Lake

Jessie Lake

Bowstring Creek

Potato Lake
(Northstar Lake)

Smith
Lakes

Bowstring Lake

Smith Lake
Extension
1898

Grave
Lake

Spider Lake

Trout Lake

Little
Bowstring
Lake

□

HEADQUARTERS
CAMP 1893

Wabana
Lake

Lawrence
Lake

Lake Winnibigoshish

Moose
Lake

Deer Lake

Prairie River

Ball Club Lake

Deer
River ◆

White
Oak
Lake

Bass
Lake

Prairie
Lake

DULUTH & WINNIPEG RAILWAY

Cohasset ◆

Grand
Rapids ◆

◆ La Prairie

Scale (miles)

0 1 2 3 4 5

▲ NORTH

Mississippi River

TO DULUTH →

Pokegama Lake

Minneapolis & Rainy River Railroad +++++
M & R Survey Line - - - -
Duluth & Winnipeg Railway (Great Northern) ++++++++
Townsites ◆

LOG DRIVES
TO MINNEAPOLIS
↓

MINNEAPOLIS & RAINY RIVER RAILROAD 1893–1904

The M&R Comes to Deer River
1893–1904

ON NOVEMBER 23, 1891, ITASCA LUMBER COMPANY Manager J. P. Sims platted the town site of Deer River located on the river of the same name.[1] Sims recognized that the spot was a gateway to expansive areas of pine and also had access to the Mississippi River for log driving and to the Duluth and Winnipeg Railroad for transportation of equipment and supplies. Indeed, it was ripe for a logging railroad. Yet, when the Itasca Lumber Company moved its rail equipment to the newly forming town of Deer River toward the end of 1893, it received scant notice. After the ILC abandoned downstream Cohasset, people were no doubt suspicious of a railroad that could disappear practically overnight. Nevertheless, the logging railroad established itself and continued to operate from Deer River for thirty-nine years, becoming an integral part of that village and sustaining the existence of settlers and other communities along its route.

The owners of the Itasca Lumber Company had great expectations for their little logging road at Deer River. By 1894, the year David Joyce died, leaving his son William to carry on the business, the company had provisionally named the new venture the Minneapolis and Rainy River Railway (M&R), although the public continued to use the old name, the Itasca Railroad, long after its official incorporation as a common carrier in 1904. The new name represented the intention that someday the rails would stretch from Minneapolis to the Rainy River on the Canadian border. Gold fever may have been the cause of such a grandiose scheme among lumbermen.

George W. Davis had discovered gold on Rainy Lake's Little America Island in July 1893.[2] Reporting on the find, the papers of the day predicted a gigantic rush to the new Eldorado. Roads to the north were nonexistent, making it difficult for prospectors, miners, and their equipment to reach the area. Only the very hardy could manage the arduous overland treks by foot and by water or by circuitous routes through Canada. Poised to become part of a direct route from Minneapolis through Deer River to the Rainy River, the Itasca Lumber Company's railroad offered a potential solution.

The owners probably had no intention of actually building a rail from Minneapolis to Rainy River. They did not have the capital for such an undertaking but expected to realize profits from the sale of their segment to a larger concern like the Soo Line or the Duluth and Winnipeg (later known as the Great Northern) that could afford to link Minneapolis to Canada. If the line were sold, it would still transport logs for the Itasca Lumber Company, which could operate its spur lines as before, saving a considerable amount on maintenance to the mainline track. By 1900 the gold rush was a bust, but the newly forming industry and population on Rainy River remained a worthy destination for a north-south railway. Efforts to merge the Minneapolis and Rainy River Railway with a larger railway system would persist throughout its history.

Immediately upon the M&R's arrival in Deer River in late 1893, J. P. Sims set up a headquarters camp for the Itasca Lumber Company twelve miles north of town at Little Bowstring Lake.[3] Crews rapidly laid the northbound track, aiming for Little Bowstring, which then became the terminus of the railroad. Further extensions would have to wait another four years while the ILC concentrated its resources upon the company's huge timber holdings on the Swan and Prairie Rivers.

Despite the company's focus on the tributaries to the east, logging did get underway in the forests around Little Bowstring Lake. Engine No. 1, the Itasca, served as the only source of motive power on the line from Deer River to Little Bowstring Lake during this period. Drawing from a limited area, the Itasca hauled out the season's cut of logs in short order. Rather than idle the engine and crew for the rest of the season, the ILC frequently rented its engine and cars to other logging firms in Wisconsin and Minnesota, including the Northern Mill Company of Brainerd, Wright and Davis at Swan River, and the Minneapolis, St. Paul and Ashland Railway south of Ashland, Wisconsin.[4]

As the pine in the Swan and Prairie watersheds approached depletion, the Itasca Lumber Company owners turned their attention back to the expansion of the Itasca

UPPER: Men working at the Smith Lake hoist, load rail cars in 1903.
ITASCA COUNTY HISTORICAL SOCIETY

LEFT: Smith Lake as it appeared in 1903. Logging hoist and rail cars are on the opposite shore.
ITASCA COUNTY HISTORICAL SOCIETY

Railroad. During the winter of 1896–1897, lumberjacks banked logs at Potato Lake (now North Star Lake) and Grave Lake in anticipation of the advancing rails. The following summer the railroad became a hotbed of activity as crews continued to push the rails northward. George Cox, previously employed on the Omaha and Soo lines, was hired as the chief construction engineer for the extension. By early May he was surveying for the most favorable routes. The *Mississippi Valley Lumberman* trade journal duly noted the progress in its May 28, 1897 issue: "Work of grading the proposed extension to the Itasca Lumber Co.'s [rail]road in northern Minnesota will be begun in a few days, as the surveyors will have had the route laid out by that time. It is the intention of the Company to extend the main line about twelve miles due north [from the Little Bowstring camp]. The line will be tapped by two spurs, one running northeast some four or five miles to Potato Lake, and the other in a northwesterly direction . . . . It is believed that this railroad will eventually become more than a mere logging road, as it runs through some of the best parts of Itasca County, which is being rapidly settled."[5]

By striking Grave and Potato Lakes as well as numerous other smaller lakes in the vicinity, the railroad turned a once inaccessible area into a logger's paradise. At Potato Lake, crews put down tracks the length of a one-mile long peninsula that jutted out from the south end of the lake. From the end of this peninsula, a trestle, built across a narrow arm of the lake, yielded a short extension due east that crossed North Smith Lake. North Smith, whose shores contained considerable pine, connected to several lakes in the Smith chain. Pilings from these trestles are still visible today.

As the summer of 1898 approached, an estimated 30 million board feet of floating logs choked the lakes from shore to shore.[6] These logs were so tightly packed that a settler could have comfortably crossed entire lakes by stepping from one log to the next. Glancing up, he would have seen the clear-cut hillsides and the hoists lifting the logs onto the log cars at the water's edge.

This staggering quantity of timber overwhelmed the little locomotive No. 1. In the summer of 1898 the Itasca Lumber Company purchased locomotives No. 2 and No. 3 along with many new Russell log cars to manage the load. Two locomotives were kept

Log train returning to Deer River.
ITASCA COUNTY HISTORICAL SOCIETY

busy at the hoists assembling trains while the third locomotive steamed into Deer River with thirty cars in tow. The haul required three to four daily runs into Deer River with an average of 100,000 feet of timber per trainload. The company cut and hauled timber throughout the summer and into the fall. In 1899 an even greater harvest in the Potato Lake area pressed the locomotive crews. Despite manpower shortages in the area's three camps, the total cut reached 34 million board feet.[7]

Concurrent with the activity at the end of the rail line, Deer River experienced a building boom when the Itasca Lumber Company started several projects in the village to support its operations. The company erected an office building and freight depot just south of the junction of the Itasca Railroad and the Duluth and Winnipeg Railroad.[*]

[*] The Duluth and Winnipeg Railroad was purchased by mining and railroad magnate James J. Hill in 1897. The railroad went through a series of name changes and in 1907 officially became part of Hill's Great Northern Railway system.

Each building measured twenty feet by forty feet. The *Itasca News* of Deer River bragged, "This will be the neatest office building in town as well as the prettiest depot this side of Duluth."[8] A machine shop and a section house sprang up south of the office and depot. The section house provided sleeping accommodations and a dining hall for the rail crews. Close by, the ILC raised housing for employees—"pleasant little dwellings . . . in a lively suburb to Deer River."[9] (Twelve years later the "suburb" would become the town of Zemple.) Rail yards for holding the expanding fleet of Russell log cars and other cars were also built in the same vicinity.

The need to cut log-driving expenses catalyzed a five-year project to span White Oak Lake with a railroad trestle. Originally used as a holding pond for Itasca Lumber Company logs, the lake was separated from the Mississippi by a slender

The Deer River depot of the Minneapolis and Rainy River Railroad.
ITASCA COUNTY HISTORICAL SOCIETY

The M&R traversed the long trestle over White Oak Lake to deposit loads directly into the Mississippi River. Shown here is the rollway on the bank of the Mississippi.
ITASCA COUNTY HISTORICAL SOCIETY

thread of land and linked only by a narrow opening. When the spring log drives started, the river men emptied logs banked over the winter on White Oak Lake into the Mississippi. Once the trestle was completed, logs could be stacked directly on the shore of the Mississippi during the winter and dumped into the river during drives, thus eliminating the expense of driving the logs through the narrow opening into the lake.[10]

In the atmosphere of optimism that prevailed in 1899, the railroad owners directed S. D. Patrick to lead a survey expedition northward to the United States-Canadian border. The primary goal of his mission was to locate the most favorable route for laying tracks for the Itasca Railroad. He was also instructed to gather information about potential timberlands, public acceptance of a railroad right-of-way, and industry in the Canadian border town of Fort Frances and its United States counterpart, Koochiching (now International Falls). It is clear that the owners were as interested in the potential of an extension to the border to generate freight traffic as they were to tap the meager pine sources of the far northern region. The Itasca Railroad owners were also looking at a possible link to the Canadian National Railway, then under construction north of Fort Frances.

S. D. Patrick took this mandate seriously, making a detailed survey of the

As men loosen the chains, pine logs hit the Mississippi to begin the long drive to the Itasca Lumber Company mill in Minneapolis. ITASCA COUNTY HISTORICAL SOCIETY

route and describing each forty-acre tract that his line crossed. Beginning at the junction of the Big Fork and Rice Rivers, the future site of the town of Bigfork, he found that a direct route to the border was possible, "nearly level and without any bad grades." However, the Big Fork River and, even more so, the Little Fork River posed difficulties for bridge building because of their high banks and dramatic fluctuations in water level. Accordingly Patrick searched for optimal points for river crossings. He also noted that tamarack, which could be used for railroad ties, grew along the route. In contrast, he found very little pine timber, although the present-day Bigfork Township contained some of the best stands noted in his survey. To the north of that was "practically nothing," with the exception of a stand of 8 to 10 million board feet some twenty miles south of Canada.

Patrick next tallied the industries of the border settlement. "Koochiching is . . . just above the falls on Rainy River, and directly opposite Fort Frances, has two stores, two newspapers, one hotel, custom house, two saloons etc. . . . and they claim a 65,000 horsepower water power [plant]. At present there are six boats running up from Lake of the Woods, freighting [supplies for] the projected Canadian [National] Railroad." Thirty more steamboats on Rainy Lake, Patrick learned, engaged in towing logs, fishing, freighting, and transporting passengers. As for the Rainy Lake gold mines, he recorded an air of confidence, even though the mines had produced little. Agricultural, fishing, and logging businesses around Koochiching were more reliable industries.

From the Rainy Lake region, Patrick made preliminary surveys for a possible spur track to run east for thirty miles to the vicinity of Nett Lake Indian Reservation, Ash Lake, Black Duck Lake, Elephant Lake, and Pelican Lake, where the Itasca Lumber Company had the opportunity to purchase some large blocks of pineland. This area did contain a good showing of pine timber, but Patrick's enthusiasm for it was tempered by the rugged bedrock terrain that would challenge the prospective railroad builder.[11]

Patrick's report was reviewed in late 1899 by F. C. Gerhard, general manager of the Itasca Lumber Company's executive and sales offices in Minneapolis. Gerhard recommended that the company extend the railway to the border immediately as it would "pay as a logging road, to say nothing as to any other [freight] traffic." Rather than building any spur tracks to reach timber, Gerhard also recommended that the Big Fork, Little Fork, and Nett Rivers and their tributaries be used to drive logs to the railroad's river crossing points for loading.[12] William Joyce and his associates were slow to act on the northward expansion of the railroad. Another six years passed before the railroad arrived at the junction of the Bigfork and Rice Rivers, the site of the newly forming town of Bigfork. By then, the economic benefits of reaching Fort Frances had disappeared. The pine timber that Patrick had observed near the border was gone, and other rail companies had entered that locale. Had Gerhard's recommendation to tap the border with haste and to link to the Canadian National Railway been carried out, the history of Itasca County may have been quite different.

Turtle Lake

When the pine stocks circling Potato, Smith, and Grave Lakes dwindled and the total haul of logs for the years 1900 and 1901 dropped to 30 million board feet, Itasca Lumber Company crews advanced the rails into new territory. The most significant extension was toward Turtle Lake. By September 1901 they had completed the grade and were spiking down steel rails. The crews also replaced older light rails with new heavy steel over the length of the railroad, improving the general quality of the track. A manpower shortage delayed plans for further track extension northward to Bigfork, forcing the company to focus its resources on cutting the timber made available by the Turtle Lake extension.[13]

The completion of the Turtle Lake extension at the end of 1901 marked a turning point for the logging railroad. No longer would it strictly be devoted to carrying company logs. In 1902 the railroad started transporting other companies' cuts and simultaneously increased its Itasca Lumber Company haul to 33 million board feet as the logs from Turtle Lake hit the rollways.[14] Even though the cut of the ILC dropped back to about 30 million board feet the following year, the railroad was busier than ever. Seaman Brothers, who specialized in cedar timber, harvested an incredible 55,000 telegraph poles and 800,000 fence posts in 1903. The combined output of other companies cutting cedar almost doubled this figure. Most of the cedar traveled to Deer River on the ILC logging train. The loaded cars were then transferred to the Duluth and Winnipeg tracks as they continued on to distant markets. It was no surprise when the February 21, 1903 Deer River newspaper argued that cedar was "fully as important a business as pine lumbering to the local development." That year the payroll of Seaman Brothers amounted to $12,000—all pumped into the local economy.[15] Deer River was developing into an important shipping point for posts, poles, and railroad ties.

The increasing quantity of timber products leaving Deer River by rail was matched by incoming freight destined for the camps to the north. These provisions were unloaded from Duluth and Winnipeg cars and transferred to Itasca Railroad cars, which conveyed the goods to Itasca Lumber Company camps on Turtle Lake and to a growing number of independent lumber camps popping up along the upper reaches of the tracks. In response, the ILC built a thirty-foot-by-seventy-five foot warehouse with a large root house to shelter provisions waiting to be shipped out. Located across the track from the depot in Deer River, the warehouse stored the incoming carloads of navy beans, cheese, sugar, flour, beef, peanuts in the shell, and tea. Ham, salt pork, and bacon were additional protein sources. Liver was particularly plentiful as were the endless coils of sausage and bolognas that the railroad crewmen wrestled off the cars at the lumber camps. The railmen, ever on the lookout for humorous names, christened their railroad the Gut and Liver—a nickname that outlived the Itasca line.[16]

The accelerating tempo of railroad traffic required better communication. To help avoid costly collisions, the M&R installed a telephone system. The crews strung the telephone line from poles raised alongside the tracks after completing the haul in 1902. By December the line stretched about thirty miles from the depot at Deer River to the camp at Turtle Lake. Train engineers stopped at calling stations along the railroad to contact the dispatcher in Deer River, who knew the location of all trains running that day and gave clearance to continue either north or south. Since this was the only telephone service in the area for many years, the Gut and Liver frequently relayed urgent personal messages and requests for medical aid for both lumberjacks and settlers in the Turtle Lake area.[17]

In 1903 a steamboat with a twenty-four-foot keel shipped out on the Itasca

The Steamer **JENNIE B.**

Is now plying the waters at the north end of the Itasca Railroad, and meets all trains for pleasure parties or land seekers crossing **Turtle Lake** TO THE **BigFork** Wagon Roads.

RATES Very Reasonable. Call at Turtle Lake Landing,

Or Address: **A. McNEIL, Capt.,**
DEER RIVER, MINN.

A 1903 advertisement for the *Jennie B.* WESTERN ITASCA REVIEW

Railroad, traveling from the Mississippi River at Deer River to Turtle Lake. Its arrival offered another convenience for both loggers and settlers. Anna Stark, who lived in the town of Ball Club, owned the *Jennie B.*, and "Captain" Archie McNeil piloted the craft. Along with a second steamboat, called the *Cassie,* the *Jennie B.* pushed the floating masses of logs gathered into rafts on the lake toward the loading hoist and trestle located between McKenzie Island and the mainland. The steamboats also ferried northbound settlers, tourists, sportsmen, and lumberjacks from the end of the rail line to Rapp's Landing on the opposite shore. At Rapp's Landing, a horse-drawn wagon transport service picked up these passengers and continued toward Bigfork on a tote road so rugged that, on at least one occasion, the settlers' children were securely tied with a rope to the wagon to keep them from tumbling out.[18]

During the years that Turtle Lake served as the terminus for the Itasca Railroad, John Lundeen, an enterprising landowner on the south end of the lake near McKenzie Island, understood the economic opportunity at his doorstep.[19] He established the town of old Marcell, named after popular railroad conductor Andy Marcell, by building a two-story, eleven-room lodge, a general store, a small sawmill, and later a saloon. Lundeen had already aggressively advertised his resort and the sale of lots

Free Homes

On the Famous **Big Fork River.**

Homesteads FOR **Thousands.**

Send 50 cents for Home-seekers' Guide. Address:
JOHN LUNDEEN,. Drawer D.
DEER RIVER, Itasca Co., MINN

BEST Hunting on EARTH   Good FISHING

John Lundeen advertised his Turtle Lake property, located at the end of the M&R mainline. This 1901 advertisement appearing in the *Itasca News* shows the M&R's route to Turtle Lake and the M&R branch to Smith Lake. The M&R's original survey route to Bigfork, which would have crossed Turtle Lake on a long trestle, is also shown.

WESTERN ITASCA REVIEW

before the last steel had been spiked down in 1901. His ads in the Deer River paper boasted of the "best hunting on earth, good fishing and homesteads for thousands," all easily accessible by rail. Lundeen's little settlement soon attracted homesteaders searching for land claims as well as settlers needing supplies. (Fifty years later, Turtle Lake, at that time a resort area, was rediscovered by Hamm's brewing company, which made the lake famous as one of four visual centerpieces it used to advertise the beer "from the land of sky blue waters.")

John Lundeen operated all of his businesses in old Marcell until 1911 with the exception of the saloon. He closed the doors of his drinking establishment in 1905, after discovering it did not suit his personality. The February 4, 1905 issue of Deer River's *Itasca News* tells the story of Lundeen's change of heart:

> After paying his five hundred dollars, getting his receipt and filing his bond for the privilege of selling booze at Turtle, John Lundeen, the prosperous hotel man, merchant and townsite owner at Marcell post office on the shore of the lake, has concluded to pull down his money and let the job to someone else.
>
> After a crowd from the nearby camps had put in a rough night at the Lundeen saloon, taking complete and full possession, telling the proprietor they would close up when they got ready, and made him take a back seat and be quiet, Mr. Lundeen made up his mind that it was bad business anyhow, and so he quit.[20]

For a brief time, Turtle Lake served as an important link in an overland route to the north. In fact, it appears that the Itasca Lumber Company considered this link as part of a feasible route to Bigfork and was surveying a line that would have taken the tracks right across Turtle Lake on a long trestle, using McKenzie Island as a stepping-stone. Problems obtaining right-of-ways nixed this plan, however, and the Turtle Lake crossing never materialized.

Wirt

During the period of expansion from 1898 to 1903, William Joyce increased his active participation in the operation of the railroad while partner H. C. Akeley gradually reduced his role. Akeley marked his retirement from the company in February 1903, when he sold out his interest to the remaining owners for the sum of $1.2 million.[21] The change in management pumped new vigor into the railroad.

The Itasca Lumber Company redoubled efforts to advance its logging railroad after Akeley's departure, but right-of-way disputes again temporarily delayed the goal of entering Bigfork. Although most settlers welcomed the coming of the logging railroad since it was the only efficient transportation in an otherwise roadless country, a few isolated landowners refused permission to cross their land. These delays finally forced management to redirect survey crews toward pockets of timber west of Bigfork. The tracks reached Jessie Lake that fall in time to set up camps for winter logging.[22] Where the track veered west to Jessie Lake, from its original northerly line, a small community formed. Here at Jessie Junction, later renamed Alder, the company section house accommodated crews as they worked on track in that locale.

During the same fall, the rapid advancement of the rails pushed past Jessie Lake toward the town of Wirt, located on the Bigfork River. More than thirteen miles of track were laid in that direction, not counting the long spur lines that tapped lakes along the way, including Little Spring, Spring, Four Town, Whitefish, Bass, and Killdeer Lakes. The spur into Whitefish Lake alone was nearly two miles long. Rails were laid the last few miles into Wirt during either 1904 or 1905.[23]

Wirt, nicknamed Rattlesnake, grew up as a rough-and-ready wilderness town on the north side of the Big Fork River. The town claimed at least one hotel, a post office, a saloon, and a restaurant run by "Rattlesnake Annie" McAllister. Lawlessness reigned in Wirt. On Saturday nights when the lumberjacks showed up in town, their heavy drinking incited fierce drunken brawls. On one occasion, according to Wirt homesteader Thelma Holloway, a rifle accidentally "blew a hole in the ceiling of the saloon. Constable George

Brusewitz went in to investigate. He left without his shirt." Another Wirt tale also testified to its rowdy nature. A drunk "climbed on the train in Grand Rapids. When asked where he wanted to go, he mumbled, 'Aw, I wanna go ta hell.' He was promptly shipped to Wirt." Since the man would have transferred from the Duluth and Winnipeg to the Itasca Railroad in Deer River, we can say that the Itasca Railroad helped him get there.[24]

On the south bank of the river opposite Wirt the company established siding tracks, where cedar posts, hewn railroad ties, and logs awaited the train. The posts and ties were piled vertically on end so the men could more easily flip the 100-pound—or heavier—posts and ties to their shoulders. When the whistle blew announcing the train's arrival, these hardy individuals ascended ramps to the flatcar beds and slammed their loads into position. Luckier workmen used the crosshaul or hoist to load the logs.[25] The company named the location of this siding Stanley, possibly after William Joyce's younger son.

Incorporation

In 1904 the railroad incorporated as a common carrier. On July 20 it was officially named the Minneapolis and Rainy River Railroad (M&R). The newly incorporated M&R was authorized to cross the counties of Hennepin, Ramsey, Anoka, Isanti, Kanabec, Mille Lacs, Aitkin, Crow Wing, Cass, and Itasca in its bid for the border. At the time, Itasca County still included territory to the north that today is known as Koochiching County. Although legally a separate business apart from the Itasca Lumber Company, the Minneapolis and Rainy River Railroad was still in practice an arm of the ILC since the same people owned the two companies.[26]

The railroad was now bound to public service as a common carrier under the rules of the Minnesota Warehouse and Railroad Commission. This commission scrutinized the M&R rates for transportation of freight and passengers to insure fair competition among all common carriers in the state. In return for some loss of control over the rates it charged, the M&R gained the power of eminent domain—the ability to lay track over private land without consent of the owners. As a result, the route north to the town of

Bigfork, which had been thwarted for several years by uncooperative landowners, opened up.

In celebration of the incorporation, the Minneapolis and Rainy River Railroad officials scheduled a special train for a public excursion from Deer River to the new settlement and headquarters camp on Turtle Lake. The *Itasca News* of Deer River reported that on July 20, 1904, the town of Deer River was practically deserted because so many citizens took advantage of the excursion. One can imagine the excitement of the sightseers, dressed in their finest clothes and packed tightly into the passenger coach and the caboose, while the train slowly made its way northward to Turtle Lake. "All took lunch with them and at the Lake [Turtle Lake] steam launches and row boats were given free for the excursionists' use and everybody had a splendid time. There were 163 in the party and when the train arrived at the depot on the return at 7:00 P. M. three rousing cheers for the Itasca [Railroad] people woke up the town."[27]

Statistics filed with the Minnesota Railroad and Warehouse Commission at the time of incorporation offer a good snapshot of the scope of operations from August 1, 1904, to June 30, 1905. During that time frame, the railroad employed fifty-four people, including office clerks, station agents, enginemen, firemen, conductors, machinists, carpenters, shop men, section foremen and trackmen, switch tenders, crossing tenders, and watchmen. Fifty-four injuries were tallied, a rate that shows how dangerous the work was. Paying passengers, who were charged three cents per mile, purchased 7,175 tickets. Fares averaged sixty-three cents.

The total freight carried on the M&R amounted to 147,703 tons with forest products dominating the railroad's reports. Most of the tonnage would have been Itasca Lumber Company logs that

Many men living near the M&R tracks earned income by hand hewing railroad ties.
VERNIE JOHNSON PRIVATE COLLECTION

were dumped into the Mississippi River for the float trip to the Akeley mill in Minneapolis. Supplies for lumber camps and settlers contributed only a little more than 1 percent of the total. The freight consisted of 1,405 tons of agricultural products, such as grains, flour, vegetables, and hay; 353 tons of livestock and meat products; 615 tons of coal and gravel; 365 tons of manufactured goods; 950 tons of other merchandise; and 144,014 tons of forest products, such as lumber, logs, posts, and poles. All of the agricultural products, livestock, meat products, and coal came to Deer River on the Duluth and Winnipeg Railroad and were transferred to the M&R for delivery.

Other statistics dealt with equipment, track and telephone line length, and fuel consumption. In June 1905 equipment was listed as six locomotives, one passenger car, two boxcars, ninety-three log cars, twenty gravel cars, and two caboose cars. A note indicated that most of the cars were fitted with automatic couplers and air brakes. Main line track stretched twenty-two miles, and the length of additional spurs added nineteen miles. The railroad had constructed more than a mile of trestles over water crossings, the longest being a whopping 3,811 feet crossing White Oak Lake at Deer River. Private telephone lines extended the entire length of mainline and spur track. Locomotives consumed 2,843 tons of bituminous coal, valued at $4.15 per ton, and 200 cords of wood, valued at $1.15 per cord.[28]

In 1893 an ambitious Itasca Lumber Company railroad had pulled up stakes and

MINNEAPOLIS & RAINY RIVER RAILWAY.

TIME TABLE

TUESDAY		
(Going South)		
Leave	Turtle Lake	7:00 a. m.
Arrive	Deer River	9:00 a. m.
(Going North)		
Leave	Deer River	2:00 p. m.
Arrive	Turtle Lake	4:00 p. m.
THURSDAY		
(Going South)		
Leave	Turtle Lake	7:00 a. m.
Arrive	Deer River	9:00 a. m.
(Going North)		
Leave	Deer River	12:00 m.
Arrive	Bass Lake	3:00 p. m.
(Going South)		
Leave	Bass Lake	3:00 p. m.
Arrive	Deer River	6:00 p. m.
FRIDAY		
(Going North)		
Leave	Deer River	2:00 p. m.
Arrive	Turtle Lake	4:00 p. m.

Freight for shipment to all points on the Turtle Lake division will be received up to the hour of 12 o'clock noon on Thursdays and Fridays at the Deer River office.

Freight for shipment to all points on the Bass Lake division will be received at the Deer River office up to ten o'clock a. m. on Thursday.

C. A. BIRKE, Agent
General office, Deer River, Dec. 12.

Timetable for passenger and freight service on the Minneapolis & Rainy River Railroad.
WESTERN ITASCA REVIEW

steamed west from Cohasset to its new headquarters in Deer River. While the people there had greeted the railroad with uncertainty, a little more than a decade later the Minneapolis and Rainy River Railroad lent an air of permanence and respectability to the little logging town. Both the M&R and Deer River were positioned for the boom years to come.[*]

---

[*] The incorporation of the railway company in 1904 for $1,000,000 included $400,000 of subscribed stock, which was divided among the owners as follows:

William Joyce: 2,140 shares, Hackley and Hume: 1,337 shares, H. C. Akeley: 400 shares, F. C. Gerhard: 120 shares, Thomas Hume: 1 share, C. H. Hackley: 1 share, Fred Bill: 1 share.

Directors for the railway were the same men. Gerhard and Bill were employees of the Itasca Lumber Company. Akeley had retired and no longer was actively involved. Hackley and Hume were essentially investors. William Joyce was the man in control (Ernst, "White Pine, Ties, and High Finance," 16).

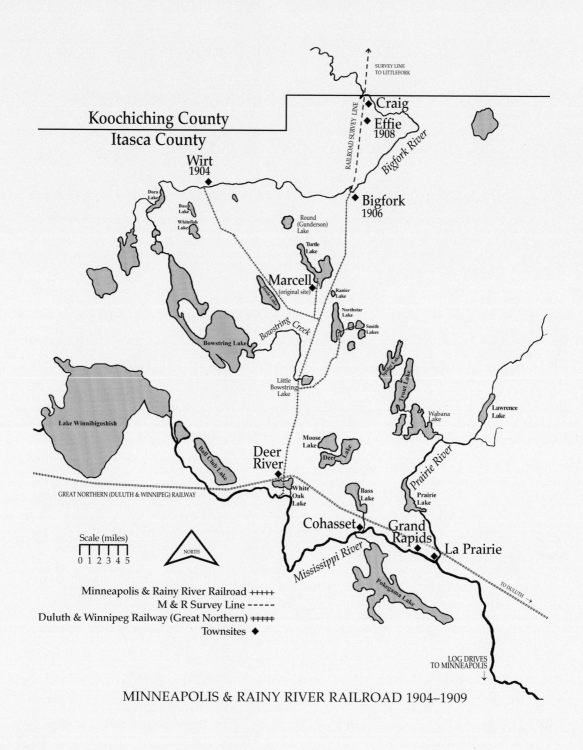

SURVEY LINE
TO LITTLEFORK

◆ Craig

◆ Effie
1908

Koochiching County

Itasca County

Bigfork River

Wirt
1904
◆

Dora
Lake

Bass
Lake

Whitefish
Lake

Round
(Gunderson)
Lake

◆ Bigfork
1906

Turtle
Lake

Tenth Lake

Marcell
(original site)

Ranier
Lake

Northstar
Lake

Bowstring Creek

Smith
Lakes

Bowstring Lake

Snider Lake

Trout Lake

Wabana
Lake

Lawrence
Lake

Little
Bowstring
Lake

Lake Winnibigoshish

Ball Club Lake

Moose
Lake

Deer
Lake

Deer
River
◆

Prairie River

GREAT NORTHERN (DULUTH & WINNIPEG) RAILWAY

White
Oak
Lake

Bass
Lake

Prairie
Lake

Scale (miles)

0 1 2 3 4 5

NORTH

Cohasset ◆

Grand
Rapids

◆ La Prairie
◆

Mississippi River

TO DULUTH

Minneapolis & Rainy River Railroad ┼┼┼┼┼
M & R Survey Line - - - - -
Duluth & Winnipeg Railway (Great Northern) ┼┼┼┼┼
Townsites ◆

Pokegama Lake

LOG DRIVES
TO MINNEAPOLIS

MINNEAPOLIS & RAINY RIVER RAILROAD 1904–1909

Bigfork or Bust
1904–1909

DURING THE PERIOD BETWEEN 1904 AND 1909, close to 100 million board feet of logs rode the rails annually from the forest to Deer River.[1] These were the boom years, when the Minneapolis and Rainy River Railroad employed 100 men and the Itasca Lumber Company operated thirty-one camps, averaging 125 lumberjacks per camp. Thundering north out of Deer River, four logging trains every twenty-four hours coasted into these camps day and night, dropping off empty flat cars for the lumberjacks to stack with logs. After negotiating the turnaround at the end of the line, the trains returned to collect loaded flat cars and then labored slowly back to Deer River under the strain of the load.[2]

The optimistic owners—William Joyce, Charles Hackley, and Thomas Hume—once again attempted to extend the railroad toward Bigfork since the M&R could now condemn right-of-way over private property. Originally surveyed to cross Turtle Lake, the proposed route was moved several miles east. The new survey line skirted Ranier Lake, the present town site of Marcell, and continued another eleven miles north to Bigfork. Survey crews pressed on nearly fifty miles beyond Bigfork, reaching the vicinity of Littlefork, just eight miles from the Canadian border.[3]

Company officials quickly learned as they extended the line that the power of eminent domain did not solve all of their right-of-way problems. They still needed to meet with individual landowners and settle right-of-way compensation. Although a resisting landowner could not, in the end, prevent the right-of-way across his land, he could delay the process, much to the dismay of the railroad management.[4] During this period of negotiations, a 1905 Bigfork newspaper reminded landowners to "be careful and reject no fair offers from the company for they will cross anyway and will use what lands they

Horse-drawn graders prepare the rail bed.
GENE MADSEN PRIVATE COLLECTION

need. . . . If you are too stubborn, you may find yourself in full possession of a lost opportunity [to negotiate your price]."[5]

In 1906 the resolution of right-of-way disputes cleared the route to Bigfork. The Minneapolis and Rainy River marshaled fifty teams of horses, a steam shovel, and more than fifty men to prepare a rail bed on the survey line. The M&R also purchased three new engines, raising the total number operated on the railroad to ten. As soon as weather permitted, two trains started hauling gravel to build up the grades. By the end of April 1906, the steel reached Horsehide Lake, only six miles from Bigfork. In the long summer days that followed, two shifts worked daily to build grade and put down steel, the second shift laboring into the night. The hot and sweaty railroad workers fought off mosquitoes, gnats, deer flies, and horse flies with an ointment of kerosene and oil. Undaunted by the miserable conditions, they laid a spectacular 3,000 feet of steel on the last day of June. Bigfork was almost in sight by the middle of July. Only three miles of steel remained to be laid.[6]

The train finally pulled into the Bigfork station the first week of August 1906. Stepping down from the passenger coach was a group of local schoolteachers who had been taking summer classes in Grand Rapids. The Bigfork newspaper reported on the marvel of the newly established rail link by printing an item that would have been mundane in any other circumstance. The trunk of C. M. King had been shipped "direct from Deer River to Bigfork."[7]

Soon after, the superintendent of the railroad, A. L. Davis, announced a special excursion to celebrate the official opening of the Bigfork extension. It was predicted that every family in Deer River would join the trip, paying a round-trip fare of $1.00 per adult and $.50 per child. However, events leading up to the September excursion dampened the celebratory mood.

Three weeks prior to the excursion, nine out of ten engineers and their firemen "left their engines 'dead' and struck for better pay," protesting that they put in longer hours for less money than any other road crew in the Northwest. General Manager Gerhard

The M&R passed through a sparsely populated countryside.
PETE BONESTEEL PRIVATE COLLECTION

acted immediately to end the dispute. The strikers accepted the compromise offered by the owners. Company policy now defined a workday as twelve hours. Overtime pay was an extra $.30 per hour for engineers and $.23 per hour for firemen—an amount reported by the *Itasca News* to be only a "slight increase" in wages. Despite the settlement, the strike rankled the owners. Management let it be known that the men who participated in the strike would be laid off as soon as replacements could be located. The record does not indicate whether the company actually carried through with its threat to replace the strikers. It probably did not, because skilled men were very difficult to find.[8]

Troubles continued to plague the M&R. Less than two weeks before the official Bigfork opening, twenty-two logging cars were reduced to splinters when a logging train derailed and hit the ditch. The heavily loaded train, pulled by the new No. 10 engine, had gained considerable momentum as it descended a steep grade at which point a loose log or a wheel failure caused one of the cars to skip the track. All of the following cars piled up into a haystack of twisted steel and jumbled logs. Miraculously, none of the men were hurt. Road crews spent two days cleaning up the mess and repairing the tracks.[9]

This and other less serious derailments, noted in the Deer River newspaper, dashed public confidence. As the day for the excursion approached, the community expressed concern about safety on the M&R. Some individuals were afraid to board the train. To allay their fears, railway officials declared, "There is no need of alarm. The special train will run slow, taking two hours to make the forty miles, and every precaution against danger is arranged." (Since the distance between the Deer River depot and Bigfork was actually thirty-one miles by rail, the train would have averaged 15.5 miles per hour.)[10]

Sunday, September 23, 1906, dawned as a perfect day. More than 100 people boarded the excursion train to celebrate the completion of the Minneapolis and Rainy River Railway to Bigfork. The train proceeded northward at the promised slow pace, pleasing the festive sightseers. Upon arrival, "the party headed by the Deer River band, led by [homesteader] Charles Coolen who carried the American flag, marched to the Big Fork hotel, then on to Lindem's store and post office, then west to Pinette's hotel and the sawmill. From this point the crowd scattered." Some rowed the dozen boats provided by the residents of Bigfork, but the majority of excursionists crossed the river in the company of homesteader Oscar Lind to visit the town's lovely park.

At 5:00 p.m. the engineer signaled the crowd with a blast from the train whistle. The celebration then ended as the people of Deer River reboarded the train and made the return trip, arriving home by 7:00 p.m. The excursion had made a favorable impression upon the participants. The Deer River newspaper remarked, "Big Fork is comprised of a lot of intelligent, wide awake people and with its upland soil and manufacturing advantages should become one of the leading cities of that section. Her people are hospitable and a visit to them is a pleasure not to be forgotten."[11] The long anticipated rail connection to Bigfork gave stability and importance to the newly developing burg in the wild solitude of the Bigfork Valley.

Immediately following the excursion, company officials arranged their yearly inspection tours. Twenty-one-year-old David Gage Joyce, son of the president of the M&R, took his annual tour up the line, stopping at the lumber camps where he was, as usual, "heartily welcomed by the employees" possibly, according to some reports, because he liked to join in their fun. Joyce traveled to many of his father's lumbering enterprises around the country as part of his education. If he were to take charge one day of his father's companies (along with his brother Stanley), he had best know the inner workings of not only the business offices but also the logging camps and railroads. A week after David Joyce's trip, President William T. Joyce, General Manager F. C. Gerhard, Superintendent W.C. LaCroix, former superintendent A. L. Davis and others met in Deer River for a second inspection tour.[12]

The excursion and inspection tours went smoothly. Still, for the railroad crews, working on the M&R was a dangerous occupation. In March 1907 the most remembered accident in the history of the railroad rocked the community.

Engineer John McVeigh, a popular twenty-two year old, was southbound on No. 5 around 5:00 in the evening when his train collided head on with the northbound No. 8. The accident took place at the Jessie Lake hoist. Both trains were running at full throttle. The Deer River newspaper reported the incident. "The No. 5 had right-of-way to Turtle

Engineer John McVeigh and conductor John McNaughton died in 1907 when two logging trains collided. The engine pictured here was running backwards at the time, pushing the log cars. As a result, the engine was not seriously damaged. ITASCA COUNTY HISTORICAL SOCIETY

Junction and with a load of 14 log cars, was going at top notch to make the hill, and just as they rounded the curve, Elmer Kemsley, the brakeman, who was riding on the engine, saw the train approaching in the opposite direction. He yelled for the others to jump, at the same time jumping from the engine. The fireman, Andrew Carlson, also succeeded in jumping before the crash, but McVeigh just had time to blow the whistle when the crash came. He was caught in the window of the cab and the empty cars, which were on the head of No. 8, piled up on him. He was badly mangled by the debris and death resulted before he could be extricated." As the trains collided, No. 5's coal car, carrying conductor John McNaughton, was hurled over the telephone wire into the ditch. McNaughton was found under the car with a toolbox lying across his broken neck.[13]

The *Itasca County Independent* squarely placed the blame for the crash on one member of the No. 8 train crew. "It seems, from what can be gathered, that conductor Andy Marcell, of the train pulled by engine No. 8 had received [telephone] orders to wait for McVeigh and [McNaughton's] train at the junction, but thinking he could reach a siding in time to pass the loaded train coming south, he had set out, unbeknownst to anyone but his crew, to make the siding." Two weeks after the accident, Andy Marcell, the well-liked namesake of the town of Marcell, sold his home and lot to another conductor and moved to Michigan.[14] The family of John McVeigh eventually pressed the M&R in court and received damages for the death of their son.

Two months after the tragic McVeigh-McNaughton accident, the construction season for 1907 began. M&R crews would have to build a bridge across the Bigfork River at Bigfork before they could lay track to the small settlement of Effie, eight miles north. Construction followed successful negotiations with Daniel Neveux, who owned the land in Bigfork on the north bank of the river. With this right-of-way secured, several carloads of supplies were unloaded in Bigfork for the railroad bridge. The owners had decided on a first-class steel span instead of a cheaper wooden trestle bridge because they were anticipating a potential union of the M&R with the Backus-Brooks railroad southbound out of International Falls. Such a union would require a heavy-duty bridge. The substantial concrete piers and abutments rose slowly from the water as the bridge crew, supervised by C. M. Lock, struggled under the effort. Not until January 1908 did the massive steel spans arrive. Placing the steel spans across the river took four more months due to adverse conditions in the dead of winter. In the meantime, the railroad grade into Effie had been finished and was ready for the rails as soon as the bridge could be completed. By early spring the bridge was functional, and the rails were laid down rapidly to the north, reaching Effie in May 1908. Among the first passengers from Effie were settlers Mrs. Andrew

Ottum and Mrs. Fred Johnson, who traveled to Bigfork and claimed to have had a very pleasant trip.[15] The bridge at Bigfork is the only surviving M&R structure. Still in good condition, the bridge is a testament to the men who built it.

The M&R: Pathway to the Bigfork Valley

The Bigfork Valley is not a valley visible to the casual observer but rather a region defined by the watershed of the north-flowing Bigfork River that drains part of northern Itasca County and part of Koochiching County. Beginning at Little Bowstring Lake on the Laurentian Continental Divide, Bowstring River picks up volume as it passes through a series of lakes and finally emerges as the Bigfork River. Near its headwaters, the Bigfork River forms a semicircle before striking its northerly run to the Rainy River on the Canadian border. The overall path of the river system resembles the shape of an upside-down question mark.

The town of Deer River lies south of and centered under the Bigfork Valley. Between 1905 and 1908 Deer River, gateway to the Bigfork Valley, bustled. "The Quigg Hotel, the Sullivan Hotel, the Loiselle Hotel, the Everton Hotel, the Mohr Hotel, the Northern Hotel, The Big Ship, the St. Peter Board and Room, the Martindale Boarding House, the Vickard Boarding House, the Christ Johnson Restaurant and John Danielson Restaurant" served up a smorgasbord of room and board possibilities to travelers, lumberjacks, and railroad men journeying into the valley.[16] Few details survive about these lodgings and restaurants. However, one long-time Deer River resident, Bazil Mayo, told of his mother's arrival in 1907 to wait tables at his uncle's boarding house. Head cook and owner Jim Martindale engaged his sister to serve three family-style meals each day. When the M&R first hired men to work on the railroad, they could eat at Martindale's and sleep next door at a rooming house until they received their checks. If they wished, the men could then arrange a payroll deduction in exchange for bed and board.

For most, Deer River was an overnight stop, not a final destination. Six days a week the train arrived in a cloud of steam and smoke at the Deer River depot, ready to pick up travelers and freight. Every Tuesday, Thursday, and Saturday the train took the northerly route to Bigfork and Effie. Every Monday, Wednesday, and Friday the train followed the northeast fork to Wirt. The train was comprised primarily of flat cars and freight cars with a smoking car for inebriated lumberjacks and a passenger coach for sober lumberjacks and travelers. As passengers jostled for seat positions on the train, popular conductor Pat Daley, a 250-pound blue-eyed burly Irishman, sauntered up the aisle, mentally cataloging the passengers as they paid their fares of $1.22 for the trip to Bigfork. Daley, wrote Bergit Anderson in her history of the Bigfork Valley called *The Last Frontier,* "knew which were new settlers, cruisers, traveling salesmen, school teachers, missionaries, saloon keepers, and lumbermen, executives or [lumber]jacks."[17] The train's slow progress irked first-time passengers who complained about the frequent stops while regular passengers resigned themselves to a long day of watching flat cars being switched on and off the train at the various lumber camps before they reached Bigfork or beyond.

A coal stove kept the car reasonably warm during the winter months, unless the

Passengers prepare to board the M&R.
ITASCA COUNTY HISTORICAL SOCIETY

The M&R opened up the Bigfork Valley to sportsmen. Here, deer are transferred from the M&R to the Great Northern Railway in Deer River.
ITASCA COUNTY HISTORICAL SOCIETY

temperature dipped to extremes. "Many were the frowns and curses directed at the incompetent stove" continued Anderson "as the passengers squirmed down into their coat collars and slapped their feet against each other to increase circulation." The cold could occasion gallantry, however, when "some lumberjack played Sir Walter Raleigh to a lady passenger by bundling her up in his sheepskin coat while he himself danced up and down the aisle to keep warm—always the friendly kind spirit of the lumberjack."[18]

At one time travelers enjoyed twenty plush-covered red seats, but over the years the car grew shabbier and shabbier. The eternal lampblack from the six or more kerosene lamps and the spittle underfoot despite "a pretentious sign above the door—'No spitting on the floor!'"—contradicted any romantic notion associated with taking the train. Coal dust and pipe smoke added to the grime. Some travelers contributed graffiti by carving their initials or a design on the windowsills to relieve the tedium of the trip.[19]

Passengers who came to homestead had stuffed their entire households—furniture, food, livestock, and, if space permitted, cut lumber—into rented boxcars. Arriving in Deer River on the Great Northern Railway (formerly the Duluth and Winnipeg) by way of Duluth from central or southern Minnesota or possibly from as far away as Chicago, their boxcars were transferred onto the rails of the M&R. When the train finally glided into Bigfork on a carpet of steam, these tired adventurers unloaded all of their worldly goods, shifting them afterward to a team-drawn wagon or sleigh and headed slowly for their homesteads.

Settlers and lumberjacks seasonally shared their seats on the train with sportsmen. When deer season opened during the fall of 1906, hunters caught the logging train out of

Deer River bound for Bigfork. Hans Hanson had the distinction of being the first to ship two nice deer by rail from Bigfork in November of that year. According to Martin Carlson, railroad employee from 1902 to 1932, each hunter could take three deer. Carlson claimed that at the season's peak the train freighted 350 deer to Deer River every other day, triggering much excitement among the children who raced from school "to see the frozen deer piled up like cord wood on the depot platform." After the Great Northern pulled into the station, the deer were taken by dray—a horse-drawn wagon with a long bed—to waiting boxcars while the hunters transferred between the well-used coach cars of the M&R to the relative luxury of the Great Northern coaches to continue their journey homeward. The *Bigfork Settler* newspaper ran an article in August 1907, boasting, "Deer, moose, bear, lynx, wolves and martin are not at all scarce in our beautiful forests and the hunters who visit this region never go home cheated."[20]

During these boom years, both passengers and freight on the railway increased dramatically. The following table indicates the extent of traffic during that period.[21]

YEAR	PASSENGERS	TONS FREIGHT	TONS FOREST PRODUCTS
1905–1906	10,176	4,127	184,000
1906–1907	11,598	5,888	338,382
1907–1908	16,046	6,642	476,499
1908–1909	22,304		346,343 combined

These were the best of times for the railroad, but they would not last. Prosperity was tied to the bounty of the forest. Northern Minnesota would repeat the saga of the continuously diminishing supply of white pine that had been recited across the United States from Maine through Michigan to Wisconsin. Both the railroad and settlers would have to face the coming troubles.

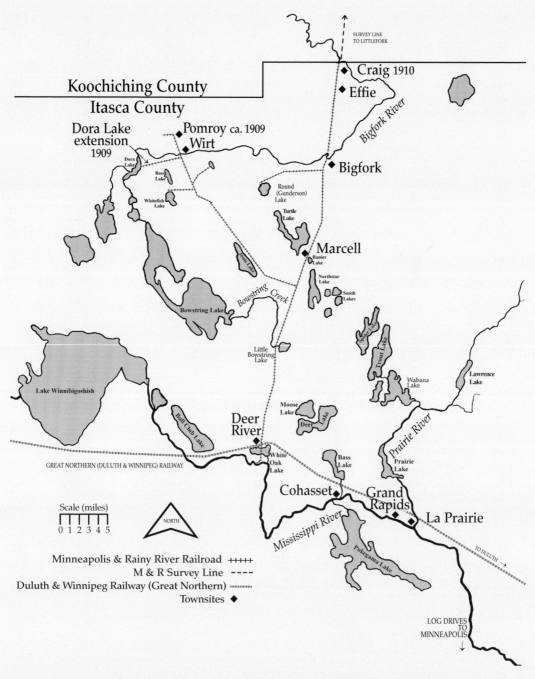

SURVEY LINE
TO LITTLEFORK

Craig 1910

Effie

Koochiching County

Itasca County

Bigfork River

Dora Lake
extension
1909

Pomroy ca. 1909

Wirt

Dora
Lake

Bass
Lake

Bigfork

Whitefish
Lake

Round
(Gunderson)
Lake

Turtle
Lake

Marcell

Ranier
Lake

Trout Lake

Northstar
Lake

Bowstring Creek

Smith
Lakes

Bowstring Lake

Snider Lake

Trout Lake

Little
Bowstring
Lake

Wabana
Lake

Lawrence
Lake

Lake Winnibigoshish

Ball Club Lake

Moose
Lake

Deer Lake

Deer
River

Prairie River

White
Oak
Lake

Bass
Lake

Prairie
Lake

GREAT NORTHERN (DULUTH & WINNIPEG) RAILWAY

Cohasset

Grand
Rapids

La Prairie

Mississippi River

TO DULUTH

Scale (miles)

0 1 2 3 4 5

NORTH

Pokegama Lake

Minneapolis & Rainy River Railroad +++++
M & R Survey Line - - - -
Duluth & Winnipeg Railway (Great Northern) ┄┄┄┄
Townsites ◆

LOG DRIVES
TO
MINNEAPOLIS

MINNEAPOLIS & RAINY RIVER RAILROAD 1909–1932

The M&R Reaches Craigville
1909—1914

ON MARCH 5, 1909, AT THE PEAK of the Bigfork Valley boom years, forty-nine year old William Joyce died at his home in Chicago. The lumber magnate left his widow and two sons in their early twenties an estate of $10.7 million, representing investments in more than twenty enterprises scattered across the country.[1] Included in this portfolio was the Minneapolis and Rainy River Railway. David and Stanley were fortunate that before their father died, he had outlined a plan for the future of the M&R as the predictable depletion of white pine approached. His plan called for extending the lines to reach more timber and exploring iron mining as a means to increase freight, or selling the railway to a larger concern, such as the Soo Line.

Before his death, William Joyce had acquainted his sons with the Minnesota businesses, since it was an established Joyce tradition to train the younger generation by immersion in the lumbering industry. David had begun making trips to northern Minnesota as a teenager. In 1902, during the summer he turned seventeen, he was employed at the Itasca Lumber Company office in Deer River under head bookkeeper Charlie Birke.[2] Three years later, in April 1905, the *Itasca News* reported, "Dave Joyce, son of an Itasca Lumber Company stockholder, came up from Chicago on his vacation, which he will spend with the lumberjacks." Already knowledgeable about the business and perhaps influenced by the strong hand with which William Joyce ruled his companies, David wasted no time in asserting his authority over what had been William Joyce's domain. In a letter directed to the managers of the Itasca Lumber Company, after the death of his father, he declared, "As you will probably find it necessary to take up with me in the near future, matters of importance, it would not be inadvisable for you to start on small matters now."[3]

David's younger brother was also familiar with the northern Minnesota enterprises, but Stanley Joyce delayed his entrance into family business by going east for a formal education. He attended Philips Academy at Andover, Massachusetts, before graduating in 1910 from Yale University's Sheffield Scientific School, which offered practical courses of study like engineering. (Admittance to Sheffield Scientific School did not require knowledge of Latin and Greek; nor did the school possess Yale's "social panache.")[4]

In July 1909, four months after the death of William Joyce, long-time professional associates as well as the managers of the Itasca Lumber Company and the Minneapolis and Rainy River Railway met with the Joyce brothers in Deer River to assess the financial status of the M&R. Their meeting culminated with an inspection tour on the railroad. David and Stanley Joyce were accompanied by two minority stockholders and business partners, H. C. Akeley and Thomas Hume. William LaCroix, president of the Minneapolis and Rainy River Railway, and F. C. Gerhard, general manager, joined the group as did land sales agent S. D. Patrick. Rounding out the party were H. W. Seaman, an experienced railroad man for the Chicago and St. Louis; William A. Remick, one of William Joyce's closest business associates in Lyons, Iowa; and a Mr. Sommers.[5]

These men inspected the physical assets of the Minneapolis and Rainy River Railway during their tour. Of the 108 miles of steel, 64 miles were mainline track and 44 miles were sidetracks and logging spurs. The rolling stock consisted of 11 locomotives, 4 passenger cars, 8 boxcars, 95 flat cars, 293 logging cars, and, according to one source, a refrigerator car. Auxiliary equipment, shops, 3 gravel pits, and 97 miles of telegraph lines completed the railroad's holdings, then appraised at about $1.7 million.[6]

M&R Spurs and Mainline Extensions

One of William Joyce's recommendations for the M&R had been to keep on extending the lines to reach more timber, and his sons methodically pursued this goal. The rail crews kept pushing into virgin stands of white and red pine during 1909 and 1910 in advance of the Itasca Lumber Company logging crews. Several spurs of notable length branched off the mainline track, reaching for pockets of exceptional pine.

The railroad crews built these spurs as quickly and inexpensively as possible, for they were not intended for permanent service. Referring to the tracks as "scratch" or "surface" grade, the railroad men simply laid the ties upon the cleared and leveled ground.[7] These ties were often hewn on the spot from timber cleared from the right-of-way. Once the timber in the vicinity of a spur was exhausted by the logging operation, the rails were taken up and used elsewhere. The spurs came and went, but the stories of the rugged characters who worked and lived alongside the tracks have survived.

Turtle Lake

Sometime between 1906 and 1909, the M&R requested permission from the Minnesota Railway and Warehouse Commission to discontinue the spur serving the original town site of Marcell on the south end of Turtle Lake. Marcell's ambitious founder, John Lundeen, loudly protested. Lundeen had created Marcell out of the wilderness by his own extraordinary effort and was incredulous at the possibility that the M&R would desert the community. The settlement, still in its infancy, would die if the M&R's tracks were removed. Lundeen took the train to Deer River to meet with state officials, certain that the Minnesota Railway and Warehouse Commission would not grant the petition forwarded by the M&R, which, as a common carrier, was compelled to operate under its regulations.

Unfortunately for Lundeen the railway prevailed, and in June 1910 the tracks were removed. Old Marcell lost any hope of sustaining itself as a community without the railway. In response, its citizens immediately formed a plan to pick up the town and move to Ranier Lake, several miles to the east. The move took place only six months after the rails had been taken up from the Turtle Lake spur.[8] This time, the citizens hoped, the town would be solidly situated upon the mainline track of the M&R. Lundeen reluctantly followed, rebuilding his general store and home at new Marcell.

Round Lake

More typical of the short-lived spurs on the M&R, the terminus of the Round Lake spur was a cluster of logging camps instead of a small community. This spur departed from the mainline track two miles south of Bigfork and tapped Round Lake. Today the lake is called Gunderson Lake, named after Charles Gunderson, logging camp foreman who worked for the Itasca Lumber Company camp at the end of the spur. Gunderson gained renown because he miraculously survived a lumberjacking accident. According to the newspaper, the *Bigfork Settler*, "Mr. Gunderson was at work at one of the large roll-ways when suddenly the great mass of logs gave way and Mr. Gunderson was buried beneath thousands of feet of logs. The crew worked like beavers to get the logs off the unfortunate man that they expected to find badly mangled if not dead. The crew had nearly reached him when the logs gave way again. When the men finally reached him, it was found that owing to the soft condition of the ground and the large skids upon which the logs were piled, that Mr. Gunderson had escaped with only a broken leg."[9]

The excellent pine and cedar timber in the vicinity of Round Lake supported several logging camps besides the Itasca Lumber Company camp. Among the supplies delivered to one of the camps on Round Lake, the M&R train crews noted peculiarly large amounts of a certain patent medicine. Don Benson, a fishing guide in the Bigfork Valley for fifty years, related a story about this patent medicine as told to him by Martin Carlson, an engineer on the M&R. A logger named Dempsey, who operated a big camp at Gunderson [Round] Lake, barred beer and liquor from his camp in order to keep the lumberjacks sober. The camp's alcoholic clerk subverted the policy by including a nationally advertised remedy called Peruna in his regular order of camp supplies. Peruna's

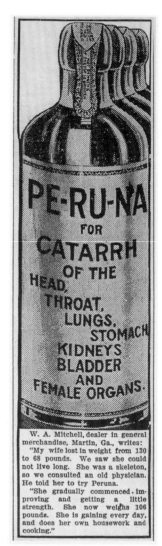

Peruna was popular among lumberjacks. They could drink the alcoholic elixir in the name of health. WESTERN ITASCA REVIEW

main ingredient—and probably only active ingredient—was alcohol. According to Benson, "It was supposed to cure anything from flat feet and on up! The train was always delivering Peruna to that camp. They [the train men] called Round Lake Branch, the Peruna Branch. They even started calling Round Lake, Peruna Lake."[10] The name stuck when the local newspaper picked up the nickname, referring to the spur as the Peruna Branch.[11]

Dora Lake and Pomroy

The mainline's western branch, which previously ended at Wirt, now expanded in two directions. One arm traveled westward five miles to Dora Lake, arriving at the lake in 1909. The other arm took a northerly course toward the tiny settlement of Pomroy, a distance of six miles.

The Itasca Lumber Company and the Northland Pine Company built the Dora Lake extension as a joint venture because the Itasca Lumber Company pinelands at Dora Lake would sustain a logging camp for a trifling two years.[12] Only hauling the log harvests of several companies could make construction worthwhile. Furthermore, the area between Wirt and Dora Lake traversed by the Dora Lake extension was almost totally swampland, expensive terrain through which to lay track. Northland Pine Company's Sam Simpson cleared and constructed a grade before the Itasca Lumber

The Jessie Junction section house provided room and board for M&R employees. The site was located at the junction of the Jessie Lake branch (also called the Wirt or western branch) with the main line. The site was later renamed Alder. PETE BONESTEEL PRIVATE COLLECTION

Company put down the ties and the M&R rail crew laid track. This section was some-times referred to as the Simpson Railway, highlighting the role Sam Simpson had played in building the extension and in operating his subsequent logging business at Dora Lake.[13]

Ranging north of Wirt, the Pomroy extension, like the Dora Lake extension, appears to have been laid primarily for the use of logging firms other than the Itasca Lumber Company. Almost nothing is known about the Pomroy spur. It was probably built just after the link to Dora Lake was completed in 1909. Around 1914 the timber com-ing out of the Pomroy district dried up.

The amount of timber and other forest products loaded at Dora Lake also declined about the same time, sealing the fate of the remote spurs. Moreover, the constantly wet ties, which had suffered from the swampy environment, had rotted so badly that only light locomotives could travel the rails, and the M&R was not about to sink capital into the maintenance of such seldom-used sections of the railroad. In 1915 it applied to the Minnesota Railroad and Warehouse Commission to abandon all service on the Dora Lake and Pomroy extensions.[14]

Faced with the prospect of losing their only efficient means of transportation, the Dora Lake loggers and settlers complained to the state of Minnesota, which then sued the M&R to show just cause for the abandonment. The resulting court testimony made the M&R case clear. Economically the railway could not justify the continued operation because of the depletion of pine and hardwoods and the sparse population. During the court case, M&R Superintendent William LaCroix was asked about the possibility of agricultural products replacing the logging tonnage on this extension. LaCroix assert-ed, "It won't be in this generation, unless they get a different class of farmers there."[15] His comment referred to the fact that subsistence farming would not increase freight tonnage and the area lacked any hope of supporting large-scale production farming. The rails lay idle until the Minnesota Railroad and Warehouse Commission granted per-mission for the removal to begin, whereupon Wirt once more became the end of the line.

Craig

On the mainline's eastern branch, which previously had ended at Bigfork, the M&R continued north past Effie to a new terminus of the line called Craig. The logging camp there remained the end of the line until the abandonment of the railroad in 1932.

The Craig extension north of Bigfork and Effie opened new timber resources. The rail crews advanced in 1910 to a point on the Bigfork River where a logging camp had recently been established by John "Smoking Jesus" Craig. A camp foreman with the Itasca Lumber Company for the previous twenty years, Craig had received his nickname "Smoking Jesus" because of his reverent abstinence from the use of all traditional swear words. He preferred instead to make up his own choice phrases, such as "Holy balls of Ireland!" when the occasion warranted it.[16] The stern Irishman also abstained from the use of alcohol and tobacco. His unfortunate death from brain cancer shortly after the M&R reached his camp on the Bigfork River was possibly the reason the camp took the name Craig.[17] Within shouting distance of the logging camp, a settlement known as Craigville also sprang up with the arrival of the M&R.

A wild reputation marked Craig throughout its existence, according to Lyle Quigg, who traveled there on the train during the summer of 1923, when he was 16 years old. He

Craig, notorious for its rowdy atmosphere, was the end of the M&R advancement northward.
GENE MADSEN PRIVATE COLLECTION

worked in Jack O'Connell's logging camp. Seventy years later he related what life was like at the end of the line:

> "That was when Craig was going full force. . . . I worked in the cook shack as a cookee. . . . I slept right in the cookhouse. The cook had the lower bunk, and I had the upper bunk. The door was right by the bunk. All hours of the night, people—drunks—would try to push the door open so that they could get something to eat. The cook was called Jimmy the Greek. If he did not want to get up in the middle of the night, he would tell them to go away. One time he had a fellow turn on him. . . . The guy grabbed the cook and was going to pull him out of bed. They had quite a fight. Jimmy the Greek was not very big, but he was tougher than nails. Jimmy finally got him outside. I was scared half the night, every night. When you went to bed, you never knew what might happen.
>
> "Several times fellows were killed while I was there. Where most of the trouble started was at the houses [brothels]. . . . I sure was glad when the fall came and I could go back to school and get out of there."[18]

Iron Ore

While the Joyce organization extended and re-routed rail line, it simultaneously pursued indications of iron deposits underlying the region traversed by the M&R. Just southeast of the M&R, the Mesaba Iron Range stretched across northeastern Minnesota in a narrow, crescent-shaped band. There a newly established mining industry had taken hold. The Mesaba's western end lay only ten miles from Deer River. Further arousing interest in the potential for iron ore was the fact that the old Wright and Davis logging railroad at Swan River—the railroad that had come very close to being built by the Itasca Lumber Company—occupied land with fabulous underground deposits of the mineral. That road now prospered as its primary haul switched from timber to the rich ore of the Mesaba.

As early as 1903, reports of good indications of iron ore were circulating in the Bigfork Valley. An article in the *Deer River Itasca News*, dated May 23, 1903, reported:

"That there is croppings of iron ore north of Deer River, supposedly broken lodes from the west point of the Mesaba range. . . .has long been suspected, and though the matter has been kept exceedingly quiet it has now leaked out that indications have proven sufficient to warrant prospect.

"The *News* has been reliably informed of good ore indications at different points between the north shore of Deer lake thence northwest about 10 miles to the vicinity of Grave lake on the Itasca Lumber Co. road. And what might indicate that large owners of land. . . . believe they have more there than land and trees, is their constant refusal to sell any kind of land in the vicinity at any price whatever."[19]

Four years later, an editorial in a 1907 issue of the *Bigfork Settler* continued to feed the excitement and wild expectations. "There are very favorable signs of iron ore in this immediate community [Bigfork] and to the careful observer it will be no surprise to see, in the near future, mines of great wealth operated here and Bigfork pass from a lumbering town to a mining town."[20]

The talk of iron was not based upon unfounded rumor. Strong magnetic anomalies, caused by the presence of iron, do underlie much of what was once the M&R right-of-way, as indicated on modern geologic maps of the area. Prospectors in the early 1900s would have been fully aware of the presence of these magnetic signatures that were comparable in strength to those found over the rich Mesaba Iron Range.[21]

It is interesting to speculate whether the builders of the M&R chose to purchase and harvest these areas of white pine because of the possibility of future mineral development. Certainly Joyce and his associates would have known about the notes from original surveys done in the 1860s and 1870s. One of the earliest surveyors of the township containing Little Bowstring Lake, the terminus of the M&R during its first years of operation out of Deer River, recorded in his journal: "I saw no signs of mineral deposit, but in some places [the compass] needle was very much affected by local attraction." Another of the early surveyors had a similar observation in Marcell Township: "I find strong indications of mineral deposits in defferent [sic] parts of the township, in some places causing my needle to vary eighty to ninety degrees in running ten chains [60 feet]."[22] The signs of mineral deposits coincided with the M&R's right-of-way.

Stanley Joyce initiated a formal search for iron deposits under the M&R tracks and the 54,000 acres of Itasca Lumber Company lands shortly after his father died in 1909. Initially Joyce requested that Oliver Iron Company do the prospecting, but when it failed to act promptly, he directed that a mining engineer be hired for the job. After spending $6,000, the ILC's only discovery proved a worthless grade of ore, located on approximately 2,000 acres of the company lands. The company again attempted to uncover usable ore bodies in 1916 and 1918. Hard-rock drilling equipment operated by the Duluth Diamond Drilling Company was hauled on the M&R to locations near Marcell and the Turtle Lake area. These drilling explorations also failed. Still, the ILC retained mineral rights on the cutover lands that it was selling just in case ore should be found in the future.[23]

Buyout Possibilities

Stanley and David Joyce continued to follow their father's strategy for making the M&R a paying investment by seeking buyout offers from other regional rail companies. Railways and investors were looking especially hard at the M&R during this period when rumors of iron deposits were rife. Interested capitalists took frequent inspection trips over the Minneapolis and Rainy River Railway.

One likely buyer was the Soo Line. Announcements of its purchase of the M&R appeared so often in newspapers that soon editors trumpeted the sale with such humorous headlines as "SOO HAS BOUGHT THE M&R AGAIN." This headline was broadcast across the front page of the December 17, 1910 issue of the *Itasca News*, along with the

The M&R passenger train typically consisted of a smoker for lumberjacks, a passenger coach for the settlers, tourists, and businessmen, and a boxcar for freight. NORTHEAST MINNESOTA HISTORICAL CENTER, DULUTH, MINNESOTA

qualifying subtitle, "Not Definite, But Considerable Rumor that the Local Line Has Been Bought up." Jokes aside, the paper had confidence that the Soo would buy. The article predicted that after the sale eighteen miles of rail would be built south from Deer River to connect to the Soo Line at the town of Remer. Almost a year later officials of the M&R and the Soo Line thoroughly examined the M&R, further cementing the belief in a Soo buyout. During this time, the M&R officials were very busy making the railway more presentable not only to the Soo Line but to other prospective buyers. Company officials particularly wanted to secure legal title to right-of-ways that previously had hinged on oral permission from landowners.[24]

Rumors of the buyout were fanned again when the citizens of the nearby town of Grand Rapids lobbied the Soo Line to lay tracks from Deer River to its community before heading south. If the Deer River-to-Grand Rapids segment were constructed, the tracks of the Soo Line would parallel the tracks of the Great Northern. Competition from a rival carrier would boost the Grand Rapids economy. "The news that the Soo had purchased the M&R was received with gladness in Grand Rapids," according to the *Itasca County Independent*. The paper went on to claim, "This arrangement would not only give Grand Rapids another railroad, but would add to the Soo's territory one of the best towns in this section."[25] Despite the great interest shown, however, the Soo Line never made an offer to acquire the M&R.

James J. Hill, an American business mogul who owned the Great Northern Railway, followed a similar track, showing interest but never acting.[26] The M&R was too much of a gamble for these potential buyers with its declining timber resources, questionable mineral deposits, and scant population to serve.

For several years Edward W. Backus, president of the Backus-Brooks companies, had also seriously entertained the idea of buying out the M&R as an addition to his own logging railroad. The Backus-Brooks road supplied raw materials for the Backus mills. These mills included the Minnesota and Ontario Paper Company, the International Lumber Company, and the National Pole and Treating Company, located in International Falls, Minnesota, and across the border in Fort Frances, Ontario. Since the Backus-Brooks road—called the Minnesota and International Railway—and the Minneapolis and Rainy River Railway were experiencing similar financial problems, Backus mulled over a consolidation as a way to stabilize his own rail interests.[27]

Backus may have envisioned a north-south railway to add to his already impressive accomplishments as a businessman. In 1910 he completed a large dam at International Falls for the generation of electrical power. There were indications that he was considering an electrified railway stretching from International Falls to Minneapolis to use the newly developed power.[28] In any case, the purchase of the M&R by Backus seemed almost a certainty to both Backus and the Joyce brothers. It appears that there was an oral agreement to that effect.

Some of the incentive for the Joyces' tapping the Craig area resulted from this ongoing negotiation with Backus. Noted the October 23, 1909 edition of the *Bigfork Settler*, "there is every reason to believe that there will soon be railroad services direct from Deer River to International Falls."[29] In 1910, as the M&R reached Craig, pilings for the railway bridge were driven across the Bigfork River as planned, ending the northward expansion of the railway. At about the same time, Backus launched a 500-strong crew to construct a thirty-two-mile rail spur south from Littlefork, using the right-of-way that had been surveyed and acquired by the M&R. When the Backus spur reached Craig, the two railways would be connected. Interestingly, the spur from Littlefork toward Craig was known as the Deer River line, in reference to the ultimate southern destination that the link would provide for the Backus-Brooks railway. It continued to be called the Deer River line until 1947, long after the rails of the M&R had ceased to exist.[30]

Backus did not act upon the proposed buyout of the M&R in a timely manner but instead "studied and figured over the M&R situation" for several years. While he studied, his railroad crews built the Deer River spur steadily southward upon the M&R right-of-way. When it reached what was known as Camp 29, across the river and two miles distant from Craig in 1914, Backus delivered his formal purchase offer for the M&R. He wrote: "Considering the physical condition of the property, including equipment, the fact that its local business cannot possibly pay operating expenses for many years to come and all other facts bearing upon the question, I have concluded that $300,000 would be the maximum amount that we could afford to consider. . . . We might want this deal, if one were made, to include your saw mill plant at Deer River. . . . You may or may not be disappointed in my figures, but I figure the property is a liability at the present time and it takes a lot of nerve to face an expenditure of from $1,000,000 to $2,000,000 in gambling that it can be put into an earning basis. . . ."[31]

Stanley Joyce, the president of the M&R, was outraged. He and his managers expected a figure in the neighborhood of $1.5 million, which was the appraised value. Joyce immediately notified Backus that any further discussion was useless and that Backus should return all of the papers that had been sent to him. It was the end of any friendship between the men and the beginning of legal skirmishes involving the use of the M&R right-of-way by the Backus-Brooks railway and the disposition of timber cut on Backus lands by the Itasca Lumber Company. After the $300,000 offer, Stanley Joyce considered the idea that Backus or any of his corporations might purchase the M&R a mere joke.[32]

The M&R Loses Steam

David and Stanley Joyce had extended the rail lines as far as they could to reach available pine stands, had prospected for iron ore, and had entertained prospective buyers for the M&R. While the search for a buyer and iron deposits were still remote possibilities, there was no question about the dwindling harvest of pine. Cedar, the livelihood of the other independent companies relying on the M&R, became a valued commodity and, for a time, rivaled the haul of white pine. Then it too became scarce. The demand for pulpwood, used in the production of paper, also increased, but it alone could not maintain the M&R. Simultaneously forest fires raged uncontrolled across the deforested white pine and cedar lands and burned into areas of still standing timber, further depleting the nearly exhausted supply.

The effect of declining white pine rippled throughout the Itasca Lumber Company. In 1911 the ILC shut down its operations in the woods, unable to locate enough pine stock to continue the large-scale harvests that were characteristic of its past. Now the company relied upon independent loggers to supply its mill at Deer River. That same year the Itasca Lumber Company's mill at Minneapolis—at one time the largest mill in the Midwest—ceased operation due to the insufficient supply of white pine logs. The M&R immediately felt the effects of the lost tonnage. One of the best locomotives, No. 8, was permanently shipped off to Manistee, Michigan, where the Joyces had partial ownership in a railway operation with at least one other ILC stockholder. Several more engines were predicted to follow No. 8. Of the eleven locomotives owned by the M&R in 1909, only five remained by 1913.[33] A discouraging report in the Bigfork paper likewise dampened hopes for the future of the railroad. "The M&R is letting a number of their men go on account of hard times. Probably they are going to quit business soon."[34] About fifty men were without employment as the shops of the M&R closed for the summer; the only trains running were the passenger trains. Some of the unemployed men did return to work that fall as logging picked up.

Trouble with the Law

Further straining the finances of the Minneapolis and Rainy River were the penalty payments and legal fees that the railroad was forced to pay due to their illegal billing practices. Originally a part of the Itasca Lumber Company, the M&R continued hauling ILC supplies for free and ILC timber at a reduced rate even after the formal incorporation of the logging railroad as a separate company in 1904. Published freight rates for shipping on the M&R ran as high as $2.75 per thousand feet for logs and other forest products, yet the M&R initially charged the Itasca Lumber Company a freight rate of $1.00.[35] Later, when it was not covering its expenses, the M&R raised the freight rate for the ILC to $1.50. Another company owned by the Joyces benefited from these lower freight rates as well. In 1904 William Joyce and a partner had erected a new mill near Deer River, eventually called the Deer River Lumber Company (DRLC), to manufacture lumber from the tree species overlooked in the lumbermen's eagerness to take out the white pine. These bills charged to the Itasca Lumber Company and the Deer River Lumber Company were just paper entries because no money actually changed hands. From the viewpoint of management, the practice of billing freight was merely a bookkeeping inconvenience, since the ILC, the DRLC, and the M&R were all owned by the Joyce organization. It is possible that the goal of the billing practices was to minimize the apparent income of the railroad, thus reducing the tax burden and boosting collective profits of the three Deer River companies.

The Minnesota Railroad and Warehouse Commission frowned upon the favoritism shown the ILC and the DRLC by the M&R, charging that such favoritism was an unfair business practice. The Joyce companies were subsequently scrutinized by state taxing authorities who demanded in excess of $12,000 for back taxes on more than $400,000 of omitted gross earnings—the discrepancy between the published and discounted shipping rates charged the ILC and the DRLC.[36] Billing rate discrimination was common among related companies at the time even though the Sherman

Antitrust Act of 1890—later strengthened by the Clayton Act of 1914—prohibited such competitive advantages as the M&R conferred on the ILC and the DRLC.

The revelations of the state investigation opened the floodgates of discontent upon the M&R. Unhappy settlers in the Bigfork Valley echoed the complaints of unhappy loggers. Mr. Herried, a Bigfork Valley farmer, testified during a December 1911 M&R rate hearing that farmers could not afford to develop their farms and ship their produce on the M&R because of excessive freight rates. Exhibits offered at this hearing featured freight bills showing that the cost of shipping from Deer River to Duluth—a distance of approximately ninety-five miles—was only slightly higher than the cost of shipping to Deer River from a place thirty miles north of town. Billing sheets from different railroads proved that the M&R's rates for the transportation of cedar ties were out of line.[37] What no doubt enraged the settlers as well was the fact that the Itasca Lumber Company shipped its own supplies, horses, and equipment free, saving the company more than $45,000 in freight fees. The Minnesota Railroad & Warehouse Commission sided with the settlers and the loggers. Lower rates on merchandise, timber products, and farm produce went into effect in late September 1912.[38]

In July 1912 the Sullivan Log and Cedar Company initiated a lawsuit against the railroad in order to recover excessive fees it had paid for transportation of logs on the M&R. During the trial, Sullivan's lawyers presented the jury and spectators with an apt metaphor for the four Joyce-owned companies in Minnesota. These four companies were the Minneapolis and Rainy River Railway, the Itasca Lumber Company, the Deer River Lumber Company, and the Northern Investment Company, a holding company for Joyce stock and stumpage. The companies were depicted as four pockets in the same suit of clothes. Since the stockholders in each of these companies were the same, the transfer of money from one company to another was like moving dollars from one pocket to another. It was nothing more than an accounting entry. The metaphor attempted to clarify the complex yet intentionally vague paper trail existing among the Joyce businesses. By the end of the court case, the jury and spectators no doubt understood a lot more about the business arrangements of these Joyce firms or were thoroughly confused. The jury awarded the plaintiff, Sullivan et al., $5,650.43 plus interest.[39]

Other independent loggers using the M&R jumped on the bandwagon and sued the railroad for the rates it charged for shipments of their logs. According to the September 27, 1913 issue of the local paper, the informality between the Itasca Lumber Company and the M&R resulted in two more judgments. Frank Seaman of Deer River received $3,445. The Minnesota Cedar and Logging Company received $1,542. Besides these judgments, the M&R incurred significant legal fees during the long trials.[40]

The same year that the Sullivan lawsuit was decided, the M&R received a blow to its passenger revenues. In 1913 the passenger fare of 3¢ per mile was reduced to 2¢ for all common carrier railways in Minnesota. The reduction, originally mandated by the state legislature in 1907, had drawn numerous legal challenges by the major carriers. After a decision by the United States Supreme Court in 1913, the reduced rate went into effect anyway.[41]

It is difficult to ascertain the true financial status of the Minneapolis and Rainy River Railroad, especially when one considers the interdependency of the Joyce enterprises. Although it had been expensive to lay track, buy equipment, gain right-of-way easements, and fight lawsuits, the M&R did increase the profits of the Itasca Lumber Company as the railroad displaced the waterways for transporting timber. The M&R was merely one pocket in the suit of clothing of the larger Joyce operation in Minnesota, and although the railroad pocket was losing ground financially, the other pockets were full of cash.

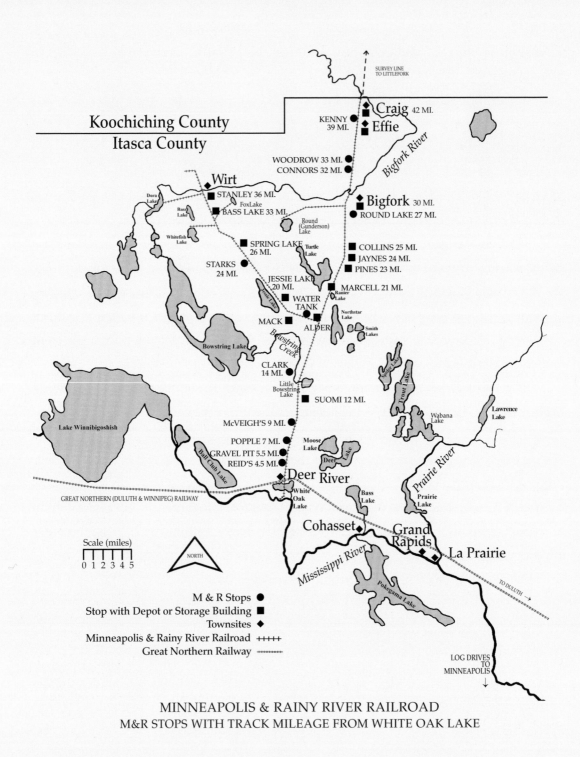

Koochiching County
Itasca County

SURVEY LINE
TO LITTLEFORK

Craig 42 MI.
KENNY 39 MI.
Effie
WOODROW 33 MI.
CONNORS 32 MI.

Bigfork River

Wirt
STANLEY 36 MI.
Dora Lake
Fox Lake
Bass Lake
BASS LAKE 33 MI.

Bigfork 30 MI.
ROUND LAKE 27 MI.

Round (Gunderson) Lake

Whitefish Lake

SPRING LAKE 26 MI.
Turtle Lake

COLLINS 25 MI.
JAYNES 24 MI.
PINES 23 MI.

STARKS 24 MI.

JESSIE LAKE 20 MI.
MARCELL 21 MI.
Ranier Lake

WATER TANK
Northstar Lake

MACK
ALDER
Smith Lakes

Bowstring Lake

Bowstring Creek

CLARK 14 MI.

Little Bowstring Lake

Lake Winnibigoshish

SUOMI 12 MI.

Squaw River
Trout Lake

McVEIGH'S 9 MI.

Wabana Lake

POPPLE 7 MI.
Moose Lake

Lawrence Lake

GRAVEL PIT 5.5 MI.
REID'S 4.5 MI.
Deer Lake

Ball Club Lake

Prairie River

Deer River
White Oak Lake

GREAT NORTHERN (DULUTH & WINNIPEG) RAILWAY

Bass Lake
Prairie Lake

Cohasset
Grand Rapids
La Prairie
TO DULUTH

Mississippi River

Pokegama Lake

Scale (miles)
0 1 2 3 4 5

NORTH

M & R Stops ●
Stop with Depot or Storage Building ■
Townsites ◆
Minneapolis & Rainy River Railroad +++++
Great Northern Railway ┄┄┄┄┄

LOG DRIVES
TO
MINNEAPOLIS

MINNEAPOLIS & RAINY RIVER RAILROAD
M&R STOPS WITH TRACK MILEAGE FROM WHITE OAK LAKE

Automobiles, Trucks, and the Great Depression

1915–1932

PROSPECTS FOR MANY RAILWAYS THROUGHOUT the country dimmed after 1914. Short lines such as the Minneapolis and Rainy River Railway were particularly hard hit, and failures were common. "Is the M&R Going to Quit?" was the prominent headline of the January 23, 1915 *Itasca News*. Later that year a poor financial report for the railway declared a deficit of just under $13,000, but the owners were not ready to surrender. Their strategy now emphasized minimizing expenses and continuing to hope for a buyout or a turnaround in the business climate.[1] The advancement of technology in the form of automobiles and trucks, however, was working against the M&R.

While Minneapolis and Rainy River officials struggled with finances, settlers in the Bigfork Valley voiced their fears of losing the railroad. C. H. Morey, general manager of the M&R, allayed these worries by announcing the purchase of two new passenger coaches. According to the *Itasca News*, they were "the equal of any car on the Great Northern." Although new to the M&R, the secondhand cars were bought at bargain prices from the Northern Pacific Railway and were almost as dilapidated as the cars they replaced.[2] Yet their acquisition assured the public of the railroad's commitment to passenger service.

A year and one-half later, the company made a minimal investment in more equipment to save employee hours and thus reduce operating costs. The *Itasca News* reported during the summer of 1916, "Manager Morey while in the eastern cities happily surprised the 'home folks' by shipping in a few days ago five new gasoline [rail] cars for the use of section crews and now the boys with

Passenger ticket issued during 1911–1912.

the shovels and bars are saving muscle and taking but a few minutes instead of hours in getting to and from work."[3] Before this purchase, the men who shoveled gravel for the rail bed and pried out faulty rails for replacement had pumped handcars to work, which consumed considerable time and energy.

Another investment, an enclosed gasoline-powered rail car seating sixteen, was used for inspection tours. This acquisition also saved the expense of dispatching a locomotive for a medical emergency, which was a common occurrence. The car looked like a small bus. Painted black, it gained the nickname of the "Black Mariah."[4]

Spuds Are Promoted as Boon to M&R

Frugality was not enough to keep the railroad running. It needed more freight. Like many of the struggling lines across the country, the M&R encouraged agricultural development as a means to boost tonnage. Potatoes in particular offered a possible substitute for lost timber since they were easy to grow in quantity and were best shipped by rail because of their bulk and weight. The idea had met with some success in the nearby community of Grand Rapids, which was shipping out potatoes in carload quantities on the Great Northern Railway. Another Joyce railway, the Tremont and Gulf, located in Louisiana, was also experimenting with agricultural products to replace declining forest products.[5]

C. H. Morey, the general manager of the M&R, and C. M. King, a successful Deer River businessman, promoted the idea locally. Morey pledged to build a potato warehouse at any station along the M&R where settlers could produce 5,000 bushels or more of potatoes. If, as one prediction asserted, 200 to 400 bushels of potatoes per acre could be grown in the fertile Bigfork Valley, a single settler with twenty-five acres could meet Morey's minimum. The railroad would not only shoulder the cost of building the warehouses but it would also buy all potatoes at market price minus transportation costs.[6]

Morey advertised the potato project widely. Besides promulgating it through newspaper notices, he displayed posters at all M&R stations and mailed questionnaires to farmers in the area asking for detailed information about their intentions to plant potatoes during the next two growing seasons. King, a proponent for better roads in the area, supported the plan by promising that "in some manner a road will be provided for every settler to get his potatoes out to the nearest shipping station, provided the settler guarantees a sufficient number of potatoes."[7]

Although the newspaper articles implied that Morey and King worked hard to develop potatoes as an agricultural commodity, no further mention of potatoes being transported by the railroad in any significant quantity was reported in the paper. The depressed local economy of the time and the reality that many of the farmers of the Bigfork Valley functioned at subsistence level meant that very few individuals could invest in equipment and preparation of new land for cultivation. Thus, the practice of shipping in substantially more produce than was ever shipped out continued.[8]

Brief Business Boom Follows World War I

The railroad's difficulties were exacerbated by wartime restraints in the timber industry. With the formal entrance of the United States into the fray on April 6, 1917, the difficulties of the logging business worsened as government regulated industry. Bemoaning the business climate, Fred Wenzel, a manager in the Itasca Lumber Company, wrote to

Nicknamed the Black Mariah, this gasoline-powered speeder shuttled not only train crews but also officials on inspection tours. On some occasions, it aided settlers in need. The M&R roundhouse in Deer River is visible in the background. ITASCA COUNTY HISTORICAL SOCIETY

Stanley Joyce, "We anticipated some difficulty in doing business under war conditions, but we certainly did not dream of the radical conditions that now exist in the way of embargoes, permits, limitations of construction and other annoyances, and if we did not look upon it as temporary, we would be very discouraged."[9] As a cost-cutting measure, the Joyces eliminated the M&R's main office in Minneapolis in 1917, moving the head-quarters for the company to Deer River and refurbishing the rural depot building to accommodate the additional staff, equipment, and records previously housed in Minneapolis. Then the M&R waited for better times.

Demand for forest products exploded after the close of the war on November 11, 1918. More than sixty carloads of timber in the ensuing months moved out daily from independent lumber camps to Deer River to fill orders for local mills and out-of-town businesses. In terms of the total amount of wood hauled, the harvest of the 1918–1919 winter months matched or exceeded "the big work of the pine of years past," reported a March 1919 issue of the *Itasca News*. Prices soared beyond everyone's expectations, top-pling all previous years' peak prices. Even with the significant rise in wages and opera-tional costs, almost everyone in the lumbering business made a profit.[10] During the post-war years, the M&R was hauling almost no pine, for the pine stocks were nearly cut over and what remained was of poor quality. Instead, the new boom in the M&R's fortune came from hauling pulpwood for paper production, railway ties, cedar posts, poles, and hardwoods. The surge in demand for forest products was short-lived. The postwar bonanza for the M&R lasted only until 1921.

Arrival of the Auto: M&R Endures Competition

The Minneapolis and Rainy River Railway virtually monopolized transportation through-out the Bigfork Valley until the onset of advancements in automotive technology after World War I. Initially there were simply no roads; later, many of the earliest wagon trails were unfit for anything but horse travel. However, as discontented settlers demanded con-stant improvements to the infrastructure of the roads in this region, they sped up the day when a journey into the interior of the Bigfork Valley by automobile was possible.

The first automobile arrived in Deer River several years before the advent of the mass-produced Ford Model T, which triggered the real surge in car ownership. Driving his auto north from Minneapolis in 1911, Mr. P. R. Brooks battled mud holes and loose sand for three days before reaching Deer River. The local newspaper chronicled the 30 horsepower Overland in vivid detail. "P. R. Brooks with his new 'devil wagon' came tearing down Division [S]treet in a cloud of dust. Dogs put up a frantic howl, dear mothers ran out with aprons streaming and crying 'My God! My Child!'. . . . After supper the family and a few friends were taken out for a spin about town, and for half an hour all business was suspended, and people poured out to the highway like at first news of an Indian outbreak."[11]

Automobiles were a common sight in Deer River by 1917. Ed Persons, a millwright at the Deer River mill, lived in Grand Rapids and daily drove thirty miles round-trip over the torturous road between the two communities. In order to defray the cost of gasoline, he sought riders, charging one dollar per trip.[12] Although Persons did not directly compete with the M&R because he did not live or work in the Bigfork Valley, he typified the coming wave of car owners who would compete with the railroad.

The next year the first automobile seen north of Deer River bounced wildly along the railroad tracks in the tiny community of Suomi, leaving a lasting impression on those who witnessed it. Two local men, Waino Anttila and Emil Hokkanen, were working near the tracks when "they heard this terrific commotion which Emil first thought to be a chimney fire in his house. On further investigation it proved to be a Model T Ford, filled with men who had come to inspect a prospective school site."[13]

In spite of the rough roads, travelers who could avoid the M&R saved time. A Bigfork citizen training to Deer River had to plan on being gone three days since the railroad only traversed the Bigfork branch on Mondays, Wednesdays, and Fridays. A settler with access to an automobile could easily make the same round trip in a single day.

As roads improved across the county, the passenger count on the M&R plummeted. In 1921 the W. R. Giberson Transportation Corporation bus line advertised its route between Bigfork and Deer River. A bus departing Bigfork daily at 7:30 a.m. reached Deer

River at 3:00 p.m. by way of Coleraine and Grand Rapids. David Zetterstrom, M&R superintendent, eventually initiated a series of protests with the Minnesota Railroad and Warehouse Commission in an attempt to block this encroachment on the passenger base of the M&R, but the commission declined to take action on the matter.[14]

Trucks intruded on the railroad's timber shipments just as automobiles and buses had eroded the M&R's passenger base. Despite their primitiveness, these trucks instantly enjoyed advantages over transport on the M&R. They could inexpensively convey timber directly from the stump to the mill, bypassing several intermediate steps required for hauling by rail. Furthermore, they did not need such carefully graded roads, climbing significant inclines without difficulty.[15]

Peter Peterson of Bigfork was a typical competitor. During the winter of 1929–1930, he trucked railroad ties to the Mesaba Iron Range mines and transported pulpwood to Grand Rapids' Blandin Paper Company, a distance of fifty miles from camp to mill. By 1931 Blandin Paper Company received the equivalent of 500 railway cars of pulpwood by truck. That same year David Zetterstrom estimated that in order to compete with the truck traffic, the railroad would have to reduce its shipping rate to about 1.5¢ per hundred weight, far below the actual cost to the M&R. Already the Minneapolis and Rainy River Railway was operating at a loss.[16]

A vehicle tally for several key roads in the county and the number of vehicle registrations in the state underscored the increasing autonomy in transportation. One road leading into Marcell from Grand Rapids had averaged 160 vehicles per day during August 1930. Statewide, Minnesota motor vehicle registrations revealed that in 1932, 611,691 cars and 108,434 trucks used the state's roads.[17] The M&R could not survive such an assault by competition.

The Last Hope for a Buyout

Many railroads endured the same troubles as the M&R when the post–World War I boom faltered. In the early 1920s, Congress investigated the possibility of merging railroads for the purpose of preserving the integrity of the nation's rail system. A proposed alignment of rails, referred to in the *Itasca News* as the Northwest group, was considered in Minnesota and other northern tier states. The companies forming the backbone of this proposed merger were the Great Northern and the Northern Pacific, which would absorb short lines like the M&R if the plan were adopted. Stanley Joyce naturally championed the plan. It went without saying that if the M&R were assimilated, the owners would receive compensation for the appraised value of the railway, and the Bigfork Valley would receive continued rail service. The plan was contingent upon the Great Northern and the Northern Pacific striking agreement on a number of details, and the fate of the M&R mattered not at all as the two giant railways wrestled with their own interests. Ultimately the merger fell apart seven years into the process, leaving the Minneapolis and Rainy River Railway without hope for the future.[18]

The Depression Starts the Abandonment Debate

The hard times that the Minneapolis and Rainy River Railway had been combating for years became even more acute as the Great Depression, catalyzed by the stock market crash of October 29, 1929, worsened. Many of the settlers who would normally have ridden the M&R simply did not have the money to spend on a fare, so they often walked long distances rather than taking the train. Those who did have money drove their automobiles. The Depression also reduced the demand for forest products, resulting in even smaller loads for the railroad. Few logging camps in the county cut timber during the winters of 1930–31 and 1931–32. Even the harvesting of pulpwood, which had been an expanding source of income for the loggers, almost stopped because the Depression forced the paper mill in Grand Rapids to consume its stockpiled wood, offsetting the need for new supplies. The extent to which logging had diminished in Minnesota is evidenced by the 1932 figure for lumber production. In that year, only 58 million board feet were harvested in the entire state, a figure substantially lower than the 70 million board feet cut by the Itasca Lumber Company during one of its peak years.[19]

Faced with such bleak prospects, we can assume that David and Stanley Joyce were forced to begin the abandonment of the Minneapolis and Rainy River Railway, yet the M&R could not simply be shut down by the decision of the owners. The railway was incorporated as a public carrier, and, as such, the Minnesota Railroad and Warehouse Commission and the Interstate Commerce Commission had to approve abandonment. Of primary concern to the commissions was the effect of losing the railroad upon the population of the Bigfork Valley. Commission officials would only make a final decision for or against abandonment after soliciting public comment and examining the financial standing of the M&R.

The directors of the Minneapolis and Rainy River Railway voted to press on with the abandonment procedure on March 13, 1931. Public response was immediate and predictably unfavorable. After all, the M&R had been a part of life in the Bigfork Valley for nearly forty years and was largely responsible for converting the area from a trackless wilderness to a region dotted with small settlements along the railroad line. This public response, however, was sentimental and conveniently ignored the fact that hardly anybody used the train anymore. (Statistics reported in the *Itasca News* some nine months later stated that the transportation of freight between November 11 and December 10, 1931, only generated $325, while the passenger count, totaling ninety for the same thirty-day period, resulted in less than $60 in fares. The low number of riders contrasts with the monthly passenger average of nearly 2,000 during the peak year of 1909.)[20]

Arguments against abandonment and attacks upon the motives of the owners came from newspaper editors as well as from settlers. A May 8, 1931 editorial in the *Bigfork Times* argued that the railroad was a public utility and couldn't stop running solely because of financial loss. More caustic commentary came from L. D. Lammon, the incensed editor of Coleraine's *Itasca Iron News*: "It has been noted by shrewd observers that capitol which has exploited the natural wealth of a district has little sentiment for the region where it got its easy money. The old Itasca Logging Company and its affiliations took a huge amount of wealth from this country. As far as we know it never made any section from which it benefited a bequeath or gift of any kind barring a few library books, donated to the county seat. It was easier to spend the money on Peggy [Hopkins] Joyce.* The Gut and Liver Line [nickname for the M&R] is the single improvement left Itasca

County from their regime. The lumbermen built no roads, no schoolhouses, no cathedrals. They left us an inheritance of deadheads in the rivers and slashings, fire menaces, and the wood ticks, which have come into Itasca County in recent years, a product of the burnings. We forget quack grass, the Canadian and Sow thistles and other pestiferous weeds brought in with their feed, and which are the worst menace that agricultural interests of the county have to contend against. Sometimes people wonder why men become anarchists, Communists or Socialists."

Lammon went on in the same editorial to temper his blast against the M&R by saying, "As logging companies go, the M&R was one of the best that operated in Minnesota. They used their labor better and treated it squarer than other concerns, while they paid fairer prices for what they purchased."[21] Lammon's favorable comments at the end of his editorial were lost on the angry Bigfork Valley residents who felt that somehow they were being cheated by the M&R.

A committee of local business people rapidly organized to research the matter and act as an informed voice to oppose the abandonment. Committee spokesmen were L. A. Rossman of Grand Rapids, H. E. Wolfe of Deer River, and James Reid of Bigfork. Rossman and Wolfe were both editors of the newspapers in their respective communities. Wolfe also held the title of superintendent of schools for the Deer River district. Reid was a logger with a sawmilling operation at Craigville.

Rossman was quick to acknowledge that the Joyce organization deserved credit for keeping the railroad in operation for the past thirty-nine years. The railroad could have applied to the Minnesota Railroad and Warehouse Commission ten years earlier to dissolve the railroad as the M&R began to lose money. Rossman further observed that the railroad's problems were neither the fault of the owners nor of the population it served but rather the result of advancing technology. He admitted that trucking was indeed impinging on the railroad's timber market but questioned the long-term sustainability of trucks. Thus he urged the public to put "every possible stick of timber or pound of freight

---

* Peggy Hopkins Joyce, famous celebrity and gold digger, was married for a short time to Stanley Joyce. The dissolution of their marriage received national attention.

upon the railroad cars. Such action is not to be done out of sympathy for the railroad but in service to the public" that needs the railroad. Rossman's final battle cry rose from the pages of his newspaper: "Itasca County must not lose the M&R!"[22]

Bewilderment over how the decision process for abandonment would proceed clouded the issues. Two government agencies were involved—one at the state level and one at the federal level—and it was unclear which had final jurisdiction. The two agencies were even at odds over where and when public meetings would be held. Public meetings were scheduled, then rescheduled numerous times. An article in the January 14, 1932 Deer River paper humorously pointed out, "There have been countless rumors and poorly founded reports afloat as to what is going to happen. . . . The safest conclusion on what is going to happen, is that nobody knows."[23]

The Showdown in Deer River

The long-delayed hearing for the abandonment application of the M&R opened February 23, 1932, before an audience of 200 at the Deer River school auditorium. In attendance were the numerous representatives of the Interstate Commerce Commission from Washington, D. C., the Minnesota Railroad and Warehouse Commission, the Minneapolis and Rainy River Railway, and the local committee against abandonment. Testimony of witnesses supporting the M&R's application consumed the entire first day, ending at 6:00 p.m. M&R officials were seeking to establish a date to cease operations and the flexibility to discontinue regular passenger service leading up to that date.

On the following day those opposed to the application spoke. Charles Hopkins, Dave Nylen, and M. H. Thompson, all loggers from Bigfork, claimed that hauling timber by truck was a passing fad. The three agreed that truck hauling was "unprofitable, that many who had engaged in it have already ceased operating, and that many others would cease to operate after this season."[24] Therefore, the M&R would be essential for future logging operations since attempts at truck logging would soon fizzle. The three men from Bigfork were not alone in their opinions. L. A. Rossman also asserted that the trucks would not last and pointed out in his editorials that "most of the trucking upon the highways is done at a loss. It is an unsound transportation process. . . . [Loggers] have bought trucks, hauled products at the going rate, paid for this service and after two or three years of hard work have found their capital gone and their trucks worn out. . . . Some day conditions [of the Depression] will right themselves and timber will be transported as it ought to be carried [on the railroad]."[25] The predictions for the failure of truck logging were clearly incorrect. Nearly all forest products in the future would be hauled by truck.

Other witnesses offered more challenges to the abandonment of the railroad. County Agent A. H. Frick testified that, in his opinion, the region was poised for rapid agricultural development, including dairying, potato growing, and land clearing. R. A. Hunt, state superintendent of timber, and Hugo Zaiser, Itasca County employee, both explained that large quantities of timber suitable for posts, poles, and pulpwood still stood on state and private lands.[26] This testimony continued into the third day.

As representatives of the public committee against abandonment, H. E. Wolfe and L. A. Rossman made their final pleas during closing statements. Both criticized testimony of the M&R witnesses and appealed to the moral responsibility of the railway. After all, citizens had settled in the Bigfork Valley because of the transportation provided by the M&R. L. A. Rossman attacked the owners of the railway, alleging inefficient management, questionable depreciation of company property, and shortsightedness in not meeting the problems of the Depression. Parting shots were also taken at the lumber barons and their cut-out-and-get-out business philosophy. At the end of his forceful delivery, cheers erupted from the audience.[27]

These criticisms aside, almost everyone acknowledged that the railway had accomplished much in the Bigfork Valley. It had opened the area for settlement. The largest towns, Deer River and Bigfork, had prospered. A string of smaller communities had established their identities along the tracks. Many different logging companies, which employed thousands directly and many more in support roles, had developed in response to the presence of the Minneapolis and Rainy River Railway. The M&R's transportation of timber products had virtually sustained the entire economy of Deer River and the Bigfork Valley prior to the advent of trucking. When called for, the M&R had not hesitated to send out special trains to transport sick or injured settlers or to provide a doctor's aid. When no other phone lines existed, the public had relied on the M&R's phone line for emergencies.

The M&R's problems were not due to poor management but instead to technological advancement. Furthermore, the financial struggles afflicting the M&R were typical of those facing the entire railway industry at the time. In fact, while the future of the M&R was being debated during March 1932, the Great Northern Railway terminated thirty years of day passenger train service in Deer River. Travelers now had to catch the night train.[28]

Sparks continued to fly after the hearings between the abrasive J. S. Burchmore, a Chicago attorney representing the interests of the M&R, and the local committee representatives, editors Rossman and Wolfe. Burchmore accused the editors of lacking good sense, while Wolfe questioned the lawyer's motives. Burchmore was quoted as saying in jest, "It is a great relief to our sense of comedy that the editors did not predict future drilling of oil" as a reason to keep the M&R. Wolfe put his newspaper to good use and punched back at Burchmore. "It may be that Mr. Burchmore has lived so long in the congested large city, that his heart and conscience have been stifled to a point where he cannot realize that out here in the great open spaces ordinary citizens, actuated only by motives to serve the common welfare, are willing to labor without compensation or prospects of personal gain, attributes not common to corporation attorneys. Therefore let us spread over his misgivings and suspicions, the broad mantle of charity."[29]

In March, shortly after the public hearing, the Minnesota Railroad and Warehouse Commission presented its ruling. It mandated a new schedule for the M&R. Three days a week the train would travel from Deer River through Bigfork to Craigville and back to Alder. From Alder, the train would take the westerly fork to Wirt before returning to Deer River. Each round trip was supposed to take seven hours to complete but typically required several extra hours. The new service would not affect any of the stops on the Bigfork or Wirt branches since these had always received tri-weekly service, but it would eliminate daily stops between Deer River and Alder. This schedule was not what the M&R management had been hoping for. They had sought an interim plan that permitted the company to schedule trains only as needed for logging. Now all management could do was anxiously wait for the Interstate Commerce Commission to deliver its decision.

In the meantime, the railroad cut its expenses by reducing the number of employees. The remaining train crew—brakeman Marion Brown, engineer Martin Carlson, fireman Harlowe Bonniwell, and conductor Harvey Martindale—did double duty by working in the repair shops on the days that the train was not running. Deer River station agent Nels Olson was now required to go out with the rest of the crew three times a week when the M&R headed north.[30]

The last train crew of the M&R. From left to right: Martin Carlson, Sherman Houser, Harlow Bonniwell, and Marion Brown. RUTH SWANSON PRIVATE COLLECTION

Only three months after the M&R implemented the new schedule set by the Minnesota Railroad and Warehouse Commission, the Bigfork Valley communities received a great shock. The initial report at the federal level, made by the Interstate Commerce Commission, indicated that the M&R would be permitted to proceed with abandonment for three reasons: the railway was losing money, truck service adequately fulfilled local transportation needs, and road improvements had destroyed the railway's business.

One new road was particularly detrimental to the livelihood of the M&R. Later designated as State Highway 38, it paralleled much of the Bigfork branch of the Minneapolis and Rainy River Railway as the highway stretched from Grand Rapids northward to Craig, connecting the intermediate towns of Marcell, Bigfork, and Effie. The M&R actually had hauled equipment crucial in constructing the northern leg of the highway, which, when completed, diverted freight from the railroad and hastened its demise.[31]

When the Interstate Commerce Commission's formal declaration allowing abandonment was released on June 28, 1932, local public officials believed that this document was still subject to final approval by the Minnesota Railroad and Warehouse Commission and that further opportunities to fight against the abandonment would be scheduled. A few weeks later the local opponents of abandonment were jubilant after the state of Minnesota announced that it would not concur with the federal decision. The editor of the *Itasca News* displayed unusual exuberance on July 14 when he printed: "Whoa! Back up and start all over again! Heck! . . . The order will be filed soon refusing abandonment. Such procedure will throw the entire matter into the courts, which in any event will mean that Emma [the M&R] will stick around for another year or two." State of Minnesota officials also assured the Bigfork Valley citizens that they would fight the Interstate Commerce Commission's decree, removing the burden of legal and travel costs from the local committee.[32]

The state initiated action to revisit the application for abandonment by saying that another public hearing at Deer River would be set. However, this process was abruptly cut short through an unexpected and brilliant trump by the railway. Management of the M&R posted notices indicating that, in accordance with the Interstate Commerce Commission ruling, it was terminating all train service on August 28, 1932. At the same time, the railroad filed for an injunction in the United States District Court in St. Paul against the Minnesota Railroad and Warehouse Commission to stop any further legal action against the M&R. David Zetterstrom and Stanley Joyce signed the posted notices.[33]

The impact of the pending federal injunction upon state government agencies was remarkable. It effectively crippled the state of Minnesota's attempt to organize a legal challenge against the abandonment. The injunction was intended to restrain the attorney general of Minnesota, the members of the Minnesota Railroad and Warehouse Commission, and the Itasca County attorney from interfering in any way with the planned abandonment or from taking any further legal action against the railway. The M&R justified the action by claiming that under the Constitution it could not be forced to operate at a loss and, furthermore, that the state had not proven that any substantial public hardship would result from abandonment. The state immediately countered that the United States District Court was without jurisdiction, that the injunction had been filed prematurely, and that the railway sought to prevent the action of the state while at the same time claiming that the state had not acted promptly. The United States District Court entered the melee at this point, declaring that it did indeed have final jurisdiction in the matter. A hearing date was set for August 22, 1932, at which time the decision for granting the injunction would be made. If the injunction were put into force, it would, in effect, result in the last whistle blow for the M&R.[34]

The state proceeded with plans for a public hearing to be held in Deer River on August 31, 1932, but this hearing never took place. An article in the *Itasca News* announced the final federal ruling a few days later. "Under a decision handed down in Federal court at St. Paul late Tuesday afternoon, service on the M&R . . . will be discontinued next Saturday. That means that the M&R is going to make just one more call on friends up the line. Better get your handkerchiefs ready!"[35]

Switching from sentimentality to anger, the editors of the local papers printed no further news about the dismantling of the railroad. The final mention of the M&R in the Deer River paper defined the changes to the mail service brought about by the loss of the train. Many of the communities north of Deer River that had previously received mail tri-weekly, according to the schedule of the M&R, would now benefit from daily mail service by automobile. "So mark down one improvement by the M&R quitting," quipped the *Itasca News*.[36]

The M&R carried its last cargo as a special request. Since the bricks for building the school at Bigfork were nearly ready for delivery, the M&R agreed to delay the starting date for track removal for two days until the railroad could dispatch this shipment.

When the M&R steamed into Deer River for the last time on August 27, 1932, the townspeople did not mask their emotions as they watched the train make its final trip. According to Bergit Anderson in her book entitled *The Last Frontier*, "Something clutched at their hearts for this railroad that had gone through pioneering hardships just as they and somehow it gave them the feeling of failing a brother who had helped them to grow . . . . Years later, when the age of speed and hurry descended on this country as elsewhere, people looked back to the time when they had a whole day to idle away, all of twelve hours to go the thirty miles from Deer River to Bigfork. Many fondly wished that the time of such complete relaxation could be again, with time to indulge in the pleasure of friendships, their own meditations, or the natural beauty surrounding them."[37]

The M&R Is Scrapped

The process of evacuating the rails began immediately. Starting at the northern ends of both spurs, crews worked south toward Deer River, not only pulling up track but also struggling to dislodge the copper wire from the M&R's telephone line. As young Darwin Holsman of Bigfork watched the men contend with the line, he remarked to the crew that he could tumble its copper wire with his single-shot .22 rifle. The incredulous trainmen scoffed at the offer, but Holsman persisted. Finally the men permitted him to prove his aim. Sure enough, the copper wire snapped instantly. Holsman now became the "favorite little boy," riding the flat car with the rest of the men as he brought down the wire. (When the authors asked him about his marksmanship, Holsman related that his mother had always told him to shoot grouse in the head or not shoot them at all.)[38]

Crews stacked the rails upon flat cars as the salvage train crept slowly back to Deer River, leaving the ties behind. By early December 1932, after three months of work, the M&R crew had taken out all of the sixty miles or 7,000 tons of track. The rails were then organized in neat piles in Deer River, where they remained for five years until they were sold to a Duluth scrap yard for $12 a ton. Since the rails had been removed for $.71 per ton and had been totally depreciated, the company profited immensely from the sale. From Duluth, the rails were loaded onto a ship bound for Japan. The ship departed with its cargo just before Japan entered World War II. Possibly the steel from these rails became raw material in the Japanese war effort. The three remaining M&R engines, along with seventy-four cars, were also sent to a scrap yard in Duluth.[39]

The last M&R engine dismantles the final sections of track in 1932.
ITASCA COUNTY HISTORICAL SOCIETY

The elimination of the train did have an effect on the smaller towns on the M&R lines. The first casualty occurred with the collapse of Alder, at the junction of the Wirt and Bigfork branches. That community had primarily served as a maintenance station for rail crews and had supported logging camps in its vicinity. Without the M&R, swampy Alder could not retain its population. When workers later dismantled the section house at Alder, members of the Lutheran congregation in the nearby community of Suomi salvaged the timbers for their new church. Craig struggled to survive but also succumbed.

The M&R existed as an entity until 1937, even though it now had no track, equipment, or business. That year the Itasca Lumber Company purchased all remaining physical assets, including landholdings and buildings. The Deer River depot, one of the last remaining structures of the Minneapolis and Rainy River Railway, burned in April 1941. Stored in the depot were company records for both the Minneapolis and Rainy River Railway and the Itasca Lumber Company as well as unclaimed luggage. All was destroyed, including the great historical wealth contained within these records.[40]

Today, the only visible artifacts of the M&R are the railroad grades, the pilings in area lakes, and the steel bridge at Bigfork. Portions of M&R right-of-ways not repurchased by property owners reverted to the state of Minnesota and are used today as snowmobile trails.

Deer River Sawmill

WILLIAM JOYCE WAS A KEY PLAYER in the events that brought a great sawmill to the shores of White Oak Lake just south of Deer River. Joyce did not initiate the idea for the mill but, in typical Joyce business style, he took control when the opportunity came. This new mill on White Oak—the last Joyce mill to operate in Minnesota—complemented his other endeavors in Deer River: the Itasca Lumber Company (ILC) and the Minneapolis and Rainy River Railway (M&R).

The mill evolved under several different company names. The Deer River mill was first associated with the Pillsbury-Watkins Company when it was formed in 1903. This business was renamed the Joyce-Pillsbury Company in 1904. In 1906 its name changed again to the Deer River Lumber Company. Eventually the Deer River Lumber Company was absorbed by the Itasca Lumber Company, Joyce's original Minnesota lumbering venture. The Joyce family was the only continuous stockholder from 1904 until the mill closed in 1921.

In 1903 W. T. Watkins, an associate of the Pillsbury timber interests, invited William Joyce to join him and the Pillsburys in the harvest of hardwoods and cedar in the Bigfork Valley. These trees had been passed over earlier because they did not float well and for that reason could never be driven downriver to Minneapolis. The best method of extracting a profit from the secondary harvest would be to manufacture lumber and other products near the stump, hence, a mill near Deer River. Joyce initially declined this offer in order to concentrate on the white pine market. At the same time that Watkins pushed for a Deer River mill, Joyce was in the process of buying the huge H. C. Akeley Lumber Company mill in Minneapolis. Dropping the Akeley name and consolidating the Minneapolis mill under the Itasca Lumber Company umbrella, Joyce now operated one of the largest white pine mills in the Midwest. This purchase, however, did not prevent Joyce from suggesting that Pillsbury and Watkins build a mill at the terminus of the M&R in the town of Deer River.[1] He committed himself to the project by agreeing to sell the two men stumpage from his landholdings and to transport the logs on his railway.

William Joyce encouraged the Pillsbury-Watkins partnership because he knew it was merely a question of time before the king of trees disappeared. All of the white pine timberland in Minnesota and elsewhere had been claimed. Once it was no longer possible to log further upstream or strike out for the north, the lumbermen would have to examine the trees neglected in the rush to harvest the precious white pine. If other species could substitute for the white pine, the logging operation's finale could be postponed.

The Pillsbury-Watkins Company incorporated in 1903. In preparation for the planned sawmill, the company logged cedar and hardwoods on the Itasca Lumber

LEFT: The Itasca Lumber Company sawmill in Deer River viewed from White Oak Lake, looking northeast.

Company property near Turtle Lake during the fall of 1903 and during the 1904–1905 logging season. These two seasons produced about $100,000 worth of timber that was banked along the tracks of Joyce's railroad, an immediate source of raw material for the sawmill as soon as it was up and running. As the next step in the mill project, the new company bought a site on the north shore of White Oak Lake from the ILC for its proposed mill. Workers then laid a spur track to the mill site.[2]

At this point Pillsbury and Watkins again invited Joyce to engage in the new lumbering business. He agreed in November 1904. Now the Joyce-Pillsbury Company incorporated to succeed the Pillsbury-Watkins organization. The *Minneapolis Journal* reported the new partnership in its December 3, 1904 edition just as the *Mississippi Valley Lumberman* trade journal optimistically announced that the proposed sawmill's electric light plant would permit 24-hour operation, making possible lumber production equal to the largest mills elsewhere in the state. Incorporators were listed as William T. Joyce, Chicago; Alfred F. Pillsbury, Healey C. Akeley, Franklin C. Gerhard, Henry P. Watson, Minneapolis; and William T. Watkins, St. Paul.[3] Initially Joyce and Pillsbury held equal shares of the controlling interest in the company. Later Joyce bought out Pillsbury and took full control of the mill.

As work on the mill progressed, men and machines were readied for action. John Schaub, foreman for the Joyce-Pillsbury mill, arrived in Deer River from New York at the end of December 1904 to start the process of hiring approximately one hundred men to work the mill's two shifts. Schaub said that he would hire as "near as possible, all married men" in an effort to secure a stable labor force.[4] Gearing up for the influx of laborers, the Itasca Lumber Company built housing during mill construction in what would become the town of Zemple. Six houses, each with five rooms, were being erected north of the shops in April 1905, and twelve cottages joined the original group that fall, all of which were rented to the employees.[5]

Progress on the new mill continued into 1905 under the direction of Franklin C. Gerhard, William Joyce's general manager of all Minnesota operations (who had come north after supervising the overhaul of the H. C. Akeley mill in Minneapolis, recently

William Joyce purchased the H. C. Akeley Mill located at 27th Avenue North in Minneapolis in 1903 and changed the mill's name to the Itasca Lumber Company. MINNESOTA HISTORICAL SOCIETY

purchased and renamed the Itasca Lumber Company mill by Joyce). In February, when the massive band saws of the Joyce-Pillsbury mill in Deer River were operational, Gerhard ordered the sawing of the necessary timbers for finishing the mill. This accomplished, the band saws bit into the logs hauled from the woods by the Itasca Lumber Company, producing 120,000 board feet of lumber every twenty-four hours. The Joyce-Pillsbury mill sawed all of the hardwoods represented in the 35 million feet of logs banked annually by the Itasca Lumber Company.[6] In the first six years of operation, the Deer River mill did not saw a significant number of pine logs. Most of the pine was still driven down the Mississippi River to the Itasca Lumber Company mill in Minneapolis.

The Itasca Lumber Company sawmill in Deer River viewed from the west.
RUTH SWANSON PRIVATE COLLECTION

Deer River immediately felt the impact of the new mill as the local population leaped from 400 to 700 in a single year. The *Itasca County Independent* newspaper of nearby Grand Rapids reported, "The payroll of the Joyce-Pillsbury mill alone is over $5000 for the past month and during the next three months it is expected that additional machinery will increase the capacity of the mill, at which time the payroll will be in the neighborhood of $10,000 per month. Several new industries are going into Deer River and with the sawmill, the Itasca Railroad [M&R] and various other industries will make this town second to none in the north."[7]

By early 1906 William Joyce had bought out Pillsbury's stock in the mill and renamed the company the Deer River Lumber Company. Now he upgraded the mill's capability by adding a planer to the mill's complement of machinery. In February carpenters embarked on the planing mill, a project they completed in a few months.[8] The planing mill was located adjacent to the main mill and housed what the local paper referred to as a box factory. In actuality, the box factory offered dimension lumber for building boxes. It was not financially practical to ship the boxes themselves out on the railroad due to their bulk, so the Deer River Lumber Company sent the correctly sized and planed lumber to its customers for assembly. Another outbuilding contained specialty-sawing equipment to produce lath—narrow slats used in the construction of plaster walls.

The addition of the planing mill finished the construction phase of the Deer River endeavor, allowing Franklin C. Gerhard to return to Minneapolis to resume his role as general manager of Minnesota operations. During his tenure in Deer River his daughter was married to W. R. Wallace, another Joyce employee. Gerhard's new son-in-law became the manager of the Deer River mill.

At the start of the season in May 1906, the Deer River Lumber Company mill commenced sawing with the additional capacity provided by the planing mill. According to the local paper, "The Company has in the mill pond about 5,000 logs with which to begin the season's runs. Manager W. R. Wallace says they will not wait for the ice to go out before starting the mill, but will have logs hauled by train to the slip." The sawed lumber—comprised primarily of spruce, tamarack, birch, poplar, and elm, plus some pine—was stacked in the yard to season before being sent to the planing mill late that summer. After planing, five to fifteen carloads of finished lumber shipped out every business day to firms in Chicago, Minneapolis, and other population centers.[9]

The sawmill and the silo-shaped burner stack dominated the skyline in the vicinity of Deer River. State of the art in its day, the mill was very efficient, making use of every scrap of wood. It featured a network of endless chain belts that conveyed lumber in various stages of processing. Carried up

The expansive lumberyard held an average of 20 million board feet of stacked lumber being dried before processing by the planing mill. RUTH SWANSON PRIVATE COLLECTION

from White Oak Lake to the cutting deck by the endless chain, each log was positioned on the steam-powered carriage by a steam-operated loader. Once properly positioned upon the carriage, the log was secured by means of clamps, referred to as *dogs*. The carriage moved back and forth carrying the log through the great blade of the band saw, each pass producing a rough slab of lumber. From there, the lumber was directed to the edger, which squared the lumber. After leaving the edger, the lumber was trimmed to length. The man employed as the grader then marked each board with chalk and sent it on horse-drawn carts to the yard to be stacked by hand one piece at a time. This lumber remained in the yard for several months or even into the next year until the moisture content of the wood fell to the desired level. After the seasoning was complete, the lumber traveled to the planer for final dimensioning and finishing before being loaded onto railroad cars for shipment.

Nothing went to waste at the sawmill. Large scraps of wood were sent to the lath mill to be resawed, while poor quality pieces were cut into 16-inch firewood for sale in Deer River.[10] Unusable scraps, bark, shavings, and sawdust fell to the bottom of the sawmill and were transported by conveyor to the burner. The burner preheated the water flowing through the pipes to the boilers that, in turn, generated the steam necessary to power the engines and other equipment such as the carriage.

There are few eyewitness accounts documenting the operation of the Deer River mill. Halga Will, a lifelong resident of Deer River, grew up in one of the company houses lining both sides of Fourth Street and recalled for the authors her father's employment at the sawmill. "When my dad, Hans Olson, worked in the mill, we would take his lunch to him because he did not come home for lunch. The lumber would come down out of the mill on a great big chain where my dad and others worked. He was a lumber grader, and he knew how many board feet there were in every board that came down. He would mark it with a big piece of chalk and send it on the way. Other men would pick off the lumber and load it on wagons and haul it to the lumberyard with horses. Once in a while my dad would let me ride on a board. When the board came to a place where somebody had to take it off the chain, they would lift me off and then take the board off.

I would run back and do it again for as long as they would put up with me."[11]

Sawmill production peaked from 1906 to 1911. Even so, crisis struck in 1907. An economic downturn left the market for hardwood lumber flat and the Deer River mill running in the red. Thomas Hume, a notable lumberman from Michigan and a partner with William Joyce in the Deer River Lumber Company as well as in several other ventures, pushed for the liquidation of the Deer River mill in order to reduce losses. Joyce stood his ground against Hume and kept the mill operating by injecting the necessary funds. By 1908 the business climate had brightened, which led William Joyce to improve the mill for spring start-up. Joyce died the following year. His two sons David and Stanley assumed control of the Joyce lumbering empire, updating and expanding the Deer River mill in 1910. By 1911 the mill employed 180 men and had started a night shift.[12]

The Deer River Lumber Company mill was conceived for processing hardwoods and softwoods other than white pine. In 1911, however, the mill added the manufacturing of white pine lumber, although the primary output remained hardwood lumber as well as cedar poles and posts along with railroad ties. This was the year that the Itasca Lumber Company mill in Minneapolis closed. Starved for an adequate supply of the big logs and stifled by the long and costly river drives, the Minneapolis mill could no longer operate efficiently. Many of the other mills in Minneapolis had already closed for the same reason; those that remained would shut down in the next nine years.[13] Now the smaller Deer River mill, located closer to the stump, assumed the work of the once mighty Minneapolis mill.

Besides improving the efficiency of operations in Minnesota with the closure of the Minneapolis mill and the transfer of production of white pine lumber to Deer River, the corporate organization also streamlined by dropping the name and the separate organizational structure of the Deer River Lumber Company. The mill was managed under the name of the Itasca Lumber Company from 1911 until the mill sawed its last log in 1921. During and after 1911, all of the logs of the Itasca Lumber Company were sawed in Deer River.

Like the Minneapolis mills, the Deer River mill faced a diminishing white pine resource that kept management personnel scratching their heads as they tried to locate trees for the next years' harvests. For the 1911 season, the ILC purchased a large tract of pineland on the Leech River near the town of Ball Club to harvest that winter. The following spring 7 million feet of logs were floated from this tract down the Mississippi and shunted into White Oak Lake through a newly constructed channel on the lake's west end.[14] The quantity of logs derived from the Leech River purchase was meager compared to years past, and production at the Deer River mill steadily declined after 1911. The drop was as much from the diminishing pine and other tree species as it was from poor market demand and low prices. World War I worsened the situation. When the brief postwar boom evaporated, the Deer River mill began the slide toward the fate of most of the large mills of that era.

In late May 1921 the mill started up for the season with a single shift. Employment had dropped from a peak of more than 250 men in earlier years to 100 men. After two weeks of operation, the log supply was exhausted because of low water levels, causing the mill to shut down temporarily until additional logs could be shipped from Bigfork on the Minneapolis and Rainy River Railway. These logs and the deadheads salvaged from White Oak Lake kept the mill operating until October 8. That day "the Itasca Lumber Company mill sawed its last log," said John Zetterstrom, son of mill superintendent David Zetterstrom. The final task was to season the lumber in the yards and plane it the following year.[15]

A long whistle had been the requiem blast for other giant sawmills along the Mississippi River. The Deer River mill paid homage to the tradition. "The 'last whistle' and a long one blew at the Itasca Lumber Companies planer mill Saturday night," reported the June 3, 1922 issue of the *Deer River Itasca News*. "All of the lumber has been planed and sold to the King Lumber Company who plan to retail it from their various yards."

The Deer River Lumber Company mill sat idle while unsuccessful attempts were made to sell the structures and equipment. Five years later, when the mill showed imminent signs of collapse and the machinery had rusted beyond use, the Joyces decided to sell the mill as scrap. The machinery had been removed for scrap iron and the lumber in the buildings was being salvaged by local farmers when a fire set by a vandal consumed what remained of the buildings.[16]

Today, the only evidence remaining of the mill on White Oak Lake is a few concrete monoliths on the shore and weathered pilings jutting out of the lake. However, the homes built by the Itasca Lumber Company for the mill workers are still standing, along with the large log home originally constructed for the mill superintendent.

Zemple

During the early 1900s more than 300 people lived in what would become the village of Zemple, sandwiched between the town of Deer River and the mill complex on the shores of White Oak Lake. The residents were employed not only at the dominant Joyce-owned sawmill and planing mill but also at a box mill owned by the Rathburn, Hair & Ridgeway Company and a veneer mill owned by Bahr Brothers. Milling was central to life in the burg. Even the road leading into Zemple was constructed of layer upon layer of sawdust, deposited on top of the swampy terrain.[17]

Zemple—or Mill Town as it was sometimes called—incorporated as a village in 1911, the same year that the Deer River Lumber Company was absorbed under the Itasca Lumber Company name. The impetus for incorporation was reported in the January 14, 1911 issue of the Deer River *Itasca News*. According to the paper, residents of the township of Otenagon, which was organized during the summer of 1910, complained that the Deer River Lumber Company's mill and lumber yard lying within the Otenagon township were not properly valued and were, therefore, underassessed. Otenagon residents living outside of the Mill Town area hoped to benefit from additional taxes if these lumber interests were assigned a higher evaluation. In order to combat this possibility, the Itasca Lumber Company challenged the legality of the procedure by which Otenagon organized, thereby gaining enough time to petition for the organization of the village of Zemple, which could then separate from Otenagon Township. Flyers announcing the vote for the incorporation of Zemple were posted on Deer River Lumber Company buildings. Most or perhaps all of those voting worked for the Deer River Lumber Company or the Minneapolis and Rainy River Railroad or in the office of the Itasca Lumber Company and were expected to vote for incorporation. This successful maneuver saved the Joyces considerable money through the prevention of higher taxes and assured them control of local government.[18] Following incorporation, the Minneapolis and Rainy River Railway depot stayed in Deer River, while the railroad yards, roundhouse, and machine shop as well as the mill and mill yard resided in newly formed Zemple.

The town was named after its largest landowner, R. T. Zempel, who was elected Zemple's first village president shortly after incorporation and was also employed as a bookkeeper for the Deer River Lumber Company mill. (According to the daughter of R. T. Zempel, the name of the town has been misspelled during most of its existence.) J. P. Martindale, Ole Berg, and Jonathan Martindale served as trustees while David Zetterstrom acted as clerk, Emil Krantz as treasurer, Morris Larson as assessor, A. W. Rice as justice, and John Larson as constable. David Zetterstrom and probably other officers also worked in some capacity for the Joyces.[19]

After the abandonment of the Minneapolis and Rainy River Railway in 1932, the company homes in Zemple sold for $100 to $150. Some of the company homes were moved off the Zemple lots to new locations on nearby farms, yet many of what were once Itasca Lumber Company homes remain on their original lots in Zemple.[20] Today the population of this quiet village near the shores of White Oak Lake hovers around sixty.

Minnesota Land Sales

BY THE TIME THE ITASCA LUMBER COMPANY exhausted its reserves of big pines and ended its active logging phase, the firm had amassed more than 50,000 acres of cutover land. Landholdings spread across three counties but were mostly concentrated within the Bigfork Valley. Reforestation was financially impractical because of the long maturation cycle of pine timber in the northern states, and, given the property tax liability, sale of the land was becoming a necessity. Frederick Weyerhaeuser, wealthiest of all

Above: Deer River management of the ILC and M&R. Seated left to right: William LaCroix, S. D. Patrick, Charles Birke. Standing left to right: Fred Scofield, Al Lindberg, Stanley Ruth. ITASCA COUNTY HISTORICAL SOCIETY

lumbermen, said flatly, "No one can hold cut-over lands and pay the present taxes."[1] Accordingly, marketing the expansive holdings became a prime function of the Itasca Lumber Company when its logging operations declined after 1911. Many of the present land-use patterns in Itasca County can be traced directly to ILC land sales. These transactions included agricultural properties, lakeside recreational properties, and lands incorporated into the Chippewa National Forest and the George Washington State Forest.

Thomas Hume, a prosperous lumberman from Muskegon, Michigan, who was a partner in the Itasca Lumber Company, had pointed out the need for land sales and agricultural development to David and William Joyce early in the history of the firm. In 1892 Hume toured the logging camps and logging railroad of the ILC, which had been based in Cohasset for barely six months. Following the inspection trip, he expressed his "surprise at the total absence of settlers" and advocated attracting farmers to Itasca County. Hume told a reporter for the *Grand Rapids Magnet* that citizens from his section of Michigan understood lasting economic success could not rest solely on lumbering. They "raised money, advertised the county, and in two years had a number of first class farmers located on the vacant lands." The Michigan lumberman claimed that Itasca County could do the same. "Your soil is far superior to ours," said Hume. "If you expect to build up substantial and live towns in this section, your people should realize that agriculture is the best thing, if not the only thing to bring it about."[2] Whether or not the local citizens heeded Hume's advice is unknown, but David and William Joyce waited more than a decade to act.

The first real interest in land sales did not occur until 1905, a year before the Minneapolis and Rainy River Railway reached Bigfork. At that time William Joyce directed his men to form the Bigfork Land Company, believing that the demand for property in the Bigfork Valley would accelerate with the arrival of the rails. S. D. Patrick, William LaCroix, Charles Birke, and W. R. Wallace, all management-level employees in the Joyce organization, incorporated this company with $50,000 worth of capital. Unfortunately Joyce's prediction proved false, and the newly formed corporation never produced any significant profits.[3]

The Itasca Lumber Company added a land sales department to market its cutover

50,000 Acres
AGRICULTURAL LAND
For Sale
By the Itasca Lumber Company, Deer River, Minn.

Why not procure a good farm. Excellent locations.

Why not have a fishing camp, or a hunting lodge, a place for recreation pleasure on one of the many beautiful lakes in Itasca county?

Why not combine business with pleasure? These lands will rapidly increase in value.

Prices and terms within reach of all

The Itasca Lumber Company continually advertised its cutover lands. This ad appeared in the 1914 *Itasca News*.
WESTERN ITASCA REVIEW

lands a few years later. It was managed by longtime employee S. D. Patrick. In late 1912 Patrick moved to Grand Rapids, the county seat, so he could conveniently meet newcomers arriving on the Great Northern in order to advance sales. At the same time, William LaCroix headed the department of land sales in Deer River. Sales sporadically reported in the Deer River newspaper in the next few years give a glimpse of the two men's activities. A 1912 issue of the *Itasca News* announced that Patrick sold property to three families from Chicago, who, in turn, promised to encourage their Illinois friends to visit the north country as prospective buyers. Patrick and LaCroix teamed the following year for another notable land sale that brought a $1,000 cash payment. Patrick sold each of three Reglin brothers of Waseca eighty acres located along the tracks of the M&R in the vicinity of Little Bowstring Lake in 1914.[4]

A regular Itasca Lumber Company advertising campaign, targeting fishermen, hunters, tourists, and farmers, offered 50,000 acres of land. The myriad lakes and expansive areas of wild countryside were a true paradise for the recreational land buyers, but the ads greatly exaggerated the potential of agricultural property. According to an article in "A Zone of Plenty," a special supplement to the *Grand Rapids Herald Review*, a man buying one of the ILC cutover timber farms for $15 to $20 per acre could harvest "more from his 40 acres than [an Iowa] grain farmer on his 150 acres" as long as the buyer raised the recommended crops. "The big paying crop is timothy and clover, the yield being from two to three tons to the acre with 17% more nutrition than that grown on the prairie farms of the middle west; potatoes are a big money making crop, average yield being from 150 to 300 bushels to the acre; head lettuce and celery are phenomenal crop yields; cucumbers raised for the pickling factory of Deer River net from $300 to $400 to the acre; strawberries are another sure crop, yielding from $600 to $1000 per acre, according to the market selling price; all small grains do well, especially oats and barley. It will thus be seen that farming in Itasca County has none of the drawbacks such as crop failures, drought, hailstorms, or tornadoes, but on the other hand there is one hour more sunshine a day than in Iowa or 30 hours more per month which is one of the reasons combined with the fertility of the soil and adequate rainfall during the season of propagation that makes this such a big crop yield section."[5]

There were more selling points as well. The advertising campaign claimed that timber left on the property after logging was often sufficient to build a farmhouse and a barn, sometimes with enough leftover logs to cover the cost of the buildings. Prospective land buyers could subsidize other expenses by buying a dairy cow or small herd and selling cream and butter to the local creameries. They were also assured of "splendid graveled roads" connecting them to rail transportation provided by the M&R, which linked to the national rail system. This transportation network would put their produce within reach of the larger markets of Duluth, Superior, St. Paul, and Minneapolis. These claims, like the declarations of high agricultural yields, glowed a bit too brightly.[6]

Many farmers who responded to the ads for Itasca Lumber Company land found their homesteads riddled with challenges. The good pine timber had felt the bite of the two-man crosscut-saw years ago, and much of the mixed timber that remained had been charred by uncontrolled slashing fires that raged over large areas. The remaining stumps frustrated everyone. One early resident was quoted as saying, "The axe would just bounce off, and the stumps wouldn't even burn." The farmers also contended with rocky soil. The stumps and boulders that surrendered only to dynamite served as testaments to the stubborn landscape. Nevertheless, these folks stayed to plant and harvest meager crops on the generally poor glacial soil for which the Itasca Lumber Company no longer had any use.[7]

Many years later, in 1919, local resident H. H. Herreid bought 380 acres adjoining the town of Deer River on the east. This particular land parcel had originally served as a farm for the Itasca Lumber Company, supplying produce and hay for the logging camps. Seventy-five acres were cultivated and another twenty-five acres were cleared. A first-rate house and barn accompanied the property. This farm, for which Herreid paid $13,000 or

$30 per acre, was one of the exceptional purchases. It was exceptional for the ILC because of the sale price and for Herreid because of the fine quality of the farmland.[8]

The Itasca Lumber Company also developed several plats to encourage the sale of some of its more valuable lakeshore property. The first of these, registered in 1911, was known as Trout Lake Park, located at the north end of Trout Lake in Balsam Township. One of the first buyers was Irv Martin, who purchased several of these lots in 1912. Martin subsequently developed a popular resort on Trout Lake. The Sherwood Forest plats were registered between 1916 and 1922 and offered the scenic beauty of Deer Lake. The Deer Lake plats were a cooperative venture among Itasca Lumber Company, Crowell Land Company, and Scribner Kelly Land Company.[9]

New Communities Are Formed

Itasca Lumber Company land sales catalyzed the birth of several ethnic agricultural communities. One Czechoslovakian settlement evolved in the northwestern part of the county near the town of Wirt through the efforts of Baclav Komarek. This native Czech and his daughter Anne arrived from Chicago in 1911 to investigate the countryside.

The Komareks' first experience of the Bigfork Valley probably was similar to that of many other families. Father and daughter were met at the Great Northern Railway station in Deer River by Komarek's brother-in-law, Cyril Stejskal, a homesteader in Max. Transferring to the M&R, the trio trained to Dora Lake, stopping to lunch at a logging camp. Years later Anne Komarek wrote in a letter that "the real fun began" after the meal when "Uncle Stejskal led us to Dora Lake where my cousin Jim was taking care of two rowboats." Scrambling aboard with their supplies, the group crossed Dora Lake and meandered south on the Bigfork River to Squaw Lake. "By that time dusk overtook us and we tramped through the woods by a lighted lantern for quite a distance. To a city girl, this was a real adventure." At last Stejskal's log house came into view, "its windows cheerily blinking the beckoning lamp light" to the travelers.[10]

On subsequent trips, Baclav Komarek brought his entire family and close family friends, enticed by the glowing accounts of the Bigfork Valley. The exhilarating climate of northern Minnesota and the close proximity of her brother, Cyril Stejskal, agreed with Mrs. Komarek, whose health had been failing in Chicago. Thrilled with his wife's renewed vitality, Baclav Komarek bought a 200-acre tract on Bass Lake, two miles south of Wirt, from the Itasca Lumber Company. The family returned north the following spring from Chicago, joined by the Prazaks. These two families collectively formed the nucleus of the Bass Lake community. To attract more settlers to the fledgling settlement, Komarek wrote articles for the *Hlasatel,* a Bohemian newspaper published in Chicago, and for the *Hospodar,* a journal for farmers. After reading the papers, other Czech families purchased land around Bass Lake, forging a Czech farming community.[11]

A Finnish community formed a few years later in what came to be known as Suomi. In 1914 Antero Wilhelm Havela and John Asiala organized the Pellervo Land Company that sold Itasca Lumber Company lands through its ads in Finnish newspapers and Havela's speaking tours.[12] Two of the company's earliest clients were Edwin and Minnie Juntunen. Minnie had moved as a child in 1905 from Suomussalmi, Finland, to Holmes City, Minnesota, very near Alexandria. A decade later the young woman married Edwin Juntunen, also from Suomussalmi. The couple rented a farm in Holmes City after their marriage. Then Edwin saw an advertisement by the Pellervo Land Company that lured him north to Itasca County to examine the land firsthand. Charmed by the countryside so similar to his Finland, Edwin Juntunen signed a contract for property and returned to Holmes City for Minnie and their ten-month-old daughter Marion.

The family boarded the Great Northern on April 22, 1917, after stuffing "three cows, two calves, 40 chickens, a pick, shovel and axe" along with their other household goods into a boxcar destined for Deer River. Pulling into the boisterous logging town after a long train ride, the tired but excited Juntunens were delayed for a night or two as they awaited the Minneapolis and Rainy River Railroad, which traveled on alternate days to Elbow Station. Even then the journey wasn't over. They still had to load their belongings onto a dray, or horse-drawn wagon, and drive to their homestead. The last leg of the journey was on an old railroad grade, the Smith Lake extension of the M&R that had been abandoned in 1904.

A few days after arriving, Minnie Juntunen carried her baby to the site of their future home. "I sat on the pile of hewn logs and looked around me. Our cow was chewing her cud, the chickens were cackling, and the roosters crowing. How homelike it already felt!"[13]

Other early arrivals to Suomi were Otto Salo, Jaffet and Edward Heikkinen, Oscar Maki, and Nestor and Richard Wierimaa. Most of the settlers came from the old country, drawn by the news that this part of America closely resembled the countryside in which they had grown up. When enough Finnish immigrants had settled in the vicinity of the M&R station called Elbow, they voted to change the name to Suomi, meaning "Finland" in their native language. The railroad was only too happy to have its station renamed by citizenry that it hoped would help the railroad prosper.[14] In the years that followed, the Itasca Lumber Company received "as many as 100 letters a day" inquiring about tracts of land in the Bigfork Valley, according to a letter that S. D. Patrick sent to David Gage Joyce on May 16, 1920.[15]

By 1928 company sales had stalled, and the remaining land became more of a liability than an asset. The Itasca Lumber Company land department had managed to dispose of about 16,000 acres of its best property. What was left had little appeal. Furthermore, as the national economy slowed in the period leading up to the Great Depression, buyers with cash were scarce. The ILC would have been content to wait for the slow economic times to pass had it not been for the complication of property taxation. The company was paying between $12,000 and $14,000 a year in property taxes to Itasca, Koochiching, and St. Louis Counties. The tax burden induced the company to drop 30,000 acres for taxes during 1928. Minnesota tax laws allowed a company to regain ownership of its tax-forfeited lands by paying back taxes and penalties on the property. Whenever a rare buyer appeared, the land office took advantage of the tax laws by paying up the taxes and thus earning the right to sell the property. Even some of the land already sold became problematic as people indebted to the ILC missed payments on their purchase contracts. When the Minnesota Forest Reserve, later known as the Chippewa National Forest, was created in 1902, neither the Joyces nor other company officials could have predicted that Itasca Lumber Company residual lands would eventually boost the acreage of the federal forest.

A Remarkable Sale

The Chippewa National Forest was the first attempt of the federal government at long-term forest management. Debate about the ethics of cut-out-and-get-out logging practices had raged ever since the inception of large-scale logging. While conservationists argued that some forests should be saved from the axe, the lumbermen vehemently disagreed.[16] The debate came to a head in northern Minnesota when loggers unlawfully harvested timber on the Chippewa Indian Reservation, just west of the Bigfork Valley. National outrage at the corruption by Bureau of Indian Affairs officials entrusted to protect timber within the reservation led to the conservationists' loud call for federal action.

Many activists pushed for the creation of the Minnesota Forest Reserve. Prominent in the movement to establish the reserve were Herman Haupt Chapman, superintendent of the North Central Agricultural Experiment Station, located in Grand Rapids, Minnesota; Colonel John S. Cooper of Chicago, an advocate for sportsmen; and Christopher C. Andrews, chief fire warden of Minnesota. Strong support also came from the Minnesota Federation of Women's Clubs and its chairwoman, Mrs. W. E. Bramhall. Most of the credit, however, goes to the dedicated efforts of conservationist Gifford Pinchot, who became the founder and first chief of the United States Forest Service a few years later. Pinchot's principles of forest management emphasized multiple-use, long-range sustainable harvest, and preservation of significant sites. Pinchot had methodically studied long-established tree-farming methods in Europe before formulating practices that he thought would work for American forests. His forest management practices, still in use, were revolutionary in his time. Had it not been for Pinchot's close friendship with conservation-minded President Theodore Roosevelt, the call for the establishment of forest reserves like the Minnesota Forest Reserve would probably have been ignored.[17]

Congress formed the Minnesota Forest Reserve with the passage of the Morris Act on June 27, 1902. Its boundary was originally defined by the Chippewa Indian Reservation in which it was located. With the creation of the reserve, administration of the forests was taken away from the Bureau of Indian Affairs and placed under the supervision of trained foresters guided by Pinchot's forest management practices. Initially, the passage of the Morris Act had no effect on the Itasca Lumber Company, since the original boundary of the Minnesota Forest Reserve lay west of Itasca Lumber Company's lands. Thirty years later the eastern boundary of the reserve—which had been renamed the Chippewa National Forest—was extended into the Bigfork Valley, allowing the government to buy up privately held lands within the region.

In 1934 the federal government bought its first installment of Itasca Lumber Company lands in the Bigfork Valley. ILC sales to the national forest continued until 1939, at which point a total of 29,498 acres had changed hands. The transactions were executed in a series of twelve deeds. The government paid the Itasca Lumber Company a total of $56,571. The average price per acre was $1.92.[18] This was a bargain for the government, relieved the ILC of most of its remaining land, and benefited the public. Outside of the national forest boundary, lands that had been dropped for taxes were eventually acquired by the state as part of the George Washington State Forest in northeastern Itasca County. The state of Minnesota did not purchase this property from the Itasca Lumber Company; it gained the land through the tax-forfeit procedure.[19]

After sales to the Chippewa National Forest concluded, it is somewhat surprising that the Joyces did not dissolve the Itasca Lumber Company. We can speculate that the company continued to exist in order to manage the mineral rights it had retained on lands it had sold in the past. Even though mining possibilities had never materialized, there were still tantalizing indications that something might lie hidden in the bedrock. David Zetterstrom, highly regarded in the Joyce organization, stayed on as the sole employee of ILC, tending to paperwork for the mineral rights. It is also possible that David Gage Joyce and his daughter Beatrice kept the company to act as a fiscal agent for their 4,500-acre estate on Trout Lake. The company was terminated two years after the death of Beatrice Joyce Kean in 1972.

The final acquisition of Joyce lands took place in 1974, when 4,500 contiguous acres that had comprised the Joyce's summer retreat, were absorbed into the Chippewa National Forest for the sum of $2 million. This final acquisition ended the Itasca Lumber Company's eighty-eight year adventure in northern Minnesota.

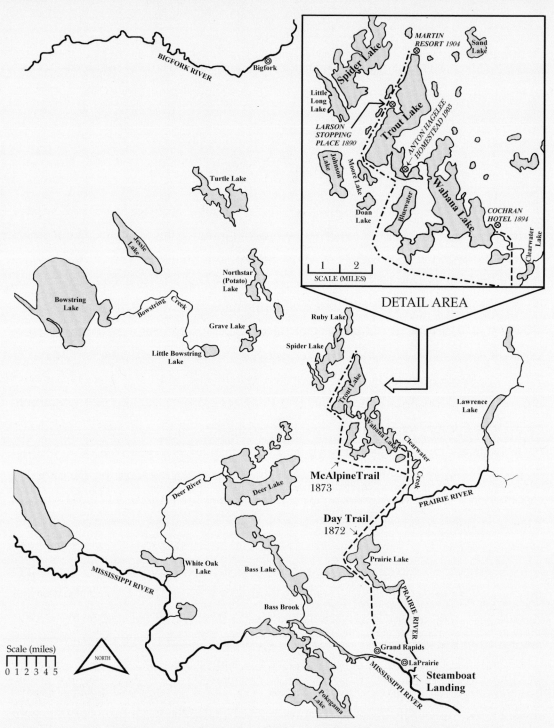

DETAIL AREA

MARTIN RESORT 1904

Sand Lake

Spider Lake

Little Long Lake

Trout Lake

LARSON STOPPING PLACE 1890

ANTON HAGELEE HOMESTEAD 1908

Johnson Lake

Moore Lake

Wabana Lake

Doan Lake

Bluewater

COCHRAN HOTEL 1894

Clearwater Lake

1   2

SCALE (MILES)

BIGFORK RIVER

Bigfork

Turtle Lake

Jessie Lake

Bowstring Creek

Northstar (Potato) Lake

Bowstring Lake

Grave Lake

Little Bowstring Lake

Ruby Lake

Spider Lake

Trout Lake

Lawrence Lake

Wabana Lake

Clearwater Creek

McAlpine Trail 1873

PRAIRIE RIVER

Deer River

Deer Lake

Day Trail 1872

White Oak Lake

Bass Lake

Prairie Lake

MISSISSIPPI RIVER

Bass Brook

PRAIRIE RIVER

Scale (miles)

0 1 2 3 4 5

NORTH

Grand Rapids

LaPrairie

MISSISSIPPI RIVER

Steamboat Landing

Pokegama Lake

EARLY LOGGING TRAILS TO TROUT LAKE AREA

Trout Lake Logging and Tourism

MOST PEOPLE FAMILIAR WITH TROUT LAKE, located north of Grand Rapids, Minnesota, recall that the Joyces built an impressive estate on its shores. The area that is now generally known as the Joyce Estate and officially titled the Trout Lake Tract was originally occupied by Native Americans, who were displaced in the late 1800s by a swelling army of lumberjacks employed by a number of logging firms, including Joyce's own Itasca Lumber Company. The first logging camp was established on Trout Lake around 1873, although adjacent Wabana Lake had a camp even earlier. Eventually Trout Lake hosted three camps as logging peaked in that vicinity. The loggers blazed supply trails that later settlers, fishermen, and hunters traveled as they explored the hundreds of area lakes. Some of these settlers started resorts. Enthralled with the bountiful fishing and hunting, tourists returned with their families year after year or even built their own summer homes. It was only after this pattern of use was firmly in place that David Gage Joyce (1885–1937) reclaimed lands cut over by his grandfather, father, and other lumbermen and built his summer retreat in 1917.

Arrival of Loggers and Surveyors

The Lorene Day family entered Itasca County in 1851. Pushing into what is now Wabana Township in 1865, these pioneer lumbermen were among the first to log the hillsides around Trout Lake, situated at the head of the Wabana chain of lakes, consisting of Trout,

LEFT: Trout Lake anchored the upper end of a chain of lakes, consisting of Trout, Little Trout, Wabana, and Bluewater Lakes. Short connecting streams tied these lakes together, and the outflow drained into the Clearwater, Prairie, and Mississippi Rivers. Trout Lake—four miles long, a mile wide, and more than one hundred feet deep—had scattered groves of red pine interspersed by white pine dotting the hillsides surrounding the lake. Loggers with an eye for pine recognized early on that Trout Lake was an ideal spot to locate a lumber camp. To supply their lumberjacks with food, the loggers built the first wagon trails northward from the LaPrairie-Grand Rapids town sites on the Mississippi River.

Wabana, Little Trout, and Bluewater. John Wesley Day, son of Lorene Day, built a camp at the south end of Wabana Lake that served him throughout the duration of his logging in the area.

The Day camp was more than twenty miles from the main supply route on the Mississippi River. Initially camp supplies were transported by bateaux, small flat-bottomed boats capable of negotiating the shallow creeks.[1] During the winter, sleds substituted for the boats. Transport proved difficult, particularly in the fall when water levels were low. To insure a reliable flow of supplies to support his lumberjacks, John Wesley Day blazed the Prairie River Road in 1872, paralleling the Prairie River north to Clearwater and Wabana Lakes. His trail originated near the intersection of the Prairie River with the Mississippi, a grassy spot later identified as LaPrairie, where steamboats could unload cargo.

While Day expended considerable effort to send supplies upstream to his lumberjack crews, getting the logs downstream was no less challenging. Day constructed crude dams at the outlets of each of the lakes in the Wabana chain to produce the surging water needed to float so many ponderous logs down the normally shallow creeks. Downstream of Wabana, more dams buoyed log drives until the logs reached the deeper waters of the Mississippi. Once on the Mississippi, river drivers coaxed the logs southward toward the distant holding booms at the Day mill in Minneapolis. L. Day and Sons ranked seventh among lumber producers in Minneapolis by 1878.[2]

The Days had already been extracting logs from the Wabana/Trout Lake area for seven years when Nathan Butler arrived in 1872 to establish the first government survey of section and township lines. After traversing the area, Butler jotted down in his survey book a note about the township's timber resources. He estimated that a minimum of 20 million board feet of white and red pine populated Wabana Township. The following year Eli W. Griffin continued the government survey in the next township to the north, western Balsam Township, out of which the future Joyce Estate would be carved. Griffin did not attempt to quantify the timber resources as Butler had done, but he did note that the area was "well timbered with various kinds of hardwoods" as well as "a large quantity

of white pine" and groves of red pine. The two surveyors would have seen the Day logging dams and so recorded in their survey books that the outlet streams of Trout and
Wabana were suitable for log driving. According to Griffin, there were only two homesteaders in the entire township encompassing Trout Lake. Emil S. Wilder and D. Y.
Wheeler had both staked out land near the west shore of Trout Lake, but there is no other
information about their fleeting land claims.[3]

Day's monopoly over the Wabana chain ended in 1873, the year that Mike
McAlpine, eventual owner of both the McAlpine Building in Grand Rapids and the
Ogema Hotel on Pokegama Lake, and a Mr. Kirkpatrick established a camp on Trout
Lake. The newcomers built their own supply trail by branching off Day's trail near the
south end of Wabana. The McAlpine Trail tracked westward, skirting Wabana Lake, then
curved northward to Trout Lake, where the trail followed an undulating course along
Trout Lake's western shore. This segment of the McAlpine Trail, parallel to Trout Lake,
eventually was incorporated into the Bigfork Trail, an informal and constantly changing
network of logging trails leading northward toward the Bigfork River. McAlpine also cut
a hay road from Trout Lake up the north side of McAlpine Brook and from there to
Bowstring Meadows near Bowstring Lake. As more and more logging companies set up
camps, the entire area became a maze of unofficial logging trails leading in every direction. Many of these trails would last only a few years and then be abandoned. (The Trout
Lake segment of the Bigfork Trail, however, has remained in service as a hiking trail until
the present day.)[4]

A constant stream of heavily loaded supply wagons now made the journey northward from the Mississippi steamboat landings at LaPrairie or Grand Rapids to logging
camps at every lake touched by the trail system. These were the roughest roads imagin-
able. The road builders simply cleared the trees and stumps from the pathway and paved
the low areas with corduroy—poles laid side by side over swampy ground. Wagon
drivers took extra precautions and sat in seats suspended on flexible hardwood poles in
order to absorb some of the shock of the ride. They also tied themselves to their seats with
leather straps as insurance against being launched from their perches. In the local jargon,

these wagons were designated "jolt wagons."[5]

The first association between the Joyce family and Trout Lake came in 1888 when the Itasca Lumber Company mounted one of its large logging operations in the Trout Lake area. Most of the pine adjacent to the shores of Trout Lake had already been cut, and loggers were building overland sled trails linking inland sites and a multitude of nearby lakes to Trout Lake. Richly timbered with pine, expansive Spider Lake became accessible by the construction of a one-mile sled trail. Other lakes tapped were Moore, Day, Little Long, and Ruby Lakes. To expedite the rush of new timber into Trout Lake, the Itasca Lumber Company needed new sluicing dams to replace the aging dams, originally built by John Wesley Day at Clearwater, Wabana, Trout, and Bluewater Lakes. William LaCroix, a talented employee of the Itasca Lumber Company, supervised the reconstruction of these dams. At the same time, J. P. Sims, Itasca Lumber Company superintendent, made improvements to the Bigfork Trail from Grand Rapids north to Trout Lake in order to guarantee the smooth flow of camp supplies. Sims had received $750 from a newly formed ad hoc county government in Grand Rapids for the Bigfork Trail roadwork on October 25, 1887, only the second such road contract to be awarded.[6]

On January 11, 1889, the *Mississippi Valley Lumberman* reported a brisk logging business. "The Itasca Lumber Company have 1,500,000 [board feet] on the banks at their Spider and Trout Lake camps. They're hauling on ice roads, one three miles, and another one and one-half miles long. Their two horse teams haul from 2,500 to 3,500 feet, and the four horse teams from 4,500 to 8,000 feet. They have 7,500,000 on the skids at their two camps."[7] Three and one-half months later, at the onset of spring ice breakup, the ILC launched its drive on Trout Lake. The logs were destined for Minneapolis.

For at least three years during the 1890s, George Moore, a contract logger for the Itasca Lumber Company, harvested pine in this region. In 1894 he cut 1.39 million board feet, representing 12,677 logs, from acreage around Trout, Little Trout, and Wabana Lakes. One contract in 1895 between George Moore and the Itasca Lumber Company specified a total area of five and one-half square miles (3,530 acres) to be logged of "all the merchantable pine logs that can be cut . . . that will scale or measure 7 inches in diameter at the small end, and that will make ⅓ merchantable lumber . . . ." This contract included Trout Lake and extended to neighboring Spider, Day, Spring, Bee Cee, Moonshine, Beavertail, Francis, Little Trout, Bluewater, Moore, and Johnson Lakes and Buckman Cove on Wabana Lake.[8] Most of the land described in George Moore's contract would become part of the yet-to-be-envisioned Joyce Estate.

A rare glimpse of logging activities on a specific piece of land that, in a few years, would

	MARK	LOGS	FEET	STAMP
Trout Lake	Kö 4	10577	1138290	KoS
Little "	"	1525	206580	"
Wabana "	"	575	46190	"
Bass "	"	688	85070	"
TOTALS		13365	1476130	

This Bill of Pine Logs records the quantity of logs that George Moore's logging crew cut for the H. C. Akeley Lumber Company, a firm closely affiliated with the Itasca Lumber Company. Moore took most of the timber from the Trout Lake, Little Trout Lake, and Wabana Lake area. The cut was certified by Minnesota's Surveyor General, who also recorded the log marks and stamps. Some of these cutover lands would later be incorporated into David Gage Joyce's northwoods retreat.
MINNESOTA HISTORICAL SOCIETY

become part of the Joyce Estate appeared in the transcript of testimony in a 1904 lawsuit. This lawsuit was brought by the Vermillion Pine and Iron Land Company against the Itasca Lumber Company regarding an ownership dispute over the timber on fifty-nine acres with shoreline on Spider Lake (Section 30, Township 58 North, Range 25 West, lots 2 and 3.) These particular fifty-nine acres contained fifty-one white pine in 1897. After the trees were cut and bucked to length by George Moore, they produced 202 logs and scaled 68,500 board feet. Moore's contract specified that the logs were to be conveyed to the shore of Trout Lake. According to his contract, Moore received about $3 per thousand board feet, $205 total for the white pine on the disputed fifty-nine acres. After Moore delivered the logs at Trout Lake, river drivers moved them downstream to the Itasca Lumber Company mill at Minneapolis. The cost for driving the logs was $.50 per thousand board feet for the segment from Trout Lake to the mouth of the Prairie River on the Mississippi. From that point to Brainerd cost $.08 per thousand board feet, and from Brainerd to the Minneapolis mill cost another $.37 per thousand board feet. The fifty-nine acres, of course, was only a tiny fraction of land around Trout Lake that was subject to George Moore's logging crews.[9]

Stopping Places

Some of the earliest successful settlers took advantage of the logging trade and movement of travelers by establishing ranches or stopping places along the Bigfork Trail. From Grand Rapids and LaPrairie, a procession of men and draft animals plodded slowly northward with their provisions, the toting of which made "immense business," according to an 1892 issue of the *Mississippi Valley Lumberman*. Of the many wagons departing for the logging camps, most were loaded with three to four tons of supplies and were pulled by teams of four to six draft animals. Proprietors of stopping places could commonly expect ten to fifteen wagons and their drivers to stop each night.[10]

One of these stopping places served travelers on the west side of Trout Lake along the Bigfork Trail. It was built and operated by Frank and Anna Larson, who came to Trout Lake in 1890 from Wisconsin after emigrating from Sweden. The couple received a formal deed to their property in 1895. Their stopping place occupied the site where David Gage Joyce would later develop a golf course as part of his estate complex.[11]

The Larsons did not stay at their homestead overlooking the turquoise waters of Trout Lake. Misfortune and opportunity led them to move twenty miles northward to a new home on the Bigfork River. On a fall day in 1897 smoke billowed up the shoreline toward the Larson ranch, which neighbored a logging camp operated by George Moore. Moore's apparently unattended camp was destroyed as forest fires sacked the cutover areas of Trout Lake. Anna Larson and her children successfully fought to save the water tank and logging sleds stored at the camp, but Mrs. Larson badly burned her hands while beating back the flames.[12] The fire was inevitable in an area denuded of big trees and covered with slashing. It also was an indicator that logging activity was drawing to a close.

Shortly after the fire, Nels Felstet, one of the first pioneers to settle at the junction of the Bigfork and Rice Rivers, met the Larson daughter, Olga. Frequenting the ranch when he now and then traveled the Bigfork Trail to Grand Rapids, Nels wooed and married the young Scandinavian woman. Following their marriage he convinced his bride's parents to vacate their home of seven years in order to found a new ranch near his homestead.[13] Frank and Anna Larson opened a post office at their ranch on the Bigfork River in 1902 and in the process formalized Bigfork as that settlement's name.

The move was beneficial for the Larsons since it was increasingly difficult to sustain a living by operating a stopping place with the decline of logging activity around Trout Lake. Farming was also out of the question at their original home because soil was poor and level ground, scarce. Frank Larson struggled even to keep his team of horses and small herd of cattle fed. However, the couple steadfastly held onto the property title for their ranch on Trout Lake. It was much too lovely a spot to relinquish.[14]

The Tourist Industry and the Summer People

At the turn of the century, people with money intent upon finding unspoiled wilderness and boundless catches of fish began making brief appearances on Wabana and Trout Lakes. An excellent network of rail transportation carried these vacationers and sportsmen from distant cities to the Grand Rapids' train depot. From midwestern states like Iowa and Illinois to the head of the Bigfork Trail in Grand Rapids was only a day's travel. A new livelihood materialized for local settlers willing to cater to the needs of these visitors.

Wabana Lake

Dave Cochran put up a two-story log home, stopping place, and boat landing at the south end of Wabana Lake in 1894. Originally he served homestead seekers and wagoneers bearing provisions to logging camps. During 1899 four fishermen from the Elgin Muskelonge Club of Illinois knocked on his door, old friends of Cochran from the days when he operated a lodge in Eagle River, Wisconsin. Cochran's place soon swarmed with sportsmen needing lodging, guiding, and boat services. In addition to his earlier Wisconsin experience, Cochran had also run a three-story hotel in LaPrairie before his move to Wabana, so it was no surprise that he expanded his quarters to accommodate the arriving fishermen. By 1901 he had invested more than $5,000 in a two-story hotel with seventeen rooms. Once the structure was completed in 1902, Cochran kept a full house the entire year as guests arrived from all over the country.[15]

Cochran ferried his guests throughout the scenic lake chain on his homemade twenty-six-foot launch, powered by a six-horsepower gasoline engine. Four years later he replaced this boat with a homemade thirty-five-foot launch capable of seating more than forty people. He also built an unpowered houseboat with a kitchen, dining room, living room, and four beds, which he pushed with one of his other boats. A fleet of rowboats docked with the rest of the watercraft. A 1904 article in the Grand Rapids newspaper lauded Cochran's hotel as "one of the best known and most popular" in the area. Cochran's price was affordable, and he promised the eager anglers their fill of Wabana Lake's black bass. For those guests tired of landing black bass, Trout Lake, only a lake away, was well stocked with the elusive fish for which it was named.[16]

The hotel rapidly emerged as the Wabana area social and civic center. Cochran, postmaster for the Wabana area, set up a post office in his hotel for local residents and guests. He also operated a general store. The hotel was the scene of many dances and weddings as well as Sunday school services. In 1910 Cochran turned over his hotel and business to Pat Taylor. The hotel was destroyed by fire in 1928, but the boat landing is still called Taylor's Landing.[17]

Trout Lake

Cochran's hotel business introduced many wealthy vacationers to the Wabana chain of lakes that included Trout Lake. Some vacationers decided to purchase land and build. In 1903, a Dr. McGee and M. S. Burroughs raised the first summer cabins on the north end of Trout Lake. A rare 1905 photo of one of these log cabins reveals elaborate cedar stick-work decorating the periphery of the large porch, curved cedar stickwork forming the railings for the front steps, and additional stickwork defining a rear porch. The distinctive style, typical of the Great Camps of the Adirondacks, was popularized in magazines of that era. When David Joyce constructed his retreat fourteen years later in 1917, it would likewise mimic the rustic Adirondack style. Joyce's cabins closely matched the McGee and Burroughs cabins, although the only decorative stickwork featured on the Joyce cabins consisted of naturally curved cedar railings for the front steps.

Year-round residents arrived along with the tourists. Anton Hagelee built his log cabin in 1903 at the opposite end of Trout Lake, high on a hill overlooking its large southern bay. Hagelee had arrived in the United States from Scandinavia in 1872 and had worked as a railroad machinist before moving to Trout Lake. He supported his large family as a trapper, fishing guide, and carpenter. Many of the first cabins on Trout Lake were probably raised with Hagelee's help. When the Joyce Estate was built, Hagelee was engaged as a carpenter and later served as a handyman.[18]

In 1904 Irv Martin established a modest beachfront log cabin at the north end of Trout Lake. He had moved from his birth state of Wisconsin to LaPrairie, Minnesota, finding work first as a lumberjack and later as a fireman on locomotives running between Deer River and Duluth. When Martin came to Trout Lake, Duluth logger John McAlpine

Just years after logging ceased in the Trout Lake area, tourists were attracted to the sporting opportunities and raw beauty of the lake-dotted countryside. This 1905 photo shows one of the many seasonal cabins erected at the north end of Trout Lake, built by local artisans, such as Anton Hagelee. The elaborate stickwork is reminiscent of the architectural style used by the Great Camps of the Adirondacks. INSET: Later photo of the same cabin on the north end of Trout Lake. IRETON FAMILY PRIVATE COLLECTION

(no relation to logger Mike McAlpine) was operating a logging camp in the same forest opening as Martin's homestead. McAlpine's crew was harvesting timber north of Trout Lake in the Ruby Lake region and landing the logs at Trout. Martin was probably counted among McAlpine's crew of lumberjacks. Two or three years later McAlpine's camp closed, leaving Martin ideally positioned as the industry in the area turned from logging to tourism.

Guests from Dave Cochran's hotel on Wabana noticed Martin's place as they toured the lakes during the years between 1904 and 1909. Some inquired about available lodging, and Martin was quick to take in boarders. Barney Kaye was one such guest, first coming to Cochran's hotel in 1900 and sometime after that to Martin's. A prominent jeweler from Elgin, Illinois, Kaye returned to Wabana and Trout Lakes year after year and eventually put up his own cabin on Trout, located at what would become the north entrance to the Joyce Estate.[19]

Through guests like Barney Kaye, Irv Martin stumbled upon his future livelihood as a resort owner. In July 1912 Martin purchased five lots or 300 feet of frontage on Trout Lake from the Itasca Lumber Company for the sum of $250. These were part of the twenty-seven lots available in the Trout Lake Park plat, created from the company's desirable lakeshore holdings after the cessation of logging. The lots were mostly 50 or 100 feet in width, although four larger peripheral lots comprised less attractive lakeshore. On his five lots Irv Martin built rustic log cabins for his clientele and started one of the first cabin resorts in the county.[20]

The cabins built on the Trout Lake Park lots by Martin and others remained somewhat uniform in

Pete Kennedy, cook for Martin's resort on Trout Lake, sounded his bugle to announce mealtime.
IRETON FAMILY PRIVATE COLLECTION

design. Initially all featured log construction and a screened-in front porch. Several of the cabins had hand railings made from carefully selected naturally curved cedar stickwork. Along the sandy beachfront, flagpoles of substantial height marked each cabin. The expansive sandy beach, a result of more than twenty years of wildly fluctuating lake levels caused by the use of the downstream logging dam, encouraged a distant setback from the water to the cabins.

Irv Martin's resort became the community center of Trout Lake Park. Martin soon hired former logging camp cook Pete Kennedy to prepare meals for both his hungry guests and the seasonal cabin owners, nearly all of whom relied upon Martin for three meals a day. Kennedy cooked nothing fancy, but in the tradition of the lumber camp, it was good food and there was lots of it. As meal time approached, the cook strolled to the lakeside dock wearing his long white apron, his trademark bugle in hand. In a manner reminiscent of the logging camps, he lifted the horn to his lips and blew its musical strains across the lake, signaling that all should gather at Martin's communal table for such typical fare as wild game, berries collected by Martin and his family, and produce from the Martin garden.[21]

As postmaster and resort owner, Martin made regular trips to Cochran's hotel and sometimes into Grand Rapids to collect mail and to keep his cook supplied with enough foodstuffs to satisfy his many guests, his boarders, and his own large family. He boated the first leg of his trip, docking at the south end of Wabana, nine miles distant, to avoid the longer and rough overland trails. Even so, the round trip to town would have taken an entire day. Martin shuttled his guests between the train depot in Grand Rapids and his resort until a livery service was established, allowing him to meet his guests at Cochran's hotel.

The preeminent pastime for residents and tourists, of course, was fishing, which lured many repeat customers to Martin's Trout Lake Resort. But the wild abandon of amateur and commercial fishermen unfortunately depleted the lake of its namesake, the lake trout, during the first years of the resort. An unidentified newspaper clipping collected by Martin's daughter described the disappearance of the fish:

"Trout Lake was well named. In the early days there were large numbers of lake trout taken from its waters. Nets were set off the spawning grounds, when the big trout came up to deposit their eggs along the rocky bars. Mr. Martin remembers one night when he put out a net and secured 60 trout varying in weight from five to twenty pounds. Parties would come all the way from Duluth to [commercially] net the trout, salting them down for winter use. Laws did not prohibit the netting or were evaded when in effect, until the supply of trout in the lake ran low, and for a number of years none were caught."[22]

Trout Lake teemed with walleyed pike, northern pike, and bass, according to an advertisement for Martin's resort which was published around 1916. The ad claimed that some of these fish weighed a whopping thirty pounds. (Although northern pike and bass could certainly be caught, it is doubtful that Trout Lake ever teemed with walleye.) Anglers casting their lines for smaller fish landed sunfish, crappies, bluegills, and perch. If they tired of the fishing holes on Trout, they ambled down an old logging trail to Spider Lake, less than a mile from Martin's doorstep. In the days before limits, these ecstatic fishermen effortlessly reeled in endless buckets of bass from the neighboring lake.

A brochure for Martin's resort also listed a few of the lakes easily accessible by canoe, namely Spider, Little Island, Sand, Burnt Shanty, One Arm, Ruby, Long, Moore, Smith, and Ole as well as the Rice River system. By throwing together a tent, a bed roll, a cast iron griddle, and grub, adventurous guests could leave behind the amenities at Martin's and paddle off on their own with only wildlife for company.

Martin kept his resort open throughout the fall, catering to as many as twenty deer hunters each season. Deer was the most prevalent game, but visitors could hunt moose, black bear, fox, wolf, bobcat, grouse, ducks, and geese. Trout Lake had an extended bird season since it did not ice over until a month after nearby lakes.[23]

In 1914, a decade after Irv Martin homesteaded on the north end of Trout, Louis A. Ireton learned of the Martin resort. Ireton's son retold the following story passed down from his father, explaining how the Ireton family became annual summer residents of the lake: A client named Camel burst into Louis A. Ireton's Cincinnati, Ohio law office, exclaiming, "Lou, I've really hit the jackpot!" Camel then related an exuberant story of returning from an outing during which his party caught 200 bass in a single day. The small ones from this incredible catch were tossed "in the slop barrel for the pigs" while only "a handful of [bass were kept] for the table."[24]

Ireton's client had discovered the place by pure luck. He had arrived in Duluth on the train and had queried the station master about fishing opportunities. The station master had advised him to continue on to Grand Rapids. Departing the train there, Camel entered the local saloon, ordered a drink, and announced his desire for some good fishing. Pointing to Irv Martin, who was also quenching his thirst before picking up supplies, the bartender told Camel that Martin's place had access to Spider Lake, the finest bass fishing in this part of the country. Camel promptly joined Martin for the fishing experience of his life.

Louis A. Ireton was quite impressed with this story and immediately posted a letter to Martin, reserving two cabins for his family for the next summer. After a fatiguing train trip from Cincinnati to Grand Rapids that following year, the Ireton family was met by Ernie Poland at the train station. His livery service extended as far as Taylor's Landing at the south end of Wabana Lake, where Irv Martin waited on shore with his motor launch to ferry the family through the lake chain to Trout Lake. An hour or two later Martin cut the motor and coasted to a stop alongside his dock. Out stepped the Iretons with their carpetbag trunk to begin a leisurely month casting for fish. The family most often chose Spider Lake for outings, landing bass for their noon picnics. The Iretons returned to Trout Lake the next two summers and purchased property on the hillside above Martin's in 1917.[25]

The year 1917 also marked the initial construction of David Gage Joyce's estate on Trout Lake. The authors cannot say when or how often Joyce's path had led him to Trout Lake in the years prior to 1917, but before committing to such a large project, he certainly had familiarized himself with the area. It is likely that he was well acquainted with Taylor's hotel on Wabana Lake and Martin's resort at the north end of Trout Lake, that he had fished the area lakes, and that he knew the local people. Joyce would later employ some of the local settlers, such as Pat Taylor, Anton Hagelee, Irv Martin, and Ernie Poland. Summer residents like Barney Kaye and Louis Ireton became casual friends.

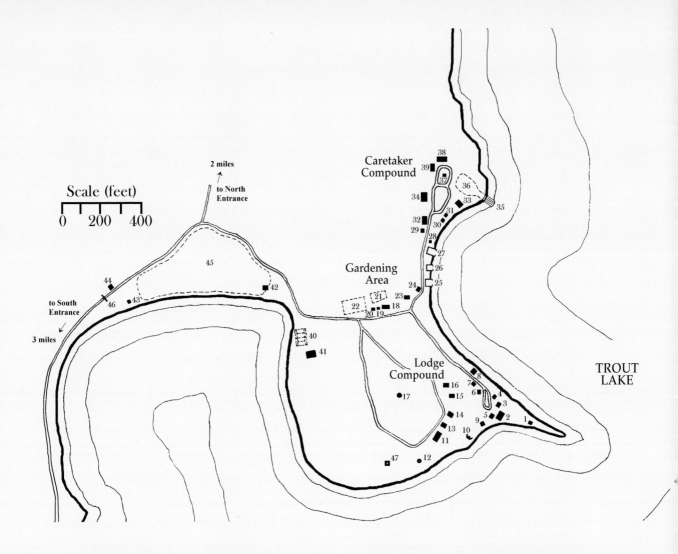

THE JOYCE ESTATE BUILDING COMPLEX

1. Bathhouse
2. Main Lodge
3. Joyce Cabin
4. Guest Cabin
5. Root Cellar
6. Gunhouse
7. Laundry
8. Icehouse
9. Playhouse
10. Barbecue
11. Peterson Cabin
12. Gazebo

13. B.C.'s Cabin
14. Mary Louise Cabin
15. Butler Cabin
16. Maid Cabin
17. Water Tank
18. Greenhouse
19. Utility Building
20. Utility Building
21. Garden
22. White Spruce
       Plantation
23. Men's Cabin

24. Powerhouse
25. Boathouse
26. Boathouse
27. Seaplane Hanger
28. Fuel Storage
29. Utility Building
30. Utility Building
31. Utility Building
32. Three Stall Garage
33. Dog Kennel
34. Caretaker Cabin
35. Seaplane /Boat Ramp

36. Seaplane Parking
37. Woodshed
38. Steel Garage
39. Barn
40. Tennis Court
41. Special Cabin
42. Golf Clubhouse
43. Pump House
44. Tool Shed
45. Golf Course
46. Gate
47. Observation Tower

David Gage Joyce

DAVID GAGE JOYCE, HEIR TO A LOGGING EMPIRE, accumulated the rare, the priceless, and the extravagant. Perhaps he first envisioned an estate of grand proportion on the shores of Trout Lake when, as a young man traveling along the Bigfork Trail to company logging camps and forest lands, he passed by the lake's clear blue waters. Regardless of when he conceived the idea, he launched construction of the estate in 1917 and called it Nopeming, an Ojibwe word for "going out in the country" or "up in the north," although Joyce's interpretation of the name of the estate was "a place of rest."[*1]

To set his dream of a rustic lodge and cabin complex in motion, thirty-year-old David Gage Joyce instructed Itasca Lumber Company timber cruiser, surveyor, and land sales department manager S. D. Patrick to merge the properties of more than seventy individuals and organizations rimming Trout Lake into an initial estate of 2,600 acres.[2] Contrary to popular belief, the lands comprising the Joyce Estate were not held exclusively by Joyce or the Itasca Lumber Company before 1915. Instead, the property was divided into a checkerboard pattern of logging interests and homestead claims. Prominent names in the logging industry such as H. C. Akeley, George Camp, and T. B. Walker appear in the records.

By October 1915 Patrick had nearly completed his task. However, the key eighty-acre parcel, the Larson ranch property commanding the point on the western lakeshore, was still owned by Frank and Anna Larson. It was on that point that David Gage Joyce expected to set the foundations for Nopeming. Details of the events that put the Larson

[*] In the midst of the formation of Nopeming, David Gage Joyce was divorced and remarried. His first wife was Roberta Acuff Joyce of St. Louis, whom he married on August 19, 1912. His second wife was Beatrice Rudolph Joyce with whom he had a daughter, Beatrice Clotilde Joyce. When the daughter was married for the second time, her name became Beatrice Joyce Kean.

property into the hands of Joyce are clouded by time. All the authors know is that on January 4, 1916, a mortgage foreclosure notice was issued to the Larsons, and on August 23, 1916, S. D. Patrick purchased the Larson property in his name, reselling it to Joyce on May 9, 1917.

While Joyce waited for the completion of the Larson transaction, he frequented the Grand Rapids area and also summered sixty miles away on Woman Lake near Walker, Minnesota. "Strong inducements were offered him to locate there," reported the Grand Rapids paper, "but the superior advantages of Itasca County turned his decision in favor of this section."[3] In reality, Joyce's longtime familiarity with Trout Lake and the advanced state of preparations for actual construction of Nopeming probably precluded a change of plans.

As 1916 drew to a close, S. D. Patrick readied Nopeming for construction. He organized work crews, ordered building materials—relying on the office of the Itasca Lumber Company in Deer River as Joyce's financial agent for the project—and located a source of standing pine and cedar trees of sufficient number, size, and quality for the raising of the lodge and eight log cabins indicated in Joyce's plans. Most of the region had been stripped of its big pine stands many years before, but Patrick, with his intimate knowledge of Itasca Lumber Company lands in the area, found a small stand of modestly sized pine near Ruby Lake, only a few miles north of Trout Lake. These trees, along with cedar, probably growing near North Star Lake, satisfied the log quota.

Patrick assigned a crew of men to cut the logs during the winter of 1916–1917. Stacked on sleds and hauled overland from North Star and Ruby Lakes, the logs crossed Irv Martin's resort and glided onto the frozen surface of Trout Lake for the final two-mile ride across the ice to Larson's Point. There, sleds and horses were relieved of their loads as the men banked the logs on the shore. At this point the crew waited until the spring ice breakup signaled the advent of the construction season.

The Great Camp Model

David Gage Joyce's plans for Nopeming closely paralleled the Great Camps of many affluent industrialists, financiers, and railroad magnates. These magnificent complexes, sequestered on majestic tracts of wilderness, evolved in the Adirondack Mountains of Upstate New York at the turn of the twentieth century. Harvey H. Kaiser's book, *Great Camps of the Adirondacks*, describes the camps in detail. The most popular model for the camps, wrote Kaiser, was exhibited in the estates of such families as the Vanderbilts and the Rockefellers. According to the model, guests motoring down the lake were greeted by "a picturesque sequence of boathouse, log gazebo, and main lodge," located on an isolated peninsula. Nopeming would feature the same. The rustic appearance of the camps idealized "the pioneering spirit and the simple life" of settlers hewing logs for their cabins out of the dense northwoods with minimal tools and the strength of their bodies.[4]

Another Great Camp characteristic—the desire "to convey a sense of wonder"—however, ran counter to any notion of simple living. In a document prepared to evaluate the historical significance of the Joyce Estate, consultant Jeffrey Hess reported that besides promoting "relaxation and recreation . . . the Great Camp [owners] sought to overwhelm their guests with marvelous contradictions: log cabins and luxuriously landscaped lawns; pristine moon-lit lakes and electrically-lighted boat houses; backwoods fishing expeditions and butlers."[5] Like guests reaching the Adirondack Great Camps from New York City, visitors arriving at Nopeming from cities like Chicago must have been amazed by Joyce's extravagance in the northwoods.

In Nopeming, Joyce joined the ranks of many seeking to emulate the Great Camp theme in building projects across the country. Well traveled, Joyce may have toured the Adirondacks and seen the camps firsthand. Knowledge of the Great Camp style was widespread. The architecture and log construction of the Great Camps were illustrated in popular magazines of the day, such as the *Craftsman* and *Home and Garden*. The National Park Service adopted this architectural style, producing such marvels as the lodges of Yellowstone and Glacier National Parks. There were also similar complexes in Wisconsin and Michigan. A nearby example in northern Minnesota is the Chippewa National Forest headquarters at Cass Lake, a massive three-story log structure displaying equally massive stonework and awe-inspiring interior log work. Even on Trout Lake, the cabins of the first summer residents featured the elaborate cedar stickwork, characteristic of the Great Camps.

Full Speed Ahead: The Genesis of Nopeming

On March 14, 1917, the *Grand Rapids Herald Review* announced that David Gage Joyce and his chief attorney F. P. Leffingwell had come to make final arrangements for the start of the construction season. Even before Joyce's arrival, more building materials, delivered on horse-drawn sleds, had joined the logs already stockpiled at Larson's Point. The moment that the snow and frost left the ground, work began in earnest. S. D. Patrick employed a local building foreman, F. L. Norman, well known in Itasca County for his fine log workmanship, along with his crew of Pete Richland, a Mr. Rupert, and the Holum brothers. Norman hired a host of other local artisans as well.[6]

After the Bigfork Trail dried out with the approach of summer, Pete Leroux, a drayman from Grand Rapids, carried lumber onto the construction site by the wagonload with the assistance of Tom Fitzgerald. Material was also barged in from Taylor's Landing on Wabana Lake through the interconnecting creeks and lakes to the point on Trout Lake, a distance of some six miles. The barge handled "lumber up to 18 feet in length," according to summer lake resident Louis M. Ireton, "and was towed by a boat with a small 4 or 5 horsepower outboard engine." It took all day to deliver the supplies to the estate and return to the landing. (Only a few years earlier the Itasca Lumber Company had floated logs on this same water route in the opposite direction.)

Norman and his workmen fashioned the main lodge out of saddle-notched and peeled cedar and pine logs. After planting simple post foundations, they wrestled the logs into place. The workmen then scribed and trimmed the logs for their final fittings. On the north wall in the undivided thirty-four-by-twenty-six-foot great room, stonemasons installed a large fireplace that would erase the early morning chill. A wraparound screen porch concealed Norman's fine log work. As a result, the exterior of the main lodge was unassuming and rather stark with dark-stained wood shingles and green trim. By contrast, sandpapered and shellacked logs in their natural hue dominated the interior of the great room and porch.

Joyce's floor plan was unpresumptuous. On the lake side to the east, the great room opened through double doors onto the wraparound, screened-in front porch. Several modest great room windows looked out through the porch to the lake. Away from the lake, the great room entered the sectioned-off kitchen area to the south and Joyce's study and library room to the north. A tiny bathroom was squeezed between the study and the north end of the screen porch.

Typical of decor for Great Camp lodges, the interior log walls at Nopeming held a menagerie of mounted animals. A ferocious-looking fisher bared its teeth at guests entering the great room. An eagle, eternally poised for a strike, soared over a parade of game bird mounts on the fireplace mantel while moose with ponderous racks surveyed the scene below. Large wildlife paintings graced the walls. David Gage Joyce continued the rustic motif as he furnished the great room exclusively with wicker furniture and grass rugs. The screened-in porch was appointed in the same style.

Joyce's Trout Lake Lodge

to point

wraparound screen porch

to Joyce cabin

Fireplace

Great Room

toilet

storage

library

Joyce study/office

flower preparation room

kitchen cooking

kitchen pantry

The point on Trout Lake shows the newly constructed Joyce Estate. The bathhouse with its huge martin house bisects the narrow spit of land extending out from the lodge. IRETON FAMILY PRIVATE COLLECTION

The interior of the lodge during the David Gage Joyce era.
JOE WALESKI PRIVATE COLLECTION

The Joyce cabin and guest cabin adjacent to the lodge. A reflecting pond complete with a small island is visible in the foreground. IRETON FAMILY PRIVATE COLLECTION

Two identical cabins were built adjacent to the main lodge, one for the Joyces and one for their guests. The dimensions of the cabins were approximately sixteen by twenty feet, not including the small screened tuck-under porch that faced the lake and the bathroom and dressing room that were added onto the central sleeping area in the back. Simple handrails of naturally curved cedar accented the steps leading up to the cabin porches. They were the only decorative flare applied to any of the building exteriors with the exception of the gazebo. The cabin interiors mirrored the rustic decor of the main lodge.

Between quick business trips to Minneapolis and Chicago that summer of 1917, David Gage Joyce diligently oversaw the work in progress at his estate. He arrived in Grand Rapids in June with his wife, Roberta Acuff Joyce, and registered at the

Pokegama Hotel for a planned stay of one month, but they remained for most of the summer. The two spent their days at Nopeming, watching the lodge and cabins take shape, returning to Grand Rapids in the evenings. During the middle of August, the couple spent several days and nights on the grounds in the nearly completed cabin before going back to Chicago.[7]

Construction continued on the estate through 1917 and 1918. Two guest cabins, a maids' cabin, and a butlers' cabin were finished on the hillside overlooking the lodge. By August of the second summer, six cabins, including the two built the previous summer, nestled near or behind the main lodge. A narrow walkway shaded with a grape arbor connected the hillside cabins. Guests could relax on benches along the walkway. Paths with stone borders and steps led from the cabins on the hill to the kitchen area at the back of the main lodge, and a gravel-covered path proceeded from the front of the lodge to the tip of the peninsula.

Next, the building crew applied their energy to the caretaker's compound that consisted of a cabin, a garage, several small sheds, a root cellar, and a small barn, all positioned a thousand feet north of the point along the shoreline. These were conventional frame construction with the exception of the caretaker's log cabin and the log root cellar, burrowed into the hillside beside the caretaker's cabin. (The log root cellar rotted after fifteen years of contact with the damp soil, and the structure had to be removed.) A few feet to the north of the root cellar, the barn sheltered several riding horses and the caretaker's milk cow.

Midway between the caretaker's compound and the lodge, another log cabin for workmen, a wood frame boathouse, a concrete and stone earth-sheltered powerhouse, and an icehouse went up. The powerhouse's gasoline-powered Delco generator provided electricity for lighting, small appliances, and water pumping prior to rural electrification of the area in 1946. Lake-harvested ice kept in the icehouse furnished refrigeration. Like the root cellar, the original log icehouse rapidly succumbed to rot and was reconstructed with solid concrete walls.

An elaborate water system laced the point, the caretaker's area, and eventually the golf course. Workmen installed a 1,500-gallon water tank on the summit of the hill behind the cabins and main lodge exclusively for irrigating the extensive lawn and gardens. To replenish the tank, one of the men switched on an electric pump at the lake and then watched for the red semaphore, attached to a float inside the tank, to indicate that it was full. It was necessary to continually clear a narrow swath up the hillside from the pump to the tank in order to keep this semaphore in sight. After the tank filled, gravity created the pressure needed to supply the faucets spaced throughout the grounds. Yet another pump, stationed at the golf course, irrigated the greens.

Drinking water for the main lodge and cabins came from a well, housed nearby. A well in the basement of the caretaker's cabin supplied water for that area.

As amazing as the extensive plumbing were the ten private telephones that acted as an intercom system among the widely spaced estate buildings and also connected the Joyce Estate with the outside world. Originally David Gage Joyce extended a cable under Trout Lake and southward to tie into the Grand Rapids telephone exchange, a necessity for his business. Since boats often ran afoul of the cable in the shallows, it had to be replaced with overhead line. Joyce's workmen put up the entire fifteen-mile span of telephone line into Grand Rapids and maintained it into the 1940s.[8]

The year 1920 marked the construction finale of the major estate buildings, including the gazebo, the observation tower, the bathhouse, the photo darkroom, and the gunhouse

The top of the bathhouse originally functioned as an observation deck. Later, an enclosed teahouse topped the structure. IRETON FAMILY PRIVATE COLLECTION

that stored David Gage Joyce's trapshooting equipment and personal collection of guns.

The gazebo was one of several spots David Gage Joyce dedicated to the observation of nature. The airy log-framed octagonal structure overlooked Trout Lake high on the hillside behind the lodge. It was the sole example of the elaborate decorative stickwork, characteristic of the Adirondack style, among the original buildings at the estate. Some afternoons at teatime the Joyces and their guests congregated at the gazebo. With only the breeze and an occasional fishing boat to disturb the water, the party must have praised the quiet beauty of Trout Lake as they sipped tea and talked.

David Gage Joyce frequented an observation tower further up the hill beyond the gazebo to read and to watch wildlife. After climbing the fifty stairs, he stepped onto an enclosed platform, where a stationary stand held a very heavy pair of binoculars for scanning the distant shorelines. Well above the forest cover of that time and 120 feet above Trout Lake, the lofty perch offered him a soaring sense of suspension over the iridescent blue waters. (The deteriorating observation tower was deemed unsafe and was the first structure removed after David Gage Joyce's daughter, Beatrice, died in 1972. The gazebo was destroyed by a storm years later.)

The bathhouse on the tip of the point served as a changing room for swimmers. There are indications that David Gage Joyce initially planned to mount a telescope on the observation deck above the bathhouse, but it was instead stationed on the lawn. Joyce and his guests used the telescope to observe deer coming to a salt lick one mile across the lake. He also noted birds such as the blue herons that he nicknamed "flying beefsteaks," according to John Zetterstrom, whose father was the manager of the estate during the 1930s and 1940s. "Maybe," thought Zetterstrom, Joyce used the moniker "because they looked so chesty when they coiled up their necks in flight."[9] On top of the original bathhouse, a huge martin house was fitted to a mast in the center of the observation deck.

The bathhouse design changed over the years. During the initial remodeling, an exterior stairway leading to the deck was crafted out of fancy Adirondack-style stickwork, echoing the work on the gazebo. Sometime during the middle 1950s, Beatrice

Joyce Kean, David Gage Joyce's daughter, converted the bathhouse into a sauna and transformed the observation deck into a Japanese-style teahouse. The walls of the teahouse were composed of sliding celluloid panels. Grass mats covered the floor. Guests removed their shoes at the entrance and slipped on sandals before seating themselves on the cushions circling a low table. Possibly Beatrice's renovation was influenced by the style of the Great Camps, whose owners sometimes incorporated Japanese teahouses and other Japanese architectural influences into their complexes.

The large copper-roofed martin house capping the original bathhouse was only one of many birdhouses that sheltered the returning purple martins at the point and on the golf course after it was built in 1923. By 1951 these houses had deteriorated. Three- and four-story martin houses that could be taken apart and cleaned were substituted for the original birdhouses. Each of these new houses accommodated approximately thirty nesting pairs of martins. Estate manager Joe Waleski Jr. remarked that when some of the new birdhouses were given an annual cleaning, they "had to be taken down with block and tackle and the Jeep or the Power Wagon" because they weighed about 400 pounds each. At the time that the estate was sold in 1974, these houses still welcomed the purple martins that returned annually to Nopeming. Without annual maintenance, these magnificent birdhouses turned to weather-beaten tenements and were removed some years later.

David Gage Joyce setting up one of two cameras that he used for stereo photography. Directly behind Joyce and centered in photo is his wife, Beatrice. JOE WALESKI PRIVATE COLLECTION

A tiny photo darkroom was built next to the gunhouse northwest of the lodge. An avid photographer, David Gage Joyce developed some of his own pictures there. He also

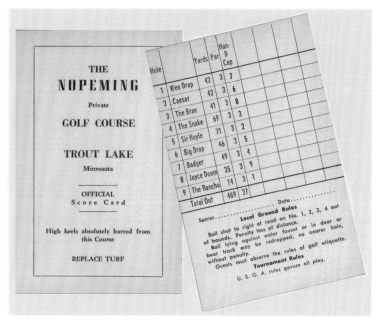

Scorecard for the Joyce Estate golf course. JOE WALESKI PRIVATE COLLECTION

THE

NOPEMING

Private

GOLF COURSE

TROUT LAKE

Minnesota

OFFICIAL
S c o r e   C a r d

High heels absolutely barred from
this Course

REPLACE TURF

Hole		Yards	Par	Han-D Cap
1	Wee Drap	42	3	7
2	Caesar	42	3	6
3	The Brae	41	3	8
4	The Snake	69	3	3
5	Sir Hoyle	71	3	2
6	Big Drap	46	3	5
7	Badger	49	3	4
8	Joyce Doom	35	3	9
9	The Rancho	74	3	1
Total Out		469	27	

Scorer . . . . Date . . . .

Local Ground Rules

Ball shot to right of road on No. 1, 2, 3, 4 out
of bounds. Penalty loss of distance.
Ball lying against water faucet or in deer or
bear track may be redropped, no nearer hole,
without penalty.
Guests must observe the rules of golf etiquette.
Tournament Rules
U. S. G. A. rules govern all play.

experimented with stereo photography. After setting up two cameras on tripods a few feet apart, he simultaneously tripped the shutters on both cameras. Joyce sent this film to Chicago to be processed as alpha lantern glass slides. Each glass slide came back with two images, one shot from each camera. When Joyce put the slide into a stereo viewer and held the viewer up to the light, he saw his photographs rendered in three dimensions.

The estate continued its expansion in 1923 with a nine-hole par-three pitch-and-putt golf course and accompanying clubhouse along the shore of Trout Lake southwest of the main lodge. Its design is attributed to a Mr. Melville, onetime golf pro at Grand Rapids' Pokegama Golf Course. Statistics appearing on an undated printed scorecard listed the length as 469 yards. The shortest hole of 35 yards was nicknamed "Joyce Doom," while the scorecard identified the longest hole of 74 yards as "The Rancho." Golf course rules permitted a player whose ball landed in a bear or deer track "to redrop" it the same distance from the hole without losing points but prohibited wearing high heel shoes while playing the sport. (Deer were particularly problematic at the estate. High heel shoes probably were not.) Two years after the course was completed, David's wife, Beatrice Rudolph Joyce, earned the distinction of scoring the first hole-in-one. Evidence of sand traps still survives today, although a significant portion of the golf course has succumbed to underbrush. A number of white pine, planted as saplings at the course's inception, now dominate the former course. Nature has also taken back the adjacent first-class clay tennis court that lay at water's edge.

Several outbuildings designed by Grand Rapids gardener and greenhouse owner Dudley Green were devoted to the cultivation of flowers and vegetables. During the 1920s the Joyces installed a sixteen-by-thirty-five-foot greenhouse 1,500 feet northwest of the main lodge. A partial basement housed an oil furnace and boiler, which circulated hot water through pipes routed beneath the potting benches. Each fall the caretaker made sure that the greenhouse oil tank was filled and the pipes and boiler were drained. Then in late winter, when the estate lay under a blanket of snow, he shoveled a path to the greenhouse to turn on the water and start the furnace, so the gardener could pot seeds for the next summer's flowers. In a small root cellar across the road from the greenhouse, one of the gardeners grew big white mushrooms during the summer. The mushrooms were primarily for the Joyces' consumption, although the staff indulged in any surplus. During the winter, flower bulbs were stored in the root cellar. Adjacent to the greenhouse, the expansive garden plot not only grew tomatoes, carrots, muskmelons, and other fruits and vegetables, but a large section produced cut flowers for the lodge and cabins.

The greenhouse did much to civilize the grounds of the estate. Nopeming was located in the midst of a sapling forest on disheveled rocky and sandy soil and lacked the natural aesthetics of the eastern Great Camps. Landscaping partially cured this problem with trucked-in topsoil to cover the area around the lodge and cabins, but flowers from the greenhouse really domesticated and brightened the grounds. A series of large floral beds in front of the main lodge divided the manicured lawn, stretching about 250 feet down the narrow peninsula to the water's edge. Alyssum, pansies, irises, gladiolus, castor beans, sunflowers, and rose and lilac bushes accented the lawn. Plantings of shrubs and trees further defined a coordinated landscaping plan. Connecting the upper and lower levels of lawn were stone stairs that extended down from the main lodge. Originally the lower level included an excavated 20-foot wide pond complete with a small island at the center. Evidently the pond or moat, as it was sometimes called, proved difficult to maintain or perhaps unnecessary with the beauty of Trout Lake only a few feet away. It was later filled in and converted to flower beds.

In 1922 the *Grand Rapids Herald Review* touted David Gage Joyce's estate on Trout

Lake as "one of the most soul inspiring recreation camps to be found between the two oceans."[10] Despite its more plebeian appearance, the Trout Lake imitation of the Adirondack Great Camps amazed those who saw it. In all, some fifty structures constituted the Joyce Estate, which cost more than $75,000. No other camp in northern Minnesota rivaled that of David Gage Joyce. The nine buildings of peeled, sandpapered, and shellacked logs emerged as works of art to a populace unfamiliar with luxury. Such unexpected comfort in a recently logged wilderness stood in contrast to the harsh and demanding experience of the average settler coming into Itasca County.

However impressive it was in northern Minnesota, the Joyce Estate was never able to fully duplicate the atmosphere of the Great Camps. The nearly flat topography of Minnesota did not resemble the rugged Adirondack Mountains. Although endowed with the most beautiful of lakes, Joyce's original 2,600-acre estate had been logged and ravaged by wildfire, and young second-growth hardwoods made for spindly forests behind his camp. Of the red and white pine, only a few slender trees on the point still prevailed. On the contrary, areas of virgin forests remained in the Adirondacks, protected in 1894 from logging by legislative action. (Article 14 of the New York State Constitution stipulates a "forever wild" policy for a portion of state lands within Adirondack State Park. It was instituted as a result of public outcry not only against the rapid and destructive logging practices that had nearly wiped out the "inexhaustible" forests of Upstate New York but also against the inept government management of the precursor to Adirondack State Park, the New York State Forest Preserve, created in 1885.)[11]

The Joyce Estate complex also fell short of the grand wilderness complexes of Upstate New York. Its rather small main lodge and cabins lacked the massive elements of eastern counterparts, and the characteristic fancy architectural stickwork was generally absent. Vacation cabins on the north end of Trout Lake, which preceded the Joyce Estate complex by more than a decade, outshined Nopeming, in terms of their decorative stickwork. Although Nopeming deserves the Great Camp designation, its status is that of poor country cousin to the wondrous Adirondack forest lodges.

The Joyce Estate Staff

In order to operate Nopeming, the Joyces hired local people as managers, caretakers, gardeners, cooks, workmen, and seasonal game wardens. For special occasions, butlers and maids arrived from Chicago. The manager oversaw finances and personnel while the caretaker, who lived year round on the estate, maintained security and supervised work on the grounds and buildings. During the estate's fifty-five years of use, a significant fraction of the surrounding population worked for the Joyce family in some capacity.

David Gage Joyce gleaned some of the skilled men that were needed to run his estate from the employees of his declining businesses in Deer River. Joyce enlisted S. D. Patrick, the man who had acquired the Joyce Estate land and supervised the estate's construction, as the first manager. Patrick had worked for the Joyces in northern Minnesota since about 1892, originally employed as a surveyor and timber estimator for both the Itasca Lumber Company and the Minneapolis and Rainy River Railway.[12] When logging operations declined, he headed the land department for the Itasca Lumber Company, selling cutover lands with the assistance of fellow employee David Zetterstrom. Patrick served as manager for the estate until his death in September 1935.

David Zetterstrom, the second manager, had moved from Minneapolis to Deer River in 1910 to work for the Itasca Lumber Company. He quickly advanced from sorting and grading lumber to upper management. As Joyce logging operations ended in northern Minnesota, the talented Zetterstrom could have transferred to an executive position at any of the Joyce companies around the country, but he preferred to keep his home in Deer River. When S. D. Patrick died, Zetterstrom assumed the role of estate manager, a position he retained until failing health forced him to retire in 1947. He died in 1948.

Management of the estate then remained in the Joe Waleski Sr. family until the estate was sold in 1974. Joe Waleski Sr. started working for the Joyces at the Itasca Lumber Company sawmill in 1918, producing lath during the final years before the mill closed in 1921. After the mill shut down, Waleski Sr. moved to Grand Rapids to find work. He tried several jobs, working in a veneer mill and the Blandin Paper Company mill and then as a police officer before Joyce hired him as a part-time general laborer and patrolman along the property boundary at Nopeming. Around 1940 he assumed the role of caretaker. He replaced Zetterstrom as manager in 1947, still retaining his position as caretaker. In 1968 Waleski Sr. retired from both positions.

Joe Waleski Jr. first visited the estate at age eight or nine during the late 1920s. He spent two days working with his dad at the end of September, cutting and stacking firewood, draining pipes, and doing other winterizing tasks. In 1951, after being self-employed for many years, Waleski Jr. was hired to maintain the golf course. He also helped his father with the duties of manager until Waleski Sr. relinquished that position. At that point Waleski Jr. became the natural replacement. He set up an office in 1968 in what had previously been the powerhouse, traveling seven days a week to Nopeming from his home in Grand Rapids. Shortly after the death of Beatrice Joyce Kean in 1972, Joe Waleski Jr. gave up his managerial position.

The first regular caretaker at Nopeming was a familiar Wabana area resident, Ernie Poland, who lived at the estate from 1919 through 1921 or 1922.[13] Poland had been a logging camp foreman years earlier in the Trout Lake area with a camp on Doan Lake, at one time called Poland Lake. When the logging era ended, Poland guided sportsmen and maintained a ferry service on the Wabana chain of lakes and, during the Joyce Estate construction, carried supplies and people from Taylor's Landing on Wabana Lake to the building site. Impressed by his service, David Gage Joyce hired Poland as caretaker.

After Poland moved on, the Joyces hired a series of short-term caretakers until Charlie and Adeline Pearson settled at Nopeming from 1928 until 1932. The young couple brought their wedding present from Charlie's father with them, a cow that supplied milk for the estate, but they decided after only a year that taking care of the cow was too time-consuming and sent her back to Charlie's father. The senior Mr. Pearson, who not only kept dairy cows but also ran a resort on nearby Sand Lake, then supplied milk, butter, and cream daily to the estate.

Charlie Pearson regularly traveled to Grand Rapids for supplies, groceries, and the semi-weekly laundry drop-off and pick-up. The round trip took all day. Pearson boated the first two miles from the estate to Joyce's steel garage at the south bay of Trout Lake, docked the boat, and drove the truck to town. After purchasing groceries and other supplies, he hauled them back in the truck to the steel garage, loaded them onto the boat, and motored back to the estate. Pearson walked part way to town in the winter or drove across the frozen lake, which made travel both risky and difficult. At spring ice breakup, when neither the lake nor the roads could be counted on, the Pearsons were sometimes stranded at Nopeming.

Adeline Pearson's duties included housekeeping and cooking. She cleaned the cabins and main lodge, dusting the game mounts and washing down the log walls before the arrival of the Joyces and after their departure. During the peak season she devoted much of her day to food preparation for the hired help. The chauffeur, game warden, gardener, golf course manager, laborer Anton Hagelee, and an occasional other employee ate with the Pearsons. Estate manager S. D. Patrick and his wife also stopped for a meal when they visited Nopeming, as did David Zetterstrom. According to Adeline Pearson, her grocery stipend of one dollar per day generously sufficed in the late 1920s and early 1930s when a loaf of bread cost ten cents.

Mrs. Pearson's duties left her with little free time, unlike her husband who experienced slack periods during the workday. On one occasion Mrs. Pearson was returning from the garden with vegetables for the next meal, when she heard a loud pounding noise coming from the boathouse as she walked by. Since she could not imagine what her husband was doing, she opened the door and saw Charlie standing by the workbench, gazing out the window at the water as he furiously hammered the bare bench top. Chauffeur Bill Ralston slept in the boat a few feet away. The two men were frustrated by too little to do and wanted to avoid angering David Gage Joyce with their idleness. Adeline Pearson concluded, "As long as David Joyce heard noise, he would not come around."

The Pearsons were replaced in 1932 by Nels and Vi Olson, who spent the next decade at the estate. Like a number of other employees at Nopeming, Nels Olson began his service with the Joyces in Deer River. He worked as freight agent on the Minneapolis and Rainy River Railway, as secretary to the general manager, and finally as depot agent. In the waning months of the M&R's existence, Olson sold passenger tickets, managed the freight, and loaded the mail on the train before he closed the depot, boarded the train, collected the tickets that he had just sold to the passengers, and remained on board for the round trip to Craig and Wirt. The last M&R train rolled to a stop in 1932, putting Olson out of a job until Joyce offered him the position at the estate. Olson gratefully accepted because of the uncertainty of making a living during the depression years. The Joyce Estate job did not pay well, but it did provide room and board, a car, and gas.

An annual task for the caretaker was the winter ice harvest that occurred around the first of each year when the ice was fifteen or more inches thick. In the 1930s caretaker Nels Olson and employee Joe Waleski Sr. worked by hand with ice saws for several days in order to complete the task. By the 1940s a crew of eight or ten men could retrieve enough ice in a single day for the following summer season. Using a motor-driven circular saw, the crew cut a field of ice into sixteen-by-thirty-two-inch blocks, each weighing 150 pounds. These were broken out one at a time with a long steel bar and hauled up on the lake surface with ice tongs. Wearing ice cleats called creepers strapped to their boots to keep them from slipping, the men slid each ice block to the edge of the lake, where they used a block and tackle to pull the ice up the wooden chute into the icehouse. Each block of ice was then insulated with snow to keep it from freezing to its neighbor. Afterward the crew insulated the entire group of ice blocks with sawdust. The tradition of harvesting ice continued even after rural electrification reached Nopeming because the Joyces preferred the transparent lake ice. Every day a hired hand toted a chunk of ice from the icehouse to the kitchen, where it was chipped to cool beverages.

One of the few guests that Nels Olson and his wife entertained in the caretaker quarters at the Joyce Estate was Marion Brown, a close childhood friend from Deer River, who, like Olson, served on the last M&R train crew. Brown had been hired by a fuel distribution business after the abandonment of the railroad and sold gasoline and fuel oil to the Joyces on occasion. According to Brown, "I never had better friends than Nels and Vi Olson. . . . We [Marion Brown and his wife] used to go out there on Saturday nights and play poker. They could not leave at night. They had to stay out there. The maid, the butler, and chauffeur would play poker with us too. The butler used to make mint juleps for us. Fred [Grenogh, the gardener,] grew the mint."

Mr. and Mrs. Olson briefly left the estate to attend the Chicago World's Fair in 1934. During this time, when the nation was still recovering from the depression, David Gage Joyce gave the Olsons fifty dollars for the fair, which, of course, was a lot of money in those days. In the evenings the domestic servants at Joyce's Chicago home treated them to the excitement of city life.

Eight years later Olson left Nopeming because Beatrice Rudolph Joyce refused his request for a raise. She "used to tell me" he explained, "that she could not afford to pay me more." This seemed absurd to Olson, who had worked so many years for the wealthy Joyce family.

Joe Waleski Sr. acted as caretaker from 1942 until 1968. Two caretakers followed Joe Waleski Sr. John Johnson and his wife, Irja, remained at the estate until 1974, the year Nopeming was sold to the United States Forest Service. Replacing the Johnsons, George Baker and his wife lived on the grounds until 1986. After that time the property no longer had a caretaker.

Getting There

David Gage Joyce established his annual pattern of visiting northern Minnesota in 1917. At first he journeyed by train from Chicago, but Joyce abandoned train travel in favor of driving his Deusenberg or Crane-Simplex when sturdier automobiles and better roads permitted the change. He devoted a minimum of sixteen hours to the trip. After arriving in Grand Rapids, Joyce took the precursor to Highway 38, a gravel road running north out of town to the Wabana road, from which he could reach Wakeman Bay of Wabana Lake. He parked his auto in a small garage on property purchased on this bay and waited for one of his employees, who, by prior arrangement, was scheduled to pick him up at his private boat landing and take him to the lodge.

In October 1925 David Gage Joyce acquired 1,900 acres adjoining the Joyce Estate from Thomas and Luella Simmons. The property encompassed Moore Lake, just south of Trout Lake. This acquisition allowed Joyce to build another boat landing on the bay of Trout Lake across from the hilltop home of estate employee Anton Hagelee. The move cut four miles from the overwater commute. At the new landing Joyce put up a larger six-stall steel garage and connected the garage site to his private telephone system. Joyce could now call the estate from the garage to request that one of his employees boat the two miles to meet him.

David Gage Joyce and his wife in front of the lodge in 1923. JOE WALESKI PRIVATE COLLECTION

Weather permitting, David Gage Joyce preferred to drive directly to the estate rather than leave his vehicle at the six-stall steel garage. If the trail was dry, it was possible to reach Nopeming from either the south or the north by taking the old Bigfork Trail segment along the western shore of Trout Lake. In 1935 three miles of the Bigfork Trail on estate property was reconstructed by Joyce to provide reliable road access to the estate from the south. After the road improvement, the garage was removed from the bay of Trout Lake and reassembled at the caretaker's compound. Joyce's rebuilding of his three-mile long driveway through the hilly terrain around Trout Lake quite impressed at least one young man. Dr. Bill Downing, who still summers on Wabana Lake, exclaimed, "Everyone was just agog that they had built the road."[14]

Social Life

David Gage Joyce traded the fast pace and humidity of Chicago for the tranquility and cooler temperatures of his northern Minnesota estate from Memorial Day through Labor Day. Throughout the summer the Joyces sent a steady stream of invitations to friends from many walks of life. Employees from Illinois, nationally known celebrities, and local friends alike visited Nopeming to trap shoot, fish, golf, boat, swim, and play croquet at the Joyce Estate.

The first visitor to the Joyce Estate was Beatrice Rudolph Eshe, wife of David Gage Joyce's chauffeur, Edward Eshe. In September 1917 she accompanied Mrs. Roberta Acuff Joyce to Nopeming to view the fall colors.[15] Sometime between 1918 and 1922 Mrs. Eshe became the second Mrs. David Gage Joyce. What happened to Mrs. Roberta Acuff Joyce is not known, but some details about the former chauffeur and husband of the second Mrs. Joyce exist. Edward Eshe visited the estate in the 1950s after both Mr. and Mrs. Joyce had died. Eshe worked for Victoria Motors in Detroit. At least twice he traveled from Michigan to Minnesota, ostensibly on business, for a stay at Nopeming. He planned to sell the Joyces' daughter, Beatrice, who had inherited Nopeming, a new car. He was successful in the sale of a Dodge Power Wagon to Beatrice; he sold a DeSoto that he had hoped to sell to her to Bobby Dahl, a Grand Rapids resident.

David Gage Joyce collected a remarkable library of first edition books.
JOE WALESKI PRIVATE COLLECTION

Both of David Gage Joyce's wives would have known Mrs. Frank Hudnell, caretaker for the Joyce hunting lodge in Illinois. Which one welcomed her to the Joyce Estate as another early guest is unclear. The record of her visit appeared in the local newspaper— Hudnell passed a pleasant week at Nopeming, expressing her keenness for northern Minnesota, "especially its clear lakes and excellent bathing."[16]

David Gage Joyce's brother Stanley was not a stranger to northern Minnesota. In July 1918, with the estate still in its construction phase, Stanley drove his new Cadillac to Nopeming with corporate attorney Frank Leffingwell for several days of relaxation. On other occasions he accompanied his mother Clotilde Gage Joyce to the estate. Stanley also came up in October after his brother had departed for Chicago and Miami. He ate with the caretakers and entertained himself, perhaps imagining a place of his own across the water from Nopeming.

The Joyces entertained celebrities as well as trusted employees and family members. One of the celebrities was Damon Runyon, a famous war correspondent in Mexico from 1912 to 1916 and in Europe during World War I. Runyon was one of the highest paid writers in New York City during the 1930s. His prolific writing career included *Guys and Dolls*. Published in 1931, the collection of stories was the basis for the 1950 Broadway musical.

Damon Runyon and David Gage Joyce loved the written word and were both book collectors. Runyon's collection of 700 books on the subject of World War I probably grew out of his work as a journalist in Europe during the war. He gave this collection to David

Gage Joyce, who later donated it to the Grand Rapids Public Library in 1929. Originally the books were housed together in a separate section of the library as the "David Gage Joyce War Library." Currently the books are shelved under the topic of World War I. Runyon's books did not fit Joyce's collecting interests, which might have been the reason for the donation. Joyce specialized in rare first-edition books by famous authors, some of which he kept in his study at Nopeming for his personal reading.

No other information has survived about Damon Runyon's vacation at Nopeming with the exception of a favorite story retold by estate manager Joe Waleski Jr., whose father was living at the estate at the time of Runyon's visit. One summer when Damon Runyon and Barney Oldfield, a national celebrity and record-setting race-car driver, were both guests at the estate, they teamed up for a fishing expedition. Runyon hooked a large fish that he finally managed to bring to the side of the boat. While Runyon struggled to land his catch, Oldfield came to his aid by shooting at the fish with his Buffalo Bill revolver. Oldfield missed the fish but managed to hit the fishing line, allowing the fish to escape.

National racing icon Barney Oldfield and his wife were frequent guests at Nopeming.
JOE WALESKI PRIVATE COLLECTION

Damon Runyon's trips to Nopeming attracted little attention, but the activities of his fishing partner, the flamboyant Barney Oldfield—portrayed in *Car and Driver* magazine as one of America's most celebrated men in the years preceding World War I— elicited regular coverage in the Grand Rapids newspaper.[17] Oldfield was the first race-car driver to break the sixty-mile-per-hour record, and, more than any other man, he popularized the infant sport of motor racing. His first racing machine, Henry Ford's legendary 999, was little more than an engine on wheels. This 1902 car lacked a body shell, an engine cowling, and even a steering wheel (using instead a tiller), but it carried him past the sixty-mile-per-hour mark on June 20, 1903.

David Joyce had admired Oldfield's racing bravado for years and even offered to buy him a sports car late in his career. William Nolan, author of *Barney Oldfield: The Life and Times of America's Legendary Speed King*, recorded a conversation between the two men at a 1915 Frank Barrieau-Jack Collins boxing match, during which Joyce made the offer:

"'I hear your contract with Maxwell expired,' said Joyce.

'Yeah,' sighed Barney. 'I got this here Bugatti that Hill brought back, but it's slow as hell. George drove it at Indy and the boys went by him like he was tied to a brick house. George tried to pick up a Mercedes for me overseas, but you know—with the war on he couldn't swing it.'

'The French cars seem to be cleaning up,' Joyce observed. 'Tell you what, Barney—I'll just *buy* you one of 'em as a birthday present. How about a Delage?'

'But, Dave, my birthday was five months ago!'

'So, who's counting the days? You want the Delage or don't you?'

'Damn right I do!'

'Then you've *got* one.'"

Unfortunately for Oldfield, noted Nolan, "the new Delage proved to be the most unsuccessful car Barney ever drove." It was nicknamed the "jinx car," possibly because of its frustrating mechanical problems. It never captured an important race.[18]

In late July 1918 Barney Oldfield and his wife arrived from Los Angeles to spend several weeks at the Joyce Estate.[19] Oldfield "is now taking a little rest from his worries of the racing game," reported the July 31, 1918 *Grand Rapids Herald Review*, "and is catching a few bass which inhabit the lakes of this section, and needless to say he is finding fishing as interesting though not as strenuous a sport as auto racing."

After a week or so of the quiet fishing life at Nopeming, Oldfield and Joyce amused themselves by driving Joyce's Cadillac to the Twin Cities. On the return trip the duo burned up the road, reaching Brainerd "in three and one-half hours," but on the way from Brainerd to Grand Rapids, "they were delayed by blowouts or a record of all-time would have been set." The August 7, 1918 *Grand Rapids Herald Review* went on to exclaim,

"Two men more capable of setting speed records could not be found." Joyce and Oldfield toured the United States from time to time, taking in the Indianapolis 500, Daytona, and state fairs.[20]

During Barney Oldfield's stays at the estate, he and David Gage Joyce frequented the golf course and Ogema Hotel on Pokegama Lake. At the hotel they attended the picnics sponsored by Grand Rapids merchants throughout the summer months that drew families to pie-eating

Special events at the Ogema Hotel on Pokegama Lake always drew large crowds. David Joyce and Barney Oldfield were often seen mingling with the locals. JOE WALESKI PRIVATE COLLECTION

contests, children's races, steamboat rides on the lake, and sporting events. Barney Oldfield was the sought-after referee for the softball games between the young ladies of Grand Rapids and the surrounding communities.

Perhaps some of Barney Oldfield's daredevil, competitive style rubbed off on David Gage Joyce. In an age before highway speed limits, Joyce attempted to break his own personal travel times whenever he could. He and Al Wellein, who sometimes stored Joyce's cars in Grand Rapids, went on a few noteworthy junkets that were related in the Grand Rapids paper. "Dave Joyce and Al Wellein returned on Saturday from a three days' trip to the Twin Cities and Red Wing [Minnesota]. They made the trip in Mr. Joyce's Crane-Simplex car and according to Al's story, they made a fast trip. Among other things they passed the Winnipeg Flier, which ran parallel to the road for a considerable distance."[21] Although it was quite a feat for the men to outpace the speeding train along the stretch of dirt road, Joyce and Wellein not long after "broke all speed records on their way to Duluth. . . . From the Pokegama Hotel [in Grand Rapids] to Superior Street in Duluth in two hours flat, a distance of 84 miles."[22]

In July 1922 the Joyces left Nopeming to motor through Yellowstone, Glacier, and Banff National Parks in their Crane-Simplex before turning south at the West Coast to explore Los Angeles and San Diego. If the weather was inclement, David Gage and Beatrice Rudolph Joyce and Elita Eshe, Mrs. Joyce's daughter by her previous marriage, deserted the car to catch the train while the chauffeur drove to a predetermined destination. The Crane-Simplex, which carried an extra large tank of gas in reserve, was a convertible sedan with canvas and celluloid side curtains. It dwarfed other automobiles of the day. The vehicle was peculiar by today's standards, for it delivered power to the wheels through a chain drive. The open chain and sprockets had to be cleaned regularly and required constant oiling by hand. Later models of the auto enclosed the chain drive to protect it from road dust. Joyce joked that he kept the chain exposed so that the chauffeur had something to do.

Joyce's fervor for the automobile and his inclination as a collector led to several notable additions to his fleet of cars. Besides a Crane-Simplex and a Deusenberg, he owned a Delage, a Cadillac, a Reo Flying Cloud, and a Packard. He later purchased a Chrysler Airflow in 1934 at the Chicago World's Fair, a car for which Barney Oldfield was a spokesman.

Trap shooting and gun collecting were other hobbies that Joyce shared with some of his guests. Twice a month all summer they shot clay pigeons on the trap range south of the golf course. Cavour and Guilford Hartley, heirs to a mining fortune, drove over to trapshoot from their neighboring estate. H. D. Powers, who owned Powers Hardware in Grand Rapids, and Jess Anthony, a terrific local trapshooter, arrived from town. Joyce also traveled 100 miles

David Gage Joyce kept several boats at his estate on Trout Lake. JOE WALESKI PRIVATE COLLECTION

David Gage is waiting to board the train to Chicago at the Grand Rapids depot. Standing closest to the parked automobile, Joyce is facing the train. JOE WALESKI PRIVATE COLLECTION

south to Breezy Point Resort for trapshooting (and socializing with his friend Captain Billy Fawcett, who owned the resort and Fawcett Publications. Fawcett's humorous and slightly risqué *Whiz Bang* magazine sold a half million copies per month in the 1920s.)

In 1938 a probate inventory for Joyce's gun collection listed "over thirty shotguns, rifles, and revolvers." One of these firearms was disguised as a walking cane, more a collector's item and conversation piece than a weapon. Sometimes in Chicago Joyce carried the unusual walking cane that camouflaged a .410 shotgun. By turning the cane handle ninety degrees, he could load a .410 shell and cock the trigger mechanism. After he returned the cane handle to its original position and removed a brass thimble-like cap at the base of the cane, the gun was ready to shoot. (During the 1960s, two estate employees, manager Joe Waleski Jr. and pilot Bud Daniels, mounted this gun on the dock, attached a forty-foot string to the trigger, and yanked the string. Pellets from the .410 shell fanned out over the lake. By firing the gun, the men assuaged their curiosity about the effectiveness and potential danger of the weapon.)

The Joyces' Annual Calendar

Labor Day marked the end of summer for David Gage Joyce. He and his wife left Nopeming for their Chicago apartment, located across the street from the Drake Hotel and within walking distance of downtown. Fall duck-hunting season enticed Joyce and sometimes his wife to leave the apartment for their hunting camp on the Illinois River. Joyce had purchased the Illinois camp, situated south of Peoria between Bath and Havana, from Mr. and Mrs. Frank Hudnell and had hired them to stay on as caretakers. After a successful shoot the Joyces returned to Chicago. David's favorite butcher dressed out the ducks, most of which were delivered as gifts to his friends.

The Joyces wintered at their Miami mansion, called Bon Aire, which was located on Biscayne Bay's prestigious Brickell Avenue. Next door was Louis Comfort Tiffany, whose father owned Tiffany Jewelry in New York. Arthur Brisbane, the highest-paid United States newspaper editor of his day, shared this exclusive neighborhood with the Joyces, as did the Wrigleys of Wrigleys Chewing Gum, who were close friends. Brickell Avenue carried the nickname of Millionaires' Row.

When business called, Joyce commuted to his Chicago offices or to the family-owned sawmills in Louisiana, but there was still plenty of time to enjoy himself at Bon Aire. He fished, swam in his private pool and in the ocean, photographed, and socialized. During the day David Gage Joyce took advantage of his ocean setting to catch sailfish from his thirty-eight-foot yacht named the *B. C.* (Beatrice C.) for his daughter. He and his brother Stanley, who owned a yacht christened *The White Cap*, shared a captain. At night Joyce went to the Miami clubs.

David Gage Joyce's appetite for entertainment seemed boundless. One morning after Joyce had been at a club until 7 a.m., he directed his chauffeur Bill Ralston to drive him to the airport. According to Ralston, Joyce "charted a plane and we flew to Havana, Cuba." Following a haircut and a shave, Joyce bought "drinks for breakfast" for the pilot, the co-pilot, the chauffeur, and himself. He also purchased Panama hats with a price tag of $125 apiece for each of them before the men flew back to Miami.[23]

As Florida grew warmer during the spring months, the Joyces boarded their private car on the Illinois Central and returned to Chicago. Right after Memorial Day weekend, they continued on to Nopeming. David Gage Joyce kept up his rotation of residences until the summer of 1936. He died the following August from a heart attack at the age of 52. Possibly contributing to his early death was his alcoholism and his fast living.

An Astounding Collection

Decades after his death, an astounding collection came to light that indicated another facet of Joyce's personality. He was a serious collector of literary works and papers. In late September 1973 David Gage Joyce's literary and letter collection was auctioned in Chicago. The *Des Moines Register*, dated October 7, 1973, recorded the event in detail.[24]

Three hundred ninety-eight pieces of literature and letters sold for $896,000. Famous correspondence by George Washington, Abraham Lincoln, and poet Lord Byron accompanied original manuscripts by Alfred Lord Tennyson, Mark Twain, Conan Doyle,

Henry Wadsworth Longfellow, James Fennimore Cooper, Edgar Allen Poe, Oscar Wilde, Robert Louis Stevenson, Harriet Beecher Stowe, Percy Bysshe Shelley, and Robert Browning among others. "A New York dealer was quoted in the *Register* as saying, 'In my 48 years in the business, this is the greatest sale. With the supreme quality of the material, there's never been anything like it.'"

The fact that no one realized David Gage Joyce was amassing these manuscripts generally surprised the dealers at the Chicago auction who couldn't even speculate about his sources for these treasures. No one knew when or why Joyce collected or how much he paid for the items. The *Register* stated that a "Chicago dealer in 1909 bought the manuscript of *The Sign of the Four*, a Sherlock Holmes novel by Conan Doyle, for $105 and presumably he immediately turned it over to Joyce." Sixty-three years later, the novel fetched $51,000, the best price for a single work mentioned in the article about the auction in the Des Moines newspaper.

Other auction favorites sold for fabulous amounts as well. Reported the *Register*, "A George Washington letter to Patrick Henry, said to be the best Washington letter in existence, brought $37,000. In the letter Washington turned down Henry's offer of a share of the financial action in a river navigation project. A Lincoln letter discussing his outlook in the 1860 election yielded $15,000; a first edition of Poe's 'Murders in the Rue Morgue,' $20,000; another Washington letter, $25,000. The Lord Byron letter, saying goodbye to his wife, brought $17,000. The manuscript of *The White Company*, another Conan Doyle book, sold for $30,000."

The auctioned autographed manuscripts attracted significant price tags too. *The Way We Live* by Anthony Trollope captured $45,000. James Fennimore Cooper's *The Pathfinder* received $34,000; Thomas Hardy's *The Distracted Young Preacher*, $19,000; and Charles Dickens' *The Best Authority*, $13,500.

The collection had remained in the hands of David Gage Joyce's only child, Beatrice Joyce Kean, tucked away in her downtown Chicago apartment for thirty-six years. It was not until after her death that her father's literary interests were revealed to the public. The proceeds from the auction flowed into the family charitable foundation.

Stanley Joyce

DAVID GAGE JOYCE CULTIVATED A DIVERSE PERSONAL LIFE that featured fast living, literary interests, and famous friends. In contrast, brother Stanley, a Yale graduate, was reserved. He stayed in the background, except for one spectacular event that, much to his discomfort, thrust him into the national spotlight for a short time. This was his brief marriage to Ziegfeld Follies girl, Peggy Hopkins, considered to be one of the most beautiful women in the world in the 1920s. In her book *Gold Digger: The Outrageous Life and Times of Peggy Hopkins Joyce*, Constance Rosenblum characterized Stanley. His "shortcomings were painfully obvious, both to him and to everyone who knew him. He wasn't especially handsome, and his employees back in Chicago found him taciturn, uncomfortable around people, and standoffish to the point of rudeness. Hardly a ladies' man, he had few friends of either sex, and he suffered especially by comparison with his gregarious older brother David. As one of his employees said bluntly, 'Stanley was a man you had to know and had to know awful well to like a damn bit in the world.'"[1] In spite of his personality, Stanley was briefly married to the much sought-after Peggy Hopkins.

The story of Peggy Hopkins and the "rather shy"[2] Stanley Joyce began in Wood's Theater in Chicago in May 1919.[3] Peggy Hopkins was performing in *A Sleepless Night*, a short-lived Broadway production that had traveled to the Midwest. Hopkins noted Joyce's regular attendance at the show in her personal diary (later published with little editing as *Men Marriage and Me*.) "Talking about men there is one who sits in the front row every night wearing horn rim glasses. He does not laugh very much, only smiles and spends his time constantly looking at me. I have asked who he is but nobody seems to know." After having supper with the wealthy lumberman a few nights later, Hopkins described Joyce as "small and quite uninteresting, or rather unpresuming." When he offered to buy her a car, Joyce suddenly appeared "very dependable looking, not the sort of man likely to lose his head at all."[4]

Joyce convinced Hopkins to stay in Chicago for several weeks after the show closed by giving her a green emerald worth $20,000 and other baubles that only the very rich could afford. Then he asked her to marry him. "Of course," wrote Hopkins in her diary, "I said that was ridiculous I did not know him very well and besides I was married already."[5] In reality, Peggy Hopkins had been separated from her second husband, Sherburne Hopkins, for some time.

Hopkins eventually changed her mind, but it took approximately seven months for her to secure a divorce. During this time Joyce provided his future bride with an apartment in New York, a chauffeur, department-store charge accounts, and fifty-dollar bouquets of fresh flowers daily. Later he sent her and Ida Smart to Palm Beach, Florida, to await news of Peggy's divorce. (Ostensibly a "stage aunt," Smart served as a liaison between Hopkins and her many admirers both before and during her marriage to Joyce.) As soon as Stanley Joyce received the document, he drove from New York City to Palm Beach in two days.[6]

Peggy Hopkins' marriage to Stanley Joyce on January 23, 1920, "happened in the strangest way," according to her diary:

> "I was cycling down-town doing some shopping when a big car came up at
> terrific speed, I was so scared I fell off my bicycle.

"The car stopped and who came running back but Stanley!

"And I was all cut up and bruised and dirty and blood was streaming down my face, so Stanley carried me to the car and drove like lightning.

"I thought of course he was going back to the hotel or to a doctor's but instead he stopped at a Justice of the Peace and I gasped, 'Where are you taking me?'

"'To be married of course,' said Stanley.

"'But I can't be married like this,' I said.

Nevertheless, Stanley Joyce carried his soon-to-be bride into the office of the Justice of the Peace where they were married in spite of Joyce's dusty clothes and Hopkins' bruises.[7]

As a wedding present Joyce bought his bride a $250,000 mansion in Coconut Grove, Florida, near Brickell Avenue, the winter address of his brother. Next to the newlyweds lived one-time presidential hopeful William Jennings Bryan. Another well-known name in the neighborhood was John Deering of International Harvester, whose mansion was valued at $22 million.

When Peggy Joyce learned that John Deering kept monkeys on his estate, she decided to purchase some herself to play in the palms around her new marble swimming pool. "The monkeys smelled a little bit of course but really one can't have everything and they are so cute," wrote Peggy. Everyone agreed with her, she continued in her diary, "except David, Stanley's brother, and he laughed and said, 'Why don't you get some alligators and put them in the pool?' He is so silly sometimes."[8]

Stanley and Peggy Joyce left in the spring for Europe after she had acquired a few items for the trip in New York. Her purchases for the week, according to her husband's calculations, cost nearly three-quarters of a million dollars—$400,000 for jewelry, nearly $100,000 for clothes, and $200,000 for odds and ends.[9] Peggy Joyce was set for Paris.

Arriving in France in May 1920, the Joyces joined other rich Americans and Europeans whose sole purpose was to amuse themselves over the summer months. Peggy now mingled with the aristocratic and monied men of Europe, but Stanley's jealous reaction to the incessant flirtations and affairs Peggy carried on with numerous accommodating gentlemen provoked frequent arguments both in public and later in their hotel room. After weeks of watching his wife's dalliances, Stanley left her in Europe and returned to Chicago to sue for divorce.

Four thousand national news articles sensationalized the divorce proceedings that ended during the spring of 1921. Even the *New York Times* kept a newsman in the Chicago courtroom during the testimony. Stanley Joyce's short marriage to Peggy Hopkins was predictably expensive. An out-of-court divorce settlement gave Peggy Hopkins Joyce nearly a million dollars' worth of jewelry, two fur coats, a Rolls-Royce, and $80,000. This was in addition to the money Joyce lavished on her during their courtship and marriage.[10]

It's hardly possible that these two had had enough time to develop a deep and enduring love for each other. Joyce was infatuated with Peggy's beauty, and Peggy was infatuated with Joyce's money. Still, Peggy Hopkins Joyce's last comment about Stanley in her diary was tender. "In spite of all the heart aches he has caused me, I can't forget that Stanley was very good to me once. I suppose you never really stop completely loving anyone you once loved a lot."[11]

What has lived on after the divorce is a commonly told story—almost certainly myth—of Peggy's appearance at Cochran's Hotel on Wabana Lake. Stanley had brought his wife to northern Minnesota to see the land on neighboring Trout Lake, where he wanted to build a retreat comparable to his brother's. Carl Clippinger, a friend of the Ireton family who summered at the north end of Trout Lake, was at the hotel as well. According to Clippinger, Peggy Hopkins Joyce, dressed like a New York fashion model complete with a very expensive pair of lizard- or snake-skin pumps, sunk her heels into the soft sand at the water's edge. "With many words, which only the lumberjacks knew," said Clippinger, she insisted upon leaving immediately for Grand Rapids in order to catch the train to Chicago.[12]

Stanley Joyce never built a northwoods retreat. The logs cut for the lodge that was to be constructed across the lake from Nopeming were sold, and the land was never even cleared. Nonetheless, to this day some refer to the point across the lake from Nopeming as Peggy's Point.

Another less dramatic and less expensive marriage to Nellie Maize Vail in 1926 also failed for Stanley. Vail's divorce against Joyce pended from 1929 until his death in 1944, at which time she received $250,000 in exchange for relinquishing all further claim to his estate.[13]

THE JOYCE FOUNDATION

Beatrice Joyce Kean

NAMED AFTER HER MOTHER, Beatrice Rudolph, and paternal grandmother, Clotilde Gage, Beatrice Clotilde Joyce, nicknamed Bee Cee, was born on March 20, 1923. Her mother was 34. Her father, David Gage Joyce, was 38. Her half sister Elita, Mrs. Joyce's daughter by a previous marriage, was in her middle or late teens. The Joyces immediately hired a full-time nurse and later a governess to care for their daughter.[1] From the age of two or three, Bee Cee also played under the watchful eye of Joe Waleski Sr. during her summer months at Nopeming. The Joyces hired Waleski as a bodyguard, because local residents claimed that gangsters haunted northern Minnesota. A few even swore that John Dillinger had been sighted angling on the lakes in northern Itasca County. Around the time Beatrice turned eight, Charles Lindbergh's son, Charles Augustus Jr., was kidnapped and murdered, attracting international coverage and reinforcing the Joyces' fear for their daughter's safety.

The Joyces were also concerned for their own well-being. At night Joe Waleski Sr. slept on the porch of their cabin on two sawhorses notched out to support a mattress and springs. According to Joe Waleski Jr., "Dad carried a [Smith and Wesson .38] pistol. The rifle was close by. On the rifle he had an eight-cell flashlight mounted below the barrel, and he had a scope on top. The rifle was a German Mannlicher."

Parental fears and the isolation of Nopeming left Beatrice with few playmates until the Joyces discovered some young companions for their daughter through their local dentist, Dr. Albert Kean, and local doctor, Dr. Henry Binet. Dr. Kean's son Dudley, who became Beatrice's second husband, recounted, "David wanted a few [children] from Grand Rapids to come to the estate to play [with Beatrice]. So Maxine and Bill Binet and myself would go out to the estate from the age of about eight. It would just be for the day, and it would be a big treat to go out and ride in the boat. At that time there was a landing at Wabana, and the garages were there so we would get in the boat and go up to Trout Lake."

Other companions for Beatrice were the son and daughter of her half sister, Elita Mallers. Mallers and her husband traveled from Chicago to summer at the estate with their children. Although Beatrice probably welcomed playmates, she did not welcome her half sister, who chummed with their mother while a jealous Bee Cee looked on. Bee Cee and Elita remained distant throughout their lives.

Dr. Bill Downing, who first met Beatrice when she was about ten years old, maintained a casual acquaintanceship with her and her mother. As teenagers, he and his brothers paddled from their summer place on Wabana Lake to Nopeming on Trout Lake several times a season. "Mrs. Joyce would be down in her flower garden by the lakeshore working," Downing recalled, "and we would land and say, 'Hello Mrs. Joyce,' and she would say, 'Oh hello. Here you are again. Won't you come up and have some lemonade.'

And so we would get out of the canoe and go up to the lodge. . . . Bee Cee would appear if she was at the estate. She was not always there. Then we would all sit around and drink lemonade and chat."

Some nights after supper Beatrice Rudolph Joyce took ten-year-old Bee Cee fishing on Moore Lake, separated from Trout Lake by a narrow strip of land. The lake was nestled within the borders of Nopeming, two and one-half miles down the Joyces' dirt road from the lodge. Nels Olson, caretaker at Nopeming from 1932 to 1942, remembered Bee Cee and her mother catching "bass just as fast as they could throw the line in." The pair would come home with "an eight gallon can full of fish" that Joe Waleski Sr. filleted. The Joyces also enjoyed fishing the other small lakes on their property. Like Moore Lake, Day Lake sported a boathouse and boat for pan fishing and picnicking. Sprawling Spider Lake, part of which bordered the Joyce Estate, was accessible by following the remnant of the McAlpine logging road, probably first used as a Native American portage trail.

Bee Cee's idyllic-sounding childhood had a darker undercurrent. Her mother did not spend much time parenting, preferring instead to tend to her own interests, such as gardening. As Bee Cee approached her teenage years, her parents drifted apart. In fact, Beatrice and her mother came alone to Nopeming the year before her father died in 1937. During this time of estrangement and death, Beatrice moved to a cabin built especially for her near the tennis court, preferring privacy and solitude to the proximity of her mother. Initially her governess accompanied her.

David Gage Joyce's relationship with his daughter was strained by his frenetic lifestyle. He was preoccupied with business at his Chicago headquarters, commuting between Illinois and Minnesota during his summer months at Nopeming. When he was at the estate, he was engrossed with socializing, birding, photography, and reading. As a result, Joe Waleski Sr. served as a surrogate father during Bee Cee's summers at the estate, fostering a fondness between them that lasted until she died. Ellen Kean Rudolph, Beatrice's former sister-in-law, felt that Beatrice was closer to Joe Waleski Sr. than she was to any other person.

The lack of attention from her parents would have a lasting effect on Bee Cee's life.

She became a difficult child to manage. According to caretaker Nels Olson, Bee Cee was a domineering youngster, who had the personality of her father. "Bee Cee ruled the roost," recollected Olson. "She would give her folks a real going over." The estate staff were not exempt from Bee Cee's autocratic temperament either. One time after her mother had purchased a gray Ford convertible sedan for her, she invited Joe Waleski Sr. to join several of her Grand Rapids friends for a trip to Duluth. Pressing the accelerator to the floor, Beatrice drove as fast as the car would go all the way to the port city, terrifying Waleski, who excused himself from all future trips. As Beatrice grew older, her sense of being neglected by her parents contributed to depression and alcoholism.

Little is known about Beatrice's early education, although she did attend both private and public schools in Miami and possibly in Chicago. She transferred to Fermata Girls School in Aiken, South Carolina, after the death of her father in 1937. Originally a large family home, the estate had been converted into a residential finishing school. Equivalent to high school, Fermata enrolled thirty or forty students, eight or ten per grade level. Fermata Girls School lay in the midst of a region known for horse breeding and horse shows, and the school catered to young women with an interest in horses. Beatrice Joyce's best friend at Fermata, Cecelia Neville Dalsemer, had grown up on a horse farm in Lafayette, Indiana, and had ridden since she was very young. Beatrice was not much of a rider. Having grown up on the shores of Trout Lake and the Florida ocean-front, Bee Cee chose to be on the swim team, captained by her Indiana friend. Academically, Dalsemer said that Joyce favored art

Beatrice Joyce reclining on the floor of the Joyce Estate lodge in front of the fireplace about 1950. JOE WALESKI PRIVATE COLLECTION

over other curriculum offerings. She continued her oil painting after she left school.

Beatrice's friendship with Cecelia Dalsemer extended beyond finishing school. Sometime after the women had graduated from Fermata, Cecelia established a pattern of summer visits with Beatrice at Nopeming. Dalsemer recalled that Bee Cee

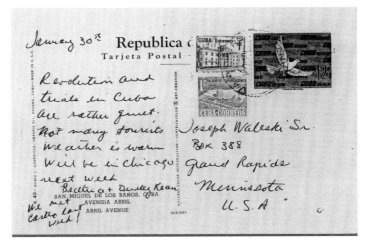

Beatrice and Dudley sent this postcard from Cuba. "Revolution and trials in Cuba are rather quiet. Not many tourists. Weather is warm. Will be in Chicago next week." They added the postscript, "We met Castro last week!" JOE WALESKI PRIVATE COLLECTION

still enjoyed swimming. She "would scare me to death because a couple of times she swam across the lake at night [a distance of approximately two-thirds mile one way]. I can remember being frightened that something was going to happen to her." Dalsemer's fear was warranted. Although Joyce was a strong swimmer, she could not be described as athletic. Beatrice reciprocated by traveling to Indiana to stay with Cecelia at the home of her parents. "She loved to visit my mother and father," said Dalsemer. Beatrice vacationed with Cecelia's family in Indiana even after her marriage to Dudley Kean.

The two women also spent some time together in Chicago. Beatrice's apartment "was fabulous," stated her finishing-school classmate. It was "filled with a lot of French antiques. A canopy bed in Beatrice's bedroom belonged to somebody like Marie Antoinette—that type of thing." Among the French antiques hung many famous artworks. Joyce owned two Diego Rivera prints, inscribed to her by the painter, an important twentieth-century muralist from Mexico. She also displayed a painting by Corot, a French Realist from the mid-nineteenth century, renowned for his landscapes. A wall-size Picasso decorated the foyer, impressing guests who stepped out of the elevator on the floor of her apartment.

Millionairess weds son of country doc

In a brief, simple ceremony in the County Building Saturday, an heiress to a $5,000,000 lumber fortune became the bride of an intern at the Passavant Hospital.

Attractive, brunette Beatrice Joyce, 25, of 233 E. Walton St., niece of the late James Stanley Joyce, multi-millionaire lumberman, was married to Dr. Dudley Kean, 25, son of a country doctor of Grand Rapids, Minn.

Judge U. S. Schwartz of the Superior Court performed the ceremony.

C. B. Bissel, attorney for the bride and a witness at the wedding, said the couple had been childhood sweethearts, despite the great gap in their family's financial and social standings.

Miss Joyce's family had a summer home in Grand Rapids, Minn., Bissel said, and had met young Kean on her vacation trips there.

It was the second marriage for Beatrice. In 1946 she was divorced from John D. Richardson, a naval officer.

Bissel said the newlyweds, who celebrated their nuptials with a private dinner in the Drake Hotel Saturday, and were planning a honeymoon in India.

After simple marriage ceremony, Dr. and Mrs. Dudley Kean receive friends at private party. Intern and heiress will honeymoon in India. (SUN-TIMES Photo)

JOE WALESKI PRIVATE COLLECTION

In 1948 Beatrice Joyce married Dr. Dudley Kean. The marriage lasted until approximately 1961. This conjecture is based on the fact that Dudley Kean's name disappeared from the Itasca Lumber Company's list of officers and board of directors that year. For the previous decade he had acted as both president of the company and a member of the board. Beatrice and Dudley stayed in touch throughout her life. A letter from former Joyce employee John P. Gregg informing Joe Waleski Jr. of Beatrice's death in 1972 suggested that they were thinking of remarrying just before she died.

This was Beatrice's second marriage. Beatrice was only a year or two out of finishing school when she married her first husband, John Richardson, a naval officer and heir to the Sawyer Biscuit Company. Their marriage took place sometime prior to 1944. She divorced him in 1946.

Heiress to a Business Empire

Beatrice lost all of her close family members when she was still a very young woman. In 1937, when she was fourteen years old, her father died at the age of fifty-two. Three years after his death, Beatrice's grandmother, Clotilde Gage Joyce, died in 1940 at the age of seventy-two. (Grandfather William Joyce had died in 1909 when he was forty-nine.) Stanley Joyce, Beatrice's uncle and her father's only sibling, died childless in 1944 at the age of fifty-seven, the year Bee Cee turned twenty-one. Beatrice's mother died in 1948 at the age of fifty-nine. Other than her half sister, Elita Mallers, for whom she felt no affection, Bee Cee had no siblings. At twenty-five, Beatrice was the last living Joyce.

Beatrice Clotilde Joyce was the first female born into the Joyce family in 100 years. Unlike the men in the generations before her, she was not groomed to take over the Joyce lumber concerns. She was sent to a finishing school, whereas the Joyce men had traditionally been trained in the field. Some also had supplemented their fieldwork with formal education. Beatrice's grandfather, William Joyce, had been sent to Shattuck, a preparatory school in Faribault, Minnesota, and later to Chicago for "an academic training" before being taken into the lumber companies.[2] Her father, David Gage Joyce, joined the family operations immediately, but her uncle, Stanley Joyce, graduated from Sheffield Scientific School at Yale University first. Although Beatrice absorbed some business clues from her father and her uncle while she was growing up, she had to rely on company executives for guidance as she sought to understand the complexity of the Joyce enterprises for which she was suddenly responsible.

Rather than shrinking from the demands of running the lumber conglomerate, however, Beatrice maneuvered her way into the Joyce companies. Al Smith, general manager of the Tremont and Gulf Railroad, remembered attending a meeting with Beatrice in 1946 at the Tremont Lumber Company offices in Winnfield, Louisiana. Tremont Lumber Company was the most important Joyce enterprise operating during Beatrice's life. By 1952 she had replaced John P. Gregg, originally from Blackduck, Minnesota, as president of six Joyce-owned ventures, including Tremont. After she became president of Tremont, her husband, Dr. Dudley Kean, whom she had married in 1948, flew to Louisiana six or seven times a year to check on company operations for his wife. Sometimes Beatrice accompanied him. On one of these trips, thirty-year-old Beatrice Joyce Kean changed company history by intervening in the yearlong strike of 1952–1953.

Gene Turner, who started working for Tremont in 1966 as comptroller, minerals manager, and director of oil and gas operations, related the story about this strike in an interview. "The strikers set fire to a bunch of stuff," said Turner, repeating the information recorded in the company ledgers. "There was a fire department, but the firemen would not cross the picket line with the fire hose. Beatrice grabbed the fire hose herself and walked across the picket lines, and she dared them to lay a hand on her! When Beatrice crossed the line and got away with it, some of the other management people decided that if they wanted to keep their job, they had better cross the line too. . . . So Beatrice got the full credit for breaking the strike, because she is the one that took the initiative and got it done."

Turner was also able to offer some insights into Beatrice Joyce Kean's business style, which differed dramatically from his own. As a businessman, he valued making a profit while Kean, who had all the money she was going to need for the rest of her life, focused on accumulating assets. "She was looking for asset management rather than revenue generation, [but] she had a hard time convincing her managers and other people of that. Rather than cut her own trees, she would cut other people's trees and let her trees grow for capital appreciation. . . . Tremont had a bunch of real ripe mature timber that should have really been cut for better growth. It did not make sense business-wise to let those old trees that were thirty to sixty years old go uncut. Their growth per year was nothing compared to a ten-to-twelve-year-old pine tree. But Beatrice would have no part of that. She was just not interested in paying taxes. . . . Was she a good businessperson? I don't know that she was necessarily a great business manager. I just think that she knew what she wanted to do as far as capital appreciation and she did a good job of staying focused on the task."

After business hours, Beatrice Joyce Kean preferred to mingle with the management rather than with their wives. Remarked Turner, "When we would get together socially, the men and women would form separate groups for discussion, but Beatrice was not interested in talking to the women. She wanted to talk business with the men. Beatrice could sit in a room with four or five conversations going on around her, and she could monitor every conversation that was going on plus keep up a conversation of her own. She had a tremendous ear for listening to other people's ideas and comments. She was a person that made up her own mind. She was very independent and strong willed."

Turner believed that Kean generally employed knowledgeable people "and she pretty much let them run the business except for the three or four times a year when she wanted to play president. As long as the management followed her overall objectives and goals, there was no problem, but if you did not, then you would hear from her." Beatrice, however, didn't always put business first. She was "a big fan of the Chicago hockey team," continued Turner. "I remember we would have a hard time having a meeting while the Chicago hockey team was playing, because Beatrice would have one eye on what was happening in the game."

While Beatrice attended to the business of Tremont Lumber Company, she also inspected her southern pine, cypress, mahogany, and cedar forests, the primary source of her fortune. Dr. and Mrs. Kean generally traveled by small aircraft to visit her southern pine and cypress forests in Louisiana, and each spring Dudley and Beatrice flew to Mexico, Guatemala, and Panama to negotiate for mahogany in order to keep the Louisiana Cypress Lumber Company sawmill from shutting down and the community of Ponchatoula, Louisiana, from becoming a ghost town. The company was predicted to exhaust its supply of the slow-growing cypress in 1957, necessitating the switch to mahogany. There was another forest as well in Canada. Beatrice's grandfather, William Joyce, had acquired timberland, primarily cedar stands, near Revelstoke, British Columbia. Both William Joyce and his sons, David and Stanley, had offered to sell these holdings, but no buyer would meet their price. As of December 29, 1951, the unharvested "600 million feet of cedar, spruce, and fir" was still expanding annually, demanding the attention of the Keans.[3]

According to Dudley Kean, many people who met Beatrice or knew of her as the owner of the vast retreat on Trout Lake were unaware of the magnitude of her business responsibilities. They assumed she was not involved in Joyce business affairs, since she summered at Nopeming. Kean said this was not the case. "Contrary to what people think in Itasca County, Beatrice worked. She had an office and she went there every day when she was in Chicago. She did not sit around."

Beatrice Joyce survived in a male-dominated business world during an era when few women secured an executive position, much less the presidency of a firm. "You would be hard put to name another female in corporate America at that time that had the holdings Beatrice had who was as much in charge of them as she was," emphasized Dr. Ellen Kean Rudolph, Beatrice's former sister-in-law and a practicing psychologist. "You have to continually remember her era, which was extremely male in that corporate zone in particular. And she functioned very well in spite of it. In spite of the fact that her family did not educate her in the business, she learned and understood every aspect of it. Probably more than anything she ever said to me, she said, 'When you go to college, you major in business. You're going to need to know that stuff.' She said that to me for years and years. Which meant, 'I had a really hard time of it [in the family business]. Don't let that happen to you [in the business world].'"

Beatrice remained active in her enterprises at least until the last years of her life, when her health was failing, according to Alvin Huss, stockholder in both the Tremont Lumber Company and the Louisiana Cypress Lumber Company. Huss was also a member of the board of directors for Tremont, starting in 1949, and, for a time, a member of the board of directors for the Joyce Foundation (the charitable entity of the Joyce companies). However, Huss diminished Beatrice's role in the history of the Joyce businesses, saying, "She was more of an honorary [company official]."

Nopeming

Beatrice loved her northern Minnesota retreat and never missed her annual stay. Once she reached adulthood, she abandoned the clockwork tradition of her parents, who arrived at the estate on June first and departed the day after Labor Day. Some Junes she skipped because of the mosquitoes, and some falls she reluctantly left for Chicago in November or even December. One winter during her short marriage to John Richardson, the couple spent a night in one of the cabins at the estate. (According to Joe Waleski Jr., Richardson was a wealthy Chicagoan, an heir to the Sawyer Biscuit Company fortune.) Caretaker Joe Waleski Sr. had started the cabin's kerosene heater in advance of their arrival. The heater malfunctioned when Beatrice adjusted the thermostat, enveloping the couple in a cloud of soot. The two emerged from the cabin with blackened faces, made all the more striking by the white haloes around their eyes. It was difficult at this time of year to operate Nopeming, since it was not designed for winter living. To keep the lodge and her cabin heated taxed the caretaker, not to mention the cantankerous plumbing that could freeze at any time. And driving across the ice or down the narrow, snow-covered road to the estate could be treacherous.

Getting There

Most often Beatrice arrived in northern Minnesota by air. Her first plane was a Sea Bee, referred to by one of her pilots as a "flying boat." This small single-engine plane could land on either its wheels on a runway or on its belly on water, important for lake landings at the estate, which had no landing strip. Beatrice recognized that the Sea Bee's slow air speed of one hundred miles per hour limited its use. For long-distance trips she maintained a second aircraft. The Twin Beechcraft D-18 was a twin engine plane with a table, a cocktail bar, and a bathroom. It seated seven or eight passengers. This plane was hangered at the Grand Rapids airport, while Beatrice was in northern Minnesota. Later she replaced the Twin

Beatrice's first seaplane, the Sea Bee. JOE WALESKI PRIVATE COLLECTION

Beatrice's second seaplane, the Grumman Mallard, could seat fifteen people. JOE WALESKI PRIVATE COLLECTION

Beechcraft with a Grumman Mallard, an amphibious seaplane large enough to accommodate fifteen people. The last plane Beatrice owned was a twin engine Queen-Aire, similar to the Beechcraft.

Bee Cee employed a succession of pilots. She flew in her early twenties with pilot John McArdle (who said of her, "She was capable and learned to fly, but mostly it was just for fun.") On one occasion the two took the Sea Bee to visit her mill in Louisiana, but commonly they flew in northern Minnesota and Canada, where she duck hunted. Soon after McArdle accepted a job with TWA, Gordy Newstrom, a well-known pioneer aviator in the Grand Rapids area, flew for her. Newstrom occasionally piloted Beatrice, her husband Dudley, and Grand Rapids mayor Louis Laurent to Montana to hunt pheasants, geese, or ducks. He also flew Beatrice to the Dakotas to hunt. Following Newstrom, Bob Myers took over the piloting duties. Bud Daniels, who had worked as an aircraft mechanic under Myers, eventually became licensed and then took charge of piloting after Myers left. Bud Daniels stayed with the job for the remainder of Beatrice's life.

Nopeming's Deer Refuge

Even though Beatrice allowed a select few to bird hunt on the estate property, she did not permit deer hunting. A concerted effort was made to keep hunters and poachers off the grounds, requiring the efforts of many hired game wardens, who patrolled the property lines each fall. Mickie Benton, wife of Beatrice's northern Minnesota attorney, recalled that "the game wardens were all good friends of Beatrice. . . . She loved the animals and she loved the birds and took care of them. . . . She always had extra people up there to take care of her property. Just during the hunting season. If they [hunters] would go onto her property, they were caught and they were punished for doing it because they had no business there. That was hers, and she wanted to keep the animals safe. She was furious if anybody would trespass. She was just livid during the hunting season, because sometimes they would try to get too close to her home, and that was a no-no because she was a very private person."

Beatrice's grandfather had maintained a deer-feeding station on the grounds of his Lyons, Iowa homestead years before the creation of the Joyce Estate, so it was not surprising that Beatrice's father, David Gage Joyce, started the practice of feeding white-tailed deer at Nopeming. Soon a large herd of deer established its range upon the estate. With the burgeoning population of deer, hunters unlawfully entered his property in search of easy game, much to Joyce's displeasure. He obtained a federal injunction—the first to be issued for such a purpose in the state of Minnesota—to protect his estate from trespassing hunters. The injunction, granted in 1925, was printed on placards and posted by the hundreds along the perimeter of the estate to intimidate the poaching element and to assist Joyce in his creation of a sanctuary for wildlife in Itasca County.[4] In 1938, the year after David Gage Joyce died, Beatrice's mother resorted to hiring men to patrol the property boundaries because the injunction proved ineffective unless the poachers could be caught red-handed. The Itasca County sheriff deputized the seasonal employees hired by Joyce for patrol duty. By land and by water, the fourteen miles of property boundary fell under the roving patrols' scrutiny, especially during deer-hunting season.

John Muhar, onetime Itasca County sheriff, who participated in the Joyce Estate patrol throughout Beatrice's life, saw "as many as 150 deer at the estate. I would go in there early in the morning during the winter to see Joe Waleski. . . . When Joe started up the Jeep [adjacent to the caretaker's cabin] and poured out the six or seven sacks of oats and cracked corn, the deer would hear that and would run after him." Another feeding station in a clearing at McAlpine Brook, located one mile to the south and along the entrance road, also attracted a large herd of deer.

Beatrice Joyce Kean remodeled the lodge interior. She followed her father's use of the Great Camp theme. Note the anaconda snakeskin stretched nearly from wall to wall above the fireplace mantel. Beneath the snakeskin, two great antlered moose flank a bison head. A Remington bronze sculpture and another small statue of an Indian and horse rest upon the mantel. Navajo rugs and baskets as well as bear rugs continue the rustic décor. JOE WALESKI PRIVATE COLLECTION

Social Life

Life at Nopeming was a series of contrasts. After driving three miles on a narrow winding forest road, visitors emerged from the dense canopy to the inviting comforts of the lodge. According to Mickie Benton, "It was not a place that was fabulous. It was quite rustic, but everything was nice." The ordinary furniture served as a counterpoint to the butlers, who offered "all the fancy wonderful drinks" while a three- or four-piece band played. "All the rugs were taken up," Benton went on, "and if you wanted to dance, then you could dance. It was a whole new world!" Benton elaborated on the frequent social outings at Nopeming. On one occasion, guests arrived dressed up as animals and were received by the animal mounts dressed up in human attire by the estate staff. "The parties were wonderful," said Benton. "I remember the first party I went to. It was a costume party and you had to come as an island. . . . I was seven months pregnant and went as Bali Hai."

During the 1950s, Beatrice gave several parties in a modest 1920s vintage wood-frame cabin without plumbing on Moore Lake's tiny island. One evening featured a uranium hunt. Caretaker Joe Waleski Jr. recounted that on a business trip to Chicago with pilot Bob Myers, Beatrice sent the pilot out to borrow two Geiger counters and some chunks of uranium ore as props for the party. On the day of the festivities some of the help hid the uranium while Joe and his brother Everett, seated in a small boat, floated the old golf-course outhouse the short distance from the shore of

The interior of the wraparound screen porch invited relaxation.
JOE WALESKI PRIVATE COLLECTION

NOPEMING

AWAY FROM CITY SMOKE!!!

PLAY IN THE WOODS!!

RELAX AND LIVE THE SIMPLE OUTDOOR LIFE!!

Come to Nopeming Lodge on
and cut a swath of your own through Northern Pine.

ENJOY:

Art Courses (Advanced)	Clotilde Kean
Art Courses (Beginning)	Swanky Franky
Nocturnal Swimming	Ester Kean
Dancing Lessons (Hula and Siamese)	Madam Beatrice
Libation Instruction (Beginning and Advanced)	P. Lawler, DGD, CCL, and NMT*
Bear Hunting	Robert Meyers
Roulette Instructions	Texas Guinan Kean
Woods Romping	Slew-foot Lawler
Art of Relaxing	B. Collinson
Elocution, Voice & Dramatics	Madam Binet
Life Saving	Kent Peterson

The names and nicknames appearing on this party invitation refer to Dudley and Beatrice Joyce Kean, their friends, and staff.
JOE WALESKI PRIVATE COLLECTION

Hunting and Retrieving Inst.	Schaun von Schloss Clinton
Sauna Courses	Steamy Lawler
Instructions in Social Graces & Deportment	J. Saxhaug
Courses in "How to Win Friends and Influence People	Baron Geza
Wild Animal Stalking	Finesse
Play Production & Scenerio Writing	Bill Binet
Course in "Cheese-cake" Photography	Jean Grear
Barbecue Courses	Pierre Kean
Julep making Instructions	Colonel Fraley
Boating (Paddle and Motor)	Dorthy Peterson
Courses in Patience & Patients	D. B. Kean, M.D.
How to Communicate with Animals	Glen Gore
Organized Play	Entire Staff

Footnote:
Staff is subject to change, as they are usually not all in attendance, however charming and equally talented substitutions are made when necessary.

Constant entertainment in immediate area:

County Fair	Seasonal
Legion Club	Not Private
Pokagama	"Cocktails only"
VFW Club	After Theater Spot
Lund's	for more genteel activity
Rainbow	Grand Rapids Exclusive Supper Club
Anything goes and usually does (Charleston Lessons Upon Request.)	

Come and feel free in Smirnoff Corner for a night's enjoyment and revelry!

Services Available

Tea House Typist	Jack Helmers
Public Steno Available?	Pat Lawler
Laundry Service	Bea Collinson
Translator	Claude
Mid-night Hauling	Everett & Bob
Photography	Izzie Cainstein

EXPERT AND COMPETENT HOUSE PHYSICIAN IN CONSTANT ATTENDANCE.

NOTHING COULD BE MORE RESTFUL AND RELAXING
THAN A WEEKEND IN THE COUNTRY!!

Write or phone for reservations:

Nopeming
Grand Rapids, Minnesota

*DGD - Dam Good Drinker, CCL - Couldn't Care Less, NMT - Not My Type

Moore Lake to the island. They discreetly positioned the outhouse behind the cabin for the guests' use. In the nearby brush they draped the bear rug from the main lodge on two sawhorses bulked up with hay to mimic the shape of a bear.

When the guests arrived at the gate of the Joyce Estate, they were told to proceed to the small Moore Lake boathouse to be ferried over to the island for a uranium hunt and a special barbecue prepared by Joe Waleski Sr. As supper was being served, tunes from the Roaring Twenties wafted out over the water from a wind-up phonograph. One of the guests complimented Beatrice on the tasty hamburgers, to which she nonchalantly replied, "You just ate beaver burgers!" Less successful was the imitation bear. Some of the guests took the trail to the old golf-course toilet, but either nobody saw the bear in the dusk, or else they stayed mum so as not to ruin the joke for the next in need of accommodation.

Beatrice loved surprising and teasing her guests. According to Waleski Jr., one evening after her Grand Rapids company arrived at the estate for supper, she chauffeured them in the box of her pickup truck back through Grand Rapids to dine at Lund's Resort on Pokegama Lake south of town. Following the meal, Beatrice returned them to Nopeming in order to get their cars and drive home. This prank added more than fifty miles to their evening adventure.

Another of Joe Waleski Jr.'s favorite stories took place at the Grand Rapids Rainbow Bar and Restaurant. On several evenings Mrs. Kean had tried to bring her Great Dane, Geza, to her table as her escort. Pointing out that the dog wasn't wearing shoes, the owner would not admit Geza. This eventually prompted Kean to order dog shoes from Chicago. The shoes resembled four small boxing gloves. She then insisted that her Great Dane be allowed in the restaurant. "Okay," said the owner, chuckling, "but keep the dog under the table so he won't disturb anyone else."

Longtime employee Katie Krueth, a maid for twenty-five years at Nopeming, confirmed that Beatrice could be "a little rascal. If the guys went out bird hunting, she [Beatrice] would ride along with them. The guys would get out of the Jeep and go into the woods, and then she would take the Jeep back to the lodge! So when they got out of the woods, there was no transportation. They would have their guns and big boots on, and they would have to walk home."

A Very Lonely Rich Woman

The people who knew Beatrice Joyce Kean felt strongly about how she related to them and were not shy about expressing their feelings. Although her staff and acquaintances were fond of relating stories about the humorous streak that she exhibited, they also revealed a demanding side to her character. Emerging from the many voices that described Beatrice is a picture of an intelligent woman deprived of love, beset by alcoholism, and depressed.

Caretaker Joe Waleski Jr. described Beatrice as an insensitive woman who only cared about herself. "Everybody kowtowed to her, not only because she had the money but because she had the power. If anyone said anything [that upset Beatrice], they would just be out." Like many of the staff, Waleski felt she could have afforded to be more generous with salaries because of her personal wealth. "At the end my salary was $400 a month," said Waleski. "It did not matter how many hours I worked. I was paid by the month. Many times I worked seven days a week. She was great for keeping me after hours. She just wanted to keep me there later."

She was "a lonely rich woman," added Katie Krueth. "A very lonely rich woman." At times demanding, she was not always an easy woman to work for, in part due to her loneliness. "I worked there [at Nopeming] from 8 a.m. to 4 p.m. . . . . It was common for her to call me up [to her cabin] at 3:30 p.m. and want me to come and sit with her and talk with her or comb her hair or just read an article out of the newspaper or anything to keep me there. She did not want me to go home." Even though Beatrice "did not pay well," Krueth acknowledged, "she was good to us in lots of ways. . . . Working there was always kind of fun. Mrs. Kean was quite a gal. I will admit that. She really was. . . . It was only the last four or five years [when her health was failing] that she pretty much stayed in her cabin." Before that "she would come down and mingle with the people and the help. She would even sit at the table and have coffee with us in her earlier years."

Katie Krueth and her husband lived about four miles from the entrance of the Joyce Estate on Pickerel Lake, adjacent to Bluewater Lake. On the rare occasion when Beatrice would visit them, "she was real neighborly and friendly," remarked Krueth. "If she ever came in and took up our time, she would always bring a bottle of liquor and she would leave it. That was her way to say thank you for your time. But she was lonely, she wanted to visit, and she wanted to visit with men. She was intelligent."

Mickie Benton, wife of Beatrice's Minnesota attorney, John Benton, felt that it was difficult to make small talk with Beatrice because she wanted to discuss business or world events. "She loved John, my John," said Benton. "I was part of it because I belonged to John. Beatrice liked men better than she liked women. I suppose maybe in her business that was who she associated with."

Beatrice Joyce Kean never had children, but she had a close relationship with Ellen Kean Rudolph, the much younger adopted sister of Beatrice's husband Dudley. Rudolph remembers first meeting her twenty-nine-year-old sister-in-law in 1952 when she was six years old. Among many first-edition books that Beatrice's father had collected was a work by Edgar Allen Poe that Beatrice read to Ellen when she visited Nopeming. "Beatrice and I would sit on dark and stormy nights and put a candle on the floor. Beatrice would read into the wee hours of the night from the book. With very wonderful drama! Then she would go like this! [Ellen clapped her hands together as Beatrice had done to punctuate a scary point in the story.] It was fun."

The works by Poe no doubt begged to be read out loud, appropriate content for the inclement weather and for the entertainment of a six-year-old; however, these works also spoke powerfully to Beatrice. As an adult, Ellen Kean Rudolph concluded that Beatrice "resonated with the melancholia of Poe's writing. Poe died young. Beatrice never expected to live a long life. She was well aware of the ages of her father and grandfather when they died. She said many times that she did not think she would be an old person."

A practicing psychologist, Rudolph reflected on Beatrice's childhood and life. "Beatrice did not grow up in a nurturing family environment," explained Rudolph. "That contributes to lifelong depression. She did not have many 'best' friends. Joe Waleski Sr.

and that whole family were good friends of hers. Her pilot and Dudley were her friends. In a unique way, I was her friend.

"Beatrice was the best model for womanhood with a high image of self," Rudolph continued. "It is just that she had such emptiness with melancholia overwhelming her with her family history and the lack of connections and the aloofness that was born out of all of that. She would have been much more of a presence if she had grown up loved . . . . After her death, I saw all of her paintings out at Nopeming. They were extraordinarily depressive, black, angry."

During the last five years of Beatrice's life, she became more reclusive. Earlier she had dined at nearby resorts, such as Mike Brown's on Johnson Lake or DeHaven's on North Star Lake, or visited nearby Grand Rapids. Now she rested, read, and watched television in her cabin at Nopeming.

One factor that shortened Beatrice's life, as it had her father's, was her use of alcohol. Her excessive drinking puzzled some of her acquaintances. "Beatrice was a very brilliant young lady," said Grand Rapids resident Dan Hoolihan, whose father had worked for the Itasca Lumber Company. "I told Beatrice one time at the Legion Club, 'Beatrice, if I had all of your money, I think I would quit wasting my time around these bars.' She said, 'Oh you would, would you? What would you do?' And I named off about twenty things, including big-game hunting in Africa and sailing around the world and all kinds of activities for having fun. Beatrice said, 'And then what would you do after you had done all those things?' So she gave me my answer."

Beatrice Joyce Kean left Nopeming for the last time on November 11, 1972. She signed her will on November 21, and less than a month later, on December 14, 1972, Beatrice died at age forty-nine. Joe Waleski Jr. received a letter shortly thereafter from longtime Chicago employee John P. Gregg, saying that she had died in her sleep of a heart attack. On her death certificate, signed by Elita Mallers, the cause of her death was listed as acute cardiac dilatation due to unknown causes. Beatrice was cremated in a plain, inexpensive casket as specified in her will. Announcements of her death were sent out in lieu of a funeral service.

Beatrice Joyce Kean bequeathed ninety percent of her net worth to the Joyce Foundation; the remaining ten percent or approximately $14,550,000 was divided unequally among eleven friends. The non-taxable inheritances went to her godchild, Maurice Neville, the son of her close friend from finishing school, Cecelia Neville Dalsemer; her ex-husband, Dudley Kean; the caretaker of Nopeming, Joe Waleski Sr.; her mother's sister, Catherine Agnes Rudolph; one of her pilots, Bud Daniels; one of her Chicago secretaries, Miss Margaret Blake; three Chicago executives—Evald O. Anderson, Kent F. Peterson, and Cushman B. Bissell; and two children of Joyce company or Joyce Foundation executives, Steven Kent Peterson and Michael Wearing.

The Joyce Foundation

The Joyce Foundation, which received the bulk of the Beatrice Joyce Kean estate, was incorporated in 1948. Beatrice Clotilde Joyce, Chicago attorney Cushman B. Bissell, and longtime Joyce employee John P. Gregg signed the Joyce Foundation incorporation papers that year. The papers were then filed with the Secretary of State of Illinois on May 19.

Cushman B. Bissell, who had provided legal advice for the Joyces and had socialized with them as early as the 1930s, recommended to Beatrice the formation of the Joyce Foundation. According to the articles of incorporation, it was "organized exclusively for religious, charitable, scientific, literary, and educational purposes."[5] Increasing taxes were a strong inducement to form the foundation. In 1909 corporate income tax was only one percent. In 1939 it jumped to 19 percent. During World War II, this tax more than doubled, reaching 40 percent, then dropped to 38 percent following the war. Many other affluent industrialists also established tax-exempt foundations at this time. By the mid-1950s more than 4,000 foundations operated nationally with combined assets around $3 billion.[6]

Initially, the foundation's board of directors—Beatrice Joyce Kean, E. O. Anderson, Cushman Bissell, Raymond Wearing, and Kent Peterson, who were Joyce company executives, lawyers, or accountants—let the assets grow. By 1962, assets exceeded $500,000. During the period of asset growth, the Joyce Foundation did not make noteworthy contributions. In 1964, donations represented less than one percent of assets. In 1968, however, the foundation granted $63,886.55, including many student scholarships to colleges in Iowa, South Dakota, Nebraska, Louisiana, and possibly in other states. These grants represented 6.66 percent of foundation assets of $956,637.

The Joyce Foundation earned a fine reputation in the world of philanthropy. Gene Turner, comptroller for the Joyce-owned Tremont Lumber Company in Louisiana, kept close ties with the Joyce Foundation. He felt the foundation supported programs and causes that Beatrice was passionate about. These included "music and arts, especially in the Chicago area, and anything to do with kids' programs. She was strong with the Boy Scouts and Girl Scouts. . . . And Beatrice was good to those kids that had polio and other problems. . . . Beatrice looked for things with a big need. She used her money pretty wisely, I think." It is possible that Kean gave to some of these causes personally as well as through the Joyce Foundation.

During the fifty-four years since Beatrice signed the incorporation papers, the purpose of the Joyce Foundation has crystallized. In 2002 the Joyce Foundation stated its mission as supporting "efforts to protect the natural environment of the Great Lakes, to reduce poverty and violence in the region, and to insure that its people have access to good schools, decent jobs, and a diverse and thriving culture. We are especially interested in improving public policies, because public systems such as education and welfare directly affect the lives of so many people, and because public policies help shape private sector decisions about jobs, the environment, and the health of our communities. To ensure that public policies truly reflect public rather than private interests, we support efforts to reform the system of financing election campaigns."[7]

The value of the Joyce Foundation has grown significantly over the years as has its grant giving. In 2002 the Joyce Foundation reported assets of $850 million. The previous year the Joyce Foundation gave grants totaling $37 million.

The Sale of Nopeming

EVEN BEFORE THE DEATH OF BEATRICE JOYCE KEAN, the possibility of owning Nopeming's Adirondack-style hunting lodge retreat, with its setting of tranquil
woods and aquamarine water, intrigued potential buyers. The sheer size of the 4,500-acre
estate had drawn the attention of state, federal, and private organizations for years. Kean's
death in December 1972 catalyzed a contest between the public and private sectors for the
purchase of the property.

According to former governor Wendell Anderson, as early as the 1930s, Minnesota state
officials had been enchanted by Nopeming and had hoped to claim it someday as a state park
or recreation area. Years later local citizen and volunteer conservationist Wes Libbey, a member
of the Minnesota Council of State Parks, approached Kean shortly before her death and suggested that she donate the Joyce Estate to the state park system in memory of her father.[1]

The federal government was also interested. Many of the district rangers from the
United States Forest Service's (USFS) Marcell District Office as well as Chippewa National
Forest Supervisor M. K. Lauritsen and forester George Campbell from the regional office at
Cass Lake, Minnesota, had eyed the lovely lakes-and-woods estate over the years. Nopeming
would be a prized addition to the Chippewa National Forest that surrounded it. Letters
archived at Cass Lake and dated during 1969 and 1972 confirm that Lauritsen and Campbell
had written to Beatrice Joyce Kean inviting her to sell her estate to the USFS.

Nopeming attracted the attention of the private sector as well. The Rajala Lumber
Company owners had first visited the Joyce Estate in 1970 for a potential timber sale. Beatrice
Joyce Kean invited Art Rajala to look at the estate's timber, probably for the purpose of creating open spaces for deer habitat. Jack Rajala, Art's son, relates an unusual story about their
business dealings. After cruising the estate on foot for pine stands, Rajala wanted one of his

employees to evaluate the hardwoods and aspen with which he was less familiar. At first Beatrice would not let anyone but Art on her property. Finally, she compromised. "It was arranged that Beatrice would supply her airplane," recalled Jack Rajala. "The cruising would be done from the air. Well, that was something that we had never heard of!" Soon after, with the necessary maps and adventurous spirits, Jack Rajala and employee Stan Ringold met Beatrice's pilot one morning in Grand Rapids for aerial cruising. During several hours of flying over the 4,500 acres, the men typed the property for species and recorded the location of various timber stands on a grid. However, Beatrice died before a timber harvest agreement was reached. As Jack Rajala recollects, it was probably during this time that the Rajalas became interested in buying Nopeming.[2]

Beatrice Joyce Kean died on December 14, 1972, without having made plans for the disposition of the property. The executors of her estate, who were also Joyce Foundation board members, arranged for appraisals of Nopeming in April 1973 and then put it up for sale. The next month the United States Forest Service called the Joyce Foundation about acquiring the property. It also contacted the Nature Conservancy—a privately funded non-profit organization dedicated to protection of habitat and endangered species—to act as a possible interim purchaser. With the aid of concerned citizens, the USFS finally rallied the political support needed to convince the United States Congress to earmark funds to buy Nopeming if the Joyce Foundation agreed to sell the property to the Nature Conservancy.

The offer from the Nature Conservancy arrived simultaneously with bids from the United States Steel Corporation, Minnesota Mining and Manufacturing (3M), and Investment Realty Solutions, Inc. 3M envisioned the estate as an executive retreat. United States Steel probably had similar intentions. Investment Realty was interested in a division of the property into lots for resale. The executors of the estate reserved the right to solicit a second bid from a lower bidder. Investment Realty Solutions, Inc. originally proposed the high bid of $1.75 million, but the Nature Conservancy submitted a higher second bid. In response, Investment Realty Solutions, Inc. offered $2 million. In a letter written to G. W. Van Gilst, USFS Director of Lands in Washington, D.C., Daniel Olin, an assistant director for the USFS in Washington, D.C., reported, "The Nature Conservancy met this bid and the Estate sold to them because they [the executors of the estate] desired the property to be undeveloped."[3]

The Nature Conservancy contributed $500,000 for this purchase from its Revolving Fund, but another $1.5 million for purchase and $500,000 for expenses came from unlikely sources. The Northwestern National Life Insurance Company of Minneapolis loaned the Nature Conservancy the additional dollars for the purchase price. According to the November 8, 1973 issue of the *Grand Rapids Herald Review,* "Wallace C. Dayton, chairman of the Nature Conservancy's board of governors, called the action 'a prime example of the cooperation that can be achieved by the business community, on one hand, and by an organization such as the Conservancy, on the other, to provide funds to preserve environmentally significant lands such as the Joyce estate.'"[4] The Joyce Foundation itself then granted the Nature Conservancy an unstipulated $500,000 to cover taxes, maintenance, and interest on the loan until the federal government could take ownership. Taxes exceeded $20,000; maintenance ran more than $5,000, and interest at ten percent cost $150,000 annually. The balance contributed to partial payment for Nopeming.[5]

Jack Rajala of Rajala Lumber Company was not aware that Nopeming had been sold. He continued to contact "friends in the industry" about funding for this valuable property. Many months slipped by before he secured the necessary capital from a "friendly family who also had lumber and forest product interests." On a business trip to Chicago, Rajala called the Kean estate lawyers to put in a bid. In conversation with Kent Peterson, an accountant for Beatrice Joyce Kean, he soon learned that he had let too much time elapse before making his offer. "We talked only a little longer," said Rajala, "but before the conversation ended, Mr. Peterson said, 'Oh, by the way, what was your offer going to be?'" Rajala responded with his bid of somewhere between $2.2 million and $2.5 million. "What!" said Peterson. "That's considerably more than we got for it." Reflecting years later upon the sale to the Forest Service, Rajala mused that the outcome "would have been to Beatrice's liking. This probably happened the way it was supposed to." The Joyce Estate was destined, as Jack Rajala realized, to become part of the public domain.[6]

Although Beatrice had not set Nopeming aside for public use, there is evidence supporting her preference for her property to become part of the public domain. According

Nelson French of the Nature Conservancy conveyed ownership of the Joyce Estate to a Unites States Forest Service representative. The ceremony took place at the Joyce Estate in August 1974. GRAND RAPIDS *HERALD REVIEW*

to John Johnson, the last caretaker during Beatrice's life, "Beatrice did not want the estate divided. She wanted it to become some sort of refuge. She wanted the federal government to take it." Marcell District ranger Melvin Goldie, local manager for the Chippewa National Forest at the time of Beatrice's death, believed that the Joyce Estate executors also preferred to sell the property to the government. "They wanted to see it remain intact, but they also wanted to get what the land was worth," said Goldie. "They were willing to work with us to see if we could pull it off, rather than have it sold to developers and have it subdivided."[7]

In early September 1974 the Nature Conservancy transferred the Joyce Estate title to the United States Forest Service. The Forest Service immediately set up an interim plan to consider all possible uses for Nopeming, which it renamed the Trout Lake Tract. The Forest Service inventoried resources such as soil, water, vegetation, timber, and wildlife. It also offered George Baker, a local resident, the opportunity to live at Nopeming in exchange for supervising the property and buildings, a difficult job due to the distance between the caretaker's cabin and the main complex of buildings. A month later, in October, at a dedication ceremony celebrating the transfer, the Forest Service presented the interim plan. The plan safeguarded the land and the buildings for public enjoyment and placed a moratorium on timber harvest. The interim plan also maintained the semi-primitive condition of the property by keeping the gates at entry points closed. This established non-motorized public use. Thus the gates, originally set up by David Joyce around 1917, continued the tradition of protecting the wild character of the land.

The process of formulating a permanent management plan for the Joyce Estate seemed to last forever. Eighteen years passed between the sale of Nopeming in August 1973 and the signing of the Trout Lake Opportunity Area governance document by the Forest Service in September 1991. The delays were due in part to Forest Service priorities and in part to controversy over the use and management of the estate.

The United States Forest Service had acquired the Joyce Estate property during a large-scale revision of the forest plan for the entire Chippewa National Forest. While the Forest Service handled this other business, the Trout Lake Tract buildings deteriorated. Vandals broke the windows and stripped the buildings of the few remaining fixtures, such as the cupboards and bathtubs. Neglected, the estate buildings played host to carpenter ants. The condition of the buildings, however, was not a major concern for the United States Forest Service. Melvin Goldie, forest supervisor during the first years of Forest Service ownership of the Trout Lake Tract, felt that the buildings should be removed and the property should return to its natural state. After all, the mission of the Forest Service was not to preserve buildings.

During the nearly two decades of hammering out a management plan, the United States Forest Service listened to the public's passionate and varied views concerning the future of the Trout Lake Tract. Itasca County had lost more than $20,000 of its annual tax base because of the federal government property tax exemption, and some of the county officials were disgruntled. Just before the death of Beatrice Joyce Kean, the county board of commissioners had adopted a resolution, stating that federal ownership of land in Itasca County caused economic hardship to its residents by eroding the tax base. The "per capita income for residents of the Chippewa National Forest [is] the lowest in the State of Minnesota and the unemployment rate [is] unreasonably high compared to other areas of the County," pointed out the commissioners.[8] They had hoped that the property would be subdivided and sold privately and that the lodge would be converted into a private resort, substantially increasing the taxes collected for these 4,500 acres. But many people in the area saw value in preserving the property. A November 15, 1973 *Grand Rapids Herald Review* editorial had argued that public ownership of the Joyce property was preferable to privatization: "It is entirely possible that the estate will have a greater economic impact on the county as part of the Forest Service than as private property. Tens of thousands will explore and admire the beauty of the area and they will spend money to reach here and stay here. Far more people may make use of the forest and spend more money than would the owners of the land if it were developed in the strictly commercial manner. It is difficult to think of a better solution for the Joyce Estate."

Other groups were also concerned with the United States Forest Service's plans for the property's lodge and cabins. Independent School District 318 suggested establishing a nature center to complement its environmental education program.[9] Bemidji State University proposed operating a biological station; the University of Illinois, a forestry camp. A group from Duluth wanted a halfway center for chemically dependent people. Some of these organizations had never visited the Joyce Estate. The fact that it included a par-three golf course, tennis court, airplane hangar, and other amenities glamorized the property. In actuality, general disrepair reigned. The Forest Service rejected all proposals, because they would directly influence the final management plan for the area. Once a pattern of use had been established, district office officials knew that it would be hard to dismantle.[10]

Letters also flowed into the United States Forest Service expressing opinions about the best way to manage the Trout Lake Tract. The main philosophical conflict lay between the individuals who supported a return to wilderness and those who rallied around preservation of the buildings for their historic value. The first group felt that the buildings should be razed, while the second wanted them saved and repaired. (An echo of this debate resounds in New York whenever Great Camp owners occasionally seek to sell to the state. The "forever wild" designation of the Adirondacks has protected the natural environment since 1892 and is at odds with any notion of protecting manmade structures. Architectural preservationists want the law changed to save the Great Camps, while environmental conservationists want to maintain the designation in order to protect the natural environment.)[11]

In September 1977 Mike Landis of the Minnesota Historical Society (MHS) alerted the United States Forest Service that an increasing number of citizens were petitioning the MHS to place the Joyce Estate buildings on the National Historic Register.[12] Responding to these citizens' fears that the Forest Service was going to destroy the buildings, the MHS embarked on a study of the estate structures. Eight years later, in 1985, the State Historic Preservation Office (SHPO) of the Minnesota Historical Society completed the evaluation of the architectural and historical significance of the Joyce Estate and nominated Nopeming to the National Register of Historic Places. "The Joyce Estate" wrote the MHS, "is historically significant as Minnesota's only known example of a family summer home built in the opulent tradition of the 'Great Camps' of the Adirondacks region of New York State."[13]

Opponents protested this decision. They argued that the Joyce Estate complex only imitated the Great Camp tradition and did not merit restoration. They felt the land, a greater testament to an earlier history, would be degraded by restoration of the buildings. Melvin Goldie and possibly other Chippewa National Forest supervisors agreed. They also were on a budget and did not wish to reallocate money and personnel from other projects to the restoration and maintenance of the Joyce Estate buildings.

Despite the opposition, the Joyce Estate was nominated to the National Register of Historic Places. Once the United States Forest Service knew they were stuck with the buildings, Howard Zeman, district ranger of the Chippewa National Forest, contacted the Joyce Foundation in May 1990 for potential restoration funds. The foundation's program director wrote back, "Somewhat to my surprise, there appears to be no interest in participation in the restoration of the complex. The original sale of the property was considered to be final. If anything, the underlying bias appears to be to allow the property to return to its natural state."[14]

Opposition continued. Members of the Zimmerman family and Carolyn Kastner, residents on the north end of Trout Lake, appealed to the Forest Service in a letter dated May 14, 1990. The residents questioned the compatibility of rehabilitating the buildings with the semi-primitive non-motorized designation for the Trout Lake Tract. By definition, this designation affords users probable solitude in a natural setting with minimum, rustic improvements. Wouldn't the restoration of some of the buildings violate this designation?[15]

In 1991 personnel from the Forest Service and the State Historic Preservation Office, along with two local residents, Kraig Dibb and Warren Jewett, hammered out the permanent management plan for the Trout Lake Tract. The fact that the Forest Service knew that the State Historic Preservation Office (SHPO) would sue if the Forest Service removed all of the buildings influenced the decision-making process. Charlie Nelson, historical architect for the State Historic Preservation Office, helped diffuse a potentially tense situation when he supported the United States Forest Service in restoring only four buildings—the lodge, two cabins, and the bathhouse—while removing all others. He argued that when people approached the estate by water as the Joyces did initially, these four buildings preserved its original Great Camp image. Placards could provide the rest of the history. This was a new preservation approach for SHPO, but it seemed to make sense. At this point SHPO officials in St. Paul doubted that they could win a court case against the United States Forest Service, given this compromise. The resolution pleased all parties, and the document to manage the Joyce Estate was signed September 12, 1991.[16]

The permanent plan complied with the Historic Preservation Act of 1966 by restoring the lodge, two cabins, and the bathhouse. With the exception of the earthen structures such as the root cellar and powerhouse, other buildings were removed. Today placards appearing near the structures catalog the history of the family. The remaining buildings coexist in the designated semi-primitive non-motorized Trout Lake Tract with a few rustic campsites and hiking trails, which are groomed as cross-country ski trails during the winter.

So far the Joyce Estate has fared well. Campers and tourists have not abused the grounds or the structures. The forest canopy gains stature annually, deer and wolf sign mark the dirt road, and one can still find solitude in the forest. It has remained true to the name Nopeming—a place up north, a place of rest.

The Shift to Southern Pine

THE ELDER DAVID JOYCE WAS SIXTY-THREE YEARS OLD when his Lyons, Iowa sawmill burned to the ground, an event that might have stifled the ambition of the average lumberman. However, neither his advancing age nor the prospect of rebuilding his mill kept Joyce from both diversifying his holdings and further investing in the lumber industry. During late summer and early fall of 1888, Joyce became a partner in the Benjamin Machine Company of Evanston, Illinois, which manufactured heavy sawmilling equipment, and also purchased an interest in a resort hotel in Hot Springs, Arkansas. To his mill holdings in Iowa and Wisconsin, he added major purchases of stock in the Langford and Hall Lumber Company of Fulton, Illinois, the Itasca Lumber Company of northern Minnesota, and the Trinity County Lumber Company of East Texas. The Fulton mill was right across the Mississippi River from his Iowa mill and the Minnesota undertaking was a logical replacement for the declining timber stocks in Wisconsin, but Texas represented a major departure from the lumbering that David Joyce was used to. The dramatically different climate, terrain, labor force, and social environment—not to mention the difficulties of controlling the endeavor from afar—challenged three generations of Joyces at every turn. Furthermore, the southern yellow pine populating the forests of East Texas in an area known as the Pineywoods was despised in the 1880s by many northern mill men. In an age when white pine was the undisputed building material of choice, Joyce's unorthodox investment in the Trinity County Lumber Company and in yellow pine proved, in time, to be remarkably astute.[1]

The Trinity County Lumber Company sprang up in 1882 from the initiative of four of Joyce's fellow citizens of Lyons, Iowa, L. T. Sloan being the principal driving force and president. Joyce knew these men well, for they had worked with or for him on several

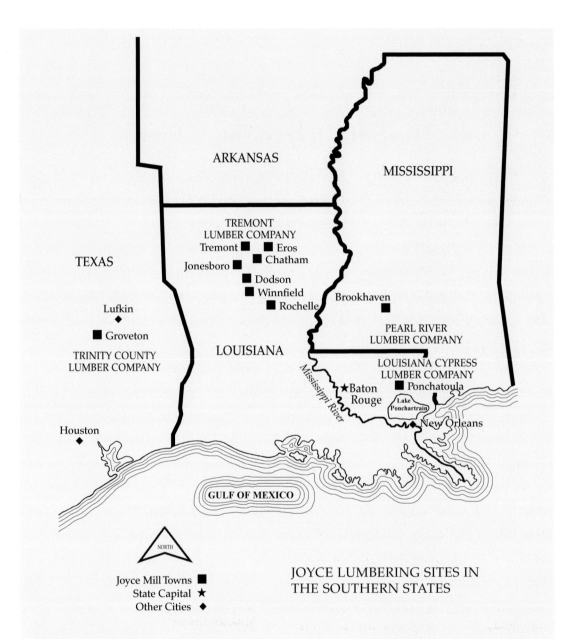

ARKANSAS

MISSISSIPPI

TEXAS

TREMONT
LUMBER COMPANY
Tremont ■   ■ Eros
■ Chatham
Jonesboro ■
■ Dodson
■ Winnfield
■ Rochelle
Brookhaven ■

Lufkin ♦
■ Groveton

TRINITY COUNTY
LUMBER COMPANY

LOUISIANA

PEARL RIVER
LUMBER COMPANY

LOUISIANA CYPRESS
LUMBER COMPANY
■ Ponchatoula

★ Baton
Rouge

Mississippi River

Lake
Ponchartrain

♦ New Orleans

Houston ♦

GULF OF MEXICO

NORTH

Joyce Mill Towns ■
State Capital ★
Other Cities ♦

JOYCE LUMBERING SITES IN
THE SOUTHERN STATES

Up to this point, *Timber Connections* has focused on Joyce activities in the Midwest and, in particular, in Minnesota. However, the most significant part of the family's lumbering enterprises took place in the South—Texas, Mississippi, and Louisiana. Southern logging and milling was the largest source of the Joyce fortune.

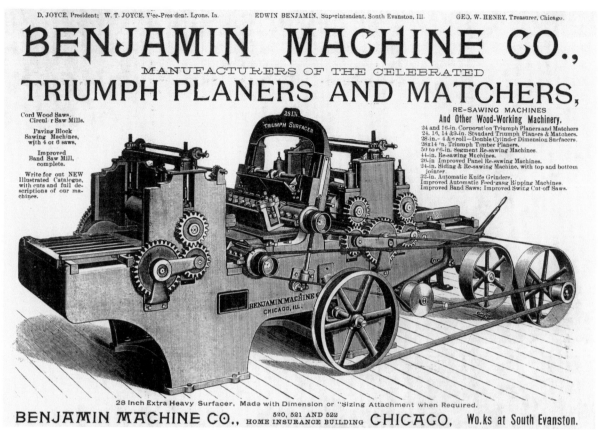

D. JOYCE, President; W. T. JOYCE, Vice-President, Lyons, Ia.   EDWIN BENJAMIN, Superintendent, South Evanston, Ill.   GEO. W. HENRY, Treasurer, Chicago.

BENJAMIN MACHINE CO.,
MANUFACTURERS OF THE CELEBRATED
TRIUMPH PLANERS AND MATCHERS,

Cord Wood Saws.
Circular Saw Mills.

Paving Block
Sawing Machines,
with 4 or 6 saws,

Improved
Band Saw Mill,
complete.

Write for out NEW
Illustrated Catalogue,
with cuts and full de-
scriptions of our ma-
chines.

RE-SAWING MACHINES
And Other Wood-Working Machinery.

24 and 16-in. Corporation Triumph Planers and Matchers.
24, 16, 14 &9-in. Standard Triumph Planers & Matchers.
28-in.- 4 &6 roll — Double Cylinder Dimension Surfacers.
28x14 in. Triumph Timber Planers.
50 to 6-in. Segment Re-sawing Machines.
44-in. Re-sawing Machines.
26-in Improved Panel Re-sawing Machines.
24-in. Siding & Re-sawing Machine, with top and bottom
   jointer.
32-in. Automatic Knife Grinders.
Improved Automatic Feed-gang Ripping Machines.
Improved Band Saws; Improved Swing Cut-off Saws.

28 Inch Extra Heavy Surfacer, Made with Dimension or "Sizing Attachment when Required.

BENJAMIN MACHINE CO., 520, 521 AND 522
HOME INSURANCE BUILDING **CHICAGO,** Works at South Evanston.

The Benjamin Machine Co. of Chicago manufactured specialty sawmill equipment. This advertisement appeared in the March 7, 1890 issue of the *Mississippi Valley Lumberman.*

projects in Lyons. It seems reasonable then to assume that Joyce knew about the formation of Trinity County Lumber Company and followed the decisions of its owners with interest. Typical of the Joyce business style, he waited for the company to prove itself sound before making his entry into the firm.

Sloan and his partners launched their Texas enterprise by first securing approximately 29,000 acres of timbered land for $41,000. This land was previously held by the Trinity and Sabine Timber Company and the Trinity and Sabine Railroad. The men spent another $9,000 to build a small sawmill to produce the first lumber. After these initial purchases, Sloan left the security of his Lyons home to become the manager of the mill, introducing his family to what was then a rough-and-ready frontier. The new company immediately prospered, and profits were turned back into improving the mill and buying additional land. Under Sloan's management, the mill gained the distinction of supplying fine lumber for interior woodwork in the state capital at Austin.[2]

The Birth of a Mill Town

Alongside the successful lumbering business, the company developed the town of Groveton, located ninety miles northwest of Houston, to house employees and their families. Originally called Grovetown, the community was named for the beautiful stand of blackjack oak trees on the site.[3] Settlement here had been limited to scattered subsistence farmers prior to the arrival of the lumber company. Ed Sims had worked a five-acre squatter's homestead on the site before the Civil War but abandoned his stake after the war's outbreak. Mose Randolph, a former slave, squatted on the property after the war. The formation of the mill town dislodged squatters like Randolph. They were replaced by a rush of new settlers, entrepreneurs, and mill employees. William "Shug" Magee put up the first saloon shack—"so small the purchaser had to back out the way he entered."[4] He and his wife next started a restaurant that served meals under a tent. New homes followed, a grocery store and a post office went up, and streets were established. Trinity County Lumber Company Manager L. T. Sloan built a home for his family by the mill property and received the honor of having the main street named after him. The company provided housing at a reasonable rental fee, donated land and lumber for a school, and, to abide by the southern caste system, created a separate school for the black population as well as segregated churches. Groveton was on its way to becoming a bona fide Texas town.

The community now possessed the largest business in the county as well as growing political clout. As a result, the townspeople prevailed in the 1882 election to change the Trinity County seat from Pennington to Groveton. County employees completed the move near the end of the year. The following year a brick jailhouse was built. By 1885 a permanent courthouse provided government functions while the business district of Groveton had expanded to include several grocery stores, a general merchandise store, four saloons, a barbershop, a confectionery, several hotels, the train depot, and a drug store.

Early Years in the Pineywoods

Called the Pineywoods by locals, East Texas was densely forested in yellow pine as well as other merchantable tree species. The 18 million-acre forested region covered approximately 14 percent of the state. Large-scale industrial logging and sawmilling had only become feasible within the interior of the Pineywoods in the 1880s when national railways penetrated previously isolated forested areas. Now trains could transport heavy mill and logging railroad equipment into the Pineywoods and return with finished lumber destined for distant markets.[5] This allowed L. T. Sloan and his partners to start their Texas lumbering business.

In the northern tier states, logging was a seasonal occupation; in contrast, in the Pineywoods, logging occurred year-round except during the years when heavy summer rains interrupted the harvest. Initially, oxen, horse, or mule teams, coupled to eight-wheeled logging wagons, conveyed logs to the mill. One of these wagons could carry only two or three of the huge logs cut from the virgin forests surrounding Groveton. A load consisting of one massive log was not uncommon.[6] These slow-moving logging wagons were no longer practical once several miles of clear-cut area surrounded the mill. A logging railroad would provide a workable solution.

By 1886 the Trinity County Lumber Company had assembled a narrow-gauge railway, among the first built exclusively for logging in the United States. The railway began with only four miles of lightweight thirty-pound rail, one locomotive, and eleven cars. It was known as the Groveton, Kickapoo and Gulf. "Kickapoo" refers to a creek crossing near Groveton, but the tracks never came close to its other namesake, the Gulf of Mexico. That year the line hauled only 1.5 million board feet of logs to the Groveton mill, but the addition of the new railway unbridled the possibilities for expanding the Trinity County Lumber Company. It is interesting to note that while David Joyce was not yet involved in the Texas company in 1886, two of its incorporators were men who had worked on Joyce's horse railway connecting Clinton and Lyons, Iowa, fifteen years earlier. Thus, Joyce's horse railway may have furnished the model needed to catapult the Trinity County Lumber Company into the era of logging railroads.

The company incorporators now enjoyed the transportation and raw materials needed to expand; however, they lacked the necessary capital and hence sought a new partner. David Joyce was the natural candidate with his financial savvy, connections to banking firms, lumbering experience, and hometown familiarity with the Lyons men. The situation was mutually beneficial, for Joyce wanted to diversify his investments. What might have initially intrigued Joyce as he considered this opportunity were the trade journal articles published during the 1880s that speculated at length about lumbering opportunities in the relatively untouched forests of the southern states.

Joyce bought his first stock shares in the Trinity County Lumber Company in 1888, six years after its formation. Within a year he owned 36 percent of the operation. Joyce steadily increased his participation in the company, eventually attaining the position of company president in 1891, the year company founder L. T. Sloan retired as president-general manager and moved back to his Lyons, Iowa home.[7] In spite of Joyce's prestigious position in the Trinity County Lumber Company, his varied interests, primarily in the northern states, limited his visits to East Texas. Joyce relied on a Mr. Graves, also an Iowa man, to serve as the new general manager after the departure of L. T. Sloan. During the next five years the Trinity County Lumber Company languished as a modestly sized producer of southern pine. Northern white pine remained the preeminent wood of commerce.[8]

Not until the closing years of the nineteenth century did lumbermen generally acknowledge the value of southern pine. This shift in thinking began to take hold as devastating forest fires and logging pressure dramatically diminished the Wisconsin white pine reserves, turning the lumber trade to its last bastion in Minnesota's northern-most forests. It was soon obvious that the Minnesota pine stocks would not last under the relentless demand for white pine lumber. Furthermore, the white pine of northern

Minnesota produced inferior lumber grades in comparison to the lumber manufactured from the larger trees that had once stood in Wisconsin and Michigan. By the turn of the century, prices soared on the remaining white pine, and the inevitable end was apparent to all.

Unlike the white pine forests, the southern yellow pine forests had scarcely been tapped, partially because of the widespread notion that yellow pine lumber was an inferior product. It was a different wood. Heavier as well as harder to cut and nail, yellow pine was, nevertheless, stronger and more resistant to rot. As white pine prices climbed and the supply became tenuous, the perceived inferiority of yellow pine suddenly vanished.

The energy many lake state lumber barons once focused on harvesting white pine quickly shifted, in many cases, to the yellow pine of the South. Lumbermen also looked west to the ponderosa pine, Douglas fir, Western white pine, and Engelmann spruce of the Pacific Northwest or south to the cypress of the Gulf States.[9] Wherever these lumbermen went, they brought with them the cut-out-and-get-out logging philosophy of their industry that had depleted the forests of the North. The Joyces were no exception.

Under these conditions, the humble Trinity County Lumber Company started its ascent toward becoming a major producer of the newly coveted yellow pine.

Sawmill Woes

David Joyce did not live to see the rise in Trinity's fortunes nor the management squabbles that aggravated his thirty-four-year-old son William, who inherited control of the firm in 1894. Keen on accurate financial accounting, William immediately pursued measures to replace his father's casual bookkeeping style, hiring a new general manager to succeed Graves. His choice, A. B. Ives, moved his family from Wisconsin to Groveton, Texas, in 1895. Ives also became the vice president of the company, second only to Joyce. In the disappointing years that followed, William Joyce lost his trust in Ives' accounting abilities. A letter he sent to his general manager and vice president in 1899 chided, "I want to have a certain method followed in the bookkeeping there as it does not make us any richer to swell our assets by carrying fictitious accounts, nor does it make us any poorer to charge them off, we want our books to make a good, clean showing."[10] Ives excelled in most areas of management, but his bookkeeping continued to fall short of Joyce's expectations.

Joyce also felt uneasy about Trinity for other reasons. Writing to a minority stockholder, he confided, "It is more or less hazardous running as an extensive a business as that [Trinity] so far from home."[11] Furthermore, with its outmoded circular saw, the Trinity County Lumber Company mill at Groveton required a major overhaul to become competitive.

In October of 1900 Joyce posted what must have been a startling letter to his mill manager. Joyce told Ives, "I want to sell out my interests in Texas when I can do so to my advantage, and I believe that the time has now arrived. I feel that I already have too many irons in the fire."[12]

Joyce pursued his desire to unload Trinity by submitting proposals to potential buyers. At first Joyce was asking nearly $1 million for the Texas company, but he dropped his price after receiving no offers. The Iowan then put forward the price of slightly more than $500,000, plus an additional amount to cover lumber in stock. The price covered the mill, 67,000 acres of timberland, and the narrow-gauge railway. One of the most likely purchasers was John D. Lacey, a prominent timber and mill broker dealing in the southern states. Lacey was unresponsive even to the significantly reduced price, leaving Joyce to assemble further proposals throughout 1901 and into 1902. Other promising buyers, preeminent lumber barons Frederick Weyerhaeuser and his partner F. C. Denkmann, considered the deal but declined to bite. Joyce pondered what to do next.

Failure to sell turned out to be advantageous for Joyce. The improving market for southern pine lumber and the impending exhaustion of the popular white pine soon reversed Joyce's opinion of his Texas investment. By 1903 he had executed an about-face and initiated an expensive rebuilding and expansion of the Trinity facilities, including a completely new mill complex and offices. F. E. Van Alstine of Chicago took control as the millwright for the project and outfitted the plant with the newest and best machinery

The Trinity County Lumber Company mill in East Texas reflected in the large millpond.
COURTESY OF KATE ATKINSON BELL

available. The new two-story mill featured two Allis-Chalmers telescopic double-cutting band saws for the initial cuts on incoming logs. Allis-Chalmers specialty saws and equipment produced finished lumber at a maximum rate of 40 million board feet annually. Next to the double-band sawmill was the two-story brick boiler and engine house, the electric light plant, and the large-capacity brick dry kilns. The planing mill, machine shops, roundhouse, blacksmith shop, and enormous storage sheds for lumber finished the complement of buildings.[13]

At this time Joyce queried his peers for a co-manager and eventual replacement for the aging A. B. Ives. A promising Michigan mill operator, W. F. N. Davis, considered Joyce's attractive financial incentives but finally refused the offer because his wife was too ill to travel to Texas. (Davis would later come back into the picture.) Joyce's second choice,

L. B. Conroy of New Orleans, accepted the position. Conroy assumed the duties of managing the mill and lumber sales, while Ives retained management of logging and railroad operations.

The new mill's machinery was humming under new management by late summer of 1904 when fate delivered William Joyce and the people of Groveton a cruel blow. After only three months of operation the main sawmill was reduced to a smoking heap of ashes and twisted metal.[14] Joyce was undaunted by this exorbitant financial setback and responded to the fire just as his father had to the burning of the Lyons, Iowa mill in 1888. He immediately called for rebuilding, relying on the original plans and specifications. Within a week, men started clearing the blackened rubble. The duplicated mill became operational in short order; band saws bit into the first logs by early spring of 1905.

Groveton Experiences Growing Pains

William Joyce's consternation with management and mill problems was rivaled by his dismay over the social problems of the wild Texas lumbering town. The booming saloon business, typical of young lumbering towns, brought trouble during a lawless period from 1890 to 1907. When the consumption of bootleg liquor bred murders and brawls, extreme measures were required to reclaim the community. Local historian Patricia Hensley chronicled Groveton's travails, citing the efforts of Methodist minister Jessie Lee, who also served as a deputy sheriff, to clean up the town. He enlisted a mob of vigilantes who marched about Groveton "destroying the saloons and running the bootleggers out." As a result of his crusades against alcohol, Lee acquired a considerable list of enemies. He wore his holster and side arms at all times in the interest of self-preservation. He did not part company with his pistols even during the Sunday service, although "he took them out of the holster and laid them on the pulpit while he delivered his sermon." Retaliators burned Lee's church and threatened his life, forcing him to practice his ministry in another community.[15]

Jessie Lee's vigilante efforts were reinforced by legitimate law enforcement. Six Texas Rangers rode into Groveton and boarded in local residences in an effort to quell the mayhem. These men were well practiced in discouraging outlaws that troubled communities like Groveton. They had ridden the Texas range for decades, ferreting out despicable characters interrupting the peace and quiet of law-abiding citizens. One evening the rangers arrived at a Groveton boarding house for supper after a grueling day of enforcing law and order. The lady of the house insisted they deposit all firearms outside the front door on the porch. The neighborhood boys seized this opportunity to stir up the rangers by touching off a few firecrackers beneath the crawlspace of the home while the men dined inside. When the first concussions sounded, the rangers' finely honed survival instincts sent them scrambling for their weapons. The table, along with food, drink, and dishes, took a ballistic course as the men focused on the most direct path to the front door. These mischievous youngsters—one of whom was the son of the owner of the house—were quickly discovered as the source of the disturbance, much to the relief of the rangers, who graciously paid for the damaged china.[16]

William Joyce voiced his disgust at the lawless faction riddling the town with violence. During the mill reconstruction in 1905 he sarcastically commented that it was "a good time for a lot of those devils to go out and shoot at each other, thereby possibly improving the community."[17] The victims of the frequent gunplay, however, were not always the troublemakers. After a disagreement between a lawyer and a Texas Ranger, the lawyer took a potshot at the ranger on Groveton's main street. The speeding bullet missed the intended target and went on to kill a second attorney standing at the door of the local barbershop.

Joyce and Trinity management were drawn into the fray as violence, motivated by racial intolerance, began to affect company employees. Maintaining a cohesive workforce when black wage earners constituted the majority of workers required delicate maneuvering. Racial tensions, virtually unknown to lumbering in the northern states, repeatedly obstructed the production of lumber throughout the South. A segment of the white population, influenced by the Ku Klux Klan, violently opposed employment of black men. But the black men had proved themselves to be valuable laborers in the hot humid southern forests. This placed the company in the middle of the conflict.

Manager A. B. Ives met one such challenge in 1900. That year his men commuted sixteen miles every morning on the company's railroad to reach standing timber. The substantial travel time lengthened the already exhausting twelve-hour workday. To ameliorate the situation, the company resorted to railroad boarding cars, essentially a mobile logging camp, to house the men in the woods during the week. But news of race riots and murders in isolated lumber camps elsewhere in Texas and Louisiana made Trinity's black contingent reluctant to occupy the new boarding cars. Ives responded with a "program of education" that quieted racial tensions. He also promised that his woods crews would be protected with armed guards.[18] After cooling the explosive atmosphere, Ives convinced the mixed race crews to return to work and to live together in the remote camps. Designated boarding cars kept the races segregated within the camps just as company housing segregated the races in Groveton.

Experience taught the Trinity County Lumber Company that whenever it moved into a new section of the forest, trouble was inevitable. Some white settlers became agitated at the sight of black workers on logging crews. These rabble-rousing local farmers threatened to burn the company's trees, sabotage the railroad, and rough up the workers. The company placated the local people by giving them token odd jobs, a strategy that effectively diminished the hostile resistance. The company's armory of .30-30 rifles also deserves some credit as a promoter of peace.

The Trinity County Lumber Company strove to bring stability within the town of Groveton as well. It maintained housing and provided water, electricity, ice, and garden plots for flowers and vegetables. The company doctor looked after the health of the town's population. Trinity also presented recreational alternatives to the corruptive saloons. A long pier led to a large open-air pavilion in the center of the company's largest millpond. The pavilion became the Groveton social center, where couples swayed to the beat of dance bands playing during the hot summer nights. On three sides of the pavilion, steps extended to the water for swimming and boating. On Sunday afternoons young men and women met at the pier and rowed out on the millpond, nestling their boats together before dropping anchor and crooning such favorite melodies as "Down by the Old Mill Stream" and "Carry Me Back to Old Virginia." Fishing from the pier was another popular pastime. In the latter part of the 1920s, a natatorium, or indoor swimming pool, was built beside the millpond.[19]

Perhaps as popular as the open-air pavilion, the company store served as a gathering place for the townsfolk. Such stores were standard features in nearly all lumbering communities. In 1905 the Trinity company store was stocked with "dry goods, clothing, crockery, glassware, groceries and provisions"—almost everything a family needed.[20] The large inventory was valued between $50,000 and $100,000 in 1912. On the store's porch, which stretched across its entire front wall, shoppers exchanged news and gossip.[21]

Crowds of people flocked to the store on special occasions like the ever-popular summer style shows on the porch. Possibly the biggest event promoted Buster Brown shoes, when Buster Brown visited Groveton. A stage was set up at the side of the company store, where Buster and his dog Tige entertained the community. Tige amazed the audience with fantastic feats, such as smoking cigarettes, finding hidden objects, and walking on his hind legs. Afterwards, children in town lobbied hard for Buster Brown shoes, Buster Brown suits, and Buster Brown haircuts. The dogs of Groveton suffered hours of training but could never quite muster the talents of Tige.[22]

Management Squabbles

Problems at Trinity exceeded those at any of William Joyce's many other companies. Much to his dismay, Joyce constantly had to chastise his managers, who seemed unable to run the business according to his directives. Trouble began during the fall of 1903 when Joyce sent his auditors to review the company records. At that time, A. B. Ives directed the company's logging and railroad operations, while L. B. Conroy managed the mill and lumber sales and presumably controlled the books. Although Joyce already knew the bookkeeping was inadequate, the audit revealed every painful detail. Ives resented the exposure and balked at assisting the auditors. Conroy followed suit by claiming that the auditors were interfering when they showed him better accounting methods.

Both managers warned that they would leave if they were forced to follow the auditors' directives. In their telegrams to Joyce, they also criticized each other in a childish, tattle-tale manner. Joyce had no time for such antics. His return telegram stated unequivocally that this was "no occasion for excitement, discord or expensive telegraphing."[23] Unfortunately the infighting persisted. After several months, Joyce refused to tolerate the unprofessional behavior any longer and moved to end the fray. "While I am not accustomed to issuing orders in an arbitrary manner or to keep continually asserting myself, I believe that I am competent to run my own business or to have it run in my way, and I propose to do this and to do this regarding the Trinity County Lumber Company to a greater extent than I have heretofore, and I want to say to both of you that I am very disappointed in you as men."[24] His stinging rebuke induced Conroy to resign. Surprisingly, Ives bowed to the criticism and continued to work at Trinity. Perhaps he felt somewhat vindicated at Conroy's resignation. In any case, Ives possessed good management skills, provided he was kept away from the company books. Joyce sent his right-hand man from Chicago, W. A. Remick, to Groveton as an interim replacement for Conroy. Ives and Remick stayed on until Joyce selected a new manager.

Joyce once again queried W. F. N. Davis of Michigan about accepting the management position. Evidently he thought Davis would be a cure-all for Trinity, for Joyce proposed an extremely attractive financial incentive—one-quarter of the company stock, free and clear. Davis accepted the offer and moved to Groveton early in 1905. Joyce believed so strongly in the ability of Davis that he issued instructions to his employees at Trinity to regard Davis's word as final in all matters.

After six months with Davis at the helm, the company seemed to run smoothly, and William Joyce began to relax. His satisfaction with Davis turned out to be short-lived, however, for news arrived in Chicago that the new manager and the auditors were butting heads. Other conflicts boiled up in rapid succession. Joyce had instructed Davis to build a standard-gauge railroad to replace the narrow-gauge logging railroad. Davis procrastinated. Davis also needled Joyce to put the Trinity County Lumber Company up for sale, but Joyce had no interest in selling. Then Davis offered to buy the company himself or get out entirely by having Joyce purchase Davis's one-quarter stock interest. Joyce retorted that Davis was under a contract and must run the company as directed. Davis responded through his attorney, an action that caught Joyce off guard. Joyce responded with dismay on March 12, 1907: "I have been in business quite a number of years. I think I am President of seventeen different corporations at the present time and am interested in many others. None of my associates have ever found it necessary to approach me through an attorney."[25]

Joyce summarily booted Davis out of the Trinity County Lumber Company after he had served one year as company manager. But Davis and his attorney were not done with Joyce. They initiated a civil suit alleging that Davis had a claim to the company stock. Joyce recognized that although Davis had never purchased his one-quarter stock interest, his contract stipulated that Davis owned the stock. Fearing that the suit was tarnishing the image of the Joyce organization, Joyce reluctantly offered Davis a cash settlement to cover the value of stock and other claims. Apparently $141,000 appeased Davis, for he made no further demands.

Joyce took a different approach after these debacles. He assumed the position of general manager of Trinity himself, making it clear that he had full authority over the company. Apparently Joyce did not spend any time in Groveton but instead maintained his rule from Chicago with the help of his son, David Gage Joyce, and two trusted men, David Batchelder Jr., and J. C. Anderson. All three were sent to Texas to appraise the company management. After the investigation, Joyce assigned Anderson the task of rebuilding the logging railroad, a project which the previous manager, Davis, had refused to begin. When Anderson successfully completed this charge, Joyce rewarded him with the general manager's position in 1908.

William Joyce was dead within a year of appointing J. C. Anderson as general manager. Joyce's two sons, David and Stanley, assumed control of his business empire, including the trouble-prone Texas operation. The propensity toward unsettled management seemed infectious at the Trinity County Lumber Company. In 1912 Stanley Joyce arrived in Groveton from Chicago to address allegations of Anderson's incompetence. After firing Anderson, Joyce came frequently to Groveton, setting up his own apartment in town so he could keep the company's progress under a keen eye.[26] A. E. Ball, another mill man from Lyons, Iowa, replaced Anderson in January 1913. Ball managed Trinity without incident for three years before he quit for personal reasons. The next manager worked only two years. It seems Sheffield Bridgewater had an irresistible urge to paint the town of Groveton red. For this purpose he purchased four railroad tank cars of red paint. The flamboyant painting fiasco sealed his fate. Baxter Stallcup succeeded Bridgewater for four years before following his predecessors out the door. Frequent turnovers in management continued until the final stick of lumber left the Trinity County Lumber Company mill in 1931.

The Logging Railroad Is Transformed

The Groveton, Kickapoo and Gulf, Trinity's narrow-gauge logging railroad, was innovative when it was built in 1886 but approached the limits of its useful life as it entered the twentieth century. The treeless void around Groveton extended outward many miles from the mill, and the light rails and old engines strained to keep up a steady feed of logs for the hungry band saws. No longer remote, the Pineywoods was crisscrossed by a grid of standard-gauge railway lines for passengers and freight that hemmed in the future advancement of the narrow gauge. Unless William Joyce's logging railroad was transformed into a full-fledged standard-gauge railway, capable of freely interchanging trains on the surrounding rail network, it would become history.

Other factors weighted the decision to update the railroad. Lumber companies owning standard-gauge logging railroads earned a division—or a share of the shipping costs—on lumber traffic from their parent company mills as well as on other freight. With the added income from divisions, freight, and regular passenger service, a standard-gauge logging railroad could possibly pay for its construction and even operate as a profitable investment. The fact that Trinity's shipping costs were high also tipped the balance in favor of updating the railroad. Since Groveton was serviced by only one interstate carrier, the Missouri, Kansas, and Texas Railway, the Trinity County Lumber Company was unable to secure competitive shipping prices for its lumber.

The Trinity County Lumber Company owned the Groveton, Lufkin, and Northern logging railroad.
COURTESY OF KATE ATKINSON BELL

Company manager Ives researched the details of converting the Groveton, Kickapoo, and Gulf. His communication to William Joyce in 1900 concluded that if a line were built through the lumber company's lands to a junction with the Houston, East and West Texas Railway, a subsidiary of the Southern Pacific, shipping costs of Trinity lumber would be substantially reduced. Ives estimated lumber-shipping costs could be cut by $1.50 per thousand board feet. This was on lumber that sold for between $3.50 and $10.00 per thousand board feet, depending on the grade.

Ives' impressive numbers tempted Joyce to consider rebuilding the railroad in 1900, but he postponed the project since, at that time, he was trying to sell the Trinity County Lumber Company. The rebuilding of the sawmill and the ongoing managerial problems at Trinity further delayed the start of the project until 1906. That year Joyce optimistically authorized the standard-gauge line, envisioned to link Groveton and Houston. By 1908 the rails reached approximately twenty miles northeast to Vair, connecting with the tracks of another short-line railroad, the Texas and Southeastern.

From there, Joyce's railroad leased the right to travel upon the Texas and Southeastern into the city of Lufkin, another sixteen miles. This accomplished, the sawmill at Groveton finally gained access to more than one major rail carrier, opening the door to competition, which assured reduced shipping rates.

After leasing the rail connection to Lufkin in 1908, Joyce and his lawyers took steps to rework the corporate structure of the railroad. They formed a new corporation called the Groveton, Lufkin & Northern Railroad (GL&N) in order to comply with state and federal regulations. These regulations required a complete separation between the railroad and lumbering operations if the railroad wanted to collect divisions. Following incorporation, the railroad received common carrier status, giving it the power of eminent domain and rights to receive divisions. In exchange for these benefits, the common carrier status mandated a commitment to public service and adherence to regulatory guidelines. On November 29, 1908, the GL&N began daily passenger and freight services between Groveton and Lufkin, a distance of thirty-six miles.

Coincidentally, after the GL&N's incorporation, the Interstate Commerce Commission (ICC) initiated investigations into short lines, such as the GL&N, and their practice of receiving divisions. Some lumber companies complained to the ICC that lumber plants that also owned railroad facilities were obtaining unfair advantages in the lumber market.[27] No doubt the lumber companies that raised the issue did not own railroad facilities and were irritated by the fact that collecting divisions effectively reduced the cost of shipping finished lumber. Put another way, a lumber company receiving divisions could produce lumber at a lower cost.

The ICC investigation of short-line divisions was a serious matter for Joyce, for he had counted on income from divisions when he built the GL&N. The Trinity County Lumber Company and the GL&N took additional steps at this point to maintain the appearance of two separate companies. Preferential shipping rates for Trinity lumber and free rights for logging trains to use GL&N tracks were eliminated. In reality, reducing these preferential shipping rates for lumber amounted to superficial compliance with the law. The two companies were owned by the same people, with Joyce serving as the principal stockholder, so the cost of GL&N shipping charges for the lumber company did not matter.

When the Interstate Commerce Commission ruled on the divisions issue, it did not fall for the two-separate-companies ploy used by companies like Trinity and the GL&N. The ICC's ruling disallowed a significant percentage of the divisions that the GL&N had been receiving. Appeals continued for several years. The GL&N tried to make the case that it was a legitimate common carrier, hauling agricultural products vital to the local farming community. Indeed, farmers around Groveton produced substantial amounts of cotton, which constituted the bulk of agricultural shipments on the GL&N. In 1911 the railroad carried 14,646 tons of freight other than lumber, which represented about twenty-seven percent of the total traffic. During this period, the company actively promoted public use of the railroad to bolster its case before the ICC. The final ruling that came in 1914 permitted the GL&N a slight increase in the division rates. Still, the revised rates affected all freight and fell short of what the GL&N had been collecting prior to the ICC action.

In spite of the ICC intervention that lowered the profits of the railroad, the GL&N still upgraded its equipment, tracks, and bridges, as it traveled further to collect timber for the mill. At the time of incorporation, the GL&N rolling stock included two coal-fired locomotives, thirty flat cars, sixteen boxcars, one passenger car, and a combination passenger/freight car, which operated on twenty-one miles of track made of sixty-pound steel rails. The Trinity County Lumber Company retained ownership of some equipment, such as logging cars and boarding camp cars, as well as a Shay locomotive.[28] A three-cylinder geared locomotive, the Shay was designed explicitly for the logging industry. Although slow and noisy, the geared Shay possessed great pulling power and personality. In fact, according to one writer, "No one who has ever known it could forget it: the sight of a Shay thrashing its way up a grade, lost in an aura of sound and smoke and steam."[29] By 1919 the original two standard-gauge locomotives had been replaced with a larger ten-wheel oil-burning locomotive and a six-wheel coal-burning locomotive. Another passenger car and a caboose had been added. To improve the economics of hauling logs from more distant forests, heavy-duty rail cars designed specifically for log hauling were purchased. Built expressly for the Trinity County Lumber Company, each of these cars had a capacity of 100,000 pounds. All of the tracks were upgraded with 110-pound rails, and all bridges were reconstructed for the heavier and presumably higher-speed traffic. The quality of the GL&N tracks permitted a major rail line, the Southern Pacific Railway, to reroute its traffic temporarily over the GL&N when devastating floods struck Texas in 1927.[30]

Although the company found it necessary to upgrade its equipment to keep pace with the demands of the sawmill, there was an alternative to extending the rails to reach the ever-receding forests around Groveton. The GL&N determined that it was more economical to lease trackage rights from other railroads than to construct its own tracks. As a result, the track length of the GL&N never grew beyond 22 miles, yet its trains traveled as far as 100 miles to reach the Trinity County Lumber Company's logging camps. GL&N trains made connections to one large tract of Trinity timber near Colmesneil, Texas, over the tracks of three other railroads. The GL&N entered into a joint maintenance agreement with one of these, the Texas and Southeastern, and even shared construction costs and ownership of the long bridge over the Angelina River.[31]

The Great Depression Fells Trinity and Its Railroad

The Trinity County Lumber Company and its logging railroad, the Groveton Lufkin and Northern, had prospered in an era of cut-out-and-get-out logging that relied on constant access to virgin timber. With no thought given to reforestation, the fate of the Trinity sawmill was preordained. Further hamstringing the lumber company was the stock market crash of 1929. The Great Depression that followed seized the economic machinery of the country, quelling any hopes of continuing mill operation. The Joyce organization responded with a prudent business decision to close the mill.

This loss deprived Groveton of its financial footing at the worst possible time. The citizens of Groveton could not help but know that their lives would be changed forever as the earsplitting gasp of the steam boilers, a traditional end-of-life salute for sawmills, echoed across the remains of the Pineywoods on December 31, 1930. Many years later, one citizen, Elmer O. Hill, described the closing of the mill: "At 12:00 midnight the steam whistle was pulled open and tied down until all the steam was exhausted, which lasted about an hour. As the whistle began to blow, it was like the giant it was; as the steam diminished, the roar turned to a whine; at last it began to make weak cries and then a sigh as its end came and we who remember the end will not forget it. Most of us who are living today were children, but we sensed its meaning."[32] Immediately before the mill closure, the GL&N railroad petitioned the Interstate Commerce Commission for authorization to proceed with abandonment, citing the impending loss of the lumber traffic, about eighty percent of its total freight. Other indicators for the survival of the railroad also looked bleak. Efforts to consolidate the GL&N into a mainline railroad, such as the Cotton Belt or Southern Pacific systems, failed to garner support since the GL&N had no importance as a strategic route. The passenger income of the railroad was falling off rapidly as automobiles grew in number. At the same time, the use of trucks chipped away at the remaining freight base of the GL&N. As the ICC's deadline for public comment neared, the local populace failed to organize any protest against abandonment. The commission granted the GL&N permission to proceed with abandonment on July 31, 1931. Service continued until the last day of 1931, when its Texas charter expired, ending the life of the railroad.

The Groveton community, already strained by national depression, reeled under the loss of mill and railroad. Its population of 4,000 plummeted to 2,000 as families moved elsewhere to find work. Ed C. Johnson, the mill superintendent who blew the last whistle, was hired as superintendent at another Joyce enterprise, the Tremont Lumber Company in Rochelle, Louisiana. Other workers went with Johnson to join Tremont. Over the next few years, the mill machinery that could be salvaged was dismantled and shipped to another mill.[33]

For forty-five years the employment provided by the Trinity County Lumber Company had allowed the citizens of Groveton to create a thriving community, and those who did not leave town to find new jobs fought to keep Groveton from slipping to ghost town status. According to Elmer O. Hill, "The people began taking inventory of what was left and how they could use it to maintain the town. By the efforts of its people and the Grace of God the town of Groveton did survive and progressed."[34]

Life after Lumbering

Even though the mill and railroad had ceased to exist, the Trinity County Lumber Company had one final mission, namely the disposal of about 90,000 acres of cutover land. Land sales proved to be problematic. Potential buyers were paralyzed by the Great Depression, and little of the vast acreage could sustain agricultural pursuits due to poor soil. With land sales stalled, Stanley Joyce contacted David Zetterstrom, land sales department manager for the Itasca Lumber Company in Minnesota, to investigate the possibility of selling the Trinity property to the federal government. Zetterstrom's encouraging report in 1934 led to negotiations with the government, succeeded a few months later by the sale of 58,000 acres for $3.75 per acre. The government absorbed the purchase into the Davy Crockett National Forest.

Just before the sale of the property in 1934, the first oil well in Trinity County began to spew a spectacular 1,500 barrels of oil per day only fifteen miles east of Joyce lands. David and Stanley Joyce responded by retaining oil rights on all of the land sold, even the parcels acquired by the Davy Crockett National Forest. Trinity County Lumber Company's oil rights on 90,000 acres immediately attracted a barrage of offers from those hoping to secure a claim in the area. Inexperienced in the domain of oil exploration and production, the Joyces sought out the best of their suitors. Three weeks after the first strike in Trinity County they leased their oil rights to the Gulf Production Company. According to the agreement, Gulf Production would pay a one-eighth royalty on all oil produced and $1.00 per ton on all sulfur produced. The hoped-for oil proved to be elusive. As the years progressed, the boom went bust. Subsequent oil strikes brought in only dribbles of crude. In 1944 a new lease on Trinity's oil rights was negotiated with the Continental and Magnolia Oil Companies. This same year marked the death of Stanley Joyce (whose brother, David, had died in 1937) and the final dissolution of the Trinity

County Lumber Company. Its lingering 30,000 acres of land was sold to another lumber company and other individuals. The oil rights to 90,000 acres were distributed to the stockholders, including Beatrice Joyce, the last living Joyce and the majority stockholder. Management of the Texas oil leases shifted to the only remaining Joyce enterprise, the Tremont Lumber Company in nearby Louisiana.

Three generations of the Joyce family had struggled with the Trinity County Lumber Company, but in the final analysis, the endeavor must be considered a success. At one time it was the longest running and the largest sawmill business in Texas, manufacturing a whopping two billion board feet of lumber over its forty-five year run.[35] Furthermore, the stockholders profited handsomely, and the company offered an entire community reliable employment during its operation.

When the Trinity County Lumber Company disappeared in accordance with the old doctrine of cut-out-and-get-out logging, it signaled the end of a business philosophy. A new doctrine of sustainable-yield logging now demanded the Joyce family's attention as the Tremont Lumber Company of Louisiana teetered between following Trinity County Lumber Company's journey to oblivion or embracing sustainable-yield logging practices.

Louisiana Cypress—The Wood Eternal

WILLIAM JOYCE MADE HIS FIRST FORAY into Louisiana in May 1900 to purchase approximately 33,000 acres of tidewater cypress lands with his Itasca Lumber Company partners, Charles Hackley and Thomas Hume. The purchase, located north of New Orleans near Lake Pontchartrain and the town of Ponchatoula, cost the trio slightly more than $600,000. The investment was sound, for cypress from the coastal region yielded some of the finest and most durable lumber of any tree species in North America. However, rather than logging and manufacturing cypress lumber, the men hoped to profit by reselling the standing cypress. Protected by a watery morass in Tangipahoa and Livingston parishes, the great solitudes of the moss-draped cypress were beyond the realm of these northern lumbermen's logging experience.[1]

Joyce and his partners continued to purchase smaller tracts of cypress in the Lake Maurepas area, immediately west of Lake Pontchartrain, as they became available in the years that followed. Timber reserves on a 1,440-acre tract located at the mouth of the Amite River on Lake Maurepas translated into 19 million board feet of cypress and 2 million board feet of gum (water tupelo). The men justified the purchase price of $75,000 by calculating that the cypress cost them less than $4.00 per thousand board feet. They bought an additional 332 acres of adjoining cypress for $12,500.[2] William Joyce felt somewhat cautious about buying unfamiliar land from afar and relied upon J. D. Lacey, his agent in Louisiana, to help him verify the location of his purchases. Writing to Lacey in one instance, Joyce confided, "I undertook to check up the deeds with the plat which you had previously sent me of the lands for which we are trading. I find it impossible to check the deeds with the plat, or to locate definitely upon the plat the lands conveyed by the deeds." Joyce then requested "government plats or some other information which will enable me to definitely locate the land conveyed."[3] William Joyce was meticulous in all of his business transactions.

Joyce's uneasiness about buying cypress lands in Louisiana was heightened while he and his partners were purchasing additional cypress tracts. The state of Louisiana challenged ownership of a large part of the property he owned with Hackley and Hume as well as the property of other lumbermen around Lake Maurepas. These parcels fell under the category of tidal overflow lands, essentially swamplands at sea level, for which the state originally charged $.25 per acre during the 1870s. In 1905, state officials believed that some of the parcels had been above sea level when sold, and, therefore, the state should not have sold the land for less than $1.25 per acre. At the time of the state's challenge, cypress lands commanded more than $50.00 per acre on the open market.[4]

After claiming that the original sales were fraudulent and that the current owners held invalid titles to their parcels, the state was placed in the awkward position of having to prove the invalidity of its 1870s sales. The state's case looked weak, but Joyce and the other cypress owners took no chances and mounted a vigorous defense over several years. In 1909 state officials reluctantly dropped their case when conclusive evidence proved that water levels on the lands fluctuated in sync with tidal motions.[5] William Joyce did not survive to see the final page turned on the tidal overflow suit. Not long after his death, his sons David and Stanley received a clear title to the property and continued to hold on to the valuable cypress lands as a speculative investment.

The cypress property, estimated to contain roughly 400 million board feet of timber, attracted the attention of several lumbermen during the decade following the death of William Joyce in 1909. In 1914 the Lyon Cypress Company offered David and Stanley Joyce, the estate of the late Charles Hackley, and Thomas Hume $4.5 million for the land, more than seven times the original purchase cost. The partners refused the offer, gambling that the value of trees could only go up. The Joyces' timber agent in the South, J. D. Lacey & Company, transmitted a number of like opportunities to the Joyces. Then, in the spring of 1919, Lacey came forward with his own plan. It called for a joint partnership between the Lacey Timber Company and a proposed timber company to be formed by the Joyce brothers, along with Thomas Hume and the Estate of Charles Hackley, to manufacture lumber from the cypress lands. E. E. Moberly, banker and lumberman from New York, would manage the operation after becoming a large stockholder in the Lacey Timber Company. The partners vetoed the plan.[6]

Proponents of one unique proposal to use the Louisiana cypress lands wanted to exploit neither the trees nor the land but the Spanish moss, which hung thickly from the lower branches of the cypress trees. George S. Clarke of the Reeves Company, New Orleans, offered in 1915 to harvest the moss—a source of fiber—on an industrial scale as opposed to the usual method of procuring the moss from individual collectors. The men engaged in collection would use long hooked poles and rope ladders to reach the aerial tresses. Clarke anticipated collecting about one railroad car of ten tons of dry moss per week, about 500 to 600 tons per year. In return, the landowners would receive a royalty of $3.00 per ton. The sum was paltry compared to the value of the cypress wood, but it generated considerable correspondence among the owners.

The chief concern over moss collection centered on possible damage to the trees. Clarke assured the Joyce brothers and their partners that the crews would exercise the utmost care when removing the moss. The lumbermen also asked whether the moss might impart some vital symbiotic factor for the survival of cypress, a legitimate question since the exact relationship between moss and tree was unknown to them. Spanish moss is not a moss at all but rather a member of the bromeliad plant family, growing from trees as silvery-gray threadlike masses up to eighteen feet long. What we know now is that the plants derive no moisture or nourishment from the host trees, using them simply as a means of support. Nor does the moss provide any benefit to the trees. Although he lacked this knowledge, Stanley Joyce still wrote to Thomas Hume in support of the scheme, saying, "I should think it would be a good thing for us to pick up this additional revenue and I cannot see why there should be any harm in taking the moss from the trees."[7] The outcome of the moss proposal is unknown since the records are incomplete.

The valuable cypress was drawing increasingly more interest from lumbermen, and the Joyce brothers knew that they were sitting on a potential gold mine. In 1919 David and Stanley Joyce signed a contract to buy out the Hackley-Hume half of the

Louisiana cypress. While William Joyce spent $318,000 for a half interest in 35,000 acres in 1902, his sons procured the other half in 1919 for a little more than $2.3 million. (This was paid in installments over several years with the final exchange occurring in 1928.) A few months after the buyout, the Joyce brothers sold just less than 15,000 acres of their cypress near Ponchatoula to Joseph Rathborne of Harvey, Louisiana, and C. Seyburn Williams of New Orleans. These two men owned and operated the Joseph Rathborne Lumber Company and the Williams Lumber Company. Rathborne and Williams jointly constructed a mill near Ponchatoula and began manufacturing cypress lumber from the 245 million board feet of timber they had just purchased. The Joyces, who collected a handsome profit on the sale, still owned 18,917 acres on which stood 238 million board feet of cypress.[8]

The remaining acreage of Joyce cypress now sat idle, but it appreciated in value with every passing year. Cypress lumber, known as the *wood eternal*, grew in its reputation as a premium product. Among the many qualities of this beautifully grained and colored wood are exceptional resistance to decay and warping. Its workability is similar to white pine, yet it possesses greater strength than white pine and can be nailed without splitting. This most desirable of woods had a narrow geographic range, making it relatively scarce. All factors combined to drive the market price of cypress lumber well beyond that of other woods.[9]

In late 1930 the Williams and Rathborne Cypress Lumber Company milled the last of the increasingly valuable cypress purchased from the Joyces in 1919. Almost nothing of the original forests of cypress was left at that time, and many of Louisiana's cypress mills had closed.[10]

The Joyces now saw an excellent opportunity to assume operation of the Williams and Rathborne mill to manufacture the rare cypress on their own land. Accordingly, in 1930, they incorporated the Louisiana Cypress Lumber Company with a capitalization of $500,000 and then purchased the idled Rathborne mill and equipment near Ponchatoula. But the Great Depression was dampening the demand for lumber, and the Joyces felt content to withhold production until the nation was once again on its feet. (In 1934 a United States Forest Service analysis revealed that Louisiana possessed 1,628,915 acres of denuded cypress lands and only 22,356 acres of intact cypress. Of the standing cypress lands, Joyce's 18,917 acres constituted the bulk of what remained in Louisiana.) Claude H. Lindsay, an employee of Joyce's other Louisiana enterprise called the Tremont Lumber Company, spent the years from 1930 to 1936 overseeing plant renovations and fashioning equipment for laying railroad tracks through the cypress swamp. The fluctuant swampland presented a challenge because it not only rose one foot above sea level but also dropped one foot below sea level. Lindsay successfully met this challenge by completing "the 'Gumbo Line' where 'the rails squish down into the muck, to rise behind with a noise like a prolonged movie kiss'."[11]

Running the Gumbo Line through the swamps was a complicated undertaking. Crews creating the footing for the rails first felled trees adjacent to each other along the survey lines. On top of the tumbled trees, they constructed the semi-stable base with sawdust, shavings, bark, chips, and more trees.[12] After this long skinny compost pile crowned by railroad ties was complete, the steel gang moved in to do its job. Railroad spurs or dredged canals fanned out from the main line into the cypress swamp at regular intervals, placing almost every nook of the forest within reach of the cable skidders.

In 1936 the Joyce-owned Louisiana Cypress Lumber Company started production for the first time under Claude H. Lindsay, company president and general manager. Lindsay knew that the process of harvesting cypress, like the construction of the Gumbo Line, was complicated by the watery environment. Prior to harvesting, a crew entered the cypress swamps to deaden the trees by girdling their trunks, a procedure that reduced the moisture content of the wood. It was important to dry the wood before moving the massive logs because there was no solid ground in the swamp. A cubic foot of dry cypress weighs half of an equal amount of green cypress, and although the deadened stands of cypress could not be thoroughly dried, at least the felled logs would float. Before felling the trees, the men wielding saws were sometimes obliged to throw up scaffolding because of the heavily buttressed bases of these trees, occasionally twenty-five to forty-five feet in circumference. The scaffolding raised the lumberjacks' footing five or six feet above the ground so they could reach the narrower part of the trunk.[13]

Crews hauled logs to rail side by two methods. Cables from the steam skidders snaked out through the swamps, drawing the logs to the train tracks so that they could be hoisted onto the Gumbo Line. Where dredged canals or natural waterways, called bayous, existed, logs were floated short distances to the rail loading points with pull boats. Every quarter mile work crews constructed pockets on alternating sides of the canal. A pull boat parked in a pocket and played out a long cable before winching the floating logs up to the boat. Then the pull boat moved on to the next pocket and repeated this process until it reached a rail loading point. There the logs were loaded onto flat cars, which made the quick journey to the Ponchatoula mill. Sixteen million board feet of cypress were harvested annually in this manner, clear-cut from about 1,250 acres.[14]

Initially cypress sales remained steady. Between 1936 and 1941 Louisiana Cypress marketed 86 million board feet of cypress, which averaged $46.00 per thousand board feet. Following World War II and the death of Stanley Joyce in 1944, only 6 million board feet of cypress left the mill each year, but the price had reached a phenomenal $130 per thousand board feet. Scant cypress remained to be cut, and harvesting second growth was entirely out of the question, for the slow-growing cypress requires at least 100 years to be marginally useful and 300 years for optimum size. In fact, many of the felled trees revealed growth rings in excess of 1,000 years, hardly a renewable resource. The best use of Louisiana's clear-cut tidewater cypress swamps was considered to be dredging, drainage, and conversion to farmland. Commercial sugar beet farms profitably operated on some of the converted acreage.[15]

The Ponchatoula mill began supplementing the rapidly diminishing cypress stocks with mahogany logs shipped from Mexico and Central America. Max Fowler, who started as a forester at the Joyce-owned Tremont Lumber Company in 1953, said that by the time he visited Ponchatoula, the mill almost exclusively manufactured imported mahogany. This kept the mill alive until approximately 1970, when the Louisiana Cypress Lumber Company merged with Joyce's greater enterprise, the Tremont Lumber Company, placing management of the cutover lands and potential oil deposits under the auspices of the larger organization.[16]

In late 1978 some of the cypress swamp, then owned by the Joyce Foundation, became the Joyce Wildlife Area. The Joyce Foundation donated 13,660 acres of swamp, located just south of Ponchatoula between Lake Maurepas and Lake Pontchartrain, and free-leased approximately 850 additional acres to the Louisiana Department of Wildlife and Fisheries with help from the Nature Conservancy in transferring property. Now the public observes Louisiana swamp ecology from a 1,500-foot long, elevated boardwalk built by this Louisiana agency.[17] Here second-growth cypress gains stature annually on its millennial journey to reclaim a lost title: monarch of the Louisiana swamps.

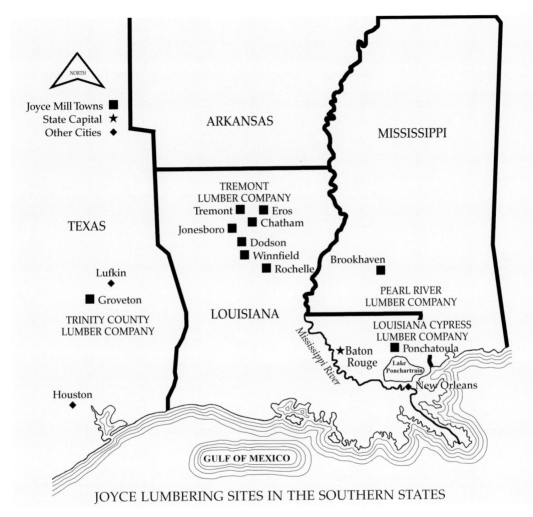

JOYCE LUMBERING SITES IN THE SOUTHERN STATES

Tremont Lumber—The Pinnacle Achievement

TREMONT LUMBER COMPANY ORIGINATED IN 1899 as a modest mill formed by several citizens of Tremont, Louisiana. William Joyce bought into the Tremont company six years later in order to bolster his investments in southern lumbering. With the strength of Joyce capital and expertise, this company evolved into an important producer of lumber nationally, operating one of the largest mills in the South. Unlike Joyce enterprises in other states that each depended upon a single mill,

Tremont expanded as an umbrella organization with multiple mill sites, nearly 200,000 acres of timberlands, and a private railway system linking all of the mills and lands of the logging business. Its defining success came as the company survived the cut-out-and-get-out logging era as well as the Great Depression. Tremont went on to prosper by embracing forest-management techniques that relied upon timber regrowth and sustainable-yield concepts.

Like Joyce's Trinity County Lumber Company of Texas, the Louisiana firm was based in the Pineywoods extending from East Texas through western and central Louisiana. Eighty-five percent of Louisiana was still forested when northern lumbermen seriously turned their attention to the state. A broad thirty- to fifty-mile swath of hardwood forests followed the Mississippi River bottoms. Upland areas supported the growth of pine species while the expansive coastal tidewater areas fostered seemingly endless cypress groves. Collectively this region represented more than "150 billion board feet of virgin timber, exceeding that of any other state east of the Pacific Coast."[1]

Even though the state harbored one of the greatest timber reserves in the nation, the development of Louisiana's lumber industry was slow. A dearth of transportation hobbled access to forests and to out-of-state lumber markets. Loggers were confined to a few good driving rivers, including the Sabine, the Calcasieu, and the Red. From the mouths of these rivers on the Gulf Coast, longshoremen hoisted lumber onto schooners that sailed to distant markets. The navigable system of tributaries, however, could touch very little of what Louisiana had to offer. As in Texas, railroads launched the era of large-scale lumbering, yet they did not significantly penetrate Louisiana's pine areas until nearly the turn of the century. Northern lumbermen, driven by the looming demise of white pine, arrived along with the rail development, infusing capital into the state's milling machinery. They joined forces with southern lumbermen to put Louisiana at the top of the chart for lumber production. In 1869 Louisiana had produced less lumber than any other southern state. However, by 1904, Louisiana mills had taken the lead in the South, sawing almost 2.5 billion board feet. Nationally, Louisiana ranked either second or third in lumber production during the years between 1907 and 1925 with the exception of 1914, when it sawed more lumber than any other state.[2]

The Mississippi Venture

A surprisingly short-term lumbering investment in the state of Mississippi ultimately led to William Joyce's Tremont venture in Louisiana. In Joyce's hometown of Lyons, Iowa, David J. Batchelder Jr., son of Lyons Savings Bank president and lumberman David J. Batchelder Sr., promoted a newly formed Mississippi lumbering enterprise known as the Pearl River Lumber Company. Young Batchelder, who owned twenty percent of the company stock, assured Joyce that the company was a fiscally sound investment for his idle cash. William Joyce knew David J. Batchelder Jr. and trusted his word. Joyce had held executive positions and directorships in Lyons banks along with Batchelder's father and had great respect for the family. After Joyce inspected the Pearl River Lumber Company books, he was convinced that the firm had genuine potential for success. In 1901 he invested in the Mississippi company. His decision would prove to be highly profitable.

The Pearl River Lumber Company had formed in 1899 in Brookhaven, Mississippi, a town located in Lincoln County, midway between Jackson, Mississippi, and New Orleans. It held impressive assets: 90,000 acres of longleaf yellow pine, a newly constructed and well-equipped mill, and a standard-gauge logging railroad with sixteen miles of track. The company was so new and had blossomed so rapidly that it carried an imposing debt, which opened a window of opportunity for William Joyce. The northern lumberman loaned $250,000 to the company to consolidate its debts and then proceeded to buy stock as well as extra blocks of timber for the mill. By 1903 Joyce was president of Pearl River Lumber Company. Even though the mill was new, he invested in more sawing capacity, boosting output from 150,000 to 300,000 board feet per day. Experience had taught Joyce earlier in his career that the key to profit was the speed of production.[3]

Joyce enlisted outstanding men to manage the Pearl River Lumber Company. David J. Batchelder Jr., who now lived in Mississippi, served as the manager to whom Joyce sent his directives from distant offices in Chicago and Lyons. Captain A. E.

Moreton, a Mississippi native, experienced lumberman, and original incorporator of the company, retained some authority as vice president. Samuel J. Carpenter, the mill supervisor, hailed from a noteworthy northern lumber family. He previously worked in his father's companies—Curtis Brothers & Company of Clinton, Iowa, and Carpenter Brothers & Company of Minneapolis.

Carpenter's astute management of the workforce met with immediate success. The mill supervisor paid Pearl River Lumber Company employees in cash at a time when most southern lumber companies paid their employees in scrip. In order to stabilize the community, he encouraged employees to build their own homes, for which the company provided land and lumber at discounted prices. In return, Carpenter expected efficiency from his employees, quickly culling slackers from the ranks.[4]

The Pearl River Lumber Company received national attention when it built a recreational center complete with electric lighting and steam heat for its employees. We can surmise that the company's intent was to improve its work force by diverting attention from the ever-present saloon business, which disquieted lumber and mill towns across the country. This new facility, supervised by the state committee of the Young Men's Christian Association (YMCA), sported a "reading room, supplied with over thirty of the best papers and magazines, and a correspondence table with supplies; an amusement room with pool, box ball, caroms, chess, checkers, etc.; a gymnasium with apparatus; tub and shower baths, a parlor and educational class room."[5] Pearl River even hired a full-time manager for the premises, who inspired the formation of several men's clubs, such as the Sunday club for bible study and a debating society known as "The Up to Date Club." In its praise of the facility, the *Mississippi Valley Lumberman* trade journal concluded, "Clean, wholesome, elevating surroundings during leisure hours make clear heads, better men and more efficient employees; and this work of the Pearl River Lumber Company not only reflects credit upon the management, but in the end is sure to prove in more ways than one, a paying investment."[6]

The words "paying investment" were prophetic for Pearl River. As northern lumbermen flocked to Mississippi, pushing land and timber values to new heights, the Pearl River Lumber Company gained a reputation as a model for other lumber concerns. In fact, the Great Southern Lumber Company sent timber and mill broker J. D. Lacey of New Orleans to William Joyce in 1905 with an offer of $2.5 million for the Pearl River Lumber Company. (Lacey was also a timber and mill broker for Joyce.) Joyce might not have been so eager to sell the best lumbering operation in his family's history had it not been for complicating factors.

Two vexing problems in Mississippi befuddled the Iowa lumberman. First, the company was losing business because of a chronic shortage of cars on the interstate rail line, the Illinois Central, which transported Pearl River's lumber products to the Midwest. Despite the complaints that Joyce lodged with railroad officials, the Pearl River Lumber Company continued to receive poor rail service. Even more frustrating to Joyce, Mississippi enacted legislation limiting the total property value of each manufacturing company in its state to $1 million. William Joyce strove to operate his enterprises within the framework of state and federal laws, but complying with this Mississippi law seemed impossible since Pearl River was worth somewhat more than $1 million. Joyce's lawyers examined the legislation to find a mechanism by which the company could legally operate. Venting his anger over the matter, Batchelder wrote to Joyce, "The more we consult with attorneys, the more we are mixed up, for where they find one thing that will do; they also find a clause that will knock it in the head."[7]

The solution was not elegant. The company splintered into three separate entities: mill, forestlands, and railroad, each valued under the $1 million limit. Through an elaborate legal shell game, the appearance of independence satisfied the laws of Mississippi even though nothing had really changed.

Thus, when J. D. Lacey arrived at the door with an irresistible purchase price, Joyce accepted. The sale netted $1,175,809, a return of $6.85 for every dollar Joyce had invested only five years before. Now this new capital needed to be reinvested. Louisiana, the last frontier in southern logging, beckoned.

Joyce Galvanizes Tremont

Once again William Joyce cast about for a promising enterprise for his surplus cash. Although several Louisiana mill owners presented investment plans to Joyce, it was the company information from Robert Jenks, president of Tremont Lumber, that most pleased the Iowan. Joyce offered to loan Jenks $250,000 in December 1905 to cover operating expenses for the mill and logging railroad. Within two months, Joyce purchased controlling interest in the company for approximately $500,000. This amount included a small percentage chipped in by David J. Batchelder Jr.

Joyce now wanted to expand his Louisiana holdings and sent his older son David along with David J. Batchelder to the Gulf State to search for likely candidates. The two men recommended the Winn Parish Lumber Company, which had its mill at Pyburn and offices in Dodson. Joyce traded $2 million for a mill, a logging railroad, and 50,000 acres of excellent pine. Tremont Lumber Company, under Joyce's direction, spent another $750,000 for the Southern Arkansas Lumber Company mill and logging railroad in Jonesboro, Louisiana, and 30,000 acres of pine. The Louisiana Lumber Company of Rochelle, fifty miles south of Tremont, was added to the collection of companies for $1.5 million. This purchase featured two double-cutting band sawmills, a logging railroad, and timberland. All of these acquisitions retained their original names for a time, operating as subsidiaries of the Tremont Lumber Company. Joyce funded his Louisiana purchases not only by the sale of Pearl River Lumber Company but also from profits made by the operation of the Itasca Lumber Company in Minnesota and the Trinity County Lumber Company in Texas. However, the bulk of the money came from bank loans.

The rapid expansion of Tremont, accomplished by snatching up neighboring mills, railroads, and stumpage, altered the past conservative business patterns of the Joyce family. Yet the purchases made sense for two reasons. Tremont's logging railways could not only link with each other but could also easily connect to five mainline railroads. As a result, the company could count on many competing mainline railroads vying for Tremont's lumber traffic, a luxury lacking in Joyce's other lumbering endeavors. Furthermore, with several mills churning out lumber, a shutdown of any one mill due to mechanical failure, overhaul, or fire would merely inconvenience the owners instead of halting production.

Joyce could now turn his energy to making his operations efficient and lucrative, focusing first on the logging rail lines. He organized the Tremont and Gulf Railroad out of an amalgamation of equipment and trackage from the earlier purchased logging roads and upgraded and extended the existing rail lines over which the railroad would haul all Joyce logs from the woods to the mills. Someday, mused Joyce, the Tremont and Gulf would catch the eye of an interstate railroad owner—if its dividend record could sparkle.

Next Joyce tackled Tremont's managerial problems, reminiscent of the troubles at Trinity County Lumber Company in Texas. As always, William Joyce demanded careful bookkeeping and regular company audits, but Tremont's Robert Jenks did not comply with Joyce's wishes. Jenks' resistance cost him his role as manager. Originally Jenks had impressed Joyce. The lumber company, incorporated by Jenks and a group of Tremont, Louisiana businessmen, had dramatically appreciated in value. The men's original investment of $50,000 had mushroomed to a capitalization of $1 million five years later. However, once Joyce discovered that both the land titles and books were askew, he attributed Tremont's phenomenal growth to "an expanding national economy" rather than to any genius on the part of Jenks.[8] After being forced from the top managerial position at Tremont Lumber, Jenks briefly worked as manager for the Tremont and Gulf Railroad, where he continued to neglect the required bookkeeping procedures. Jenks further revealed his failings by getting into personal financial predicaments, placing his remaining Tremont stock at risk of being gobbled up by outsiders. Disgusted, Joyce removed Jenks as manager of the logging railroad. Samuel J. Carpenter, a Midwest lumberman who had served as the mill supervisor at the Pearl River Lumber Company, now headed both logging railroad and milling operations at Tremont. Carpenter owned approximately ten percent of the company stock.[9]

Joyce remained unhappy with Tremont executives even after the removal of Jenks from management. Despite Carpenter's rapid and shrewd company improvements, customers at times were dissatisfied with the lumber they received from the logging firm, and sometimes orders went unfilled. Joyce frequently traveled to Louisiana himself to troubleshoot. Finally, in 1908, he sent his cousin, George S. Sardam, to correct the company sales problems.[10] Sardam was trustworthy. He had followed William's father, David Joyce, to Iowa, and had successfully operated the Joyce-owned Fulton mill in Illinois across the river from Lyons, Iowa, for years. After Sardam completed his mission at Tremont, he continued to busy himself in other aspects of the business until Carpenter, irritated at the intrusion, threatened to resign. Sardam immediately returned to Iowa. At this point, Joyce blew up and, frustrated with both Sardam and Carpenter, assumed more executive control of Tremont, reducing the men in management to puppets. The next year he died.

After the death of their father, the Joyce brothers seriously considered selling Tremont. The young men had watched William sell Pearl River at a remarkable profit and wondered if they could follow suit with the sale of Tremont. The Frost Company entered into negotiations for the purchase of Tremont, and a detailed contract was drawn up. At the time Tremont carried a price tag of about $17 million, which covered the vast timber holdings on 164,000 acres and a varied array of subsidiary companies, including the Louisiana Lumber Company of Rochelle, Winn Parish Lumber Company, Tremont & Gulf Railroad, Eros Printing Company, Tremont Land & Improvement Company, and the Tremont Naval Stores Company. The sale, however, was not completed, for the logistics of trying to appraise Tremont, the large price tag, and a depressed lumber market caused the Frost Company to back out of the negotiations. Tremont remained in Joyce hands.[11]

It had become clear that the complicated corporate structure of Tremont needed streamlining. In 1910, after the sale to Frost fell through, the Joyce brothers directed a reorganization. Two subsidiary lumber companies, the Winn Parish Lumber Company and the Louisiana Lumber Company, were dissolved, and their mills, timber, and other assets were merged into the Tremont Lumber Company. The sales and accounting department of Tremont moved from the executive offices in Chicago to the management offices at Winnfield, Louisiana. From there, Samuel J. Carpenter directed the logging, manufacturing, sales, and accounting departments. Relying on Carpenter more than their father had, David and Stanley appointed him president of the company. David assumed the vice presidency and Stanley, the secretary-treasurer position. Directors of the company were David Joyce, Stanley Joyce, Thomas Hume of Muskegon, Michigan, Eugene Carpenter of Minneapolis, and Samuel J. Carpenter of Winnfield. The Joyces still held the majority of company stock.

The Evolution of Tremont's Mills

By the end of Tremont Lumber Company's first decade, five mills labored simultaneously to convert forests into lumber. Founder Robert Jenks had constructed two of these mills, one at Tremont and the other at Eros, before William Joyce took control of the firm. Jenks had built the mill at Eros, ten miles from Tremont, to accommodate logs up to forty feet long, since the Tremont mill could not handle logs exceeding twenty-two feet.[12] Mills at Jonesboro, Pyburn, and Rochelle joined those at Tremont and Eros after Joyce took

The Joyce mill at Rochelle was one of the largest mills in Louisiana. Company housing appears in the foreground. When the mill closed in 1946, the town disappeared as well. LOUIS R. SAILLARD PRIVATE COLLECTION

control of Tremont Lumber Company. He either modernized or rebuilt each of these mills in order to increase their efficiency. In 1908 Joyce's mills, spread out across sixty miles in north central Louisiana, collectively sawed 90 million board feet of lumber.

The mill at Rochelle became the premiere Tremont manufacturing plant in 1910, following several years of reconstruction. In a letter to the stockholders, David Joyce stated that the Rochelle mill "is without doubt one of the very best mills in the South. In fact, we boast and maintain that it is the best mill in the South." (Regrettably the letter does not offer any substantive data to support this claim.) Joyce went on to say that Tremont would focus its manufacturing operations at Rochelle.[13]

The modernized Rochelle mill made some of the older mills obsolete. David Joyce officially discontinued the original Tremont mill and the Pyburn mill as soon as the virgin timber in their vicinities disappeared. The community of Tremont, the namesake of the company, quickly became a ghost town along with Pyburn. After 1915, only the Eros mill remained to complement the Rochelle mill.[14] Eros typically could mill 35 million board feet of lumber annually, while Rochelle manufactured 50 million board feet (a production that increased to 62 million after 1920 when the company added a hardwood mill at Rochelle with an annual capacity of 12 million board feet.)

In spite of the expanded capacities of the mills, the Joyces curbed production in 1916. Tremont Lumber Company executives met in St. Louis with twenty-five other southern pine manufacturers to discuss tumbling lumber prices. Tremont agreed to reduce its output by 10 million board feet at the lumber industry's request. The decision to curtail lumber output "was circulated through the industry by personal contact and telephone to avoid written documents that might reach the Anti-Trust division of the Justice Department."[15] This industry-wide curtailment must have served its purpose because prices climbed during the next two years. With the rebound, Tremont Lumber Company dropped the restrictions and hit its historic peak production level of 111 million board feet of lumber in 1918.

Production dropped after 1918. Tremont Lumber Company averaged 80 million board feet of pine lumber every year from 1919 until 1926. The Eros mill went up in flames that year, slashing Tremont's production almost in half. The gigantic Rochelle mill still manufactured about 46 million board feet of lumber annually until 1931, when output plummeted as the country slipped into an economic slump that became the Great Depression. By the end of 1932, Tremont's annual yield fell to 24 million board feet of lumber. To make matters worse, the price of lumber plunged to a record low of sixteen dollars per thousand board feet because of a populace unable or unwilling to buy.

In 1932 the National Recovery Administration tried to reverse the abhorrent economic conditions by adopting the Lumber and Timber Products Code that set standards for the lumber industry. Lumber manufacturers accepted price fixing and production limits. They made sense in a time of depression. But the code also established higher wages for workers. The government theorized that higher wages would increase the buying power of workers, thus stimulating the economy. While lumber manfacturers wanted an improved economy, they doubted that the establishment of a minimum wage standard for workers would benefit their profit margins. Workers now grossed $0.24 instead of the customary $0.15 an hour. The mandated wage increase upset David Joyce, who wrote to Louisiana manager W. T. Murray on August 19, 1933: "I think we should make every effort to follow Mr. [President] Roosevelt's plans but I do think there is a limit to further losses. If we cannot operate on a fair basis meaning living up to the accepted code and paying fair salaries and eliminating further loss to the stockholders we should discontinue [Tremont Lumber Company]."[16]

Manager W. T. Murray took Joyce's words to heart and strove to run Tremont profitably. He planned to offset the increased wages by improving efficiency and by milling only high grades of lumber with correspondingly high market values. Since the sawmill was operating well below its capacity, it seemed appropriate to experiment with manufacturing methods. Murray began selective cutting in the forests, bringing in only premium saw logs and thus increasing the grade of finished lumber. At the mill, Murray conserved valuable wood by replacing gang saws with band saws that were less wasteful. Band saws gave the sawyers more control, allowing them to optimize the value of each board produced. By 1936 both demand and prices for lumber rebounded. Tremont had successfully weathered the worst of the Great Depression.

Murray's selective cutting program had unexpected benefits for the future of Tremont. Taking only the best trees from the forest reduced damage to the smaller under-story trees. These remaining trees, invigorated by the new openings to light and moisture, doubled their growth rates. The surviving trees also provided natural seeding of second-growth trees. Murray's intention was to use the new growth as a source of pulp for nearby papermills. With time, the second growth would prove to be more valuable for use as saw logs. Inadvertently, Murray had "set the stage for the rebirth of the Tremont Lumber Company as a company with a future."[17]

Still, it took Tremont another decade to face the most important hurdle to its con-tinued operation: its forest management practices. Since 1913, the state of Louisiana had endorsed reforestation, but Tremont had not followed the state government's lead. That year Urania Lumber Company President Henry E. Hardtner—known as the "Father of Southern Forestry"—signed a reforestation contract with the state for 25,719 cutover acres. This occurred almost thirty years before Tremont accepted reforestation.[18] Cut-out-and-get-out logging had served as the modus operandi for the Joyces in Wisconsin, Minnesota, Texas, Mississippi, and Louisiana, and as long as the Joyce organization could buy virgin stumpage, its members scoffed at milling second-growth trees. Not until approximately 1941 did Stanley Joyce face the fact that Tremont only owned enough virgin timber to keep the mills sawing logs for four more years, motivating him to explore sustainable yield. Even so, Tremont would not fully embrace the concept of sustainable yield until it was virtually sawing the last stick of old-growth timber. Fortunately for Stanley Joyce, some of Tremont's lands had naturally regenerated a second-growth forest, becoming the crucial link between the exploitation of the virgin forest and the reliance upon managed tree farming.

The year 1946 marked the next major crisis in the Louisiana lumbering enterprise: the Rochelle mill was not able to efficiently manufacture lumber from the smaller second-growth saw logs. Despite the fact that Tremont's lumber at the time had risen to a price of nearly $60 per thousand board feet, profits were consumed by ever higher labor and manufacturing costs. This drove the decision to close the Rochelle mill—the heart of Tremont operations—and purchase a much smaller mill at Chatham, located along the Tremont and Gulf Railway. Almost overnight the thriving mill town at Rochelle became another Louisiana ghost town. The modest output of the Chatham mill kept the Joyce retail lumberyards in Iowa in lumber until a new mill was built in Joyce, a few miles from Winnfield. This mill was designed to process smaller second-growth pine, employing the most modern equipment available. Named for the company's major stockholding family, the Joyce site was selected because of its central location to the company's best remaining timberland holdings near truck and rail transportation.[19]

Pine orchards were set aside for producing turpentine. In this photo a worker "chips" the trunk to promote the flow of sap.
UNITED STATES FOREST SERVICE PHOTO. COURTESY OF THE FOREST HISTORY SOCIETY, DURHAM, NORTH CAROLINA

Tapping Turpentine

The pitch of the yellow pine and the turpentine distilled from it, also referred to as naval stores, gave Tremont a modest source of income from trees deemed too small for lumber manufacture. The term *naval stores* took its name from the products made from the pitch of the pine tree, which were vital to the building and maintenance of sailing vessels. In fact, it was the need for naval stores that influenced the British establishment of the first colonies in Virginia. Production of naval stores was a well-established industry in the South, supported by the extensive southern pine belt that stretched from

Workers periodically collected pinesap in the pine orchards. Full barrels were then transported
to a central location for distillation into turpentine.
UNITED STATES FOREST SERVICE PHOTO. COURTESY OF THE FOREST HISTORY SOCIETY, DURHAM, NORTH CAROLINA

Virginia through Louisiana and part of Texas.[20]

Workers turpentined on Tremont land from 1904 until 1925. Tremont had set aside
a 6,000-acre pine orchard for pitch extraction as part of a business partnership with the
New Orleans Naval Stores Company. The mutually beneficial agreement, initiated in
1904, let Tremont concentrate on production, while the New Orleans Naval Stores
Company rendered expertise and managed sales.

The technique for turpentining is vaguely reminiscent of that for maple syruping.
Tremont employees "chipped" or cut diagonal grooves into the trees in the turpentine
orchard and caught the oleoresin (pitch) that oozed from the wound into metal or clay
cups. About every three weeks, workers gathered the oleoresin, stopping at each tree to
scoop the thick resin out of the cups into buckets. The collectors periodically emptied
their buckets into large barrels that were hauled by horse and wagon throughout the
orchard. Full barrels were delivered to a distilling plant for processing.

The favorable Louisiana climate allowed tappers to work the trees from March through November. Some work continued through the winter months when controlled burns removed the accumulation of debris and undergrowth from the pine orchards, thus preventing a larger killing wildfire. Men engaged in chipping and collection generally lived in the woods where they worked. They stayed in mobile sleeping shacks, moved from time to time much like the mobile camps used by loggers.[21]

Once it mastered the art of turpentining, Tremont incorporated its own subsidiary, the Tremont Naval Stores Company, to manage production and sales. By 1907 the company operated a distillery plant, valued at $5,000. In a ten-year period ending in 1916, however, total earnings from naval stores amounted to only $21,775, a fraction of Tremont's earnings as a whole. Probably because of the small return, the Tremont Naval Stores Company was abandoned in 1919 in preference to leasing the pine orchards to independent companies such as the Western Naval Stores Company and the Gullican-Chipley Naval Stores Company. Tremont profit from naval stores remained insubstantial, and in 1925 the practice of turpentining on company lands ended. At that time the total book value of turpentine assets, about $730,000 (based on the value of pine orchards and future production), disappeared without explanation from the company financial reports.[22] The market may have simply vanished with the development of cheaper petroleum-based products.

Racial and Ethnic Strife

Managing a racially and ethnically mixed labor force in Louisiana required the same delicate balance of company policy that it had in Texas. Without its black workers, Tremont's lumber operations would have been severely hampered. Tremont likewise attempted to give newly arrived immigrants fair treatment, sometimes over the explosive protests of the established population. Strained as relations were at times, all of the manual laborers did the same work in the woods and in the mills although white workers typically were promoted to skilled jobs or management positions in preference to their black coworkers. The company, constrained by southern social customs, also supported racial segregation by maintaining separate housing.

In July 1907, during a period when heightened racial tension gripped this section of Louisiana, the daily Tremont and Gulf trains that transported Tremont's black workers from Pyburn and Jonesboro to the woods became the target of shotgun-toting snipers. Tremont had not experienced violence prior to this attack. While the company grappled with the shootings, some farmers in Winn Parish anonymously warned Tremont's lumber and railroad manager, S. J. Carpenter, that they planned to run his black employees out of the parish. Carpenter suspected that the agitating farmers were responsible for the sniping, but he also knew that a Winn Parish jury would fail to convict and jail the men. He then hired a private detective to collect sufficient evidence to bring charges of "'lying in wait and shooting in attempt to commit murder,'" a crime for which the accused would be held without bail. Carpenter knew that the subsequent court proceedings could put the perpetrators out of circulation for up to six months.[23]

Another racial clash in 1907 resulted in the temporary slowdown of the Tremont mill at Eros. In a letter to William Joyce, S. J. Carpenter explained the events as he observed them:

A traveling salesman, accompanied by a teacher from the local school, attempted to obtain payment for a picture they claimed an Eros colored woman had purchased. The woman indignantly retorted that she had not ordered the picture, and, had in fact, not received anything like it. When the two men insisted, she forcibly drove them from her house. The salesman and teacher retreated to the white section of town and soon had an armed mob collected. The mill manager intervened and succeeded in convincing the mob that the woman should be heard in the mayor's court. The hearing was held and the woman fined a small amount for disturbing the peace. After paying the fine she and her husband started out of the mayor's office, but on the steps of the building she was clubbed by the still indignant teacher and someone started shooting at her husband. At the sound of the first shot every Negro in hearing started for the woods and soon the Negro quarters were completely deserted.

The mill, which had been running night and day, limped along for several days with its small white force until the Negroes returned from their hiding places.[24]

A more serious incident occurred when thirty-five Bulgarians and Macedonians, who had recently docked at New Orleans, were hired by the Tremont and Gulf Railroad just after the panic of 1907 had depressed the national economy. These foreigners were paid in cash because, according to James G. Russell, Tremont timekeeper, the manager of the Dunham logging camp "deducted a percentage of their pay for himself each week."[25] Other company employees did not realize that the manager was skimming the foreigners' salaries. They observed only that these thirty-five individuals received weekly cash payments, while they, on occasion, were paid less frequently, depending on the cash flow of the company. The misunderstanding was exacerbated by the local employees' fear of losing jobs to the immigrants and a general suspicion of foreigners. A riotous mob "of farmers, merchants, mill hands, gamblers, and bootleggers from the surrounding country" descended upon the Bulgarians and Macedonians.[26] The mob injured the immigrants, killing one of them, and destroyed their dwellings and possessions. Fleeing the Dunham logging camp during the melee, the immigrants followed the train tracks to the nearby Chathamville railroad depot, where the mob again caught up with them. The immigrants continued their flight into the countryside, camping north of Chathamville. There another mob—this time of black men—set upon them, killing one more and robbing them of their remaining belongings. As soon as word of the fracas reached Tremont manager S. J. Carpenter, he rallied aid for the survivors and sheltered them in company buildings at Tremont and Eros.

This time Carpenter sought to punish not only the perpetrators but also other people in Jackson Parish, particularly some of the merchants at Chathamville, who had encouraged the mob. He gathered enough evidence to arrest five members of the mob, three of whom were later found not guilty by a jury of peers and two of whom went to prison for a brief time. Carpenter simultaneously sued the other individuals for compensation for the victims' families. Winning the suits was not important to him. His main intent was to financially threaten the mob supporters by involving them in expensive legal proceedings. In this way Carpenter hoped to prevent future outbreaks of racial violence.

The conflicts taught Tremont executives important lessons about the high price of challenging the local racial and ethnic intolerances. Tremont never again hired a large group of immigrants, acquiescing to the prejudice of its workers and communities. In the aftermath of the 1907 violence, Tremont focused on easing tensions and fostering good public relations in the towns where it operated mills.

Company Stores

Like executives in many logging and milling towns across the country, Tremont Lumber officials commanded great power over the lives of the citizenry through the institution of the company store. Most employees spent their wages there, many times by outright coercion. Before 1915, employees received wages in the form of celluloid checks issued in denominations of $.05 to $1.00.[27] These checks, just like the scrip issued in the woods to lumberjacks, could be redeemed conveniently only at the company store. While three-fourths of the workforce chose to shop there, the remaining workforce stubbornly shopped at non-company stores, settling for a discounted value for their checks. The discount subtracted from these celluloid checks by the town merchants represented the same amount that Tremont charged the merchants when they cashed in the checks at the lumber company.

Lumber companies used the checks, or scrip, to the detriment of workers, inducing the state of Louisiana to pass legislation in 1908 that directed the companies to stop the practice of discounting checks. The intended outcome of offering employees more shopping freedom predictably did not sit well with Tremont's managers, who wanted to keep employees buying company store goods. By devising a complicated questionnaire for employees to complete, the company manager made it so difficult to use the checks anywhere except at the company store that the legislation did not help Tremont workers. Finally, in 1915, U.S. currency replaced scrip, ending the forced dependence on the company stores.

Labor and Unions

The authoritarian control lumber companies exerted over almost every aspect of their employees' lives led to a rising movement to unionize the lumber industry. This movement was set in motion during the financial panic of 1907 that led to depressed prices and wages. By 1910 the economy had rebounded, but wages in the lumber industry remained low. These low wages contributed to the formation of the Brotherhood of Timber Workers, whose message of "equal rights for workers, a living wage, and just consideration of abuses" echoed across the Gulf States. Mill owners in Louisiana called the Brotherhood "socialistic and anarchistic" and united to fight the union threat. In 1911 these mill owners shut down eleven pro-union mills in the state, fired and blacklisted all employees with union affiliation, and launched a war of rhetoric in an attempt to undermine the union movement. Tremont initiated its own campaign to suffocate union tendencies.[28]

The company portrayal of the union as evil and anti-religious apparently cast serious doubt in the minds of the common laborers. Tremont mill workers at Rochelle, who met at the request of the company doctor, formed the Anti-Timber Workers League of Rochelle, Louisiana. The white and black workers separately passed resolutions to keep the union out of their community.

Black workers gathered in their church at Rochelle to hear fire-and-brimstone testimony from an unidentified orator regarding their future should the union take hold. They were told that if they voted for the union, they would "see death, hell, and destruction staring you in the face." Accordingly, the group drafted the following unedited resolution on August 29, 1911:

> Rochelles dream and pray our Father who are in Heaven if the unioun come
> we are gone to the devil. O! Lord, let thie will be done but please don't let the
> unioun come. If the unioun comes where will we go. The mills are all running

very slow and if we stay we will turn to whay when the mill is closed down just one day she will never get here so help us God we hope it will end in the Land of Nod[29]

Unlike Rochelle mill workers, Jonesboro mill employees saw potential value in the Brotherhood. In response, S. J. Carpenter followed the example set by other mill owners in Louisiana and temporarily shut down the Jonesboro mill in order to eliminate union sympathizers. The dry weather at the time gave Carpenter an excuse for the action, since the water in the log pond fell below its usable level. In October 1911, workers were laid off until a new well could be put in or until the rains returned. Union activists, however, never saw an order to return to work. While workers forfeited wages during the shut-down, Tremont received some compensation for the lost production at Jonesboro from the union-busting fund of the Southern Lumber Operators Association. For a time, Carpenter's actions derailed any further union sentiment at Tremont mills.

During the next year the Brotherhood of Timber Workers affiliated with the Industrial Workers of the World (IWW), a move culminating in the decline of union activity in the South. The IWW's reputation for radical violence, Marxism, antisegregationism, and anti-religious tendencies alienated southern workers and gave mill owners more rhetorical fuel. The union lost what little momentum it had left after a large and violent riot on July 7, 1912, at Graybow, Louisiana: "Before the offices of the Galloway Lumber Company . . . Union president, Emerson, tried to speak. Almost immediately shooting commenced, and the crowd, numbering about 150, screamed and sought cover. Eyewitnesses estimated that about three hundred rounds were fired, the shots coming from both the company offices and union members in the crowd. Three men were killed [union men], a fourth later died of his wounds, and more than forty were wounded."[30]

Fifty-eight of the sixty-two union men arrested were indicted. After spending time in the parish jail, all were found blameless by a jury, largely because the original volley of gunfire erupted from the company offices rather than from the ranks of the union crowd. But the trial bankrupted the union, and bad publicity ricocheted across the nation.

By 1914 the Brotherhood of Timber Workers ceased to be a factor in southern mills.[31]

In 1919 labor agitation peppering the South made Tremont management nervous once again. The IWW, in collaboration with the American Federation of Laborers, sought support through a campaign promoting the eight-hour workday. As a member of the Southern Lumber Operators Association, Tremont hired two of the association's secret agents to pose as workers in Tremont's various mills. The two men visited with the other workers on the job and found the workers, for the most part, happy and unsympathetic to the union movement. That eased the minds of Tremont executives but not enough for them to let down their guard. Management continued to support the Southern Lumber Operators Association and sustained its own drone of anti-union propaganda. In this way, Tremont successfully prevented unionization of its mills through the 1930s.

Rather than Tremont's anti-union efforts being solely responsible, it may have been the company's generally fair treatment of workers that also kept the unions at bay. This became apparent as another problem distressed the southern lumber industry during World War I. Black families migrated in mass when the growth of northern industry promised higher paying jobs and a better life. This seriously depleted the southern labor force, creating worker shortages at many lumber companies. After the war, workers had no incentive to return to lower paying jobs in the South. To its credit, Tremont preserved a stable workforce throughout this labor crisis.

The Tremont and Gulf Railroad

In 1902 Robert Jenks, then president of Tremont Lumber Company, founded the Tremont and Gulf Railroad (T&G) to carry his estimated 600 million board feet of yellow pine from the woods to the Tremont Lumber Company sawmill. The Tremont and Gulf was first and foremost a logging railroad, but Jenks also added a coach car for public transport. From its inception, the T&G "was a remarkably busy operation," according to railroad historian Louis Saillard. A 1905 railroad timetable indicated that each day, three log trains stocked the sawmill with timber while one passenger train and one mixed train made

The Tremont and Gulf Railroad was an offshoot of Tremont Lumber Company. One of its engines was this Shay locomotive. Geared wheels allowed the Shay to pull loads up steep inclines. LOUIS R. SAILLARD PRIVATE COLLECTION

round-trip runs over the original nine miles of line.[32]

When William Joyce bought the controlling share of Tremont in 1906, he directed Jenks to extend the T&G's reach. The track entered Winnfield, approximately forty miles south of Tremont, on September 5, 1907. Soon after, spurs in various directions connected the T&G with the larger mainline railroads as part of Joyce's greater plan to make his line economically self-sustaining.[33] It is worth noting that Joyce's other railroads, the Groveton Lufkin and Northern in Texas and the Minneapolis and Rainy River in Minnesota, followed the same patterns of development and eventual decline as the Tremont and Gulf, although the T&G outlived its sister lines by many years.

The Tremont and Gulf Railroad reorganized as the Tremont and Gulf Railway during 1907. In a letter from Chicago, dated May 1, 1908, William Joyce explained the reorganization to his railroad's board of directors: "The Tremont & Gulf Railway Company is the outgrowth of the Tremont & Gulf Railroad, which in its initial stages was merely a logging road, with rather poor grades of alignment. The road has been practically re-constructed at large expense, all heavy grades and bad curves eliminated, and the extensions to Pyburn and Rochelle are completed. Our property is now in all respects a standard railroad."[34] These changes allowed the T&G tracks to carry the heavy engines and loads of mainline railroads.

With the improvements in place, the Tremont and Gulf Railway could collect divisions—a percentage of shipping costs—whenever cars from the surrounding systems were switched onto its tracks. However, William Joyce's vision of collecting divisions was soon crippled by government intervention. Less than a year after the Tremont and Gulf Railway upgrade, the owners became embroiled in a legal battle with the Interstate Commerce Commission (ICC), as did many other industrial roads with parent companies. (The Joyce railroads in Texas and Minnesota were among those suffering from the same government scrutiny.) As some of the lumber companies without railroads complained, the close relationship between the railroads and their parent lumber companies benefited the parent companies, giving them an edge in the market. From the competitors' viewpoint, the percentage of shipping costs received by the lumber railroads amounted to a rebate. The ICC determined that this was, indeed, the situation and demanded that lumber companies and their railroads separate their interests.[35] William Joyce did not live to see the final resolution of the legal battle. He died in March 1909, whereupon his two sons inherited the legal challenges that Tremont faced.

Even if the sawmill and railroad were now two distinct companies on paper in accordance with the wishes of the ICC, David and Stanley Joyce still controlled both. David assumed leadership of the sawmilling company while his brother Stanley took the reins of the railroad. The railroad still existed primarily to serve Tremont Lumber even though it carried other freight to supplement its earnings. Stanley Joyce, in consultation with his brother, continually refined the railroad to accommodate the changing needs of Tremont Lumber Company mills. As mills were added or abandoned, rail service followed suit. The rail network peaked at 120 miles of track in 1908, but typically the T&G operated with 70 miles of mainline and 20 miles of spurs.[36]

Stanley Joyce made sure that T&G equipment kept pace with new developments in the industry. When oil was locally available in 1923, the Tremont and Gulf improved efficiency by modifying its steam locomotives to fire with oil rather than coal. The T&G also built a fueling station that could store fifty tank cars of oil, in case of an oil worker strike.[37] Rolling along behind the T&G engine fleet, 215 flat cars, 150 freight cars, 84 logging cars, and 8 passenger cars joined the equipment roster over the years. The T&G dispatchers communicated with train crews through a telephone system instead of the traditional telegraph to insure safety and efficiency on the busy line. It was one of the pioneers nationally to employ a telephone system for railroad use. The Winnfield *Comrade* bragged that the T&G complement of engines and cars was the "very best obtainable. . . . The Tremont and Gulf is one of the best equipped in the State."[38]

The railroad hired its own mechanics to service its engines. Master mechanic Jesse Corley explained, "'We did all our own [locomotive] work on the T&G. We were known for our maintenance, and I never had an ICC inspector tie up an engine on me for a defect.'" According to Corley, what prompted the formation of the T&G's maintenance department was a locomotive repair job on engine No. 25, done by the Tremont Lumber

Company shop at Joyce. "The Tremont Lumber shop at Joyce rebuilt the engine for us, installing super heat, universal steam chests and the Southern valve gear. They charged us so much for the work that afterward we rebuilt all the engines ourselves."[39]

Timber prevailed as the primary haul on the T&G through 1926. Freight peaked that year when the T&G carried more than 62 million board feet of timber in 15,436 log cars to the mills in Eros and Rochelle. In 1934, in the grip of the Great Depression, the T&G haul decreased to 15 million board feet of timber, transported in 3,738 cars. By 1938 logs arrived at the sawmills more frequently by truck than by rail. Stifled by the growing competition from trucking, the T&G carried a mere 8.5 million board feet on 2,120 cars to the Rochelle mill in 1941. This represented only 33 percent of its freight. By 1944 log and lumber tonnage had dropped to 23 percent of the total freight conveyed on the T&G.

The significant drop in logs and finished lumber shipped on the Tremont and Gulf forced it to look for other traffic after 1926. The transportation of oil from the surrounding oil fields supplemented company freight in 1927, after the T&G laid track from Rochelle to Waggoner to pick up the black crude. With encouragement from T&G management, farmers enthusiastically grew hefty watermelons, stocking 200 cars with the fruit each year for ten years until 1936, when national overproduction killed incentives for farmers to participate in the watermelon venture. After the watermelon market collapsed, the company abandoned any further produce programs. During the early 1940s, the T&G extended its track to connect with track owned by the Brown Paper Company. The Tremont Lumber Company conveyed pulpwood to the paper producer over this line. About 5,000 cars of pulpwood sent that first year, 1943, to the paper mill boosted T&G's earnings. The T&G shipped out salt from a mine in Winnfield as well.[40]

T&G donations to the campaign funds of local officials, although never large, also aided the finances of the railroad. So did the friendship between general manager Al Smith and his childhood buddy, Huey Long, dictatorial governor of Louisiana from the late 1920s until his murder in 1935.[41] According to Joyce business historian Joseph Ernst, Smith capitalized "on his friendship with Long [and] convinced him to reduce the

[rail]road's tax assessment by 25%. The reduction order was written on a plain memo pad, which became invaluable to the road."[42] This tax break helped counter the fact that the railroad was operating in the red throughout the 1930s.

The late 1940s marked the beginning of the end for the T&G. In 1948 management responded to the recommendations of a New York firm hired to address the railroad's severely declining freight hauls. The retiring of the old mainline connecting Eros and Tremont was one cost-cutting measure. Management also phased out the T&G's steam engines and pressed more efficient diesel engines into service. In one year, the diesels saved $50,000 in expenses. Even with the savings, the railroad continued its decline. A decade later, on June 3, 1959, the Interstate Commerce Commission approved the sale of the T&G to the Illinois Central for $625,000.[43] The Joyce family was now out of the railroad business in Louisiana after more than a half century of ownership.

The Tremont and Gulf might not have profited as a company, yet its owner, Stanley Joyce, averaged an eight percent annual return. Joyce's "total return from the road" was "$2,126,317 or 230 percent of the $925,000 with which he bought the road in 1915."[44]

The South lost one of its last short-line railroads with the passing of the T&G, and railroad aficionados lamented its passing. Lucius Beebe wrote a classic account of short-line railroads in his now famous tome, *Mixed Train Daily,* published in 1947. His portrayal serves as a fitting epitaph for the T&G, whose "motive power [was] among the most beautiful in the South." According to Beebe, "More, almost, than any other surviving and tangible evidences of the pre-industrial yesterday, the little railroads inclined to the contours of the countryside and, in an age when the locating of extensive cuts and fills was unknown, they came to a sensible agreement with the landscape, a compromise with nature. Their rights of way skirted the hillsides and courted the level meadows, ran as one with the towpath and the toll road and crossed placid waters under the shelter of graceful covered bridges. At times the forty-pound rail, indifferently secured to ties innocent of chemical preservatives, wound through sunflecked woodlands . . . and under the theatrical arches of elms already old when there was no railroad there at all. . . . This [was] the mixed train, daily."[45]

Railroad historian Lucius Beebe in his book *Mixed Train Daily* commented on the picture-perfect condition of the T&G at a time when other short-line railroads let their cars slip into general disrepair. He penned: "A copy of the *Illustrated London News* would not seem out of place on the writing desk of the crummy [caboose] of the immaculate Tremont and Gulf's daily run between Winnfield and Waggoner." This photo records a reenactment of a T&G run using the restored engine. LOUIS R. SAILLARD PRIVATE COLLECTION

Oil: A Slippery Gamble

As the T&G trains made their daily runs across the Louisiana landscape, far below the tracks of the railroad, deep in the earth, another landscape of salt domes and oil pockets existed. Casual oil prospecting on Tremont lands started in 1910. That year the company spent $2,500 on drilling. None of the exploratory holes struck oil, but the prospect of striking oil tantalized company officials as drilling rigs hit crude on surrounding properties, particularly after 1920.[46] In 1925 Tremont's first oil strike sent a wave of jubilation through the company ranks. Although the first oil well "sanded up within four hours," it confirmed the presence of oil on Tremont land.[47] At least one company official, W. T. Murray, wanted Tremont to expand its business into the realm of oil production. Others felt uneasy about this new industry in which they had no expertise. Milo Gabriel, one of the Tremont Lumber Company directors, wrote to Tremont executives on March 1, 1926, "I always felt and still feel that the manufacture of lumber is where we are going to make our money and I only hope that the management of the mill will not devote too much of their time looking for oil instead of the production of lumber."[48] Seconding Milo Gabriel's observation, David Gage Joyce complained that there was "'too much oil' in the organization." He instructed Tremont's management to concentrate on lumber production and leave the black gold in the hands of experienced oil men.[49] Nevertheless, Joyce recognized the potential of an oil bonanza and wanted to keep his options open, adding, "In view of the possibility of large oil developments coming in the Tremont territory, it might be best for the company to keep very substantial [cash] reserves."[50] At about this time Stanley Joyce halted the practice of marketing cutover lands for fear of selling an undiscovered fortune in oil concealed under some stumpy field.

Starting in 1926, Tremont leased drilling and production rights to independent companies. The Louisiana Oil and Refining Company received the first contract. That summer the firm drilled or was in the process of drilling more than thirty-nine wells on Tremont lands. Eighteen of the wells produced a combined output of approximately 1,000 barrels of oil per day. In spite of the initial hullabaloo over oil, Tremont's share of the profits was somewhat disappointing, amounting to only $112,000 that year.[51] In time, Tremont owners appreciated the oil and gas royalties earned from the oil fields, especially while weathering the depression of the 1930s and the discouraging volume of lumber sales of the mid-1940s. Throughout the years after the discovery of oil, royalties provided five to seven percent of Tremont's cash flow.[52] More significantly for Tremont's future, the vision of a truly great oil find resulted in the retention of cutover lands. Some of these cutover lands were very rapidly regenerating new forests. The possibility of finding oil on the cutover lands thus served to encourage the transition from cut-out-and-get-out logging to sustainable tree farming.

Years later, after the deaths of David and Stanley Joyce, oil production at Tremont would figure more prominently in the company's operation. In 1966 Gene Turner, an experienced petroleum accountant, joined Tremont as a comptroller but also headed up oil and gas operations. Working under Turner, twelve to fifteen employees managed the details of the oil-leasing business. The scope of operations covered the leasing of oil rights in Texas on lands that had once belonged to Joyce's Trinity County Lumber Company. Although the Joyces had sold the Texas lands when the company was dissolved, they had retained the oil rights.

Tremont Lumber Company: The Final Years

Beatrice Joyce Kean was the last living Joyce when Tremont entered the modern era of forest management, a period characterized by managed cutting and reforestation. Under her authority the Louisiana enterprise could have been liquidated with the demise of old-growth southern pine. She chose instead to grow new forests in anticipation of future harvests. Some of Tremont's lands had regenerated to second growth without any help. The company could build upon nature's gift.

In 1950 Tremont hired forestry graduate Joe Burns and three woodsmen to select the trees for each annual harvest, using managed cutting and silviculture techniques. According to Burns, Tremont initiated the first planting program the year he was hired. His forest crews weeded out the undergrowth and undesirable trees as well as reforested the open areas. In 1952, 180,404 acres of Tremont lands were publicly certified as a tree farm. Praise for Tremont's efforts was noted in the 1952 centennial edition of the Winnfield newspaper. "Under Mrs. Beatrice Joyce Kean, now Tremont president, the company has continued the reforestation with the planting of thousands of loblolly pine seedlings. . . . For 1952–53, the company proposes a mammoth planting of 1,500,000 seedlings over 1500 acres."[53] Tremont's foresters not only took care of Tremont timber but also advised other landowners in the area about forest management practices.[54]

Reforestation was a new concept for many members of the lumber industry, but the need for upgrading mill equipment had always demanded the attention of lumbermen. In 1960 the call for more housing and materials nationwide forced another cycle of modernization of the Tremont mill at Joyce, Louisiana. From 1960 to 1963, the company spent $2 million in order to accomplish the "highest hourly" production in the South, allowing the Joyce mill to manufacture enough lumber "every hour to build two modern spacious homes."[55] Tremont specialized in the production of dimension lumber for the construction industry. Approximately seventy-five percent of its harvest was milled as two-inch stock, resulting in an annual total of 45 million board feet of manufactured lumber.[56] The new highly automated plant, which eventually added plywood and log chip mills, optimized each log. Even the most miserable-looking scrap yielded potential as a "valuable commodity, primarily as wood chips for the paper and pulp industry."[57]

In 1967 another $2.5 million built a 44,000-square-foot state-of-the-art plywood mill with an annual production of 57 million square feet of three-eighth-inch pine plywood. It was one of the first plywood plants in this part of the country, according to Gene Turner. Pine plywood was shipped to almost every state. In the late 1960s Tremont spent more money on its mills and equipment and manufactured and distributed more lumber products than during any other period in its seventy-year history by continuing good sustainable-yield practices.[58]

Tremont also engaged in multiple-use forest management. The company harvested and renewed its forest while attending to watershed protection and wildlife habitat. Maintaining 350 miles of access roads through its timberlands for the work of foresters and loggers, Tremont encouraged local sportsmen and their families to recreate on company lands, opening company roads to public use. According to *Forests and People*, a publication of the Louisiana Forestry Association, "Not a single acre of Tremont's holding [was] placed under a 'posted' [no trespassing] sign."[59]

Crown Zellerbach Canada Limited, a multi-national lumbering conglomerate, purchased Tremont in 1974 after the death of Beatrice Joyce Kean. When Crown Zellerbach took over, Beatrice Joyce Kean's legacy of promoting asset growth was lost as the company liquidated the forest to maximize income. Crown Zellerbach did, of course, replant, a necessity in the modern age of lumbering. The selling of Tremont ended the Joyce business reign, and the Joyce name disappeared from the lumber industry after more than a century of logging in the Midwest and South.

Notes

In citing works in the notes, shortened titles have generally been used. Works frequently cited have been identified by the following abbreviations:

BFS   *Big Fork Settler*
CNF   Chippewa National Forest
GRHR   *Grand Rapids Herald Review*
GRM   *Grand Rapids Magnet*
HHP   Hackley Hume Papers, Michigan State University Archives and Historical Collections
ICHS   Itasca County Historical Society
IN   *Itasca News*
MHS   Minnesota Historical Society
MVL   *Mississippi Valley Lumberman*

One important source of information for *Timber Connections* is an unpublished manuscript commissioned by the Joyce Foundation in the 1950s. The working title for the manuscript was "Forest Frontiers: The Joyce Search for Stumpage 1856–1945." Two individuals contributed to the research and writing of this manuscript: Herbert O. Brayer and Joseph Ernst. Brayer was the earlier writer-researcher. His work, called "New England Beginnings," was incorporated into the larger text by Ernst.

Chapter 1
[1] Herbert O. Brayer, "New England Beginnings," 4.
[2] Stanley E. Moore, letters to Joseph Waleski Jr., 16 March 1975, 14 May 1979, 25 May 1979.
[3] Brayer, 7.
[4] The Salisbury Association. Salisbury Cannon Museum. April 2, 1999, http://www.salisburyassociation.org/scm/about themuseum.htm.
[5] Stanley E. Moore, letter to Joseph Waleski Jr., 16 March 1975.
[6] Brayer, 11.
[7] Ibid., 7.
[8] George W. Hotchkiss, *History of the Lumber and Forest Industry*, 595.

Chapter 2
[1] Cited in William M. Gage, *The Coming Together of the Keyes and Gage Families*, 261.
[2] Ibid., 262.
History of Clinton County, Iowa, 1879, 489.
[3] Brayer, 16.
[4] Gage, 264.
[5] "Golden Sawdust," *Times–Democrat*, 18 November 1962.
[6] Hotchkiss, 589.
[7] Ibid., 588–589.
George Bernhardt Hartman, "The Iowa Sawmill Industry," *The Iowa Journal of History and Politics*, 76, 78.
Lyda Belthuis, "The Lumber Industry in Eastern Iowa," *The Iowa Journal of History and Politics*, 136.
[8] Hotchkiss, 588.
[9] Ernst, "The Mississippi Mills, 1856–1899," 7.
[10] Ibid., 10–11.
[11] Ralph W. Hidy, Frank Ernest Hill, and Allan Nevins, *Timber and Men*, 40.
Ernst, "The Mississippi Mills, 1856–1899," 11. *Portrait and Biographical Album of Clinton County, Iowa*, 692.
[12] *Lyons City Advocate*, 21 July 1869, 3.
[13] Clinton County Historical Society, *History of Clinton County Iowa*, 1976, 98. Hotchkiss, 594. *Portrait and Biographical Album of Clinton County, Iowa*, 692. "Our Table of Lumber Manufacture," *MVL*, 14 December 1877. G. W. Sieber, "Sawmilling on the Mississippi: The W. J. Young Lumber Company 1858–1900," 52.
[14] Quoted in Hidy, Hill, and Nevins, 43.
[15] Ibid., 43.
[16] Ibid., 68.
[17] Agnes Larson, *History of the White Pine Industry in Minnesota*, 137.
[18] Quoted in Hidy, Hill, and Nevins, 74.
[19] Brayer, 30. Clinton County Historical Society, *History of Clinton County Iowa*, 1976, 89. Connie K. Heckert, *Lyons: One Hundred Fifty Years North of the Big Tree*, 146.
[20] Brayer, 32.
Benjamin F. Shambaugh, *Biographies and Portraits of the Progressive Men of Iowa*, 517. Hotchkiss, 595.
[21] Everett A. Streit, "Once Upon a Time," *Clinton Herald*, Souvenir Edition, n.d. Heckert, 61.
[22] Brayer, 32–33.
[23] Ernst, "The Mississippi Mills, 1856–1899," 18.
[24] "D. Joyce's Mill Burned," *MVL*, 13 July 1888.
[25] *MVL*, 13 July 1888.
[26] *MVL*, 31 August 1888. *MVL*, 19 July 1889.
[27] *MVL*, 22 February 1889. Ernst, "The Mississippi Mills, 1856–1899," 21.
[28] "The Middle Mississippi District," *MVL*, 1 July 1892. *MVL*, 25 November 1892. *MVL*, 22 September 1893.
[29] Ernst, "The Mississippi Mills, 1856–1899," 24.
[30] *MVL*, 8 October 1895. *MVL*, 30 August 1895. *MVL*, 22 October 1895. *MVL*, 8 March 1895.
[31] Ernst, "The River Mills Go Hungry,

1900–1909," 19, 26. Clinton County Historical Society, *History of Clinton County Iowa*, 1976, 97, 109.

[32] Larson, 374–375. Ernst, "Lumber Markets, 1860–1899," 18–19.

[33] Ernst, "Lumber Markets, 1860–1899," 1, 9–10. Ernst, "The W. T. Joyce Company, Iowa Merchants, 1894–1915," 9.

[34] Quoted in Ernst, "Lumber Markets, 1860–1899," 15.

[35] Ibid., 16.

[36] Larson, 382.

[37] Ernst, "The Midwest Lumber Market, 1910–1945," 6–7.

[38] "Joyce Lumber Co. Will Move," *Clinton Herald*, 27 January 1921.

[39] Clinton County Historical Society, *History of Clinton County Iowa*, 1976, 99. Ernst, "The W. T. Joyce Company, Iowa Merchants, 1894–1915,"1.

Chapter 3

[1] An important source for this chapter is Walter G. Hoar's *History Is Our Heritage*, chronicling the history of the Shell Lake Lumber Company. Only direct quotations from this source will be cited.

[2] Frank Alexander King, *Minnesota Logging Railroads*, 16.

[3] Robert C. Nesbit, *Urbanization and Industrialization, 1873–1893*, 71. "Piece Stuff," *MVL*, 21 April 1899. John N. Vogel, "The Round Lake Logging Dam: A Survivor of Wisconsin's Log-Driving Days," *Wisconsin Magazine of History*, 176–177.

[4] *MVL*, 4 August 1882. "Correspondence, Shell Lake," *MVL*, 2 March 1883. "Weyerhaeuser Concerns Elect Officers," *MVL*, 28 September 1884.

[5] *MVL*, 9 December 1881.

[6] A. L. Stouffer, *The Story of Shell Lake*, 56.

[7] "The White Pine Lumber Cut of the Northwestern Mills During 1892," *MVL*, 20 January 1893.

[8] Hoar, 102–103.

[9] *MVL*, 13 May 1881.

[10] "Shell Lake," *MVL*, 3 February 1882.

[11] *MVL*, 13 April 1884.

[12] Ernst, "The Mississippi River Mills, 1856–1889," 20. *MVL*, 28 March 1890. Larson, 157–158.

[13] E. Ward Winton and Kay Brown Winton, eds., *Historical Collections of Washburn County and the Surrounding Indianhead Country*, Vol. 1, 1980, 189. *MVL*, 26 July 1889. Stouffer, 60. *Shell Lake Watchman*, 13 August 1891.

[14] *MVL*, 29 July 1887. *MVL*, 23 December 1887. Advertisements, *MVL*, 20 January 1893, 1 January 1897.

[15] King, 52.

[16] Ibid., 14, 16.

[17] Stouffer, 10.

[18] *MVL*, 27 March 1885.

[19] Quoted in Hoar, 64.

[20] "Logging Notes," *MVL*, 1 March 1889.

[21] *MVL*, 1 July 1887.

[22] Ralph W. Andrews, *This Was Logging*, 144–156. Malcolm Rosholt, *The Wisconsin Logging Book: 1839–1939*, 21–22, 34.

[23] "In the Woods," *Shell Lake Watchman*, 11 June 1891.

[24] *Shell Lake Watchman*, 13 August 1891. Stouffer, 52.

[25] Rosholt, 35, 60.

[26] "The Northern Wisconsin," *MVL*, 4 March 1881.

[27] Randall Rohe, "Lumber Company Towns in Wisconsin," *The Old Northwest*, 409–437.

[28] Winton and Winton, eds., 188. "Shell Lake," *MVL*, 2 June 1882.

[29] "Shell Lake," *MVL*, 2 June 1882.

[30] "Prevention of Forest Fires," *MVL*, 31 August 1894.

[31] "A $10,000 Blaze," *Shell Lake Watchman*, 1 October 1891.

[32] "$1,645,000 Lumber Fire In Chicago," *MVL*, 3 August 1894.

[33] Quoted in Ernst, "The Wisconsin Mills, 1880–1906," 12.

[34] "White River Lumber Company Wiped Out," *MVL*, 3 August 1894.

[35] "Piece Stuff," *MVL*, 31 August 1894. Hidy, Hill, and Nevins, 92.

[36] "The Loss at Barronett," *MVL*, 7 September 1894.

[37] Barronett Bombers & Cloverleaf 4-H Clubs, *A Journey Through Barronett*, 13, 15.

[38] Ibid.

[39] Ernst, "The Wisconsin Mills, 1880–1906," 11.

[40] Hoar, 108.

[41] Quoted in Hoar, 110.

[42] Winton and Winton, eds., 198.

[43] "It Shows Confidence," *Shell Lake Watchman*, 27 September 1894.

[44] "Piece Stuff," *MVL*, 31 August 1894. *Shell Lake Watchman*, 4 October 1894.

[45] *MVL*, 14 September 1894. "Logs and Logging," *Shell Lake Watchman*, 25 October 1894.

[46] *MVL*, 1 March 1895. "Logs and Logging," *Shell Lake Watchman*, 25 October 1894.

[47] Ernst, "The Wisconsin Mills, 1880–1906," 13. *Shell Lake Watchman*, 22 November 1894.

[48] *MVL*, 9 August 1889.

[49] "Piece Stuff," *MVL*, 31 October 1890. *MVL*, 9 December 1892.

[50] "A Great Lumberman," *MVL*, 7 December

1894.
[51] "In Memory of David Joyce," *MVL*, 14 December 1894.
[52] "A Useful Life Ended," *Shell Lake Watchman*, 6 December 1894.
[53] *MVL*, 11 January 1895.
[54] Winton and Winton, eds., 193.
[55] Ernst, "The Wisconsin Mills, 1880–1906," 20, 22.

Chapter 4

[1] "The East Bank of the Mississippi," *MVL*, 26 October 1877. Skip Drake, telephone conversation with Susan Hawkinson, Grand Rapids, Minn., 24 September 1999.
[2] Larson, 275–288.
[3] Ernst, 104.
[4] Articles of Incorporation, The Itasca Lumber Company, Illinois Secretary of State, 30 August 1886.
[5] "D. Joyce Becomes A Stockholder In The Itasca Lumber Company," *MVL*, 10 May 1889.
[6] "The East Bank of the Mississippi," *MVL*, 26 October 1877. "The First County Officials," *GRHR*, Golden Jubilee Supplement, 16 July 1941. *MVL*, 2 September 1887. Douglas Blanz, telephone conversation with Warren Jewett, Pengilly, Minn., 23 January 1998.
[7] "Minneapolis, Friday, May 10, 1889" *MVL*, 10 May 1889. Ernst, 107.
[8] "D. Joyce Becomes A Stockholder In The Itasca Lumber Company," *MVL*, 10 May 1889.
[9] Ernst, "From Canada to the Gulf 1888–1900," 10.
[10] "On The Mississippi," *MVL*, 30 May 1890.
[11] "Will Build Thirty Miles of Logging Railway," *MVL*, 26 July 1889.
[12] "Minneapolis, Friday, July 26, 1889," *MVL*, 26 July 1889.
[13] "Commencing Work," *GRM*, 24 September 1893. "Brief History of Matters Relating to Swan River Logging Company, Limited," 16 September 1899, Swan River Logging Company folder, Karjala Research Center, ICHS.
[14] *MVL*, 2 March 1894.
[15] Ibid.
[16] Hidy, Hill, and Nevins, 107–108.
[17] "Logging by Railroads," *MVL*, 1 February 1895. "The Secret Out," *GRM*, 9 August 1892.
[18] "Logging by Railroads," *MVL*, 1 February 1895.
[19] "Log Cut On The Upper Mississippi," *MVL*, 13 December 1895.
[20] "Logging by Railroads," *MVL*, 1 February 1895.
[21] "Log Cut Is Much Smaller," *Itasca County Independent*, 30 April 1908.

Chapter 5

[1] "The East Bank of the Mississippi," *MVL*, 2

November 1877.
[2] "Transportation History was Recorded in Itasca," *GRHR*, Anniversary Edition, 19 September 1934. "County of Itasca: The New Northern Empire," *GRM*, 11 June 1891.
[3] King, 14. Ernst, "From Canada to the Gulf, 1888-1900," 21.
[4] *MVL*, 8 January 1892. *MVL*, 29 May 1891.
[5] "Local," *GRM*, 9 July 1891. "Local," *GRM*, 12 November 1891.
[6] King, 35, 195. *LaPrairie News*, 4 November 1893. "Local," *GRM*, 22 October 1891.
[7] "Local," *GRM*, 30 July 1891.
[8] Ibid.
[9] "The New Logging Railroads," *GRM*, 13 August 1891.
[10] "New Election Precincts," *GRM*, 4 October 1892.
[11] *MVL*, 9 September 1892.
[12] "A Pleasant Pleasure Party," *GRM*, 7 June 1892.
[13] *MVL*, 1 January 1892. *MVL*, 1 April 1892. *MVL*, 9 September 1892.
[14] "Local," *GRM*, 10 January 1893.
[15] Jessie M. Lawrence vs. Itasca Lumber Company, Itasca County District Court transcript #236 (1893), MHS.
[16] Ibid.
[17] R. E. White vs. Minneapolis and Rainy River Railroad Company, Itasca County District Court transcript #2411 (1909), MHS. "Local," *GRM*, 18 April 1893.

Chapter 6

[1] Gladys Erola, *Along Memory Trails*, 1.
[2] Grace Lee Nute, *Rainy River Country*, 73.
[3] *GRM*, 12 September 1893.
[4] *MVL*, 7 May 1897. *MVL*, 21 May 1897.
[5] "Locals," *IN*, 30 April 1898. "News Notes," *MVL*, 28 May 1897.
[6] "Many Logs," *IN*, 9 July 1891.
[7] "Locals," *IN*, 11 June 1898. "Many Logs," *IN*, 9 July 1891. *MVL*, 8 July 1898. "Locals," *IN*, 26 August 1899.
[8] "Locals," *IN*, 2 September 1899.
[9] "Locals," *IN*, 7 May 1898.
[10] "Locals," *IN*, 16 May 1903.
[11] S. D. Patrick to Itasca Lumber Company, Minneapolis, 11 November 1899, HHP.
[12] F. C. Gerhard to W. T. Joyce, Chicago, 15 November 1899, HHP.
[13] "To Extend Line," *IN*, 28 September 1901.
[14] "Locals," *IN*, 13 September 1902.
[15] "The Cedar Output," *IN*, 21 February 1903. "Locals," *IN*, 28 February 1903.
[16] Erola, 4. "Locals," *IN*, 29 June 1901.
[17] "Locals," *IN*, 20 December 1902. Mrs. Oliver Juntunen and Mrs. Arvo Maki, *50 Years and More:*

Suomi, 14.
18 "Another Boat on Turtle," *IN*, 20 June 1903.
19 "Free Homes," *IN*, 1 June 1901.
20 "Lundeen Quits," *IN*, 4 February 1905.
21 "Big Lumber Deal," *IN*, 31 January 1903.
22 "Locals," *IN*, 3 October 1903.
23 Report of the Railroad and Warehouse Commission, 1905, State of Minnesota, Minnesota State Archives, MHS. Linda Roubalik, "Story of a Community," 2, Minnesota State Archives, MHS.
24 Roubalik, 4.
25 Ida Carver, "A History of Wirt, MN," 5.
26 *MVL*, 22 July 1904. "Minneapolis & Rainy River Road," *IN*, 23 July 1904. Report of the Railroad and Warehouse Commission, 1905, MHS.
27 "Many Enjoyed Turtle Lake," *IN*, 23 July 1904.
28 Report of the Railroad and Warehouse Commission, 1905.

Chapter 7
1 John Zetterstrom, "The Story of a Logging Town," Minnesota State Archives, MHS.
2 The Deer River Federated Woman's Club, *Deer River Yesterday and Today*, 18.
3 Minneapolis & Rainy River Railway, Right of Way Section Drawings, [1904], Itasca County Courthouse, Auditor Office. "Local Items and News in General," *BFS*, 15 March 1906.
4 *BFS*, 9 May 1907.
5 *BFS*, 25 May 1905.
6 "Locals," *IN*, 31 March 1906. *BFS*, 26 April 1906. "Rails to Bigfork," *IN*, 28 April 1906. Effie Bicentennial Committee, *The Land of "Homestead Days*," 21. "Locals," *IN*, 30 June 1906. "Locals," *IN*, 14 July 1906.
7 "Local Items and News in General," *BFS*, 9 August 1906.
8 "They 'Walked Out,'" *IN*, 1 September 1906.
9 "A Bad Wreck," *IN*, 15 September 1906.
10 "Excursion Tomorrow," *IN*, 22 September 1906. Minneapolis & Rainy River Railway, Right of Way Section Drawings, [1904], 84.
11 "M. & R. R. Excursion," *IN*, 29 September 1906.
12 "Locals," *IN*, 17 November 1906. R. E. White vs. Minneapolis & Rainy River Railway Company, Itasca County District Court, Transcript #2411 (1909), MHS.
13 "Two Killed in M. & R. R. Wreck," *IN*, [16 March 1907].
14 "A Bad Collision," *Itasca County Independent*, 16 March 1907. *IN*, 30 March 1907.
15 *BFS*, 9 May 1907. *BFS*, 21 November 1907. *BFS*, 23 January 1908. *BFS*, 14 May 1908.
16 The Deer River Federated Woman's Club, 46.
17 Bergit Anderson, *The Last Frontier*, 84–85.
18 Ibid.

19 Ibid.
20 *BFS*, 15 November 1906. The Deer River Federated Woman's Club, 18. "Hunting in Bigfork Sportsman's Delight," *BFS*, 15 August 1907.
21 Ernst, "White Pine, Ties, and High Finance," 20.

Chapter 8
1 Ernst, "Still Building," 1. Ernst, "Texas Timber and Trouble," 11.
2 "Locals," *IN*, 3 May 1902.
3 Ernst, "Retreat in the North," 4.
4 Constance Rosenblum, *Gold Digger: The Outrageous Life and Times of Peggy Hopkins Joyce*, 76–77.
5 Ernst, "Organizing Louisiana Timber," 14. Ernst, "Lumber Markets, 1860–1899," 19. *BFS*, 1 July 1909.
6 Ernst, "White Pine, Ties, and High Finance," 19.
7 Minnesota Cedar Logging Company vs. Minneapolis & Rainy River Railway, Itasca County District Court transcript #5542 (1913), 136, MHS.
8 *BFS*, 23 June 1910. *BFS*, 12 January 1911.
9 Don Benson, interview by authors, tape recording, Talmoon, Minn., 14 February 1994. *BFS*, 20 May 1909.
10 Benson, interview.
11 *BFS*, 23 September 1909.
12 State of Minnesota vs. Minneapolis & Rainy River Railway, Itasca County District Court Transcript #5953 (1916), 363–364, MHS.
13 Plat map of Stanley, Recorder's reference A47, 1908, Itasca County Courthouse, Recorder Office.
14 "Before the Railroad and Warehouse Commission of the State of Minnesota," *IN*, 15 May 1915.
15 State of Minnesota vs. Minneapolis & Rainy River Railway, Itasca County District Court Transcript #5953 (1916), 376, MHS.
16 John Craig [grandson of John Craig], interview by authors, tape recording, Grand Rapids, Minn., 16 October 1994.
17 *IN*, 7 October 1911.
18 Lyle Quigg, interview by authors, tape recording, Deer River, Minn., 28 April 1994.
19 "Iron Ore," *IN*, 23 May 1903.
20 *BFS*, 31 January 1907.
21 Aero Magnetic Map of Minnesota, Map A-4, [Chicago]: Chandler, 1983. Itasca County Courthouse, Surveyor Office.
22 William J. Trygg, 124, 137. See bibliography for complete Trygg citation.
23 Correspondence between the Itasca Lumber Company and the Duluth Diamond Drilling Company, May 27–31, 1916, HHP. Ernst, "Retreat

in the North," 10.

24 "Is Another Road Coming This Way?" *IN*, 20 August 1910. *IN*, 31 August 1912. *BFS*, 7 September 1911. *Itasca County Independent*, 16 February 1911.

25 *Itasca County Independent*, 26 January 1911.

26 *Encyclopedia Britannica*, 25th ed., s. v. "Hill, James J." Ernst, "Retreat in the North," 20.

27 Nute, 89.

28 Nute, 89–90, 106. "M. & R. Connection Soon To Be Made," *IN*, 23 March 1913.

29 "Bigfork," *BFS*, 23 October 1909.

30 Nute, 104.

31 Edward W. Backus vs. Minneapolis & Rainy River Railway Company, Itasca County District Court, Transcript #7405 (1921), Exhibit A letter dated 27 January 1914, MHS.

32 Nute, 104. Edward W. Backus vs. Minneapolis & Rainy River Railway Company, Itasca County District Court, Transcript #7405 (1921), affidavit of James Stanley Joyce, 28 July 1921, MHS.

33 *IN*, 21 December 1912. Ernst, "Retreat in the North," 4. *IN*, 16 December 1911. Minnesota Forestry Board, *Third Annual Report of the State Forester* (31 December 1913): 38.

34 *BFS*, 25 May 1911.

35 J. C. Sullivan et al. vs. Minneapolis & Rainy River Railway Co., Itasca County District Court, Transcript #4950 (1913), 141, MHS.

36 "State is After M. & R. for Rebating," *IN*, 8 October 1910. J. C. Sullivan et al. vs. Minneapolis & Rainy River Railway Co., Itasca County District Court, Transcript #4950 (1913), 236–237, MHS.

37 "M. & R. Rate Hearing," *IN*, 23 December, 1911.

38 "Evidence All in on M. & R. Rates," *IN*, 3 February 1912. "Reduction in Rates on M. & R. in Effect," *IN*, 28 September 1912.

39 J. C. Sullivan et al. vs. Minneapolis & Rainy River Railway Co., Itasca County District Court, Transcript #4950 (1913), 303, MHS.

40 "More Judgments Against Itasca Road," *IN*, 27 September 1913.

41 "State Wins R.R. Rate Fight," *IN*, 14 June 1913.

Chapter 9

1 State of Minnesota vs. Minneapolis & Rainy River Railway Company, Itasca County District Court, Transcript #5953 (1916), 28, MHS. "Court Holds M. & R. Must Run All Branches," *IN*, 30 January 1915.

2 "Court Holds M. & R. Must Run All Branches," *IN*, 30 January 1915. Ernst, "Retreat in the North," 20.

3 "Gas Cars on M. & R. Ry.," *IN*, 29 July 1916.

4 Ibid.

5 Ernst, "To Mill and To Market," 9.

6 State of Minnesota vs. Minneapolis & Rainy River Railway Company, Itasca County District Court, Transcript #5953 (1916), 491, MHS.

7 "Potato Warehouses Proposed on M. & R. Ry.," *IN*, 29 January 1916.

8 State of Minnesota vs. Minneapolis & Rainy River Railway Company, Itasca County District Court, Transcript #5953 (1916), 362–363, MHS.

9 Ernst, "Retreat in the North," 8.

10 "Much Timber Being Shipped," *IN*, 15 March 1919.

11 "Deer River's First Automobile," *IN*, 6 May 1911.

12 *IN*, 19 May 1917.

13 Mrs. Oliver Juntunen and Mrs. Arvo Maki, *50 Years and More: Suomi*, 8.

14 *IN*, 21 May 1921. Ernst, "Retreat in the North," 22.

15 "Timber Trucking Being Extended," *GRHR*, 20 November 1929.

16 Ernst, "Retreat in the North," 22.

17 "Check Cars on County Roads," *GRHR*, 24 September 1930. "Heavy Cars, Trucks, Trailers, Increase," *IN*, 21 January 1932.

18 "Railway Rumors Poorly Founded," *IN*, 2 January 1930. Ernst, "Retreat in the North," 23.

19 "Quiet Winter Anticipated in Itasca County Logging Camps," *GRHR*, 29 October 1930. Larson, 402.

20 Ernst, "Retreat in the North," 24. "Would Stop Train Service Jan. 31st," *IN*, 21 January 1932.

21 "No Sentiment," *The Itasca Iron News*, 1 May 1931.

22 "The Minneapolis & Rainy River Railroad," *GRHR*, 18 November 1931. "The Rainy River Road and the Truck," *GRHR*, 25 November 1931. "The Railroad and Itasca's Taxpayers," *GRHR*, 2 December 1931. "There Must Be A Way Out," *GRHR*, 9 December 1931.

23 "M. & R. Matters Up On February 23rd," *IN*, 4 February 1932. "Railway Hearing Starts Reports," *IN*, 14 January 1932.

24 "Railway Hearing Is Attended By Crowds," *IN*, 25 February 1932.

25 "The Rainy River Road and the Truck," *GRHR*, 25 November 1931.

26 "Railway Hearing Is Attended By Crowds," *IN*, 25 February 1932.

27 "M. & R. Hearings Ended Thursday," *IN*, 3 March 1932.

28 "Trains Off, Mail Service Crippled," *IN*, 3 March 1932.

29 "How Editors Are Loved By Corporation Attorneys," *IN*, 14 April 1932.

30 "New Schedule Now On M. & R. Lines," *IN*, 3 March 1932. "M. & R.R. Railway Line," (1680 file), CNF.

31 "Will Start Paving Work Next Tuesday," *IN*, 26

May 1932. James E. Rottsolk, *Pines, Mines, and Lakes: The Story of Itasca County*, 91. "Historical Background–Suomi Hills Area," Suomi Hills Area Management Plan, May 1973, 42, CNF.
[32] "Interstate Body O.K's Abandonment," *IN*, 7 July 1932. "State Will Refuse Road Abandonment," *IN*, 14 July 1932.
[33] "Grants Request to File Petition," *IN*, 28 July 1932. "Says Road Will Quit Next Month," *IN*, 28 July 1932.
[34] "Abandonment is Now Before Court," *IN*, 4 August 1932.
[35] "Court Rules in Favor of Railway," *IN*, 25 August 1932.
[36] "All Towns North Have Daily Mail," *IN*, 1 September 1932.
[37] Anderson, 86–87.
[38] Darwin Holsman, telephone conversation with authors, Bigfork, Minn., 6 November 1994.
[39] Ernst, "Retreat in the North," 27. Bazil Mayo, telephone conversation with authors, Deer River, Minn., 8 November 1994. King, 41.
[40] Ernst, "Retreat in the North," 28. "Fire Razes Deer River Landmark," *Duluth Herald*, [? April 1941].

Chapter 10
[1] Ernst, "White Pine, Ties, and High Finance," 13.
[2] Ibid., 13–15. *IN*, 13 August 1904.
[3] *MVL*, 2 December 1904. "All Mills Now Down But One," *The Minneapolis Journal*, 3 December 1904. *MVL*, 18 November 1904.
[4] "Locals," *IN*, 24 December 1904.
[5] "Locals," *IN*, 8 April 1905.
[6] *IN*, 19 November 1904.
[7] "Is A Good Town," *Itasca County Independent*, 15 July 1905.
[8] "Mill Stock Sold," *IN*, 31 March 1906.
[9] Ibid.
[10] William A. Byers, interview by Joseph Waleski Jr., Deer River, Minn., n.d.
[11] Halga Will, interview by authors, tape recording, Deer River, Minn., 15 March 1994.
[12] Ernst, "White Pine, Ties, and High Finance," 22–23. *IN*, 11 January 1908. *IN*, 6 May 1911.
[13] Larson, 399.
[14] Ernst, "Retreat in the North," 24–29. *IN*, 25 November 1911.
[15] *IN*, 21 May 1921. *IN*, 4 June 1921.
[16] Ernst, "Retreat in the North," 29.
[17] Quigg, interview.
[18] ["Otenagon Disorganiz'd"], *IN*, 14 Jan. 1911.
[19] *IN*, 16 March 1912.
[20] Will, interview.

Chapter 11
[1] Quoted in Hidy, Hill, and Nevins, 149.

[2] "How it Appears to a Stranger," *GRM*, 25 February 1892.
[3] Ernst, "Retreat in the North," 9. "Locals," *IN*, 19 August 1905. Ernst, "White Pine, Ties, and High Finance," 20.
[4] *IN*, 14 December 1912. *IN*, 5 April 1913. *IN*, 23 May 1914.
[5] "50,000 Acres Agricultural Land For Sale," *IN*, 20 June 1914. "Itasca County Farm Lands," *A Zone of Plenty, Itasca County, Minnesota*, a special supplement to the *GRHR*, 30 August 1922, 23.
[6] "Itasca County Farm Lands," *A Zone of Plenty, Itasca County, Minnesota*, 30 August 1922, 23. "Map of Minneapolis & Rainy River Railway and Itasca County," Fred A. Bill papers, MHS.
[7] Quoted in Roubalik, 7.
[8] *IN*, 28 June 1919.
[9] Plat map of Trout Lake Park, Recorder's reference A79, 1911, Itasca County Courthouse, Recorder Office. Plat maps of Sherwood Forest, Recorder's reference A87 and A104, 1916–1922, Itasca County Courthouse, Recorder Office. Agreement of sale, Itasca Lumber Company and I. A. Martin, 20 July 1912, Nadine Martin Scrapbook: "My Trout Lake," Karjala Research Center, ICHS.
[10] Anne Komarek, letter, MHS.
[11] Ibid. Roubalik, 6.
[12] Juntunen and Maki, 6.
[13] Quoted in Bill Marshall, "The Gut and Liver Line," ICHS newsletter, summer 1989.
[14] Juntunen and Maki, 7. "Excerpts from 'Story of Suomi' in 'School Echoes,'" Karjala Research Center, ICHS.
[15] Ernst, "Retreat in the North," 14.
[16] Gifford Pinchot, *Breaking New Ground*, 206.
[17] Ibid, 204, 206. Larson, 317.
[18] Bill Hink to authors, CNF, Cass Lake, Minnesota, 25 July 1994.
[19] Ernst, "Retreat in the North," 17.

Chapter 12
[1] *GRM*, 10 March 1892. James E. Rottsolk, *Mines, Pines, and Lakes: The Story of Itasca County, Minnesota*, 12. "Wabana District Has Interesting History," *GRHR*, 10 August 1929.
[2] "Wabana District Has Interesting History," *GRHR*, 10 August 1929. Keith W. Matson, "A Sample Survey for Cultural Resources on the Trout Lake Tract," August 1994, 4, Chippewa National Forest.
[3] William J. Trygg, "Abstracts from Original U. S. Land Surveyors' Field Notes in Minnesota," 107–108. Original survey map, "Township No. 58N. Range No. 25W. 4th Mer.," MHS.
[4] "Wabana District Has Interesting History," *GRHR*, 10 August 1929. Mike McAlpine,

interview by C.C. Kelley, Grand Rapids, Minnesota, n.d., Karjala Research Center, Itasca County Historical Society.
[5] Rottsolk, 13, 85.
[6] "Wabana District Has Interesting History," *GRHR*, 10 August 1929. *Logging Town: The Story of Grand Rapids, Minnesota*, Compiled by Workers of the Writers' Program of the Work Projects Administration. n.p., 1941, 31.
[7] "The Upper Mississippi," *MVL*, 11 January 1889.
[8] *Vermillion Pine and Iron Land Co. vs. Itasca Lumber Co.*, Itasca County District Court, Court transcript and exhibits #1294, #1295, (1904), MHS.
[9] Ibid.
[10] *MVL*, 1 January 1892. "Wabana District Has Interesting History," GRHR, 10 August 1929.
[11] Historical American Buildings Survey–Joyce Estate, HABS No. MN-146, 5, CNF. Deed book N, Itasca County Courthouse, Recorder Office, 191. Matson, 6.
[12] *MVL*, 15 October 1897.
[13] Patricia E. Navratil, *Trails Through the Northwoods*, 4. Anderson, 18–19.
[14] James Knight, *We Homesteaded*, 35, 102.
[15] "Wabana District Has Interesting History," *GRHR*, 10 August 1929.
[16] "Waubana's (sic) Beauties and Attractions," *GRHR*, 17 September 1904.
[17] "Wabana District Has Interesting History," *GRHR*, 10 August 1929.
[18] Matson, 6–8. Louis M. Ireton, self-narrated tape recording, 1970-1971, Ireton private collection.
[19] Martin Summer Homes, Minnesota Historic Properties Inventory Form, 1980, Karjala Research Center, ICHS.
[20] Agreement of sale, Itasca Lumber Company and I. A. Martin, 20 July 1912, Nadine Martin Scrapbook: "My Trout Lake," Karjala Research Center, ICHS. J. Baggott property abstract, authors' private collection.
[21] Ireton, tape recording.
[22] Newspaper clippings, [1937], Nadine Martin Scrapbook: "My Trout Lake," Karjala Research Center, ICHS.
[23] Ibid.
[24] Ireton, tape recording.
[25] Ibid.

Chapter 13
[1] This chapter relies predominantly on the following sources: Historical American Buildings Survey–Joyce Estate, CNF, and the authors' interviews with Joseph Waleski, Jr., Marion Brown, John Johnson, Nels Olson, Adeline Pearson, and Ellen Rudolph.
[2] Application of Itasca Lumber Company to register real estate title, 2 October 1915, Torrens file 323, Itasca County Courthouse, Recorder Office.
[3] "Will Build Home on 'Big Trout,'" *GRHR*, 14 March 1917.
[4] Harvey H. Kaiser, *Great Camps of the Adirondacks*, 64, 161.
[5] Jeffrey Hess, "Chapter 1: Objectives and Methodology," *Cultural Resource Overview: Joyce Estate: Trout Lake Tract: Chippewa National Forest*, 47.
[6] "Will Build Home on 'Big Trout,'" *GRHR*, 14 March 1917.
[7] *Itasca County Independent*, 9 June 1917. *GRHR*, 1 August 1917, *GRHR*, 15 August 1917.
[8] "A Zone of Plenty, Itasca County Minnesota," *GRHR*, 30 August 1922, 17.
[9] John Zetterstrom, interview by authors, tape recording, Golden Valley, Minn., 10 August 1994.
[10] "A Zone of Plenty, Itasca County Minnesota," *GRHR*, 30 August 1922, 17.
[11] Kaiser, 8–9.
[12] "Mrs. S. D. Patrick Died Last Monday," *IN*, 26 May 1932.
[13] "Wabana District Has Interesting History," *GRHR*, 10 August 1929.
[14] Dr. William Downing, interview by authors, tape recording, Grand Rapids, Minn., 16 June 1994.
[15] *Itasca County Independent*, 1 September 1917.
[16] *Itasca County Independent*, 2 July 1919.
[17] Brock Yates, "10 Best Race Drivers of All Time," *Car and Driver*, 49.
[18] William Nolan, *Barney Oldfield: The Life and Times of America's Legendary Speed King*, 186–188.
[19] "Locals," *Itasca County Independent*, 3 August 1918.
[20] Donald L. Boese and Richard R. Cain, *Grand Rapids Companion*, 195. Motor Sports Hall of Fame, Barney Oldfield, <http://www.mshf.com/hof/oldfield.htm> (April 7, 1998).
[21] *GRHR*, 1 August 1917.
[22] *GRHR*, 15 August 1917.
[23] William Ralston to Joseph Waleski, 11 February 1978.
[24] George Mills, "Discover Literary Treasure Amassed by Clinton Tycoon," *Des Moines Register*, 7 October 1973.

Chapter 14
[1] Quoted in Rosenblum, 89.
[2] David Grafton, "Peggy Hopkins Joyce, Inc.," *Forbes 400*, 68.
[3] Rosenblum, 77.
[4] Peggy Hopkins Joyce, *Men, Marriage and Me*, 116–118.

5 Ibid., 119.
6 Rosenblum, 95.
7 Joyce, 130–131.
8 Ibid., 142.
9 Rosenblum, 91.
10 Ibid., 104, 108, 115.
11 Joyce, 195.
12 Louis M. Ireton, tape recording.
13 "James Joyce Dies; Services Here Friday," *Clinton Herald*, 4 January 1944.

Chapter 15
1 This chapter is based extensively on interviews conducted by the authors. All interviewees are cited in the chapter and listed in the bibliography.
2 P. B. Wolfe, ed., *Wolfe's History of Clinton County Iowa*, 1060.
3 Ernst, "White Pine and Cypress," 8.
4 "Injunction Made Permanent," *Itasca Iron News*, 16 July 1925.
5 Articles of incorporation, The Joyce Foundation, State of Illinois, Office of the Secretary of State.
6 *Encyclopedia Britannica*, 25th ed., s.v. "corporation tax." *Encyclopedia Britannica*, 25th ed., s.v. "philanthropy."
7 The Joyce Foundation, <http://www.joycefdn.org/foundation/aboutintro.htm> (August 19, 2002).

Chapter 16
1 Northwestern National Life Insurance Company, Public Relations Department, press release, Minneapolis, 8 November 1973, CNF. Wesley Libbey, presentation to Itasca County Commissioners, 5 June 1997, Hawkinson and Jewett private collection.
2 Jack Rajala, interview with authors, tape recording, Deer River, Minn., 14 October 1994.
3 Olin to Gilst, 17 May 1974, 5420 files, CNF.
4 "The Nature Conservancy purchases Joyce estate," *GRHR*, 8 November 1973.
5 Geoffrey S. Barnard, telephone conversation with authors, 6 July 1994.
6 Rajala, interview.
7 John Johnson, interview with authors, Deer River, Minn., 17 January 1994. Melvin Goldie, telephone conversation with authors, Cadillac, Mich., 14 November 1994.
8 Itasca County Commissioners, Resolution No. 8-72-6: "Opposition to Federal Acquisition of County Lands," [7 August 1972], CNF.
9 Robert Block to Michael Hathaway, 3 December 1973, CNF.
10 Summary of respondents, n.d., CNF.
11 Kaiser, xiii-xiv.
12 James K. Lyle to Forest Supervisor, 28 December 1977, CNF.

13 Jeffrey Hess, "Chapter 3: Statement of Significance," *Cultural Resource Overview: Joyce Estate: Trout Lake Tract: Chippewa National Forest*, 57, CNF.
14 Joel D. Getzendanner to Howard A. Zeman, 16 May 1990, CNF.
15 Carolyn Kastner, Mark W. Zimmerman, and James P. Zimmerman to Floyd Marita, William F. Spinner, and Howard Zeman, 14 May 1990, Hawkinson and Jewett private collection.
16 Chippewa National Forest, Trout Lake Opportunity Area: Documentation of Analysis, 12 September 1991, CNF.

Chapter 17
1 This chapter relies extensively on the unpublished work "Forest Frontiers: The Joyce Search for Stumpage 1856–1945" by Joseph Ernst. Only direct quotations from this manuscript will be cited.
2 Patricia B. Hensley, ed., *Trinity County Beginnings*, 66. Kate Atkinson Bell, ed., *Journey to Jubilee: Groveton, Texas, USA*, 83–84.
3 Elmer O. Hill, "The Town of Groveton, Trinity County, Texas," Hensley private collection. Hensley, "An Application for an Historical Marker for Groveton, Texas, Seat of Trinity County," 5, Hensley private collection.
4 Ibid., 4.
5 "Plain and Simple: Sawmill folks at home," *Crosscut*, Third Quarter, 1996.
6 Willie A. Burch, "Sawmills and Railroads," Hensley private collection.
7 Bell, 84.
8 Hensley, "An Application for an Historical Marker," 10.
9 Hidy, Hill, and Nevins, x, 211.
10 Ernst, "David and William: Retrospect and Revision," 9.
11 Ernst, "Texas Timber and Trouble," 2.
12 Ernst, "From Canada to the Gulf," 25.
13 "Publishers Department," *MVL*, 9 December 1904. "One of the Finest and Best Mills in the State," *The Trinity County Star*, 3 March 1905, Hensley private collection.
14 "Publishers Department," *MVL*, 9 December 1904.
15 Hensley, "An Application for an Historical Marker," 13.
16 Patricia Hensley, telephone conversation with authors, Dallas, Tex., 4 December 1998.
17 Ernst, "Texas Timber and Trouble," 18.
18 Ernst, "From Canada to the Gulf," 19.
19 Bell, 26, 31, 92. Hensley, "An Application for an Historical Marker," 15–16.
20 Hensley, ed., *Trinity County Beginnings*, 66.
21 Hensley, "An Application for an Historical

Marker," 13.
[22] Bell, 29.
[23] Ernst, "Texas Timber and Trouble," 6–7.
[24] Ibid.
[25] Ibid., 11.
[26] Robert S. Maxwell and Robert D. Baker, *Sawdust Empire: The Texas Lumber Industry, 1830–1940*, 199. Burch, "Sawmills and Railroads," Hensley private collection.
[27] James Boyd, "Fifty Years in the Southern Pine Industry," *Southern Lumberman*, 15 December 1931, 63.
[28] Bell, 84.
[29] Quoted in Maxwell and Baker, 65.
[30] Bell, 84, 87.
[31] Ibid.
[32] Hill, "The Town of Groveton, Trinity County, Texas," Hensley private collection.
[33] Hensley, "An Application for an Historical Marker," 17–18. Hensley, ed., *Trinity County Beginnings*, 423.
[34] Hill, "The Town of Groveton, Trinity County, Texas," Hensley private collection.
[35] Hensley, "An Application for an Historical Marker," 18.

Chapter 18
This chapter relies extensively on the unpublished work "Forest Frontiers: The Joyce Search for Stumpage 1856–1945" by Joseph Ernst. Only direct quotations from this manuscript will be cited.
[1] Statement of taxes for 1900 on lands in Parishes of Livingston and Tangipahoa, La. purchased by Hackley and Hume and Wm. T. Joyce, in May/June 1900, HHP. James E. Fickle, *The New South and the "New Competition": Trade Association Development in the Southern Pine Industry*, ix.
[2] Documents regarding cypress lands, 1904–1906, HHP. Sale of Property by William Lee Wright to Hackley & Hume Co. Ltd. and Wm. T. Joyce, 11 May 1908, HHP.
[3] W. T. Joyce to J. D. Lacey & Company, 10 March 1906, HHP.
[4] State of Louisiana vs. Hackley, Hume & Joyce, 19 December 1906, HHP. "The Latest News in All Louisiana," *The Daily Picayune*, 1 April 1907, HHP. Rachael E. Norgress, "The History of the Cypress Lumber Industry in Louisiana," *The Louisiana Historical Quarterly*, 997.
[5] J. F. Coleman to Messrs. Farrar, Jonas, Kruttschnitt & Goldberg, 5 March 1909, HHP.
[6] Thomas Hume to J. D. Lacey & Co., Muskegon, Mich., 19 June 1912, HHP. Thomas Hume and James Stanley Joyce to J. D. Lacey & Co., Chicago, 10 October 1917, HHP. James D. Lacey Timber Company, Plan, [April 1919], HHP.

[7] James Stanley Joyce to Thomas Hume, Chicago, 28 April 1915, HHP.
[8] Tentative Memorandum of Agreement, 2 June 1919, HHP. Documents regarding transfer and sale of cypress lands, 1923–1928, HHP. John P. Gregg to Hackley & Hume Co. Limited, Chicago, 3 February 1923, HHP. William T. Joyce Company to Hackley & Hume Co., Limited, Chicago, 17 January 1920, HHP.
[9] "Merits of Cypress Wood," *MVL*, 23 February 1883.
[10] Norgress, 1047.
[11] Quoted in Ernst, "White Pine and Cypress," 11.
[12] Robert Love, telephone conversation with authors, La., 14 July 1994.
[13] Norgress, 979.
[14] Survey notes, 12 February 1902, HHP. Love, telephone conversation.
[15] Norgress, 984, 1049, 1056.
[16] Max Fowler, telephone conversation with authors, Hodge, La., 13 November 1994. H. E. (Gene) Turner, telephone conversation with authors, Winnfield, La., 20 July 1994.
[17] Love, telephone conversation.

Chapter 19
[1] "Lumbering: a Louisiana Story of Progress," unidentified newspaper article in Creighton Collection, Winnfield Museum, Winnfield, Louisiana. "The Early Years (1875–1904)," *Forests and People*, 4–5.
[2] John Collier, "The Southern Pine Story," *Forests and People*, 43. "The Early Years (1875–1904)," *Forests and People*, 4–5. Rachael E. Norgress, "The History of the Cypress Lumber Industry in Louisiana," *The Louisiana Historical Quarterly*, 1045.
[3] "Making Good in the South," *MVL*, 5 February 1904.
[4] Ibid.
[5] "A Good Investment," *MVL*, 4 March 1904.
[6] Ibid.
[7] Quoted in Ernst, "The Pearl River Adventure 1901–1905," 12.
[8] Ernst, "Louisiana Lumber 1906–1909," 2.
[9] William Joyce to Thomas Hume, 15 September 1908, HHP.
[10] Trial Balance sheet, Southern Investment Company, 30 June 1908, HHP. Joyce directed that a holding company called the Southern Investment Company be incorporated in Maine for $5 million in order to protect Tremont's minority stockholders. All of the finances of the many Louisiana companies then could be managed from the holding company.
[11] Agreement between Southern [Investment] Company and Frost Company, 15 February 1910,

HHP. Trial Balance sheet, Southern Investment Company, 30 June 1910, HHP.
[12] Louis R. Saillard, "Tremont & Gulf: Return of a Legend," *Railfan & Railroad*, 52.
[13] David G. Joyce to the stockholders of the Southern Investment Company, Chicago, 20 August 1910, HHP.
[14] Ibid.
[15] Ernst, "And Let the Trees Grow," 19.
[16] Quoted in Ernst, "And Let the Trees Grow," 21.
[17] Ibid., 22.
[18] "Lumbering: a Louisiana Story of Progress."
[19] "Tremont: After 70 Years, Looking to the Future," *Forests and People*, 9+. "Rochelle Mill to Suspend Operations Soon," [*Winn Parish Enterprise*], 7 February 1946.
[20] *Encyclopedia Britannica*, 1957 ed., s.v. "naval stores." Cover photographs and inside cover text, *Forest and Conservation History*.
[21] Ibid. *Winn Parish History: Winnfield, Louisiana*, 25.
[22] Assets and Liabilities Statement, Southern Investment Company, 31 March 1907, HHP. *Winn Parish History: Winnfield, Louisiana*, 25. Assets and Liabilities sheets, Tremont Lumber Company, 1925–1926, HHP.
[23] Quoted in Ernst, "Louisiana Lumber 1906–1909," 14.
[24] Ibid., 21.
[25] Ibid., 16.
[26] Quoted in Ernst, "Louisiana Lumber 1906–1909," 14.
[27] Ibid., 22.
[28] Ernst, "And Let the Trees Grow," 26–27.
[29] Quoted in Ernst, "And Let the Trees Grow," 28.
[30] Robert S. Maxwell and Robert D. Baker, *Sawdust Empire: The Texas Lumber Industry, 1830-1940*, 133.
[31] Ibid.
[32] Saillard, 52.
[33] "Railroads Reaching Winnfield," *The Comrade*, special edition, Winnfield, Louisiana, 24 July 1908.
[34] Corporate Records and Proceedings, Tremont & Gulf Railway Company, Chicago, 1908, Susan Hawkinson and Warren Jewett private collection.
[35] Ernst, "To Mill and to Market," 5.
[36] "Railroads Reaching Winnfield," *The Comrade*.
[37] Saillard, 54.
[38] "Railroads Reaching Winnfield," *The Comrade*.
[39] Saillard, 54.
[40] Ibid., 55.
"Tremont & Gulf Railway Company," [*Winn Parish Enterprise*], 10 September 1936. Al Smith, telephone conversation with authors, Jonesboro, La., 30 October 1994.
[41] W. Adolphe Roberts, *Lake Pontchartrain*, 328–339.
[42] Ernst, "To Mill and to Market," 12.
[43] Saillard, 57.
[44] Ernst, "To Mill and to Market," 13.
[45] Lucius Beebe, *Mixed Train Daily*, 7.
[46] Trial Balance sheet, Southern Investment Company, 30 June 1910, HHP.
[47] Ernst, "And Let the Trees Grow," 45.
[48] Quoted in Ernst, "And Let the Trees Grow," 46.
[49] Ibid.
[50] Thomas Hume to unknown, Chicago, 5 May 1927, HHP.
[51] Contract "B," Tremont Lumber Company, 1926, HHP. Thomas Hume to unknown, Chicago, 5 May 1927, HHP.
[52] H. E. (Gene) Turner, telephone conversation with authors, Winnfield, La., 20 July 1994.
[53] "Tree Farming By Tremont Assures Perpetual Harvest," *Winn Parish Enterprise*, 1952, Centennial Edition, section 5: 2.
[54] "Tremont: After 70 Years, Looking to the Future," *Forests and People*, 45.
[55] Tremont Lumber Company, "Tremont: 70th Anniversary," 6, 19.
[56] Ibid., 6.
[57] "Tremont: After 70 Years, Looking to the Future," *Forests and People*, 45.
[58] Turner, telephone conversation. "Tremont: After 70 Years, Looking to the Future," *Forests and People*, 9. Tremont Lumber Company, "Tremont: 70th Anniversary," 22.
[59] "Tremont: After 70 Years, Looking to the Future," *Forests and People*, 45.

Glossary of Logging Terms

band saw: A saw with a cutting blade that consisted of a continuous loop of steel strung tightly between two large rollers. Later versions included cutting teeth on both edges of the band so that logs could be ripped in both directions as the carriage moved back and forth. Band saws began replacing circular saws in large sawmills in the 1880s.

board foot: A quantity of raw timber or finished lumber equal in volume to 12 inches by 12 inches by 1 inch.

buck, bucked: In logging, to cut felled timber to specific length i.e. 8', 10', 16'.

common carrier: A railroad incorporated under state and federal regulations that was given common carrier status. Common-carrier status allowed the use of eminent domain or the confiscation of private property for right-of-way purposes. The common carrier status also required a commitment to public service.

gang saw: A bank of saws used for cutting many planks of lumber from a squared timber in a single pass.

high-wheel skidder: A device for skidding logs in the absence of snow. The high-wheel skidder consisted of two large wagon-style wheels, typically about twelve feet in diameter, connected by a single axle and drawn by means of a long tongue harnessed to oxen or horses. One end of the log(s) was chained beneath the center of the axle, suspended several feet off the ground, while the opposite end of the log was allowed to drag along the ground.

hoist: In logging, a device that lifted logs from the water by means of cables and pulleys at a loading point usually on a lake or river. A steam skidder, horses, or oxen provided the power.

kerf: The width of the saw cut as determined by the thickness of the saw blade. The typical circular head saw had a kerf of one-quarter inch while the band head saw had a kerf of one-eighth inch.

lath: Lumber in the form of thin slats, lath was used in plaster wall construction. Sawmills produced lath from wood deemed unfit for high quality lumber or from the smaller scraps left over from the sawing process.

log sorting: During log drives, the separation of logs and their assembly into rafts according to log stamps and bark marks on each individual log.

log stamps and bark marks: A unique identifying symbol on a log, usually an impression hammered into the end and/or cut marks made in the bark with an axe.

Middle Mississippi: The segment of the Mississippi River bordering the states of Iowa, Illinois, and Missouri. The Middle Mississippi was home to a large sawmilling industry.

narrow gauge: The distance between railroad-track rails. Any spacing smaller than the standard of 48.5 inches is considered to be narrow gauge.

planer: In lumber production, a machine that planed lumber after seasoning (drying) in the sawmill's lumberyards. This machine gave lumber its final dimensioning and finishing.

rail weight: Weight in pounds per foot of rail. In the late 1800s, a 30-pound rail would be classified as a light-duty rail. A 110-pound rail would be classified as a heavy-duty rail.

red pine: Norway Pine.

rollway: In logging, an inclined ramp that was constructed at the point where logs were unloaded from railcars. After crews removed chains from a load, logs tumbled from the cars onto inclined ramps that usually directed the logs into a river, lake, or sawmill pond.

Russell car: An early form of railroad car designed specifically for logging. Independent trucks allowed any length of log to be transported by rail. Because of the high number of accidents associated with their use, Russell cars were eventually abandoned in favor of flatcars.

section house: A building providing room and board for the crews responsible for maintaining railroad grades, tracks, and ties.

siding: A length of railroad track parallel to the main line track or spur track. Empty logging cars were placed on the siding for loading.

spar tree: In high-lead logging, a tree that supported overhead cables. Used in pairs, these trees were stripped of all branches and stabilized by guy ropes or cables.

spur: A railroad track branching off the main track. On logging railroads, spurs were built only for temporary use and were removed after the timber in the vicinity of the track was depleted.

standard gauge: The distance between railroad-track rails. A spacing of exactly 48.5 inches is called standard gauge.

steam skidder: In logging, a machine that consisted of a small steam engine geared to a cable reel. The steam skidder was used to move logs from the stump to a loading area. The simplest use of the skidder was to play out the cable, attach it to a log, and then engage the engine.

trestle: A railroad bridge constructed to carry railroad tracks over lakes and river crossings. Red pine or cedar pilings driven into the lake or river bottoms were the foundation for constructing a trestle.

Bibliography

Secondary Works

Anderson, Bergit. *The Last Frontier*. St. Paul: Bruce Printing Co., 1941.

Andrews, Ralph W. *This Was Logging*. Seattle: Superior Publishing Company, 1954.

Barronett Bombers and Cloverleaf 4-H Clubs. *A Journey Through Barronett*. Shell Lake, Wisconsin: White Birch Printing, Inc., 1978.

Beebe, Lucius. *Mixed Train Daily*. New York: E. P. Dutton & Company, Inc., 1947.

Bell, Kate Atkinson, ed. *Journey to Jubilee: Groveton, Texas, USA*. Groveton, Texas: Groveton Ex-Students Association, 1980.

Belthuis, Lyda. "The Lumber Industry in Eastern Iowa." *The Iowa Journal of History and Politics* 46, no. 2 (April 1940): 115–155.

Boese, Donald L., and Richard R. (Dick) Cain. *Grand Rapids Companion*. Grand Rapids, Minnesota: Grand Rapids Centennial Committee, 1991.

Boyd, James. "Fifty Years in the Southern Pine Industry." *Southern Lumberman* 144 (December 15, 1931): 59–67.

Cain, Dick. *LaPrairie: The Road Back*. LaPrairie, Minnesota: City of LaPrairie, Minnesota, 1990.

Carver, Ida. *A History of Wirt, Minnesota*. n.p., 1985.

Clinton County Historical Society. *History of Clinton County Iowa*. Clinton, Iowa: Clinton County Historical Society, 1976.

Collier, John. "The Southern Pine Story." *Forests and People* 13, no. 1 (1963).

Cronon, William. *Nature's Metropolis: Chicago and the Great West*. New York: W. W. Norton & Company, 1991.

The Deer River Federated Woman's Club. *Deer River Yesterday and Today*. Deer River: n.p., 1973.

Deer River (Minnesota) Area Centennial Calendar, 1998.

"The Early Years (1875–1904)." *Forests and People* (First Quarter 1981).

Effie Bicentennial Committee. *The Land of "Homestead Days."* Effie, Minnesota: n.p., 1976.

Erola, Gladys. *Along Memory Trails, A History of Deer River*. Deer River, Minnesota: Western Itasca Review, n.d.

Fickle, James E. *The New South and the "New Competition": Trade Association Development in the Southern Pine Industry*. Chicago: University of Illinois Press, 1980.

Forest & Conservation History 39, no. 1 (January 1995).

Gage, William M. *The Coming Together of the Keyes and Gage Families*. Baltimore: Gateway Press, Inc., 1986.

Grafton, David. "Peggy Hopkins Joyce, Inc." *Forbes 400* (October 23, 1989): 68–70.

Hartman, George Bernhardt. "The Iowa Sawmill Industry." *The Iowa Journal of History and Politics* 40 (1942): 52–93.

Heckert, Connie K. *Lyons: One Hundred Fifty Years North of the Big Tree*. Clinton, Iowa: Lyons Business & Professional Association, n.d.

Henry Ford Museum. *Barney Oldfield*. April 7, 1998. <http://www.hfmgv.org>.

Hensley, Patricia B., ed. *Trinity County Beginnings*. Dallas: Curtis Media, 1986.

Hess, Jeffrey A. *Cultural Resource Overview: Joyce Estate: Trout Lake Tract: Chippewa National Forest*. St. Paul: State Historic Preservation Office (SHPO) of the Minnesota Historical Society, 1987.

Hidy, Ralph W., Frank Ernest Hill, and Allan Nevins. *Timber and Men: The Weyerhaeuser Story*. New York: The Macmillan Company, 1963.

History of Clinton County, Iowa. Chicago: Western Historical Company, 1879.

Hoar, Walter G. *History is Our Heritage*. Shell Lake, Wisconsin: White Birch Printing Company, Inc., 1968.

Hotchkiss, George W. *History of the Lumber and Forest Industry of the Northwest*. Chicago: George W. Hotchkiss & Co., 1898.

The Joyce Foundation. *About Us*. February 13, 2003. <http://www.joycefoundation.org/about/aboutmain-fs.html>.

Joyce, Peggy Hopkins. *Men Marriage and Me*. New York: The Macaulay Company, 1930.

Juntunen, Mrs. Oliver, and Mrs. Arvo Maki. *50 Years and More: Suomi*. n.p., 1967.

Kaiser, Harvey H. *Great Camps of the Adirondacks*. Boston: David R. Godine, Publisher, Inc., 1982.

King, Frank Alexander. *Minnesota Logging Railroads*. San Marido, California: Golden West Books, 1981.

Knight, James K. *We Homesteaded*. New Brighton, Minnesota: Printcraft Inc., 1975.

Larson, Agnes M. *History of the White Pine Industry in Minnesota*. Minneapolis: University of Minnesota Press, 1949.

Little, Elbert L. *The Audubon Society Field Guide to North American Trees: Eastern Region*. New York: Alfred A. Knopf, 1980.

Logging Town: The Story of Grand Rapids, Minnesota. Compiled by Workers of the Writers' Program of the Work Projects Administration. n.p., 1941.

Long, Katherine, and Melvin Erickson. *Clinton: A Pictorial History*. Rock Island, Illinois: Quest Publishing, n.d.

Maxwell, Robert S., and Robert D. Baker. *Sawdust Empire: The Texas Lumber Industry, 1830–1940*. College Station, Texas: Texas A&M University Press, 1983.

Mississippi Valley Lumberman, 1877–1912, January 14, 1944.

Motor Sports Hall of Fame. *Barney Oldfield*. April 7, 1998. <http://www.mshf.com/hof/oldfield.htm>.

Navratil, Patricia E. *Trails Through the Northwoods: A History of the Bigfork Trail*. 2d ed. Bigfork, Minnesota: Northwoods Press, 1976.

Nesbit, Robert C. *Urbanization and Industrialization, 1873–1893*. Vol. 3 of *The History of Wisconsin*. Edited by William Fletcher Thompson. Madison: State Historical Society of Wisconsin, 1985.

Nolan, William F. *Barney Oldfield: The Life and Times of America's Legendary Speed King*. New York: G. P. Putnam's Sons, 1961.

Norgress, Rachael Edna. "History of Cypress Lumber Industry in Louisiana." *The Louisiana Historical Quarterly* (July 1947): 979–1059.

Nute, Grace Lee. *Rainy River Country*. St. Paul: Minnesota Historical Society, 1950.

Pinchot, Gifford. *Breaking New Ground*. New York: Harcourt, Brace, and Co., 1947; reprint, Washington, D.C.: Island Press, 1987.

"Plain and Simple: Sawmill folks at home." *Crosscut* (Texas Forestry Museum Society, Lufkin, Texas) (Third Quarter 1996):3.

Portrait and Biographical Album of Clinton County, Iowa. Chicago: Chapman Brothers, 1886.

Roberts, W. Adolphe. *Lake Pontchartrain*. The American Lakes Series. New York: Bobbs-Merrill Company, 1946.

Rohe, Randall. "Lumber Company Towns in Wisconsin." *The Old Northwest* 10, no. 4 (1984–1985): 409–437.

Rosenblum, Constance. *Gold Digger: The Outrageous Life and Times of Peggy Hopkins Joyce*. New York: Metropolitan Books, Henry Holt and Company, 2000.

Rosholt, Malcolm. *Lumbermen on the Chippewa*. Rosholt, Wisconsin: Rosholt House, 1982.

—. *The Wisconsin Logging Book: 1839–1939*. Rosholt, Wisconsin: Rosholt House, 1980.

Rottsolk, James E. *Pines, Mines, and Lakes: The Story of Itasca County, Minnesota*. Grand Rapids, Minnesota: Itasca County Historical Society, 1960.

Saillard, Louis R. "Tremont & Gulf: Return of a Legend." *Railfan & Railroad* (July 1994): 52–59.

The Salisbury Association. *Salisbury Cannon Museum*. April 2, 1999. <http://www.salisbury association.org/scm/aboutthemuseum.htm>.

Shambaugh, Benjamin F., Ph.D. *Biographies and Portraits of the Progressive Men of Iowa*. Vol. 2. Des Moines, Iowa: Conaway and Shaw, 1899.

Stouffer, A. L. *The Story of Shell Lake*. Shell Lake, Wisconsin: Washburn County Historical Society, 1961.

"Tremont: After 70 Years, Looking to the Future." *Forests and People* 20, no. 1 (1970): 9, 44–45.

Tremont Lumber Company. "Tremont: 70ᵗʰ Anniversary." Joyce, Louisiana: Tremont Lumber Company, 1969.

Vandersluis, Charles. *Mainly Logging*. Minneota, Minnesota: Minneota Clinic, 1974.

Vogel, John N. "The Round Lake Logging Dam: A Survivor of Wisconsin's Log-Driving Days." *Wisconsin Magazine of History* (Spring 1983): 170–191.

Wauseon, Ohio. *Barney Oldfield*. April 7, 1998. http://www.stopat.com/wauseon/barney.htm>.

Winn Parish History: Winnfield, Louisiana. Winnfield, Louisiana: Winn Parish Historical Society, 1985.

Winton, E. Ward, and Kay Brown Winton, eds. *Historical Collections of Washburn County and the Surrounding Indianhead Country*. Vol. 1. Shell Lake, Wisconsin: Washburn County Historical Society, 1980.

Wolfe, P. B., ed. *Wolfe's History of Clinton County Iowa*. Indianapolis: B. F. Bowen and Company, 1911.

Yates, Brock. "10 Best Race Drivers of All Time," *Car and Driver* (January 1985): 49.

Primary Sources

Miscellaneous

Aero Magnetic Map of Minnesota, Map A-4. [Chicago]: Chandler, 1983. Itasca County Courthouse, Surveyor Office.

Articles of Incorporation, The Itasca Lumber Company, Illinois Secretary of State. 30 August 1886.

Articles of Incorporation, The Joyce Foundation, Illinois Secretary of State. 19 May 1948.

Backus-Brooks vs. Minneapolis and Rainy River Railway, District Court transcript #7405 (1921).

Bonesteel, Pete. Private collection. Minneapolis, Minnesota.

Chippewa National Forest Archives, Forest Supervisor's Headquarters, Cass Lake, Minnesota.

Creighton Collection, Winnfield Museum, Winnfield, Louisiana.

Eckert, Ena. Private collection. Bigfork, Minnesota.

Hackley & Hume Papers, Michigan State University Archives and Historical Collections, East Lansing, Michigan, 1886–1974.

Hawkinson, Susan, and Warren Jewett. Private collection. Grand Rapids, Minnesota.

Hensley, Patricia. Private collection. Dallas, Texas.

Ireton Family. Private collection. Trout Lake, Minnesota.

Johnson, Vernie. Private collection. Effie, Minnesota.

J. C. Sullivan et al. vs. Minneapolis and Rainy River Railway, District Court transcript #4950 (1913).

Jessie M. Lawrence vs. M&RRR Company, District Court transcript #236 (1893).

Karjala Research Center, Itasca County Historical Society, Grand Rapids, Minnesota.

Madsen, Gene. Private collection. Bigfork, Minnesota.

Minneapolis and Rainy River Railway, Right of Way Section Drawings, [1904], Itasca County Courthouse, Auditor Office.

Minnesota Cedar Logging Company vs. Minneapolis and Rainy River Railway, District Court transcript #5542 (1913).

Minnesota Forestry Board. Third Annual Report of the State Forester, 31 December 1913.

Minnesota State Archives, Minnesota Historical Society, St. Paul.
Plat maps and other documents, Itasca County Courthouse, Recorder Office.
R. E. White vs. M&RRR Company, District Court transcript #2411 (1909).
Saillard, Louis. Private collection. Baton Rouge, Louisiana.
State of Minnesota vs. Minneapolis and Rainy River Railway, District Court transcript #5953 (1916).
Swanson, Ruth. Private collection. Deer River, Minnesota.
Tubbs, Ann. Private collection. Clinton, Iowa.
Vermillion Pine and Iron Land Company vs. Itasca Lumber Company, District Court transcript #1294, (1904).
Waleski, Joe. Private collection. Grand Rapids, Minnesota.

Unpublished Works
Brayer, Herbert O. "New England Beginnings" (The Joyce Foundation, Chicago, [1957]).
Ernst, Joseph. "Forest Frontiers: The Joyce Search for Stumpage 1856–1945" (The Joyce Foundation, Chicago, [1957]).
Sieber, G. W. "Sawmilling on the Mississippi: The W. J. Young Lumber Company 1858–1900." Ph.D. diss., University of Iowa, 1960.
Trygg, J. William. "Abstracts from Original U.S. Land Surveyors' Field Notes in Minnesota" as a supplement to "Appraisal Report: Historical and Economic Background Land and Resource Evaluation Study of Royce Area #482, Located in St. Louis, Itasca and Koochiching Counties, Minnesota"(compiled for Bois Forte (Nett Lake) Band of Chippewa Indians, 1971). Uncatalogued material at Itasca Community College library, Grand Rapids, Minnesota.

Newspapers
Bigfork (Minnesota) Settler, 1905–1911.
Clinton (Iowa) Herald, 1944.
Clinton (Iowa) Mirror, 1872.
Comrade (Winnfield, Louisiana), July 24, 1908.
Des Moines Register, October 7, 1973.
Duluth (Minnesota) Herald, April, 1941.
Eastern Itascan (Nashwauk, Minnesota), 1990.
Grand Rapids (Minnesota) Herald Review, 1904–1991.
Grand Rapids (Minnesota) Magnet, 1891–1894.
Itasca (Coleraine, Minnesota) Iron News, May 1, 1931; July 16, 1925.
Itasca County (Grand Rapids, Minnesota) Independent, 1908–1918.
Itasca (Deer River, Minnesota) News, 1898–1932.
LaPrairie (Minnesota) News, 4 November 1893.
Lyons (Iowa) City Advocate, 1869–1873.
Minneapolis Journal, December 3, 1904.
Times-Democrat, (Davenport-Bettendorf, Iowa), November 18, 1962.
Trinity County (Groveton, Texas) Star, March 3, 1905.
Watchman (Shell Lake, Wisconsin), August 13, 1891.
Western Itasca (Deer River, Minnesota) Review, 1995.
Winn Parish (Louisiana) Enterprise, September 10, 1936; February 7, 1946.

Interviews

Interviews conducted by authors
TC = telephone conversation, PI= personal interview (tape recording)

Geoffrey Barnard	Nature Conservancy staff member	TC	6 July	1994	Minneapolis, Minn.
Don Benson	Bigfork Valley resident	PI	14 Feb.	1994	Talmoon, Minn.
Mickie Benton	friend of Beatrice Joyce Kean	PI	14 Feb.	1994	Grand Rapids, Minn.
Estes Boseman	Tremont Lumber Co. employee	TC	6 Nov.	1994	Winnfield, La.
Marion Brown	M&R employee	PI	2 Feb.	1994	Grand Rapids, Minn.
Joe Burns	Tremont Lumber Co. employee	TC	16 July	1994	Jonesboro, La.
Lyle Coolen	Bigfork Valley resident	TC	23 June	1994	Bigfork, Minn.
John Craig	grandson of ILC employee	PI	16 Oct.	1994	Grand Rapids, Minn.
Agnes Cyrus	daughter of Nopeming carpenter	TC	23 June	1994	Grand Rapids, Minn.
Cecelia Dalsemer	friend of Beatrice Joyce Kean	TC	5 Aug.	1998	Santa Barbara, Calif.
Tim DeWitt	Deer River resident	PI	15 Mar.	1994	Deer River, Minn.
Mary Doherty	Winn Parish librarian	TC	16 June	1994	Winnfield, La.
Dr. William Downing	Wabana Lake resident	PI	16 June	1994	Grand Rapids, Minn.
Violet Edge	Bigfork Valley resident	PI	14 July	1994	Marcell, Minn.
Dr. Joseph Ernst	Joyce business historian	TC	6 July	1994	Southbury, Conn.
Hubert Evensen	Bigfork Valley resident	PI	4 Nov.	1994	Bigfork, Minn.
Max Fowler	Tremont Lumber Co. employee	TC	13 Nov.	1994	Hodge, La.
Charles Foy	Clinton, Iowa resident	PI	18 Apr.	1994	Clinton, Iowa
Melvin Goldie	USFS Ranger, Marcell District	TC	14 Nov.	1994	Cadillac, Mich.
Paul Haws	Joyce Lumber Co., employee	TC	15 June	1994	Omaha, Nebr.
Carl Heide	Bigfork Valley resident	PI	4 Mar.	1994	Spring Lake, Minn.
Bill Hill	Deer River resident	PI	28 Jan.	1994	Grand Rapids, Minn.
Darwin Holsman	Bigfork Valley resident	TC	6 Nov.	1994	Bigfork, Minn.
Alice Hoolihan	daughter of William LaCroix	PI	9 Oct.	1994	Grand Rapids, Minn.
Dan Hoolihan	son of ILC employee	TC	14 Nov.	1994	Grand Rapids, Minn.
Mahlon Howe	Deer River resident	TC	2 Feb.	1994	Deer River, Minn.
Alvin Huss	The Joyce Foundation board	TC	12 July	1994	Chicago, Ill.
Ethel Ikola	Bigfork Valley resident	TC	15 Mar.	1994	Deer River, Minn.
Louis Ireton	Trout Lake resident	TC	16 June	1994	Trout Lake, Minn.
Cavour Johnson	Joyce Estate employee	PI	17 Jan.	1994	Grand Rapids, Minn.
John Johnson	Joyce Estate caretaker	PI	17 Jan.	1994	Deer River, Minn.
Oliver Juntunen	Suomi resident	PI	26 Jan.	1994	Suomi, Minn.
Carolyn Kastner	Trout Lake resident	TC	26 June	1994	Trout Lake, Minn.
Dr. Dudley Kean	Beatrice Joyce's former husband	PI	9 June	1994	Grand Rapids, Minn.
Katie Krueth	Joyce Estate housekeeper	PI	7 Feb.	1994	Squaw Lake, Minn.
Marvin Lauritsen	Chippewa Natl. Forest Supervisor	TC	20 Nov.	1994	Rhinelander, Wisc.
Izzy Lekander	Bigfork Valley resident	TC	5 July	1994	Deer River, Minn.
Robert Love	La. Dept. of Wildlife and Fisheries	TC	14 July	1994	Baton Rouge, La.

Bazil Mayo	Deer River resident	TC	25 June	1994	Deer River, Minn.
John McArdle	Joyce Estate pilot	TC	5 July	1994	Grand Rapids, Minn.
Frances Moore	son of M&R engineer	TC	16 July	1994	Grand Rapids, Minn.
John Muhar	Joyce Estate game warden	PI	31 July	1994	Grand Rapids, Minn.
Maurice Neville	godchild of Beatrice Joyce Kean	TC	29 July	1998	Paso Robles, Calif.
Gordy Newstrom	Joyce Estate pilot	PI	10 Jan.	1994	Grand Rapids, Minn.
Nels Olson	Joyce Estate/M&R employee	PI	20 May	1994	Deer River, Minn.
Stan, Ned, Dave Patrow	sons of M&R employee	PI	25 Apr.	1994	Bigfork, Minn.
Laddie Pearson	Joyce Estate caretaker	PI	25 Jan.	1994	Sand Lake, Minn.
Lyle Quigg	son of ILC employee	PI	28 Apr.	1994	Deer River, Minn.
Ben Rajala	Bigfork Valley historian	PI	11 Feb.	1994	Grand Rapids, Minn.
Jack Rajala	lumberman	PI	14 Oct.	1994	Deer River, Minn.
James Ronnfeldt	Clinton, Iowa caretaker's son	TC	18 Apr.	1994	Goose Lake, Iowa
Dr. Ellen Rudolph	Beatrice Joyce's former sister-in-law	TC	23 Jan.	1994	Williamsburg, Va.
Dr. Ellen Rudolph	Beatrice Joyce's former sister-in-law	PI	24 Sept.	1994	Grand Rapids, Minn.
Newell Searle	Nature Conservancy employee	TC	5 July	1994	Minneapolis, Minn.
Al Smith	T & G Railway employee's son	TC	30 Oct.	1994	Baton Rouge, La.
Vern Snell	son of M&R employee	TC	25 June	1994	Grand Rapids, Minn.
Jim Tarbell	DNR employee	TC	2 Feb.	1994	Deer River, Minn.
Eunice Thompson	daughter of Tremont employee	TC	30 Sept.	1994	Jonesboro, La.
Ann Tubbs	Clinton architectural historian	PI	19 Apr.	1994	Clinton, Iowa
H. E. (Gene) Turner	Tremont comptroller	TC	20 July	1994	Winnfield, La.
Jean Warner	Gage family historian	PI	17 Apr.	1994	Clinton, Iowa
Halga Will	daughter of ILC employee	PI	15 Mar.	1994	Deer River, Minn.
John Zetterstrom	son of ILC employee	PI	16 Aug.	1994	St. Paul, Minn.

interviews conducted by Joseph Waleski Jr.:

William A. Byers	son of ILC employee	PI	[1985]		Deer River, Minn.
Vic Huju	M&R section crew member	PI	20 Feb.	1990	Deer River, Minn.

self-narrated tape recording:

Louis M. Ireton	Trout Lake summer resident		1970–1971

Acknowledgments

Timber Connections has been a work in progress for the past ten years, and a project of this duration only comes to fruition through the support of many individuals. We wish to extend our gratitude to those who provided information and to those who read our drafts right up until the day the book went to the designer.

The authors first wish to thank Howard Zeman, former district ranger for the Chippewa National Forest, for his part in setting our book in motion in late 1993. His staff at the district office in Marcell, Minnesota, opened their files for our initial research as did the staff at the Chippewa National Forest headquarters in Cass Lake, Minnesota.

The following spring we contacted former Joyce Estate caretaker Joe Waleski Jr., whose family worked for the Joyces for more than fifty years. He spent hours patiently telling and retelling the stories of life at the estate from the 1920s through the early 1970s. His wife Ruth gracefully added her memories as well. We are especially grateful to the Waleskis for working with us throughout the long process of writing *Timber Connections*.

Without question the most important source of information for the Joyce lumbering operations was an unpublished manuscript drafted during the 1950s and commissioned by the Joyce Foundation. Dudley Kean, former husband of Beatrice Joyce Kean, flew to Chicago to pick up the manuscript, entitled "Forest Frontiers," at the Joyce Foundation offices. Joseph Ernst wrote the Joyce business history, and, without his manuscript and our telephone conversations with him, *Timber Connections* would be missing some of its breadth and depth. We are indebted to these men.

We also enlisted the help of many others. Our hired researchers, Marcy Frantom in Louisiana and Robert Seger in Iowa, enthusiastically and diligently pursued answers to our questions, doing the legwork we did not have time or funds to do ourselves. They became as interested in our project as we were. Likewise, Groveton, Texas historian Patricia Hensley regaled us with tales about the Texas Rangers riding into Groveton, Texas. She also gave us details about the formation of that community as a result of the arrival of the Trinity County Lumber Company. Robert Saillard in Louisiana, railroad fan and author, provided information about the Groveton, Lufkin, and Northern Railroad. In Clinton, Iowa, John Ward took us upstream on the Mississippi River in his cabin cruiser toward Joyce Island and Joyce Slough. Joan Isaacs, Charles Corwin, and Jim Raich—local history aficionados—helped us with details concerning the Minneapolis and Rainy River Railroad and the Itasca Lumber Company. Jodi Maki—former director of the Itasca County Historical Society—stayed late many nights at the office so that the authors could read the *Mississippi Valley Lumberman* and the numerous files that related to the logging history in Itasca County. The staff at the *Western Itasca Review* newspaper office in Deer River allowed the authors to read paper copies of the *Itasca News* going back to the early 1900s. Ellen Kean Rudolph talked with us for hours about her former sister-in-law Beatrice Joyce Kean. Interviews with more than ninety individuals provided interesting personal anecdotes. Many thanks to all of these people who gave so willingly of their time.

A number of individuals agreed to read chapters of the book and helped us clarify our thinking. Steve Downing, Katherine Dodge, John Hawkinson, Mark Hawkinson, Cynthia Driscoll, Todd Driscoll, Annie Erickson, Dick Cain, and Skip Drake read drafts of various chapters. Mike McGinnis read all of the Minnesota chapters. As librarian of Itasca Community College during most of our years of researching and writing, he also tracked down material and introduced us to individuals in the Grand Rapids area who had similar interests and projects. Catherine Winter, University of Minnesota–Duluth journalism instructor and former Minnesota Public Radio reporter, read early drafts of the chapters over a three-year period when the authors weren't sure what they wanted to include from their voluminous collection of research material. Catherine kept the authors writing through the most challenging years. The writing process would have been much more difficult if it were not for the insights of all of these individuals. Thanks to each of you.

During the last year of our writing *Timber Connections*, editor Teresa Alto made one remarkable suggestion after another. Hardly a single line of the manuscript escaped her red pen. Her willingness to read sections of drafts at short notice kept the final chapter revisions moving along. Graphic designer Krista Matison and writer Ann Ryan also made useful suggestions. Thank you. Your keen eyes were vital.

Itasca Community College administrators and staff have supported *Timber Connections* from its inception in 1993. Dr. Larry Dukes, provost that year, reduced Susan's teaching load to accommodate the research and writing of the book. Other past and present administrators, Dr. James Clarke, Dr. Michael Johnson, and Dr. Barbara McDonald, continued to support the writing of *Timber Connections*. Itasca Community College librarians, Pat Akerman and Steve Bean, assisted in the acquisition of research material. The staff of ICC's computer services department, Larry Baker, Chad Haatvedt, and Bonnie Blooflat, helped the authors with technical considerations.

Thanks also to Lisabeth Dilley for typing early research notes, to Heather Hawkinson for reading final drafts out loud, and to Dolores D'Agosto for proofreading.

The authors would like to thank the staff of each of the following organizations and libraries not previously mentioned: Beltrami County Historical Society, Bemidji, Minnesota; Clinton County Historical Society, Clinton, Iowa; Forest History Center, Grand Rapids, Minnesota; Forest History Society, Durham, North Carolina; Grand Rapids Area Library, Grand Rapids, Minnesota; Iron Range Research Center, Chisholm, Minnesota; Itasca County Courthouse, Grand Rapids, Minnesota; Itasca County Historical Society, Grand Rapids, Minnesota; The Joyce Foundation, Chicago, Illinois; Louisiana Political Museum and Hall of Fame, Winnfield, Louisiana; Michigan State University, University Archives and Historical Collections, East Lansing, Michigan; Minnesota Historical Society, St. Paul, Minnesota; The Nature Conservancy, Minneapolis, Minnesota; Northeast Minnesota Historical Center, Duluth, Minnesota; Texas Forestry Museum, Lufkin, Texas; Washburn County Historical Society, Shell Lake, Wisconsin.

Finally we would like to thank the friends, family members, and perfect strangers who have listened to us talk about *Timber Connections* for the past ten years.

Index